YOUTH MINISTRY
MANAGEMENT TOOLS 2.0

EVERYTHING YOU NEED TO
SUCCESSFULLY MANAGE YOUR MINISTRY

MIKE WORK / GINNY OLSON

 ZONDERVAN®  youth specialties

ZONDERVAN

Youth Ministry Management Tools 2.0
Copyright © 2014 by Ginny L. Olson and Michael A. Work

YS Youth Specialties is a trademark of Real Resources Incorporated and is registered with the United States Patent and Trademark Office.

This title is also available as a Zondervan ebook. Visit www.zondervan.com/ebooks.

Requests for information should be addressed to:

Zondervan, 3900 *Sparks Dr. SE, Grand Rapids, Michigan 49546*

Library of Congress Cataloging-in-Publication Data

Work, Mike, 1961-
    Youth ministry management tools 2.0 : everything you need to successfully manage your ministry / Mike Work and Ginny Olson.
        pages cm
    ISBN 978-0-310-51685-9
    1. Church work with youth. I. Title.
BV4447.W6685 2014
259'.23—dc23   2014009126

Cover design: Lucas Art and Design
Interior design: Matthew Van Zomeren

Printed in the United States of America

HB 08.05.2021

CONTENTS

INTRODUCTION

A vision without a task is but a dream,
A task without a vision is drudgery
A vision with a task is the hope of the world.
Church Window in Sussex England, c. 1730

Many of us in youth ministry share a vision: Tribes of adolescents encountering God, families healed, churches reenergized, communities rolling up their sleeves and serving each other. But since we're usually mired in a bog of details surrounding those dreams, our vision can get cloudy—or slowly dissipate altogether.

One of our goals in writing this book was to help youth workers to get out of the bog and back on track with their vision. Those who are merely ankle deep in the muck can discover here fresh ideas and variations on old practices. Those who sense they're sinking fast can find a lifeline in *Youth Ministry Management Tools 2.0*. This book will help youth workers do more than merely survive the tasks of ministry—it will show you how crucial those tasks are for accomplishing your vision.

Our vision as developers is to help you succeed in all facets of youth ministry management. Our task as authors was to write a book to facilitate that success. We hope God will use our vision and our task to impact adolescents and their families for the kingdom through your work and your skills.

Interact with this book. Read the narrative, underline it, dog-ear it, scan it, slap sticky notes on it. Play with the forms. Get your team to wrestle with the case studies. Ask, "How can I use this stuff?" "How can it help our ministry run better and more smoothly?" "What do I need to do because of what I'm reading?" Gobble it all up or nibble at it a piece at a time.

▶ *Rookie youth workers* will find ideas in *Youth Ministry Management Tools 2.0* for handling tasks that are basic to long-term youth ministry. There are case studies to get you thinking, forms you can adapt and tweak, and checklists to help you anticipate and track details of ministry.

▶ *Youth workers who are less structured* (read: "disorganization is my middle name") will find systems, methods, and forms that are easily adaptable to your needs. No more developing procedures from scratch.

▶ *Veteran youth workers* can use this book as a tool to train interns or key volunteers, as a resource manual to dip into periodically, and a storehouse to supplement (perhaps even re-approach) your already effective ministry practices.

Having an organized ministry is important and will actually help broaden your reach and impact. But at the end of the day this is all about the teenagers God has entrusted to you. We don't think for a moment that organizing is the goal. Loving and caring for teens is the goal.

CAVEATS AND WARNINGS

We've done our best to make sure everything is accurate, but this book is not to be taken as legal counsel. Run critical decisions, policies, and forms by your church or organization's lawyer and insurance company.

Throughout the book we reference resources and products. These are not endorsements but rather tools and sites we've found helpful. We're sure we've missed a number of great ideas and resources. Let us know what they are and we'll include them in future editions.

HAVING TROUBLE WITH A WEB ADDRESS?

Internet addresses listed in this book were current at the time of publication—but there's no way we can guarantee these addresses are current as you read these words. But we'll do our best to keep them updated at ministrymanagement.com. If you have trouble with an URL and the correction isn't posted on the previously mentioned Web site, please contact us via email (ymmt.ginny@gmail.com) to let us know if you've found the correct or new URL—or if the URL is no longer operational.

PART 1

STRATEGIC FOUNDATIONS OF YOUTH MINISTRY

1 BUILDING A FOUNDATION

CHAPTER OVERVIEW
- ▶ The Four Components of Youth Ministry
- ▶ The Three Touchstones of Leadership

One of the very first things we learn about God is God is both creative and administrative. In the beginning of Genesis, God creates the heavens and the earth. God then goes on to separate darkness and light, water, and ground, and categorizes the animals. A calendar of seven days is set, including a day of rest. From the get-go, we see a mix of creativity and organization. We also see God giving pastoral care in interactions with Adam about his loneliness. Early on God institutes policies (e.g., don't eat the fruit from the tree in the middle of the garden) not for the sake of policy but for the protection of people and the pursuit of God's purposes.

From the beginning we see that God desires us to be relational, creative, organized, and purposeful. God had a plan and set the desired course for creation. Yet we youth workers spend a lot of time making decisions that we hope are moving us forward on our desired course.

If you ask a group of people in a windowless room to close their eyes and spin around and then point north, when they open their eyes, they will be pointing in every direction. Some will be pointing in the right direction; others, not so much. This is a fairly accurate representation of how some youth workers lead: they're spinning around, trying to move in a direction they believe to be north, but often they're without tools to navigate. The result is that they may or may not make it to their destination. By placing one foot in front of the other with no sense of direction, it's possible to get miles off course. A philosophy of ministry and a philosophy of leadership provide those inner compasses to direct a leader and his or her followers to true north.

DEVELOPING A PHILOSOPHY OF MINISTRY

The most effective youth workers understand why they do what they do. And they can articulate it to others. "What is your philosophy of youth ministry?" is the one interview question that often stumps those who haven't done the hard work of formulating their philosophies of ministry and leadership.

There's no formula for developing a ministry philosophy, but there are some areas to consider. Based loosely on the work of educational philosopher William Frankena, the following components can help you clarify what you believe about ministry and how it should be lived out. Understand that there are whole seminary courses about philosophy of youth ministry. This is just a primer to get you started:

HAVING A PHILOSOPHY OF MINISTRY is necessary not only when you're the leader but also when you're interviewing for a position. One mistake some new youth pastors make is they take the first position they're offered. During the interview stage, confirm that your philosophy matches the church's. This will save you much heartache (and headaches).

COMPONENT #1—PRIMARY PURPOSE

If you think of a philosophy of ministry in terms of a building, this is the foundation upon which everything else is built. When the storms of ministry blow away everything else, this is the concrete slab. It's your ideals, your values, your theology, your beliefs about God and ministry. It answers the questions about why you're here and why you're doing what you're doing—which is helpful when it's 3 a.m. at the lock-in and the second kid just threw up.

How do you discover the primary purpose? Think about what makes youth ministries different from other organizations that help adolescents, such as the Scouts or the YMCA. Ask yourself, why is youth ministry important to the church or the local community? Or, why do you want to invest in youth ministry at this point in your life? As you formulate ideas to address these questions, keep asking the question "Why?" until you hit the core of your beliefs. For example, "We believe that God wants to rescue adolescents." Play the curious toddler and repeatedly ask, "Why?" Why do you believe God wants to save adolescents? From what? To what? Why do you think it's necessary that they're saved?

Or "We believe adolescents are the church of today and tomorrow." Why do you believe the church is critical? Why is it important that adolescents are part of it either now or in the future? What does this say about your view of God? Of the church? What do you base that view upon?

We tend to rush to sayings and Bible verses without putting any thought into our choices. What we end up with is a slogan masquerading as theology. Keep pushing into this component until you're satisfied you're at the foundation of what you believe.

COMPONENT #2—PERCEPTIONS OF PEOPLE

Each of us comes with a perception of adolescents, their families, the church community, and other leaders. These perceptions are what make up component #2. Our perceptions are often formed by our experiences and our theology, both current and past. For example, if we rebelled as adolescents, if we're drawn to news stories dealing with the dark side of teenage behavior, or if we were raised in churches that strongly emphasized human transgressions and depravity, we may tend to see students as having a sinful nature that's fully intact. On the other side of the spectrum, if we had relatively chaos-free teenage years with families who thought we could do no wrong, if we focus on how teenagers are changing the world for the better, or if we were raised in churches where the term "sin" was rarely spoken but "grace" was used habitually, we may view students as essentially good at their cores.

Our beliefs about components #2 and #1 are critical in the development of a ministry philosophy. If, as we note earlier, component #1 in a ministry philosophy is the foundation, then component #2 makes up the structural beams. The rest of a ministry philosophy is built on these two components. That's why it is so important to wrestle with what we think and believe about our primary purposes and what our perceptions are about people. It's easy to leave these unexamined and just replicate what we've experienced or heard about, but we end up developing ministries built on sand rather than bedrock.

The development of component #2 requires that you grapple with the question, "What do I believe about adolescents as well as their surrounding networks?" The way you answer that question will deeply impact your ministry. If you believe people are essentially good, then you're likely to have a ministry with few, if any, rules and guidelines. Taken to an extreme, there can be an immature naiveté blind toward potentially troubling behaviors. This leader may believe that students innately know on a retreat when it's time to call it a night and will sleep in their own beds, so having a curfew is unnecessary and distrustful. Or when interviewing volunteers, this leader sees background checks as a waste of time and potentially divisive in the church, so why bother? This leader doesn't believe anyone would willingly seek to harm an adolescent.

On the other side of the spectrum: If you believe people are basically sinful, then you're likely to lead ministry marked by many rules and lots of chaperones who have been closely vetted, with strict safety measures at events. (One youth pastor hired a security guard to watch the church during a lock-in, both for those who might come in and those who might sneak out.)

Veteran youth pastors realize that the reality of component #2 is somewhere in the middle, where adolescents are made in God's image (good) and yet have fallen away from the original design (evil). They are creation, but creation in need of redemption. These youth pastors do the hard work of examining their beliefs and studying theology along with adolescent development, science, and pop culture. They investigate adolescent trends and talk with parents, teachers, and community leaders. Seasoned youth workers live in the tension between being wise as serpents and innocent as doves (Matthew 10:16), and their philosophy reflects it.

COMPONENT #3—FOCUS

This component doesn't mean a random emphasis based on the latest youth ministry blog or conference. Rather, the focus of a youth ministry flows out of the primary purpose (#1) as well as the perceptions of people (#2). For example, if a youth pastor believes God is all-powerful and loving and desires a relationship with God's creation (#1), and believes adolescents are made in God's image and yet have fallen away from the original design (#2), then perhaps the focus of the ministry is to be a safe and loving place to ask dangerous questions, build strong relationships, and consider a life dedicated to following God.

One way to help develop #3 is to ask, "What do we want the ministry to be known for?" For example, if the ministry targets adolescents who have no home and experience poverty and violence, you may want to be known as a ministry that helps adolescents develop strong, holistic, internal and external support systems and will advocate for them when they cannot advocate for themselves. Still stuck? Suppose the local news is profiling your ministry: What would they concentrate on? Or if you had to write a summary of the ministry in 140 characters, what would it say?

Another example: Say the ministry is predominantly made up of homeschooled kids. If the perception (component #2) is that these students study hard all day in relative solitude, the ministry may decide to focus on building a community marked by play and recreation. But if the perception is that adolescents are at a prime age to learn the deep things of God, the ministry may focus on being a mini-seminary.

Having a ministry that's focused allows you to know what opportunities to say "yes" to and what to say "no" to. If the ministry is focused on helping students succeed spiritually and academically, it means you say "no" to starting up a skate park but "yes" to a donation of new computers. Not that a skate park is bad. In fact, if you start getting skaters coming to the ministry, it might mean partnering with a ministry in town that hosts a skate park in its parking lot. Being focused requires that you network with other ministries and resources in order to truly be representative of the body of Christ. If you look at Jesus' ministry, he knew his purpose, he knew the people he was called to reach, and so his ministry was laser focused. His focus allowed him to fulfill his call.

COMPONENT #4—PRACTICES

Once you know what your focus is, you can develop your practices. Practices are the tangible programs, events, habits, and customs of the youth ministry. Good practices are grounded on good beliefs. For example, you have a greeter team not because the ministry's had one for five years, but because the volunteer team wants to make sure that every kid who walks through the door feels welcome. They realize that if students feel welcomed, they may be more open to hearing from God.

As the leader of the ministry, you should be able to explain how a mission trip, service project, drama team, tutoring ministry, or Bible study are in line with the focus of the youth ministry (#3). You should be able to articulate how these programs or events address the needs of the students (#2) and how they are connected to your primary purpose (#1). If you can't make a clear argument, then you have to question if this practice is right for this ministry at this time.

A rookie mistake in youth ministry is starting with practices without working on the first three components. Inexperienced youth pastors take ideas and events that they've seen in other ministries and transfer them into their context without evaluating if that's the right decision. Too often, youth pastors implement what they've experienced or what they've picked up at the latest youth ministry conference. But they fail at knowing why they're doing what they're doing. So when a parent pushes back about the high cost of a mission trip, the youth pastor weakly defends his or her actions with, "But we've always done one," or worse, "But other groups do them and see life change." A stronger response comes from knowing how a mission trip fits into the ministry's primary purpose (#1) and this particular audience (#2) and being able to explain it clearly to the parent.

Here are just a few examples of practices and when it might be helpful to use them in ministry. These aren't clear-cut categories, but general suggestions to get you thinking.

PRACTICE	USE WHEN YOUR GROUP	SPECIFICS
Discussion	Has deep questions they want addressed Needs to talk about life circumstances Is intellectually curious	Small groups, debate teams, fishbowls, mentoring
Experiential learning	Needs to feel, not just think Knows the pat answers and needs to be challenged Needs to see things from a different perspective	Simulations, case studies, journaling, art therapy, creative worship, role playing, ropes courses, challenge courses
Spaced learning	Needs to increase retention by interspersing an intellectual activity with a physical one	Bible study and basketball, Scripture memory and skateboarding, language acquisition and an obstacle course
Lectures	Wants to learn more about a specific topic Needs intellectual encouragement or challenge Has more students who prefer to learn by listening	Master teacher, sermons, presentations, video series
Collaboration	Needs to learn how to work together Needs to understand how different gifts are needed to accomplish the goal Has a strong desire for community	Service groups, worship task force, dance team, technology team, app development group
Demonstrations	Wants to understand a concept from beginning to end Needs to see an idea displayed	Object lessons, experiments, modeling
Active learning	Needs to not just do things but to reflect on what they are doing so they can retain and apply it Has students who learn by doing rather than listening	Camps, retreats, service projects, student preachers and teachers, peer discipleship, book or movie reviews, debates

As was said at the beginning of this section, there is no formula for a philosophy of youth ministry. Your philosophy will change and evolve as both you and the ministry learn and grow. By grappling with these four components, you should be on your way to having a good explanation of why the ministry does what it does and laying a strong foundation on which to build a ministry.

DEVELOPING A PHILOSOPHY OF LEADERSHIP

A leadership philosophy is a combination of your values, beliefs, and principles that direct your decisions and actions as you lead others. We all have a philosophy of leadership, whether we can articulate it or not. It shows up in how we treat those around us, especially how we treat those who have little or no power. Jesus gets at this in Matthew 19:14 when he rebukes the disciples with this comment, "Let the little children come to me, and do not hinder them, for the kingdom of heaven belongs to such as these."

> FISHBOWLS ARE A DISCUSSION TECHNIQUE where one group sits in the middle talking about a topic, book, or perspective. Another group sits in a surrounding circle and observes. There's a designated time for feedback from the observer group. They then switch places. This technique is helpful when examining an issue from multiple perspectives or in working through conflict.

If you want to know someone's philosophy of leadership, watch their actions and listen to their words, as well as their silence. Some leaders reveal a philosophy of leadership marked by strength and power, while others portray a value of collaboration and community. And still others embody a laid-back, avoid-conflict-at-all-costs kind of leadership philosophy. As with the ministry philosophy, it's crucial that youth workers do the hard work of explaining what their approach is to leadership.

One way to formulate a leadership philosophy is to consider three touchstones: knowing, being, and doing. What does a leader need to know? Who does a leader need to be? And what does a leader need to do?

TOUCHSTONE #1—KNOWING

The first touchstone, "knowing," requires that a leader have a sufficient knowledge base from which to make decisions. A youth leader doesn't need to be an expert in all areas of ministry, but he or she does need to have a curious mind about themes such as adolescent development, Jesus' style of leadership (and others in the Bible), team dynamics, change management, character qualities of a godly leader, decision making strategies, conflict resolution, family systems, and more. These topics, and others, play a role in guiding leaders as they think about ministry. You don't need a degree in youth ministry to be a youth pastor (though it helps), but you do need a strong, reliable knowledge base to guide your decisions. A small group with senior girls and 6th-grade boys probably won't work. Do you know why? And a volunteer team won't stay around if you always tell them what to do but never ask their opinion. Do you know why? The ministry vision changes every six months and attendance keeps dropping. Do you know why? A strong leader is inquisitive and constantly learning.

What do you think a youth leader must know to be effective?

TOUCHSTONE #2—BEING

Knowledge alone provides a skewed compass. History is replete with leaders who had knowledge without character; some who carried out horrendous acts in the name of God and were able to motivate others to join them. So along with knowledge, there must be a focus on "being." *In the Name of Jesus* author Henri Nouwen writes: "Immediately after Peter has been commissioned to be a leader of his sheep, Jesus confronts him with the hard truth that the servant-leader is the leader who is being led to unknown, undesirable, and painful places. The way of the Christian leader is not the way of upward mobility in which our world has invested so much, but the way of downward mobility ending on the cross." (Nouwen, 81)

In order to succeed as a youth ministry leader, one must seek to embody certain core values and character qualities, such as a respect for humanity and creation, a deep love for adolescents and their families, a loyalty to God and God's call, integrity reflected in a connection between knowledge and behavior, or courage to live out the vision and call of God. (In the next chapter, we'll explore this further.)

What character qualities do you believe youth workers must possess?

TOUCHSTONE #3—DOING

It's one thing to "know" what to do and to "be" a person of character, but a true leader must actually "do" the work of leading. James 2:18 states it this way: "But someone will say, 'You have faith; I have deeds.' Show me your faith without deeds, and I will show you my faith by what I do." This "doing" flows out of one's knowledge and character. Leaders get themselves into trouble when they preach one thing and actions take a different direction. To be a leader marked by integrity, your actions need to be aligned with your brain and your soul.

Think through what a youth pastor needs to do in your context in order to be an effective leader. Here are just a few leadership behavior commitments:

▸ I will always treat others with honor, no matter how much or how little power they have.
▸ I will seek to resolve conflict as soon and as directly as possible.
▸ I will forgive, and pursue forgiveness, quickly.

▸ I will regularly encourage team members and do whatever I can to help them succeed in ministry.

▸ I will keep my commitments, even when it's uncomfortable or inconvenient.

▸ I will strive to have clear and consistent communication with all those reached by our ministry.

What are the practices or behaviors a leader in youth ministry needs to embody?

In working through your philosophy of leadership, keep going back to these three touchstones and reflect on the key questions for each one:

#1—What do you think a youth leader needs to know to be effective?

#2—What character qualities do you believe are essential for a youth ministry leader to possess?

#3—What are the practices or behaviors a leader in youth ministry needs to embody?

Your responses to these questions form your philosophy of leadership. For an additional exercise, read through the Gospels and examine how Jesus utilized the touchstones in his leadership.

A strong leader must possess a foundation of knowledge and seek to embody core character qualities, principles, and values—and then act accordingly.

RECOMMENDED RESOURCES

▸ *This Way to Youth Ministry: An Introduction to the Adventure* by Duffy Robbins, YS/Zondervan

▸ *Teaching for Reconciliation: Revised Edition* by Ron Habermas, Wipf & Stock Publishing

▸ *In the Name of Jesus: Reflections on Christian Leadership* by Henri J. Nouwen, Crossroad/Faith & Formation

▸ *Exploring Leadership: For College Students Who Want to Make a Difference* by Susan R. Komives, et al. Jossey-Bass Publishing, 2nd edition (2006). (Note: This is not a ministry book.)

FORMS

▸ Philosophy of Youth Ministry

▸ Philosophy of Leadership

2 STRATEGIC PLANNING

CHAPTER OVERVIEW
▶ The Nine Pieces You Need to Develop a Strategic Plan

W hen firefighters arrive at a burning building, they first assess the situation before advancing. It's potentially dangerous to make decisions before seeing the fire and understanding what's going on. They are asking questions such as: *Are there lives at risk that can be saved? What is the possible risk to our team?* If they decide action is needed, they then ask: "Where's the best place to enter? What might be the source of the fire? What resources can we access right now? What do we still need? Where will we place the firefighters, and will we have a way out?" The lead firefighter is constantly assessing the risk and monitoring the team's progress toward its goals.

In essence, a strategic plan.

DEVELOPING A STRATEGIC PLAN FOR YOUR YOUTH MINISTRY

In youth ministry, we have a lot coming at us, and it's dangerous to walk too far without a plan. Jesus had a strategic plan. We see evidence of that in Luke 10: 1-11, 17-20, Luke 18:31-33, Matthew 28:16-20, and in many other passages. He was clear about his vision, values, and mission—and he communicated it to his followers.

Too many youth workers have a bag full of great tricks that last about three to six months, and after they go through them, they don't know where to go or

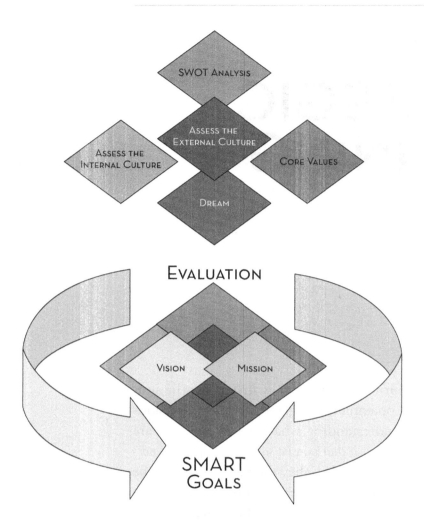

what to do. A good strategic plan will help youth workers navigate beyond these first few months and lay foundations for years to come.

Before you start the strategic planning process, ask yourself if you can objectively enter into the process and if you have the capacity to do so. If not, find someone who can honestly and fairly critique the ministry and lead the process. This is one of those times when it's worth seeking assistance from the beginning.

The following is a flexible guide for creating a strategic plan, which uses "pieces" rather than "steps." Think of putting together a mosaic rather than working a linear progression. Some people prefer starting with core values while others start with the mission or with a SWOT analysis (i.e., Strengths, Weaknesses, Opportunities, & Threats). You need to figure out what works for you in your context.

Piece #1: Assess the Internal Culture

As a leader you need to become very familiar with the mission, vision, and values of your church or organization. The mission and vision of the ministry you're leading should always flow with the larger ethos of the church, not against it. Read through the last several annual reports. Examine the budgets—they often tell you what a church really values. Also, study any congregational surveys. Talk with people who have been there for a long time and are conversant on the history of the church and/or youth ministry. Find out who the heroes and the villains were. Discover the key moments in the ministry's backstory; when did they shine brightest and what brought about the difficult times? Meet with students and families who've left the ministry and listen to their stories.

PIECE #2: ASSESS THE EXTERNAL CULTURE

One size does not fit all when it comes to a ministry plan. It's tempting to take the latest trend in youth ministry and slap it upon your current context. The problem is that such a tactic usually has a shelf life of about six months to a year. Just as the apostle Paul changed his ministry approach depending on the context (Acts 17:16-34), it's vital that you create a strategic plan based on your context.

Get out a map and draw a line around the geographic area where your students live and investigate what's in that odd-shaped circle. It's important that you understand not only the ministry you're called to, but also the community in which you serve. As you explore the community, spend time answering the following questions:

▶ What is our geographical location and how does it impact our ministry?
▶ Ministry in a rural setting is different from a suburban one, which is different from an urban one. For example, some rural youth ministries have to plan around harvesting schedules and hunting season. Urban ministries may have to consider more resource, scheduling, or transportation challenges. Suburban ministries may face challenges that are a blend of the other two. You need to take into consideration the resources and the challenges in your location. Does your location have lots of events and programs competing for your students' attention, or is your ministry the only gig around for miles?
▶ What's the population you're serving?

  • Are you in a community that's graying, or is the majority under the age of 18?
  • Is the population changing due to migration or work opportunities?
  • What's the median income of the community? Is that the same for your church? It might not be the same since some churches are commuter churches where people don't live in the same area where they worship. Which factor do you need to account for when you plan?
  • How many households are in your community? How many people are

WHY IS A STRATEGIC PLAN IMPORTANT?

A conversation between Alice and the Cheshire Cat in *Alice's Adventures in Wonderland* reminds us why:

"Would you tell me, please, which way I ought to go from here?"

"That depends a good deal on where you want to get to," said the Cat.

"I don't much care where—" said Alice.

"Then it doesn't matter which way you go," said the Cat.

"—so long as I get SOMEWHERE," Alice added as an explanation.

"Oh, you're sure to do that," said the Cat, "if you only walk long enough."

there per household? Are they primarily single-parent families, or are there two parents per household? This may impact when you schedule programs and what type of programs you plan.

- When it comes to education, how many schools are there? Is the community building or closing schools? The consequences of this are momentous for a youth ministry.
- What's the typical level of educational attainment? Is that the norm in your church as well?
- Are there local community colleges or universities? This has implications for young adult ministry, a frequent "shoulder" ministry of youth ministry (the other "shoulder" being tween or late elementary school ministry). This also might be a place to recruit interns.

As you examine these and other community demographics, it helps you discern what you should emphasize in your ministry. For example, if a number of key businesses have pulled out of the community recently, you may want to consider having free or low-cost events and consider focusing on resources addressing youth homelessness or employment opportunities for students and their families. Or, if there's a population boom of young families in your town which results in several new elementary schools being built, you may want to concentrate on developing a strong middle school ministry in anticipation of that growth. Analyze your demographic findings with two questions in mind: What challenges does this bring? What are the opportunities?

PIECE #3: DREAM

Keep the cultural analyses at the forefront of your mind and begin to dream about what the ministry could, and should, look like in light of your findings. Nehemiah is a great example of a strategic dreamer. In Nehemiah 1, he hears about the needs in Jerusalem. In chapter 2, he travels around the city so he can see its state and needs firsthand. As you walk or drive around the community, ask God to show you its needs that your ministry might address. Is it youth homelessness? Is there a need for a community drop-in center?

One church that developed out of assessing community needs is Lawndale Community Church in Chicago. It started as a Bible study for high school football players led by "Coach" Wayne Gordon. As it started to grow, Gordon began asking what the community needed, and he perceived a desire for a safe place to do laundry without having to leave the neighborhood. He was able to get a washer and dryer and use them to create a safe space where he and others could reach out to the community. That same commitment to listening to the community has continued throughout Lawndale's history. From that original "Laundromat" a church was birthed that's thriving, along with a health care center that sees more than 150,000 patients a year, a community development corporation, an after-school program, a community arts youth program, a hip-hop church, and more.

As you travel around your community and your ministry site, use your senses to imagine the youth ministry that could develop there.

- What do you hear? Maybe leaders listening to students pour out their hearts. Or students seeking God in prayer. Or laughter echoing out the windows of the sanctuary.
- What do you see? Perhaps students greeting visitors with smiles. Or a senior praying with a 7th-grade boy. Or students walking the streets, serving the neighborhood.
- What do you smell? Possibly it's the smell of hundreds of middle school feet after a massive lock-in. Or the scents of incense as the historically rebellious sophomores try leading experiential worship for the first time.
- What do you taste? Beyond Skittles and Mountain Dew, maybe you taste the rice cakes and pita bread for communion because they reflect the changing population of the community.
- What do you feel? Maybe you feel a crush of students packed into a basement to pray. Or you feel a quick hug from a leader grateful to be on the team.

Then, either in solitude or with a group of trusted leaders, continue the process by doing a brain dump. Jot down all the words you hope will describe the ministry in three years (five is too long). Ask God to guide you as you work through the following statements:

- List qualities that will characterize the youth group (e.g., caring, others-focused, marked by prayer, authenticity, joy, etc.).
- Describe the types of students you hope will attend.
- Picture how many leaders you'll need.
- Imagine new ministries based on the students you hope to attract.
- Explain the spiritual growth you anticipate for students.
- List types of outreach you hope to perform and the growth that will result.

▸ Name service and missions trips you would like to run with your students.

▸ Articulate the kind of relationship that you and other leaders will have with parents and community leaders.

▸ Clarify a plan to develop skilled volunteers who love adolescents.

▸ Describe your group's relationship with the community.

As you develop a sense of what God might be about in your ministry, write it down. Habakkuk 2:2 says, "Then the LORD replied: 'Write down the revelation and make it plain on tablets so that a herald may run with it.'" [NIV] This way you can come back to it during times of frustration and confusion, to remind you why you're pursuing ministry in this way.

IBM INITIATED A PROCESS RECENTLY in which it invited 319,000 employees to participate in an online "values jam." As a result, they determined that their actions would be governed by these three values*:

Dedication to every client's success
Innovation that matters, for our company and for the world
Trust and personal responsibility in all relationships

* http://www.ibm.com/ibm/values/us/

PIECE #4: DETERMINE YOUR CORE VALUES

As you scrutinize your ministry dream, what values float to the surface? A value is a navigating principle or belief that guides and motivates both students and leaders. These are the proverbial "hills to die on." The youth ministry values should reflect the values of the larger church or organization.

What are the non-negotiable values the ministry should uphold, values that you will quit over rather than violate?

▸ We seek to glorify God in everything that we do.

▸ We believe students and leaders should always be treated with respect.

▸ We are a safe place to ask dangerous questions.

▸ We are focused on Jesus.

▸ Our ministry is guided by God's word.

▸ We build relationships with students and other leaders that are healthy and God-centered.

▸ We believe joy and creativity need to pervade what we do.

▸ We believe we're called as Christians to meet the needs in our youth community, whether physical, mental, spiritual, or emotional.

PIECE #5: SWOT ANALYSIS

Once you've either scrutinized the macro cultures that your ministry is set in, dreamed a little, and/or identified your core values, take a step closer and analyze your ministry in light of those other pieces. Put together a group of select leaders, parents, recent alumni, and current students who can clearly evaluate the current state of the ministry and invite them to participate in a SWOT analysis—i.e., examining the ministry's Strengths, Weaknesses, Opportunities, and Threats. Strengths and Weaknesses are more internally focused whereas Opportunities and Threats deal more with external factors.

This is a helpful process when you're evaluating the whole ministry or when you're starting up a new project or sub-ministry. It's a good idea to do it once a year to make sure you're heading in the right direction.

Strengths: What does your ministry have going for it? What are its assets? Here are some potential strengths:

- A great volunteer team with proven relational skills and commitment to God and students.
- Reputation for integrity, innovation, and serving the needs of students, their families, and the community.
- Strong relationships with parents and community leaders.
- Easy location for students and their families to reach.
- Support from the whole church body.
- A strong and active board of directors.
- It's well funded.

Weaknesses: What puts your ministry at risk for growth? Here are some possible weaknesses:

- Students have a low level of commitment.
- Church leadership doesn't want the ministry to reach out beyond church kids.
- Youth pastor has weak communication and/or administration skills.
- Parents don't see church as a priority.
- The worship style doesn't connect with the students.
- Previous leadership lacked integrity, resulting in a sharp drop in student attendance.
- The youth ministry doesn't have a permanent place to meet—it keeps getting moved from room to room or house to house, resulting in students feeling unsure of where they're gathering that week.

Opportunities: What factors are present in the community that could help the ministry thrive?

- Located in an area that's booming with new housing.
- Local university with students who are interested in serving.
- There aren't any other youth ministries in the area.

▸ There aren't any other youth ministries targeting the types of students you're called to reach.

▸ There's a huge elementary school population preparing to enter middle school in one to two years.

▸ A nonprofit organization is looking for a partner to start a college-prep program.

Threats: *What factors in the community could cause the ministry to fail?*

▸ There's a huge, exciting youth ministry serving the same population.

▸ A local industry is closing, and it employs many of the families in your congregation.

▸ There's an influential family in the church who doesn't like what the youth ministry is focused on and may pull funding if it doesn't change direction.

▸ Students have school and sports schedules too busy to include ministry activities.

▸ The college ministry has high demands and involves a large percentage of your volunteers.

Have someone take notes during the SWOT analysis. Pay attention to the interplay between the four categories. For example, it might be that an Opportunity is a new regional middle school is being built a block from the church. Does the ministry have enough volunteers to handle the influx of students? "Yes" puts it in the Strength category; "No" means it goes into the Weakness area.

> "THE VERY ESSENCE OF LEADERSHIP is that you have a vision. It's got to be a vision you can articulate clearly and forcefully on every occasion. You can't blow an uncertain trumpet." —Theodore Hesburgh
>
> "WHERE THERE IS NO VISION, the people perish." —Proverbs 29:18
>
> "LEADERSHIP IS THE CAPACITY to translate vision into reality." —Warren Bennis

PIECE #6: DESCRIBE A VISION

A vision is a picture of a preferred future, one that you're seeking to create. It should be only a couple of sentences and should be descriptive and challenging. How do you get a vision? Some leaders prefer to get away and take time to pray, read, think, and then come back to the group with their description of what the ministry is (hopefully) going to look like in the near future. Others prefer to pray and discern the vision as a group. Either way, the youth ministry vision should fit with the vision of the larger church.

One way to get a vision of the ministry is to ponder the following statement: "If, in two years, we are phenomenally successful, describe what we look like and what we're doing." You, as the leader may define "success" one way while other leaders define it differently. Go back to your core values. The vision should reflect them.

It's okay to have some variance in the answers, but if one leader says, "The kids are all sitting around a table reading their Bibles in Greek" and another says, "The youth room is packed with students from 10 different high schools who have never stepped foot in a church before," realize you're dealing with different visions. Those leaders will pull the ministry in their preferred directions unless there's a clearly articulated vision from you, the ministry leader.

Here are some examples of corporate, government, and nonprofit visions. Notice how they are describing, albeit briefly, a preferred future:

- Boeing: People working together as a global enterprise for aerospace leadership. How will we get there?
  - Run healthy core businesses
  - Leverage our strengths into new products and services
  - Open new frontiers
- Salvation Army International: We see a God-raised, Spirit-filled Army for the 21st century — convinced of our calling, moving forward together. We will . . .
  - Deepen our spiritual life
  - Unite in prayer
  - Identify and develop leaders
  - Increase self-support and self-denial
- U.S. Secret Service: The vision of the United States Secret Service is to uphold the tradition of excellence in its investigative and protective mission through a dedicated, highly trained, diverse, partner-oriented workforce that employs progressive technology and promotes professionalism.

PIECE #7: ARTICULATE A MISSION

The mission should be articulated in one or two clear, motivating statements that flow out of the vision and describe why you exist as a ministry. Your mission statement articulates what you do and why you do it. It also measures new ideas that are proposed. A new idea can be measured against the mission to see if you should

TRY THIS

To make sure the youth ministry's mission is being clearly communicated, ask students, volunteers, parents, board members, and members of your church staff to answer the question: "What is the mission of our church's youth ministry?" Said another way, "Why do you think we exist?" When you compile the answers, you'll most likely discover such perceived purposes as—

  to teach responsibility
  to help confirm students'
    beliefs
  to keep kids out of trouble
  to reach and disciple young
    people
  to have fun
  to get to know God
  to keep kids from going to
    another church in town
  to share the Good News
  to fight drugs and crime

Use this exercise to discern what you need to do to make sure the mission is clear to the whole church community, not just to you.

MISSION STATEMENTS

In *The Path: Creating Your Mission Statement for Work and for Life,* Laurie Beth Jones writes that there are three simple elements to a good mission statement:

1. It should be no longer than a single sentence.
2. A 12-year-old should easily understand it.
3. Someone should be able to recite it by memory . . . at gunpoint.

proceed with it, set it aside for now or say, "It doesn't fit." For example, if your mission is to reach the skater community in your neighborhood, and someone wants to start a Bible quiz team because they LOVED being on the Bible quiz team in high school, it's probably safe to say that program is not a fit, based on your mission. It might be a question of timing: it's not a fit right now. Or it might be a question of culture: while Bible knowledge is important, a competitive quiz team may not be the best educational method.

A word of warning as you put together your mission statement: be careful not to substitute a slogan for a mission statement. A slogan might emerge out of a mission statement as a way to paraphrase it in a few words, but people have a difficult time understanding what the ministry does. For example, "Loving Jesus. Loving Students" is a slogan but not a mission statement. It doesn't tell what you do or why you do it. It might be useful on a T-shirt or as a tattoo, but not as a mission statement.

Here are some business and nonprofit examples of mission statements:

▸ The American Red Cross: The American Red Cross prevents and alleviates human suffering in the face of emergencies by mobilizing the power of volunteers and the generosity of donors.

▸ Catholic Charities: The mission of Catholic Charities agencies is to provide service to people in need, to advocate for justice in social structures, and to call the entire church and other people of good will to do the same.

▸ Coca-Cola:
  • To refresh the world . . .
  • To inspire moments of optimism and happiness . . .
  • To create value and make a difference.

▸ Walmart: We save people money so they can live better.

▸ McDonald's: To be our customers' favorite place and way to eat and drink.

▸ Starbucks: To inspire and nurture the human spirit — one person, one cup, and one neighborhood at a time.

▸ Compassion International: In response to the Great Commission, Compassion International exists as an advocate for children, to release them from their spiritual, economic, social, and physical poverty and enable them to become responsible and fulfilled Christian adults.

PIECE #8: DEVELOP YOUR GOALS

Once you've done the hard work of dreaming, assessing, analyzing and articulating, write down the goals that will help you accomplish the vision and mission. This is where you get specific and practical. A common acronym to describe goals is SMART: Strategic, Measurable, Assignable, Realistic, and Time-Based.

Strategic: What's written down on the calendar, what programs are created, what initiatives are developed—all of these should fit with the mission and vision. For example, if your mission is to create a safe place where students can ask dangerous questions about God and life, then a strategic goal would be to create small groups of students and leaders where there would be freedom and safety to wrestle with difficult doubts.

Measurable: The goal should be written in a way that you know whether or not you've accomplished it. For example, in starting the small groups, it would be a measurable goal if you wrote: "We will start *five* new small groups."

Assignable: Every goal should have one person or group responsible for carrying it out (e.g., "*Chris* is responsible for making sure that five new small groups are started."). If no one is responsible for the goal, it likely will never be achieved.

Realistic: If your ministry has 15 students, having five small groups is unrealistic . . . right now. Or if you're in a culture where small groups are awkward, don't force the idea but figure out another way to reach your goal of community building.

Time-based: Goals need to have deadlines (e.g., "We will start *five* new small groups by *November 1.*") Come November 1 you know if you have achieved your goal, or if you need to revisit and adjust it.

PIECE #9: EVALUATE

We move fast as youth workers, and there's a lot on our to-do lists. And if we're honest, evaluation is uncomfortable for most of us. What if we "failed"? If we don't pause to evaluate, we'll never know. We'll also never know if we reached our goals. Periodically, schedule times of evaluation for the ministry and programs. By asking the following questions, it keeps it about the programs instead of about evaluating a person. If you're intent on producing constructive results, gather a group of objective thinkers to help examine the ministry. Pose these questions to them:

What should we keep?

This could be anything: having donuts at Sunday school, the style of worship, small groups, summer mission trip, or our focus on discipleship. These are the things the ministry is doing well and should continue doing, or being.

RECOMMENDED RESOURCES

▸ *Advanced Strategic Planning: A 21st-Century Model for Church and Ministry Leaders,* by Aubrey Malphurs, Baker Books

▸ *The Fifth Discipline Fieldbook: Strategies and Tools for Building a Learning Organization,* Peter Senge, Crown Business

▸ *Strategic Planning for Nonprofit Organizations: A Practical Guide and Workbook,* Michael Allison and Jude Kaye, Wiley Publishing

FORMS

▸ SWOT Analysis
▸ Evaluation Tool
▸ Defining a Ministry Vision
▸ Defining a Personal Vision

What should we toss?

It might be a good idea in theory, but it isn't working right now. Maybe it's a sacred cow that's ready for a barbeque. Maybe it's time to get rid of that three-day lock-in.

What should we add?

What will make the ministry stronger and better able to fulfill its mission? Perhaps it's developing a ministry with students on the autism spectrum. Or, "We need to develop a ministry that focuses on the parents of middle schoolers." Or, "We need to design a purposeful mentoring program for under-represented students seeking to go to college."

What should we tweak?

This area includes things that are going pretty well, but need an adjustment (e.g., "The worship on Sunday morning needs to integrate younger students" or "We need to broaden our ministry to include post-high school students who are attending the community college" or "We need to add fifteen more minutes for prayer on Wednesday night.").

If we could see into the future, strategic planning would be a piece of cake. Most of us operate like firefighter wannabes: We get the call that there's a fire, and we rush into the burning building without a plan—but with a lot of passion to save those caught inside. We need to think like the veteran firefighters and put time into strategic planning before we blast ahead and put ourselves (and others) in danger. The strategic plan reminds us during those times when the heat is intense or the fire is smoldering of where we're going and why we're doing what we're doing.

PART 2

YOU AND YOUTH MINISTRY

3 EMPLOYED AS A YOUTH MINISTER

CHAPTER OVERVIEW

If you can do anything else in life besides youth ministry, do it. Youth ministry requires a strong sense of calling from God, powerful passion, and a good dose of vision—especially midway through a lock-in when you've just discovered a group of sophomores tagging the church sign outside.

The answer to the question, "Should I go into youth ministry?" may wind up being a yes or a no; but the journey to the answer winds through family, friends, and acquaintances and follows the hills and valleys of your life. Here's a list of questions to ask yourself and your friends and family to affirm your direction:

▶ Who else in my life agrees that I'm cut out for professional youth ministry?
▶ Does my ministry supervisor concur with my decision to become a youth ministry professional?
▶ What does my former youth pastor think about me doing full-time youth ministry?
▶ What experiences make me believe I'm making a good decision (volunteer, camp counselor, intern)?

▶ Have I "shadowed" a youth pastor and seen a cross-section of programming—everything from midweek small groups to weekend retreats to parent meetings? Have I observed mundane as well as crisis times?

▶ What does my family (spouse, parents, children) think about my desire to do full-time youth ministry?

▶ How much time have I spent listening for God's guidance?

▶ Is there anything about me—sins I don't give up or impossibly annoying personality traits—that would make it difficult for me to be in full-time ministry?

▶ Have I discussed my professional direction with a career counselor?

A CAREER IN YOUTH MINISTRY

The dream has kept you awake nights. As you've talked with friends, you've caught yourself pounding the table about the importance of working with adolescents. Your journal entries underscore this passionate theme. Whether you're an upper-level student considering your first full-time position or in your thirties and considering a midlife career switch to youth ministry as a full-time profession, this chapter will start you in the process.

Veteran youth workers offer these tips on discerning if youth ministry is the right direction in which to move:

▶ Look for a place to volunteer with people who can help you become a better youth worker. Suck their brains clean of everything they know about youth ministry. At the end of the season, ask them to act as your references.

▶ Kids who want to get into a great college figure out in high school what it will take to get accepted. Yet too often potential youth workers fail to do this. If you're thinking about entering the youth ministry field, figure out what experience and knowledge you can get *now*.

▶ A helpful practice for me was reflecting on my life and thinking about experiences when I was really energized. I realized what those experiences had in common: When I was organizing groups of people to do things, when I was creating community, and when I was discussing ideas with people—especially when those ideas pertained to God.

▶ Getting youth ministry experience early on in your decision-making process and making time to reflect on your experiences can undergird your confidence in your decision to either enter into or turn away from ministry among adolescents.

YOUR RÉSUMÉ
What Should a Résumé Look Like?

The same rules apply for a youth ministry résumé as for résumés for other professions. A well-done résumé is primarily a tool to get your foot in the interviewer's door. A poorly prepared résumé will find a spot in the circular file.

Even though youth ministry allows for a lot more creativity and freedom than most professions, you should still be fairly conservative with your résumé unless you know the organization really well.

Your résumé should be:

No more than one page long. The exceptions: If you've been in youth ministry for 10 or more years or if you're making a midlife career switch, you can stretch the résumé to no more than two pages.

Printed with black ink on white, ivory, or gray paper. Head to an office-supply store and buy résumé paper with matching envelopes. Use a heavier, high-quality paper—not what you find in your laser printer or copier.

Printed in a legible font. Using serif fonts makes for the easiest reading because the tags, or serifs, naturally draw the eye to the next letter. (This is a serif font; this font is without serif.) Choose a font that draws attention to your experience, not to the font itself. Stay away from funky, unless you're applying for a job that places a high value on creativity. Besides, your basic funky fonts tend to look cheesy rather than hip.

Set with a one-inch border all around. Resist the urge to cram the page full of information. Give the gist of what you want to say and leave plenty of white space. It looks sharper and more professional.

Without typos or grammatical errors. Make sure you have it carefully proofed. Seriously, this is a BIG deal. Check the information carefully for your references.

Accurate. Make sure everything is true. You can be fired for inaccuracies on your résumé.

A résumé should not:

► include handwriting;

REAL LIFE

During a recent search for candidates to fill a youth ministry position, I (Mike) received 100 résumés. Out of those 100 responses, I received 10 phone calls. Of those 10 callers, only three candidates knew how to handle the call. Two candidates were clearly clueless, and the remaining five callers were almost rude in the way they followed up on their applications: "I called to find out where the process is," and "So when can I expect to hear from you?"

If ministry is primarily about relationships, learn how to come across as a relational person as you look for a ministry. Don't just sit by the phone waiting for it to ring—do your part: Pray, write your résumé and get it out there, meet with people who can help you sharpen your interviewing skills, make follow-up calls. If you're serious about moving to a specific area, go there—fly, drive, run, walk—and meet with churches.

By the way, just in case any of your contacts decide to call, you may want to change the message on your voice mail. Do you really want potential employers hearing you imitate Bart Simpson or make weird sounds?

- ▸ state a salary expectation;
- ▸ contain personal information such as weight, height, age, race, physical health, place of birth, or marital status. Do not include photos, number of pets, children, or spouses. These are factors that can cause a future employer to be accused of discrimination. Rather than take the chance of being accused, they may toss the résumé. (Besides, it looks very unprofessional.)

FasTrack

Ask several people to proofread your résumé. If no one is available, read it backward. It slows you down, and you're more likely to catch any errors. Many résumés get tossed after the first reading because they have too many typos or other errors.

A personal Web page

This can work. An easily navigable site may graphically convey your ministry philosophy, demonstrate your creativity, and show that you're technologically astute (or at least you can fake it). Keep it simple and clean in design. Don't make yourself bigger than you really are. Looking too good to be true is a turn off.

Blogs

If you have a blog, keep it up to date. Review what you've written. Is there anything you've posted that's not congruent with the church to which you've applied?

LinkedIn

Don't underestimate the power of this online tool. It's a great way to network and connect through people with whom you're already in relationship. You can create Facebook pages for professional purposes, but LinkedIn is specifically for your professional network. Google LinkedIn to learn more. Here's a simple overview straight from its Web site:

LinkedIn is the world's largest professional network with millions of members and growing rapidly. We can help you:

Establish your professional profile and control one of the top search results for your name.

Build and maintain a broader network of professionals you can trust.

Find and reconnect with colleagues and classmates.

Learn about other companies.

Leverage powerful tools to find and reach the people you need.

Tap into the knowledge of your network.

Discover new opportunities.

REVIEW YOUR SOCIAL MEDIA PRESENCE

Look carefully at your Facebook, Twitter, Instagram, LinkedIn, and other accounts. Prospective employers sure will. Google your name and see what comes up—and don't forget to check what images arise.

NEED HELP?

Head to a FedEx Office or UPS store, Staples, or another copy shop. They have the hardware, software, resource books, and paper to do the job right. Don't skimp on quality. You're selling yourself. Show that you care.

WHAT SHOULD A RÉSUMÉ SAY ABOUT YOU?

Tons of books on creative résumé writing are available, and a wealth of Web sites reveal the fine points of résumé writing—monster.com for one.

But remember that a résumé is a jumping-off spot for interview conversations. You only want to give the church a taste of what you can do, not overwhelm it with the whole smorgasbord. Arrange your résumé according to your strengths and weaknesses and according to the job you're applying for. If you're a recent college graduate with minimal job experience, include leadership positions you held in school, such as resident assistant or newspaper editor. If you've been out of school for a while, put your experience first and your education at the end. A youth ministry résumé should include these basic components (not necessarily in this order):

Résumé Component 1

Biodata

At the top of the résumé, include:

- Your name
- Phone (with area code)
- Email address
- Home address
- Any temporary addresses (e.g., "From May 23 to August 14 I can be reached at Camp of the Blue Frogs.")

SMART TIP

Develop a personal board of directors you can tap when you're making critical decisions. These are people whose discernment, discretion, and insight you value. They may not all be close friends, but they are familiar with your life. They could be mentors, former youth pastors, relatives, college professors, or best friends.

REAL LIFE

I (Mike) received a résumé that listed incorrect phone numbers. I had to ask why would I trust this person with the lives of high school students if he couldn't manage to get the right phone numbers for his references.

Résumé Component 2

Personal Objective or Long-Term Goal

Focus your résumé with this statement—make it specific enough to land you the right interview, but avoid too narrow a focus if you're interested in related jobs, as well. If you write, "I am seeking a position in a drama ministry that will allow me to use my skills in acting, directing, and scriptwriting," you've disqualified yourself from being considered for directing extended care programs for latchkey kids—which could have a drama component. Your personal objective statement lets the potential interviewer know if you could be a right fit for the available position.

Sample Objective Statements

"I am seeking a position as a high school pastor that would allow me to use my gifts and abilities to reach high school adolescents for Christ."

"My objective is to use my passion and experience in ministering to teens as a director of a growing student ministry."

"I am seeking a one-year internship in the area of youth ministry in a town-and-country church setting."

"My goal is to find a challenging youth pastor position in an urban church that has a desire to reach adolescents in the community."

"My goal is to continue my career in youth ministry."

Résumé Component 3

Educational Background

Here's where you describe your formal education—courses taken at universities, seminaries, community colleges. (Save the mention of training taken at seminars or conferences for later.) Name the schools you attended, the degrees you received, and your major and minor areas of study. Don't even think about fudging. Many churches will check your credentials. If you didn't graduate with a degree in youth ministry, you may also want to list courses you took that are applicable to youth ministry, such as counseling, adolescent psychology, public speaking, small-business management, curriculum development, practical theology, methods of biblical study, or small group dynamics.

Résumé Component 4

Experience

Experience can include both professional employment and volunteer leadership experience. List your most recent employer or ministry and position first, and work backward. Include the dates of your employment or service. Depending on your experience, you may want to exclude certain jobs that don't pertain to your objective. Just make sure you don't leave any large, unexplainable gaps in your employment history. People who read résumés are smart. They read between the lines. Literally.

Summarize each job experience. You can use full sentences, phrases, or bullet points, depending on your style preference. When writing up your experience, use active words like *designed, selected, developed, evaluated, coordinated, planned, led, facilitated, envisioned, organized, executed, implemented, managed, assessed, oversaw, created, supervised,* and *maintained.*

SMART TIP

If God is calling you, say yes. Then talk to a career counselor who can help identify issues that can trip you up in youth ministry: insecurities, areas to work on, strengths, etc.

As you describe the job, emphasize the skills you've exercised that apply to youth ministry: organized groups of people . . . led and coordinated projects . . . resolved conflict between staff . . . setup procedures and practices . . . maintained a budget . . . coordinated a team . . . developed a curriculum . . . created a new program.

Be truthful. Don't fall for the temptation to exaggerate. The youth ministry world is not that large. If your story doesn't totally add up, it's likely you'll be found out.

Résumé Component 5
Honors, Special Achievements, Memberships and Activities, Additional Education

Use common sense here. Is it really important, for instance, that the church/organization knows you were elected "the student with the best manners"? (Well, maybe it is.) In this section, highlight areas of notable achievements as a way to offer insight into who you are personally. Emphasize elements that communicate leadership and teamwork. Here's where you include any youth ministry-related seminars, conferences, and workshops (e.g., YS Team Training Events and National Youth Worker Conventions, membership in other student organizations).

PDF It

Convert your résumé to a PDF. It's the best, most professional way to send your résumé.

Résumé Component 6
References

To make your résumé as flexible as possible, write "Available upon request" in the reference section instead of listing names and phone numbers. This way you may offer different references for different positions. For example, if your high school youth pastor was the college roommate of the senior pastor of the church that's hiring, it may (or may not) be a good idea to include his or her name. People move, after all, and area codes change—you don't want a wrong number on your résumé.

SMART TIP

After you reply to a potential employer by email, follow up right away with a good old-fashioned letter. Handwritten notes are also a nice touch.

Create a sheet of references to send out when they're requested. Include names, positions, organizations, phone numbers, email addresses, business addresses, and relationship to you.

When choosing whom you'll ask to be a reference, consider former employers, youth pastors, professors, and mentors. You want people who can give direct feedback regarding both your character and your abilities. (Don't include your mother or your babysitter in third grade.)

Here's a crucial step—*Talk to your potential references ahead of time.* Ask, "Do you feel that you know me well enough to be a reference?" This gives them an easy out if they don't think they can be a good reference.

If they agree to be references for you, get permission to use their names and find out where they prefer to be contacted (at work or at home). Let them know the position and the organizations or churches to which you are applying. Then make sure you have their correct contact information.

If your job search takes more than a year, call your references to give them a heads-up on your job search process. If it's been more than three years since you've talked with them, they're probably not the best choice for a reference any more.

YOUR COVER LETTER

Whether you send your résumé by email or snail mail, include a cover letter to introduce yourself, explain how you heard about the position, and highlight relevant experience or skills you especially want a potential employer to notice in

FASTRACK

Include on your professional résumé bio, long-term goals, education, experience, honors, and references.

the résumé. You may also want to include a sentence saying your present employer does or does not know you're seeking a new position, thus alerting them to the level of confidentiality needed.

Make sure you personalize the letter to every situation. This is very important. Visit the ministry Web site and get the correct spellings of the pastor's name or the hiring manager's name, as well as the church or organization's name. Print the address on the outside of the envelope—don't hand-address it.

Name the position for which you're applying and where you can be reached (in case the cover letter gets separated from your résumé). End by thanking this person for his or her consideration and noting you'll follow up in the next two weeks. This way, you keep the ball in your court and don't have to sit around waiting for the phone to ring. Just make sure you actually do call. That communicates initiative and follow through.

When you call, know exactly what you want to say. Don't just call to chat, but don't read from a script, either. And don't make the potential employer feel uncomfortable or pressured. It's not the time to say, "Gee, I really thought you would have called by now," or "Where are your priorities?" or "Am I in the top 10?"

Start the call by saying something like:

"I'm following up my letter from last week . . ."

"I wanted you to know that I am very interested in discussing the position with you . . ."

"I would really appreciate the chance to talk with you further about this ministry opportunity. You have my contact information if you think I might fit the profile of the person you are looking to lead this ministry . . ."

"I know you are busy, thanks for taking my call and for your time. I look forward to hearing from you . . ."

RÉSUMÉ DOUBLE SPEAK

Facilitated a study in biblical literature in the original language. (Led a Bible study for junior high guys using the King James version.)
Visionary implementer of change. (Repainted the youth room in the church basement.)
Directed a team of creative entrepreneurs. (Oversaw babysitting fundraiser for confirmation class.)
Thrives on challenge. (Drove a bus for four hours with 35 high schoolers and one chaperone, all of whom came down with food poisoning at camp. What else can you throw at me?)
Skilled in conflict management. (Separated two girls fighting over the bathroom mirror at retreat.)

FINDING A YOUTH MINISTRY JOB

Where do you begin to look for a youth ministry position? Here are a couple of ideas to help you in your search:

DENOMINATIONAL OFFICES

Denominations usually keep a list of churches looking for youth pastors. They may also be able to tell you a little bit about the history of each position (why the last person left, for starters).

NETWORK

Talk to youth workers in your area to learn who's thinking about moving or what positions are open. Also contact the National Network of Youth Ministries (*www.youthworkers.net*), an organization that specializes in linking youth workers together.

Youth Specialties' Web site (www.YouthSpecialties.com)

Youth Specialties maintains an area for individuals, churches, and organizations to post open positions.

Publications

Several magazines (*Christianity Today*, for one) list job openings in their want-ad sections.

Local universities, Bible colleges, or seminaries

Contact local Christian schools or seminaries to learn what churches and organizations have posted job openings with them. Talk to their career counselors, as well as to those in their youth ministry or Christian education or Christian formation departments.

Youth ministry conferences

At some conferences or conventions you can post your résumé on a community bulletin board.

Job Descriptions

A well-written job description is a beautiful thing. Too often, however, they also are rare. But the job description developed by the church should be your guide in your interview process. It will likely be used at a later time to review your performance should you be hired. Don't lose it.

Job descriptions generally are: Generic summaries copied from another ministry, well-developed summaries created by a hiring team to help choose the best fit, or a reactionary document developed in response to a previous bad hire. Or it's a combination of all three. Regardless, the job description requires careful attention on your part.

Take time to read it and be prepared to answer questions based on the areas identified as priorities. A good interview team will expect you to be familiar with their documents. While you may be in discussion with several ministries, their search is the only one they care about.

By carefully reading the job description, you should be able to pick up on important themes, priorities, and problems from the past. A good list of questions will help you determine what the ministry is really expecting.

INTERVIEWING FOR A POSITION

A good interview follows good preparation: Know the church, know the community, know yourself.

PREPARING FOR THE INTERVIEW

So your stellar résumé prompted the longed-for call and—good news—you got the interview. But before you book your flight, make the following preparations—otherwise your blind date might end up a horror story rather than an anniversary tale.

Familiarize yourself with that particular church or organization

Find out as much as you can about the ministry with which you're interviewing. That way, you walk in primed to ask key questions and explore the significant issues. There are a couple of ways to do this:

The formal way is to request annual reports, denominational information, mission statements, and informational brochures. Also check their Web site; this is generally an excellent source of information. Look not only for what the church says but also what it omits. How often does the youth ministry get mentioned? What percentage of the church budget is dedicated to the youth ministry?

Take time to learn about key staff you're interacting with on social media—what they value, their hobbies, musical interests.

Do you really want this job? If you do—study, study, study. Learn as much as you possibly can.

The informal way differs with each situation and must be approached delicately. You may want to call former youth pastors, counselors, the church secretary (typically a gold mine of information), or students. State the purpose of your call and then listen.

Caveat: Resist asking negative questions. Instead frame them like this:

▸ What is this youth ministry known for?
▸ What are its strengths?
▸ What areas need growth?
▸ Why did the last youth pastor leave?

Call youth pastors from churches in the area to get their perspectives. You may want to ask, "When you think of First Church, what comes to mind? How do community members perceive First Church?"

When you've done your homework, prepare a list of questions based on what you've gleaned.

Familiarize yourself with the community

Youth pastors on a job search generally take a look at the church with which they'll interview. But unless you're planning on living at the church 24/7, you need to check out the surrounding community. One of the easiest ways to do this is browsing local newspapers on the Internet. Along with checking out housing costs, get a feel for what's going on in the public schools, recreational opportunities, cultural offerings, the crime rate. If you're married, is this a place where your family will feel comfortable? If you're single, is this a place where you'll find like-minded people, or will you feel isolated? When you're single, you don't take your support system with you; rather you must start from scratch. That can be great in your 20s, but in your 30s or beyond, how will you feel about living a great distance from your extended family and friends? These are issues to consider as you look at the position.

PREPARE YOURSELF

Before the real interview, conduct a practice interview. Get some friends together, buy them pizza, and have them do a practice interview with you. The only way to get better at interviewing is to do it.

Don't hesitate to ask about interview dress code—then dress a step above. The more experienced you are, the less you have to worry about how formally you dress—your résumé and experience will carry you. But if this is one of your first two jobs, compensate by dressing well. Look at your clothing purchases as an investment in your career. Bring a variety of types of clothing to help you be best prepared for whatever unfolds during your visit.

Bring a prepared message with you. Again, you never know what they might ask you to do. What if the high school Sunday school teacher gets sick at the last moment? Guess what? You're now the guest speaker. Plan on it.

Bring breath mints. Stick a couple loose ones in your pockets so they're easy to reach.

Be careful what you eat before you interview. Butterflies don't mix with spicy food. Let's just leave it at that.

THE INTERVIEW

An interview can trigger the same emotions as a first date. You feel nauseated as well as excited. You can't wait for it to start; you can't wait for it to be over. You want to impress; you also want to be yourself. And the big question . . . do you attempt a goodnight kiss? Following these practical tips can make the interview go a little more smoothly:

Arrive alone. Nothing screams *insecure* more than bringing an uninvited friend or even a spouse. Don't bring your husband or wife unless specifically invited to do so.

Arrive on time. A good saying to remember is, "To be early is to be on time; to be on time is to be late. To be late is not to be!" Get to the church about 15 minutes early. Walk around and get a feel for the place. Pick up any brochures you haven't seen yet. Check in with the receptionist about five minutes early.

FasTrack

Before your interview, get to know the organization and its community.

Smile and say hello. Smile at the interviewer; make direct eye contact; say, "Hi, I'm (first name) (last name). It's a pleasure to meet you." Offer a firm but not-bone-crushing handshake. Focus on coming across in a warm, professional manner.

Listen for and remember names. Call members of the interview team by name. This communicates that you are interested in people. This is a big deal. And it's an important part of your ministry with students.

Come with good questions. Be ready to ask some good questions. Don't be afraid to respectfully ask hard questions when necessary.

Let the interviewer initiate the first part of the interview. Just follow the interviewer's lead in the pacing and the direction of the interview. Prepare short and to the point answers. Don't ramble. This is one of the most common mistakes.

Questions you may be asked at an interview:

- ▶ Share your faith journey.
- ▶ Why do you feel called to youth ministry?
- ▶ What is your philosophy of youth ministry?
- ▶ Why are you interested in this church or ministry?
- ▶ What do you know about our church? (*In the corporate world, this question is a test to see if you've done your homework. It's the same way in the ministry world. At one church I know of, this is the defining question. If you don't have something to say, the interview is over—no matter how strong your résumé is. No church wants someone who's just looking for a job. It wants someone who can be committed to the place.*)
- ▶ What are your strengths? Weaknesses?
- ▶ In what areas do you need to grow?
- ▶ What would you do in a situation like this? (*This question provides huge clues to what have been issues in the past. If you're asked questions about discipline or punctuality or communication, odds are that was a problem for the previous youth pastor.*)
- ▶ What are your views on—? (*This could be anything from your views on homosexuality to your approach regarding social justice. It all depends on the church and the agenda of the interviewers.*)

- Where do you see youth ministry going in the future?
- What does a successful youth ministry look like?
- What would you do in your first three months at our church?
- What is your style of teaching?
- What are your salary expectations?
- What is your view on mission trips (retreats, camps)?
- Why do you want to leave your current situation? (By the way, when you're asked about your present or past employer, say only positive things. The interviewers don't want to know the dirt, and if you're too negative, they'll begin to wonder if they'd be hiring someone divisive.)

Exhibit these attributes: Enthusiasm, confidence, energy, dependability, loyalty, honesty, and a strong work ethic.

Critical Questions You Must Ask

You need to get clear answers to the following questions before you ever agree to take a position:

How often are performance reviews completed and how are raises determined? You'll find out if you'll be locked into your starting salary for the rest of your tenure or if you can negotiate a raise. Are raises based on merit or on life circumstances (i.e., getting married, having kids, buying a house)? Are raises based on gender or marital status? (It still happens.) Veteran advice: Negotiate the salary you want up front; don't plan on making up the difference in a raise. If the church starts you at a certain amount but promises to raise you to a higher amount within the first two years, get it in writing. Promises fade quickly once you're hired.

If the ministry is considered successful in three months, what will that look like? In six months? In one year? This tells you more about the church's philosophy of ministry than any Web site ever will. It may deny being about numbers, but if your interviewers describe a successful ministry as being "packed out," "crammed with kids," or language like that, you know immediately how you'll be evaluated.

Why did the last youth pastor leave? If this raises the least bit of suspicion, reframe this question and ask it again. For example: "Talk to me about staffers who didn't make it here and why" or "Tell me who has been a staff hero in the past and why" and "Is the former youth pastor one of them? Why or why not?"

Are you hiring me to be the pastor to every kid or to train and equip the adults? In other words, will your primary focus be building relationships with students or building a team of adults? The answer you seek will be different based on your season of life.

What has been the youth ministry budget? How do you see that changing in the future? Is the youth pastor's salary included in that? Listen for what the youth ministry receives from the total budget and listen for the reasoning. It may be that there were no adolescents up until a year ago when the church experienced huge growth. It may also be that the increased budget is due to the youth pastor's proposed salary. You may take the job—but have only $800 a year to work with.

What are the church's expectations for numerical and spiritual growth? Listen for which piece they focus on. Which seems to be a priority and why?

How often are job reviews done? Who conducts them? What happens to the results?

Who will supervise me and how much time will I spend with this person? This is especially important if you are expecting to be mentored by the senior pastor or someone else. You may be interested in the position because it would mean being able to spend time with him or he may only expect to see you on the platform Sunday morning and at church meetings.

If someone were to ask you about me a year from now, and you responded that I've exceeded expectations, what would I be doing?

If someone were to ask you about me a year from now, and you responded that I'm barely surviving, what would I have done or not done? This question may be the way to get at the heart of why the last youth pastor left.

What's the process for determining and approving what the youth ministry does? a) Does everything get approved by a youth committee? b) Does the senior pastor approve everything? or c) Do you have sole authority to make decisions?

What other expectations are there outside of youth ministry? Does the church expect you to preach on a regular basis? Visit nursing homes? Perform weddings and funerals? Fill in when the nursery hits overload?

Has the staff ever had a paycheck withheld because the church was short of money? If so, when? And how was that communicated to the church?

What happens when the church is behind budget? Again, how is that communicated to the congregation?

What does a typical week look like? If you're expecting to work 45 hours a week and they're expecting 60, you're headed for a major confrontation. Get it out in the open before you start.

What about outside speaking engagements? Find out their policy for staff speaking to groups and camps outside the church. Are you allowed a certain number of days per year for that? Does it come out of your vacation time? What about honorariums—can you keep them or do you need to turn them over to the church?

Where will my office be located? This isn't about having a corner office with huge windows. It's about having a place that's easily accessible to the public and won't isolate you from people. Because of the amount of counseling that goes on, your office should be in a central location with a window in the door, not tucked under the basement stairs where people need a map to find it.

What technology will I have? Now's the time to ask for what you want. If possible, choose what you prefer using. Also inquire about software, Internet access and upgrades. What about cell phones? Who pays for your cell phone bill?

Will I have an administrative assistant? How many hours a week? With whom am I sharing this person? Who has priority? What is the assistant's base of computer knowledge?

What are the three most important qualities a staff member can possess? What does this church do well? What does this church measure? What does this church regularly celebrate? The answer to these questions will tell you much about what is important at this church.

What is this church known for in the community?

In five years, what will the church look like?

In five years, how do you hope the youth ministry looks?

What is this church really about? What is important here?

Responding to Inappropriate Questions

Churches are notorious for asking inappropriate, and sometimes illegal, questions such as:

- How old are you?
- Did you ever smoke pot and, if so, did you inhale?
- Is your spouse planning to work?
- Do you have any medical conditions we should know about?
- What's your ethnic heritage?
- What year did you graduate from high school?
- Who's going to take care of your children if you're hired for this position?

You may choose to answer the questions or respond with one of the following statements:

- "I'm willing to answer your question, but before I do, I'd like to know why you're asking it." This alerts the interviewer that they've crossed a boundary, but that you're willing to cooperate (if you are).
- "I'll answer your question, but you need to know that I'm uncomfortable in doing so." Wait and see what their response is before you continue.

▸ "I'm not sure I understand the question. Help me understand what you're getting at."

▸ "I'm sorry. I don't feel I can answer that question. Is there something else you'd like to ask?" You leave them wondering why you won't answer, and risk not getting the job. But if they're really that out of line, do you really want to serve there?

Questions to think carefully about before asking:

▸ So, how much are you paying?
▸ How can I get fired?
▸ Got any good gossip?
▸ Do the pastors ever go out for happy hour?
▸ Do I get my name on the church sign by the street?

Finishing the Interview and Follow-Up

Wrap up the interview. When the interview is coming to a conclusion, smile . . . make direct eye contact . . . say something like, "It sounds like a great opportunity. I look forward to hearing from you" . . . and offer another firm-but-gentle handshake.

What if it's a phone or online interview? Phone interviews can be tricky if more than two people get on the extensions. Some churches believe it's great to have the whole search committee at the phone interview. Sometimes you can be on the phone with seven other people. Suggest Skype or Google Hangout as a potential solution or another video-based option. If you're on a phone, be on a landline if at all possible.

As the unfortunate candidate, you have no way to avoid this chaos. Just be prepared for several people talking at once (to each other and to you) and for awkward periods of silence. Make the best of the situation by finding out who's on the other end and what their roles are (and take notes). Be sure to answer the questions you're asked. Make your answers concise. Don't ramble. Ask for feedback ("Do you need me to clarify that?"). Frequently use their names in the discussion.

Follow Up the Interview

Within a day after the interview, follow up with a handwritten thank-you note. An email is also fine, but the personal note is more powerful. Make sure to thank the interviewer for his or her time and express your continued interest in the position (if that is indeed the case). If you decide that you're no longer interested in the position, let them know your decision either by letter or phone call (again, email is not acceptable).

People wonder how long they should wait to hear from the church about the next step. If you have not heard from the church after 10 days to two weeks, it's perfectly acceptable to call and ask about the status of the process. In fact, persistent (not annoying) follow-up usually communicates that you're eager and a self-starter.

Churches want people who don't see their positions as just another "job" but will be as enthusiastic about being a part of their community as they are. Just watch your tone. Persistently communicate with a positive attitude until the outcome is clearly stated.

RECOMMENDED RESOURCES

An excellent resource for the legalities involved in hiring church workers is *Selecting and Screening Church Workers*. It's published by Church Law and Tax Report, a division of Christian Ministry Resources, 704/821-3845. This company specializes in the legal side of ministry and has many excellent, user-friendly resources.

THE JOB OFFER

If you remember nothing else, remember this: *Get everything in writing.*

NEGOTIATING THE OFFER

The interviews have gone well. You like the church; the church likes you. It looks like there's going to be a wedding. But before you say, "I do," negotiate the prenuptial very carefully. Does it feel awkward? Yes, but as uncomfortable as it feels to talk about money and ministry in the same breath, you live with the reality of paying for a roof and food and utilities, among other necessities. Your best plan is to negotiate for what you want at the beginning. Once you've taken the position, you can't go back and ask for more. The good news is that the more ministry experience you have, the easier it gets to negotiate the initial package.

The job offer can include several different elements—at least base salary and benefits (insurance, retirement). Beyond that, it can include housing, continuing education, auto allowance, and more. It depends on everything from your education and experience to the church's philosophy, experience, and financial soundness. If this is your third job and the church's fifth youth pastor, it's going to be much easier to negotiate an offer than if this is the first for both of you.

Take some time to find out what you're really worth. Talk to youth ministry veterans to get a feel for what the going salary rate is for someone with your education and experience. Try not to sell yourself too high or too low. And spend some time clarifying your expectations of the job and putting it in writing before you sit down to negotiate. If your requests are acceptable to the hiring board, have them written into your contract. Youth pastor after youth pastor has echoed this advice: *If you don't have it in writing, you don't have it.*

The Compensation Package

In a nutshell, *compensation* is what you get paid—either through dollars or benefits. Your compensation package will be influenced by whether you are licensed or ordained. If the following elements of a compensation package are foreign concepts to you, talk with your denominational offices or with a tax adviser familiar with churches or faith-based organizations.

Researching youth ministry salaries is a challenge. Some churches use local teacher salaries as a point of reference for youth worker salaries. There are some published salary guides online, but the best ones generally have a cost.

There are several factors that can affect your base salary, including:

Education. If you have a M.Div., your salary should be higher than an employee with a Bachelor of Arts or an Associate of Arts. If it's not, it tells you that the church doesn't value educational experience. Is that a warning for you? The reality of increased student loans to repay goes with the increased degree. Compare your annual salary expectations with one denomination's base salary ranges for youth pastors:

- Bachelor's (of Arts or Sciences) with no experience
- BA with some experience
- Master of Arts in Christian Education (M.A.C.E.) or Master of Divinity (M.Div.)
- M.A.C.E. or M.Div. with experience

Experience. If you come with a B.A. and no graduate-level studies but bring eight years of experience, negotiate a salary that compensates for experience. Other professions do; so should the church.

Community cost-of-living. How much will it cost to live in this community? Renting a house in Red Oak, Iowa, costs less than renting an apartment in the Silicon Valley. Too often youth pastors eager to get jobs underestimate how much it will cost to live in a given area, and they end up working extra jobs just to pay the bills. Several Web sites can do a cost-of-living analysis for you. Google should be a big help on this one.

Comparable salaries. It's helpful to put your position into perspective by comparing it with other professions with similar job requirements. A rule of thumb for recent college graduates is to learn what the area's first-year high school teachers are paid. The school system knows the cost of living for the community. If you have an advanced degree and experience, find out what counselors, principals, and medical personnel in the area are paid. You may also want to call your denominational offices to request salary guidance.

When is it appropriate to bring up salary expectations?

Salaries in youth ministry vary widely. Don't waste your time or the time of the church if the suggested salary isn't even close to your expectations. If you're a veteran and the church is looking for a veteran, you'll probably be fairly close in expectations. But the earlier you are in your career, the earlier in the interview process you need to bring up salary to discover any mismatch right away.

If the church contacts you, during the initial contact, ask these three questions: What's the greatest strength of the church? Where do you see it going in the future? Can you tell me the salary range?

If you contact the church, don't bring up salary. You may end up wasting some time, but that's better than being perceived as only interested in the money.

What About Housing?

It's rare but not unheard of for churches to include housing in youth pastors' compensation packages. They may have an old parsonage or apartment that they add into the arrangement. If that is part of the offer, find out these facts:

- ▶ Is this considered nontaxable income?
- ▶ How does the fact that you are (or are not) licensed affect your taxes in this sphere? (You need to discuss this with your tax adviser.)
- ▶ What housing costs does the church pay for, and what are you responsible for? You may need to pay the utility bills, which sounds like a great deal until you see that it costs $350 a month to heat the behemoth.
- ▶ Who is responsible for the upkeep? Usually, it's you. Do you have time to spend repaving driveways, painting shutters, and fixing screens and leaky pipes on a 75-year-old house? And who pays for the repairs?

The church may want to consider giving you the option of home ownership with a housing allowance or a parsonage with an equity allowance. Again, talk over these issues with your tax adviser.

Taxes, Cost-of-Living Increases, Bonuses, and Benefits

Ask how much of an increase the staff receives each year. If they do not give cost-of-living increases, you're technically losing money each year. Inquire if bonuses are given when ministry goals are exceeded. Also ask if merit-based raises are given, and if so, how often and how are they determined?

Retirement. Some churches have mandatory pension plans if you're licensed or ordained. Others have matching plans—they will match your retirement contributions up to, say, five percent of your salary. If you're a recent college graduate and still paying off student loans, investing in your retirement can seem like the last thing you need to consider. But you should start investing immediately. The money you invest in your twenties will increase far beyond the money you invest in your thirties and forties. Find a trustworthy financial adviser and have a long conversation about your future.

Insurance. Find out what insurance is covered by the church's plan:

- Medical? (If you have a family, are they covered? Do you need to pay any extra for their coverage?)
- Dental?
- Disability?
- Life?
- Liability?
- Accidental death and dismemberment?

FICA. A youth pastor, like a senior pastor, often qualifies as self-employed. If you are considered self-employed, it's your responsibility to make quarterly tax payments to the government (both state and federal). Some churches pay the employer's share of the youth pastor's Social Security payments. Check to see your church's policy. And—talk with a tax expert.

Time off. Expect a minimum of one full day off a week—the norm for some churches is two. Don't accept partial days off—like being off a Friday afternoon and a Tuesday morning. Employees need a full day to disengage and relax.

Vacation. The length of your first year's vacation depends on when you start. If you start in June, you usually get half the number of days written into your contract. A piece of advice—don't even touch a position that offers less than two weeks of annual vacation. Ministry is such a time- and energy-intensive profession that you need that time to refresh and renew.

Find out when your vacation is increased. An example is receiving an additional week of vacation—up to five weeks a year—for every three years on staff. For an experienced youth pastor, four paid weeks annually is appropriate. Sometimes churches that can't afford a large base salary offer more vacation time. If that seems to be the case with the interviewing church, you may negotiate more vacation time in lieu of the higher salary.

Is vacation time accrued? Meaning, do you start the year with full vacation or do you "earn it" as you go?

SMART TIP

A youth pastor asked a board member why a new staff person with less experience was getting paid more. "Because you didn't ask for more when you started," said the board member. Whatever you think about that board's salary-setting policies, the point is clear: The time to ask is before you accept.

Compensation time. Ask what the church's policy is on giving you time off after a time-intensive event (e.g., a mission trip or weekend retreat). If they blink rapidly and mumble, "Whazzat?" run . . . fast! Some churches expect you to show up at the 8 a.m. staff meeting despite the fact you were gone all weekend with the senior highers. These churches usually don't keep youth pastors for long.

Reasonable comp time would be one extra day off (not to be confused with your regular days off) for every weekend retreat, and three extra days off for every weeklong event. You also should ask if you can store up comp time and use it later in the year, or if they expect you to use that time the week after you get back.

Holidays. Typically holidays are some of the most heavily scheduled times of the year in youth ministry. Is holiday time off for the staff scheduled in light of this?

Sabbatical. What is the church's policy on staff sabbaticals? Do pastors get three-month sabbaticals every five years? Do they ever get longer sabbaticals? Do they have to be used for certain purposes (study, continuing education) or can they be used for special projects (spending time with missionaries overseas, pursuing your desire to be a NASCAR driver)?

Sick days. Can these be stored up for future use or are they "erased" at the end of the year?

Continuing education. Anywhere from three days to two weeks is appropriate for study leave. This allows you to attend a conference or take an intensive course at a local seminary.

Consider Professional Expenses

These are expenses that should be included in the job but should not be factored into your compensation package.

Car allowance. You should be reimbursed for using your car for ministry purposes. This can come as a monthly sum or as a per-mile reimbursement. If it's the latter, retain all receipts and keep a mileage log that includes date, destination, miles driven, and purpose of trip. Any drugstore or discount store will have a small notebook for this purpose in their stationery section, and there are a number of helpful apps available for your smartphone.

Continuing education. One way a church can honor its staff members is to

REAL LIFE

A new youth pastor relates the following story: I had been on the job for several months and was planning to head home for the holidays. At staff meeting I reminded everyone that I would be gone until after the New Year. After the meeting the senior pastor called me into her office to correct me—I could only take three days of vacation, she explained, since I had had only a week of vacation coming to me my first full year (the same amount as the church secretaries) and hadn't been there the full year yet.

I went to my files and found the original job posting that said "two weeks of vacation a year." When I showed it to the pastor, she was mildly surprised but quickly agreed. Saving that piece of paper saved me the extra week I was due.

encourage them to continually sharpen their professional skills. They should offer enough money to cover at least a weeklong conference (registration, airfare, and food and lodging). The church may offer tuition and textbook reimbursement. If it expects you to get a seminary degree, will it cover those expenses (either partially or totally)? Will it cover your ordination or licensing process? Will you still have money to attend youth ministry conferences?

Another question you need to ask a church before saying yes to employment: How committed is it to your development? Is it willing to invest in your education? What about conferences? How about your library? Ask now, not later.

Subscriptions. They can be used for books or magazines to help you in ministry. *iPad* magazine subscriptions? How about your Amazon Prime membership?

Hospitality. If there's an expectation that you will entertain people involved in your ministry, or even in the larger church, will the church reimburse you for these expenses?

Denominational gatherings. If you're attending a denominationally affiliated church, you may be expected to attend certain denominational events. The church should pick up those expenses.

Counseling stipend. Ministry is one of the most stressful careers. More and more churches understand that pastoral staff members may need counseling. Does the church view counseling as part of overall health care? Does the church provide an annual stipend for counseling? Does it provide a special fund? Does it have a relationship with a local therapist who provides counseling on a sliding-fee scale?

WHAT IF YOU DON'T LIKE THE OFFER?

Don't be surprised or dismayed if you don't like the first offer. That's all it is, an offer. It's perfectly acceptable to come back with a counteroffer. Just make sure you can articulate why you want the changes.

Here are some helpful tips in negotiating:

Find out who's your advocate. Is there a pastor or someone on the search committee who can go to bat for you as you ask for an increase? It's always better to have someone other than you to act as an advocate.

Be clear and respectful. Some churches have the philosophy that you're serving God, so it's okay if you're poor. Others have sacrificed to get the money for this position and are paying what most of the people in the congregation make. Respect their sacrifice, but also be very clear about what you need and why you need it.

Don't spiritualize it. Don't assume it's God's will that you take what you're offered. God probably doesn't want you to eat tuna fish and macaroni and cheese for years. If the church doesn't go for your counteroffer, you could say something like, "I don't think I can make that work. Thank you for considering me. I've appreciated getting to know your congregation. Should circumstances change, please feel free to contact me again." Your response may cause them to reevaluate the offer and get you what you need.

FasTrack

You're making what could be a long-term commitment. Be sure the compensation package and job requirements are a fit for you.

JOB REVIEWS

Annual reviews are all over the board in churches. Some are very diligent in the use of annual reviews, and reviews play a key part of the annual budget process. For others, feedback is few and far between.

Know what you're getting into. Set clear goals with your pastor/supervisor or the team you're accountable to. Don't be afraid to push this process, politely. It's for your own protection. Find out what really matters. Is it . . . staying within your budget, protecting the facility, getting X number of students into small groups, seeing X amount of community service, growing by a certain percentage, planning a certain number of activities, or eliminating the complaints the pastor has received the last 18 months? Your target and the church leadership's target should be aligned.

Is the ministry focused on transactions or transformation? Are staff conversations primarily focused on spiritual matters and people's lives—or is it program-focused and numbers-focused? Again, pay close attention. Reviews in each of these environments will look very different.

Study what the ministry celebrates. It's likely those will become the things you're evaluated on. Also—what does the ministry carefully measure? What's the focus of staff meetings?

Ask to see a copy of the annual review when you begin in your role. Discuss how the process will look with your supervisor. The focus of your ministry is students and the leadership of that ministry—but the evaluation process may measure things you're not aware of and will likely play a significant part in your happiness and future financial position.

NEGOTIATING A RAISE

Circle the answer most appropriate to your current frame of mind:

a. Your salary is never enough.
b. Consider yourself lucky for getting paid to play.
c. At least you know what to negotiate for at your *next* job.

Salary discussions in the church are challenging. The financial reality for those of us who are in ministry is that we could likely make more money by doing some other job. But we aren't doing that job. We are in ministry. That doesn't mean, however, that we should not hope to receive fair, reasonable, and competitive compensation for our ministry roles in order to provide for ourselves.

What it means to provide varies by local settings—costs of living vary greatly across the US. And people can live on vastly differing amounts of money based on their approach to personal stewardship.

So, who doesn't want a raise? Don't be afraid to talk about your needs or your desire for a raise. Generally, raises today are tied to either a simple cost of living number or they are tied directly to performance.

Our best opportunity for negotiating is when we are hired. Once we are hired, we are working under a covenant agreement.

Be very careful—if your church hires you with a low salary promising to see what it can do to get you a good raise in the first couple of years, know you're taking a risk. Be especially careful if this promise is tied to how the church budget grows . . .

Your mantra should be "under-promise and over-deliver." Surprise your pastor/board with your work ethic. Follow through on assignments. Return calls and emails. Clean up the church van when you finish an event. Learn the names of all your students, as well as their parents. Borrow something? Return it. Use the church fellowship hall? Leave it cleaner than you found it. Take out your own trash after an event. Study enough before you teach—your students deserve your preparation. Bring the receptionist his or her favorite Starbucks drink for no special reason. Turn in all receipts. Yup—all of them.

You just might get a raise.

LEAVING WELL

The way you leave a ministry is just as important as the way you come into it.

In just about every ministry, there comes a time to move on. The motivation for the move can be your sense of God's call, changing life circumstances, a desire to be closer to family, or stock options. Research shows that the average person will hold down three careers and 12 jobs in a lifetime, and the numbers continue to climb.

You can be moving toward something (a better offer, more challenge) or away from something (conflict between you and the senior pastor). So in your excitement to move on to new ventures, take some time to think about how you're going to close this chapter of your career.

One youth pastor's resignation schedule:

Wednesday—tell the senior pastor

Friday afternoon—notify associate staff at a meeting called by the senior pastor

Friday night—notify the volunteer staff at a special meeting

Saturday morning—notify the parent leadership team at a regularly scheduled meeting

Sunday morning—announce it to the youth ministry

IF IT'S YOUR DECISION . . .

There are several aspects you need to consider:

Time Frame

Once you decide to leave, you generally give at least two weeks' notice—but stay no more than 30 days. "But there's no way they can replace me in 30 days!" you say—and you're right. But after two weeks you typically become a lame-duck leader. You'll be excluded from certain conversations and meetings. And rightly so. ("You don't need to be at the planning day because, after all, you're not going to be around.")

You've chosen to move on, and so will the church.

By choosing to stay *fewer* than two weeks, you don't allow the ministry or the church to say goodbye. Both sides will need time to tie up loose ends and mourn and celebrate together. The only reason it's appropriate to leave with less than two weeks notice is if there are extreme matters of integrity at stake (e.g., the church is choosing to overlook the fact that the pastor is in an extramarital affair). Even then, prayerfully consider staying for two weeks for the sake of the youth ministry.

Attitude

This job may have been the worst ever. Truth be told, you believe it should be called "The First Church of Purgatory." But now isn't the time to act on those feelings. Dramatic resignations where you walk into the elder meeting, announce in no uncertain terms that they're instruments of Satan, and swagger out as they sit there stunned and weeping play well only in your imagination.

Reason for leaving

People are always excited to support someone who's leaving to follow a dream or pursue a next step in development. If you emphasize that you're leaving because of something going on in the organization, church members feel awkward and even rejected because they are choosing to stay. You may choose to disclose the whys to your inner circle, but the congregation won't know the story—and probably shouldn't.

Moving on

Here are the Youth Worker General's warning signs that indicate it may be time for you to move on:

- ▸ The senior minister starts to distance himself from you. He offers no back up when the women's ministry wants to take over the student room.
- ▸ There's little or no communication with leadership (e.g., they go on a leadership retreat to Maui and don't tell you about it).
- ▸ They keep you out of the public eye. You aren't even trusted with announcements.
- ▸ Leadership shows little or no interest in what's going on in youth ministry. Fifteen street kids have become Christians this year, and does anyone up there care?
- ▸ Your budget is cut—deeply cut. Now you have to pay for everything yourself. You say you already do.
- ▸ Rumblings and criticism against the youth program are entertained—like when the deacon chairman finally snaps and accuses you of not liking his nephew.
- ▸ You return from vacation and your office has been turned into the break room.

Be careful with what you say

Now's not the time to air dirty laundry or blast the church. Quite honestly, it will have very little impact and will only associate a bitter taste with your time of ministry.

Determine to not say anything negative to anyone or about anyone in the church. Even if rumors start flying, choose to maintain integrity. If there are issues that need to be dealt with, go to the appropriate person or people. Resolve to follow Matthew 18:15-17 and have your personal board of directors or close friends hold you accountable. Don't use social media as a place to lash out.

Realize that the church will continue

Early in our careers, we tend to believe the ministry will fall apart without us. We also are convinced we need to have a say regarding who replaces us. The harsh truth is that *we are replaceable* and that, generally, we have no right to a say regarding our successors.

Deal with your emotions

If this is a pleasant parting of the ways, you'll experience the normal paradox of sadness and excitement. However, if you're leaving amid anger and frustration, you'll need to figure out how to vent those emotions in a constructive manner. This may mean visiting a therapist for a session or two, getting out your journal and writing, or sitting with your network of local youth workers who have proven that they can keep their mouths shut. This is not the time to let the students or the volunteer team in on the dark side of this decision. Remember—they're staying.

FRUSTRATED?

What do you do with all the anger and frustration? In a private journal, write out your thoughts and feelings about the situation. Depending on the depth and seriousness, consider seeking a professional counselor with whom you can confidentially share these things.

Don't over-spiritualize

If you truly sense God is leading you on, you can say that. But don't put it all on God if that's not the case. Students can always detect a snow job. Figure out a way to communicate your resignation clearly and honestly.

If possible, don't leave without having another job lined up

It's very difficult to search for a job when you're unemployed. Unless circumstances are extremely difficult where you are, wait to resign until you have somewhere else to go.

FASTRACK

Leave for something, not because of something.

Writing a Resignation Letter

Make it short and to the point. This is not the time to write your Oscar acceptance speech or crucify the senior pastor and the board. Address it to the senior pastor or your supervisor and send copies to the chair of the board, head elder, or the appropriate parties in your organization (if in doubt, ask the senior pastor).

If you're leaving on good terms, say how much you enjoyed your time at the church and how they will remain in your prayers and in your heart. Cite the fact that you're resigning effective on such-and-such date. (Some people recommend that you leave the date blank until you've discussed it with your senior pastor.)

If you're leaving on strained terms, just include a statement that you're resigning and the date that it's effective. If at all possible, bless the church in some fashion (e.g., "My prayers will be with you during this time of transition."). Remember, once it's written and delivered, it's over. You can't edit it or take it back, and you won't have control over who sees it.

Whom Do I Notify?

Step 1
Talk with the senior pastor or your direct supervisor.
The ministry world is small and word travels fast. Your senior pastor needs to hear it from you, not someone else. Set up a meeting in a private place (not the church lobby as he's heading out the door to pick up his kids). Your church's policy manual may spell out how resignations are handled—or not handled. Follow those guidelines.

FASTRACK

If leaving is your decision, propose a departure timeline and maintain a positive and constructive attitude.

If you have a close relationship with your pastor or supervisor, consider bringing her into the loop prior to your resignation. Maybe let her know when you're starting to seriously consider a change. Learning of it after the fact may feel like a slap in the face to her. Each situation is different, but if you can risk being honest you may save the relationship over the long term. Also, your sharing may open up a discussion of issues in your present ministry situation. It may even lead you to reconsider looking somewhere else.

If you have written your resignation letter, bring it with you. If not, discuss what should be your last day and when you'll formally submit the letter. Ask him how he wants to handle the process. More than likely, he will not have a plan. You should. Suggest how you would like it handled and get his agreement. Many times he will concur with your suggestion. That said he may need some time to get back with you.

FASTRACK

Let your supervisor or senior pastor know when you're in the final stages of interviewing, and it looks like a done deal. If it's not a good working relationship at your current church, wait until you've accepted the position and then let your leadership know as quickly as possible.

Step 2
Meet with the associate pastors and staff.
Although your colleagues should know of your decision (preferably through you telling everyone in a meeting), caution them that you aren't making your resignation public for several days and ask that they keep the news confidential until you can tell the necessary parties yourself. And don't expect them to keep quiet for more than a week. After seven or eight days, the news gets filed in the brain's general info folder and easily becomes public knowledge. And—social media, texting and email make it easier than ever to leak the news.

Step 3
Meet with key leaders and parents.

Again, caution them that your resignation must remain confidential because you want to announce it to the students yourself. After telling them, answer questions they may have. You will need to lead them through the process. Don't expect them to know what to do. They'll probably sit stunned and feeling a little betrayed. This is especially true if you're leaving them for another youth ministry. For whatever reason, it's sometimes easier for parents and ministry teams to accept your resignation if you are heading to adult ministries, missions, or something outside of youth work.

Step 4
Announce it to the students.

Tell students about your resignation at a time when they will naturally be together, either on a Sunday morning or during small group. Make sure you tell them before it's announced at a church service. Be ready for the emotion you may face. Students handle news like this in different ways. If your ministry has experienced a lot of changes, don't be surprised if they are angry, cold, or unresponsive. Some may actually get up and walk out while others sit quietly.

If you are the third youth worker for a high school junior, be ready for some anger. Students may feel like you've betrayed them. If you've been at the church for a longer period of time, students may be deeply saddened (or relieved). It may be hard for them to understand how they will go on. This is especially true of junior highers. For them, the ministry is over. You need to help them see that God still loves them. Also, let students know that you're available in the next few weeks to talk if they want. They may not take you up on it, but it provides a certain sense of security for them to know you're available.

FasTrack
After telling the senior pastor that you're leaving, notify other paid staff, leaders in the youth ministry, and finally the students. All of this needs to take place within a week. Remember: As soon as you announce your resignation, you're not in control of the process. You take your cues from the leadership of the church.

What If It's Not My Desire To Leave?

It's always painful when it's not your choice to leave a position. But how you depart in these circumstances will say a lot about your character. Take the high road. Determine not to speak negatively about the church or anyone in the church, except to your therapist, journal, trusted friend, or accountability group.

It's normal for churches to include the phrase "at will" in an employment contract. It means that they can let you go whenever they want to. Unfair? Sometimes. Unfortunate? Always. Is it the norm? Thankfully, no. Caveat: If you feel that you've been unjustly discriminated against (perhaps because of race, gender, marital status, or age), seek legal counsel immediately. Do not accept the offer to resign (in lieu of being fired) or a severance check without first talking to a lawyer. By choosing to resign rather than be fired, you can make your case harder to prove in court.

Make sure you ask when your last day is, how students and staff will be notified of your departure, and what kind of severance package there will be. Hopefully, the church will provide some kind of financial assistance until you can get on your feet.

Be cautious of a sudden meeting where someone demands an immediate decision (unless you know why he or she is asking for your resignation). Don't be forced into a hair-trigger choice. Ask for a day (or two) to consider how you should respond. Then go and seek wise counsel. One youth worker was released from his church and was given no concrete reason when he asked why. He asked the church for severance pay for six months or until he found a new position, whichever was shorter. The church debated, then agreed to his request.

No matter what the circumstances of your leaving, it will be stressful for you. Make sure you have a support team to walk you through this—people who will pray for you and with you, who will listen to you, and who will give you wise counsel.

WHEN YOU LEAVE

REAL LIFE

One of the most helpful things my predecessor did was to leave me a note that profiled all the volunteers with their quirks and preferences, as well as observations on how to best work with them. I felt like I was ahead of the game before I even met with the team.

What can you take with you?
- ▶ Copies of fliers, management notebooks, copies of your computer files
- ▶ Books that the ministry bought for your professional library (You may want to verify this with your senior pastor or church administrator.)
- ▶ Personal items
- ▶ Leftover pizza

What should you leave behind?
- ▶ Originals of fliers, management files, and notebooks
- ▶ The computer and ministry files. Make sure you delete any personal files and email accounts. (Rule of thumb: It's best not to use a ministry

RECOMMENDED RESOURCES

- Go to www.churchlawandtax.com for the latest issue of their *Compensation Handbook for Church Staff*. This resource is very helpful to see if salary package is in the right range for the position, church size, location, etc.
- Search for "cost of living" for numerous sites and calculators that will help you find out how much it will cost to live in your new location. For example, http://www.bankrate.com/calculators/savings/moving-cost-of-living-calculator.aspx compares your current location to your future location.

FORMS

- Critical Questions You Need to Ask in the Interview
- Job Description
- Job-Interview Prep Checklist
- Job-Interview Questions You May Be Asked
- Résumé – Experienced 1
- Résumé – Experienced 2
- Résumé – Still in School
- Job Search Job Offer Checklist

computer for personal stuff. Technically, the church owns anything on the computer.)

- Ministry-specific books such as curriculum, training resources, etc.
- Make sure you give all personnel files, confidential computer files, counseling files, medical history forms, and other confidential information to someone who will keep them locked in a restricted area.
- Computer back-up drives
- Archives: photos, T-shirts, posters, brochures.
- The moment your resignation becomes effective, make sure you turn in your keys and church credit card (if you have one) for your own protection and have it documented that you did so.

Do a good job of leaving things in order. You should leave your files and office in better shape than you found them.

Starting and ending well are equally important. Your life is a story—make sure you live it well so that others can tell your story well. Set an example for leaders coming behind you. Staff members serving alongside you, and especially leaders to come, are taking notes. The students and families you have invested in surely are quietly observing. Resist (or even run from) the temptation to share any type of frustrations on social media. Buy a journal and record your deep feelings and honest prayers there.

Our actions (and angry words) speak louder than we think.

Yes, sometimes it's difficult to leave well. But choose to take the high road even if you have been hurt or wronged. Choose to pray for those you have served. Thank, honor, and bless the leaders as you go. Love well. Finish well.

4 MANAGING YOUR LIFE IN MINISTRY

CHAPTER OVERVIEW
- ▸ Time Management
- ▸ Setting Priorities
- ▸ Setting Boundaries
- ▸ Planning for Your Future

Although most of us had good elementary school teachers who made sure we understood the basics of reading, writing, and math, few of us have mastered the "other" basic skill—time management. Our efforts to organize are shaped by our personality styles, the systems of time management we use (or don't use), the environment of our churches, and our life-stage in ministry.

Too often our offices are littered with legal pads covered with scribbled notes, sticky notes, and reminder notes overflowing onto the floor. Those precious reminders could be blown into oblivion by a small gust of wind (whether from an open window or from your door when the senior pastor bursts in with news of a hastily scheduled meeting that night—your third in four nights). You must decide on one location for your to-do list and your appointment reminders, as well as for keeping up with important phone numbers and tidbits of information.

Why put everything in one place, you ask?

SCHEDULE IT
Buy and use a calendar—paper or electronic. But pick one. Stick with one. It's as simple—and as terrifying—as that.

REAL LIFE

Ministry veteran Darrell Pearson drove 90 minutes to meet with a stressed youth worker in need of time-management advice. "Can you wait a few minutes?" asked a staffer at the church. "Seems that an appointment with a volunteer just came up for Brad."

An hour later, Brad and Darrell finally went to lunch, but they only had 45 minutes together. Darrell then drove the 90 minutes home. By the time he got home, he had invested more than five hours.

- Because you can easily view an extended record of critical tasks and information at all times (especially helpful for visual people).
- Because you always know where to look for important information (the best way for disorganized people to actually find things).
- Because you'll have a natural organizational framework—that means you can make plans, confident that you're available.

TIME MANAGEMENT

For your best chance at getting organized, be sure to choose a method of information management that fits your personality and style. Then stick with it. For each entry of projected dates that you place on your working calendar, ask these questions. Is there:

- A clear and defined purpose?
- A facility to reserve?
- Transportation to arrange?
- A Web site to update, and/or flier to design, print, and mail?
- Staff to secure?
- A clear and approved budget?
- Other church communication pieces to which you must submit info?

Your approach to time management will also depend on your personality. Personality-appropriate time-management methods include:

- The creative type carries a leather journal and a box of 64 colored pencils to draw in her days the way she wants.
- The fly-by-the-seat-of-the-pants type writes reminders on his jeans.
- The indecisive type uses seven different versions of information tracking—at the same time.
- The auditory learner dictates his schedule to voice mail.
- The visual learner slaps sticky notes on her cubicle—a method that flunks the portability test.

GETTING STARTED

A number of effective tools are available to help you get organized—traditional printed calendars and planners can be found at office-supply stores. Planners vary in style, size, and available space for scheduling. Pick one that fits you. On the technology side—smartphones have built in calendars and a growing number of customizable calendar apps to suit your preferences. There are a growing number of great planning apps as well. The choices and options can be overwhelming, so take time to review the options and talk to other youth workers.

With technology, be sure to ask:

- Does it integrate with my church's IT or database system?
- Can other people view my calendar simply?
- How easily can others connect with my schedule?
- How easily can I actually use it?

Browse the possibilities, ask friends and coworkers what they use and why, pick a style that complements your personality, and commit to using it for three months.

It's been said that if you stick with something for 21 consecutive days, you're well on your way toward forming a new habit. Forming effective organizational habits (as opposed to living by unsupportive, unhelpful habits) is no different. You can replace old habits with new ones.

FasTrack

The foundation of managing your time is finding a system and or device that places important information in one place.

Don't be afraid to get help, either. Ever considered a time-management seminar? Find one and go to it. The investment is worth the results. (Given the complex demands on our time, managing this area of life can be hard to just figure out on our own.) Many seminars are simply careful explanations of detailed time-management systems, along with plans for integrating their systems into your life.

Worth the Time

Evaluate/First ask yourself:

- Is it simple to understand and easy to use?
- Will it really make my life better?
- Does it have the features I really want and need? (Can you live without bells and whistles you'll rarely, if ever, use?)
- What do the product reviews say about the variety of options?
- What do my "smartphone smart" friends recommend?
- Can I get by with a used one? (Okay, so your used smartphone wouldn't sport the newest screen, shape or button configuration, but often the older technology is still very helpful AND affordable.)

Low-Tech Calendars

Month-at-a-view calendars. These large, laminated wall calendars are available in many forms and varying graphic designs at most office-supply stores.

- ► Simple planning forms:
  - Monthly Planning
  - Weekly Planning

- ► 12- or 18-month calendars. Fill in simple calendar squares with the following information:
  - all major events (retreats, trips, mission projects, etc.)
  - staff meetings and parent meetings
  - special events (outreaches, community service, fundraisers)

Monthly
Planning
page 350

Weekly
Planning
page 351

Earlier in the book we discussed understanding your church's ministry goals and how to set your ministry goals within that context. You'll read about taking a personal retreat where you articulate your vision for your personal life and for your ministry. "In my dreams," you retort. "I'm already four days into this month. Who can think about long-range vision and personal retreats at a time like this?" If you just want to know how to get through these next four weeks, the Weekly Planning and Monthly Planning forms will put you in action so you'll still have a job after you spend time vision making.

Try using the forms like to-do lists rather than in-depth planning tools. Simply make several photocopies of each form, punch holes, and place the sheets in a thin three-ring binder. At least you'll have a place to capture ideas that come to you while you're waiting for that elusive stretch of time during which you will do serious goal setting and planning.

Not a physical notebook user? Create an e-notebook in Evernote. Place these same forms there. It will store your forms locally and in the cloud, can set reminders, and can be shared with others.

Another way to use the forms is to fill out the Priority Scale worksheet. Instead of prioritizing one day's tasks, though, order milestone tasks or events facing you in the coming month. Complete the worksheet as explained on page 310. As you total the "votes" for each of the nine items you're ordering, list those prioritized results on the monthly or weekly plan-

EVERNOTE

Evernote makes it easy to remember things big and small from your everyday life using your computer, phone, tablet, and the Web. Have access to your notes across multiple platforms. Key features of Evernote: Create text, photo, and audio notes; clip Web pages including text, links, and images; synchronize your notes across your devices; search for text within snapshots and images.

ning sheet. Finally, fill in the appropriate blocks with calls, notes, or ideas that reflect your progress toward reaching the goals you've listed.

Electronic Calendars

Smartphones

The essential hand-held devices are lightweight, designed for use as personal organizers. Most enable users to carry a ton of info with them or let you download articles and music, organize your week, keep your assistant informed of your schedule, find important numbers and addresses, operate from one schedule on multiple devices, receive and read your email, send text messages across the room during boring meetings (when you should be paying attention . . .). These are just a few of the things your smartphone can help you do.

FasTrack

A planner is a good fit when it gets used and when it helps you be more effective.

A typical smartphone is lightweight, has a bright screen and a battery that lasts . . . until you can't find a plug to recharge. (Hint: Get a mophie® recharger and carry it with you in case you run out of juice.) Be sure to get a protective case—and do what you can to protect the screen. A cracked screen is EXPENSIVE. In addition to including such applications as a word processor, spreadsheet, calendar, and address book, smartphones can act as notepads, appointment schedulers, social media connectors, cameras, portable credit devices and can connect you wirelessly so you can send and receive information of just about any kind imaginable.

Choosing a Smartphone

The Apple iOS and the Android are the most popular, dependable operating systems and certainly have the greatest number of applications developed. CNET has great reviews.

Your friends have great ideas and experiences to share with you. We confess to being partial to iPhones, but the Android operating system is pretty sweet also—ask your friends what they use. Ask your students what they use.

"Hold it. I'm a broke youth worker. I have no cash for luxuries like this. So stop feeding me all this info . . . I'm resigned to using my yellow pad and the pocket calendar our church gives to new members." If money's the only thing that's stopping you, try this simple idea to get a smartphone (or maybe even a tablet or laptop) in three easy steps:

1. Put out the word at your church, starting with your supervisor, that you're looking to upgrade to a smartphone.
2. Let people know you don't need a brand-new one—you want to buy a used one from someone who's upgrading.
3. Wait by the phone. You will be getting a call shortly. People really are generous and, if asked the right way, love to help.

Expectations and Time

Church congregations often expect youth ministers to be competent in:

- family counseling
- computer science
- theology
- graphic arts
- communication
- church history
- church politics
- sports
- multimedia
- cultural issues
- eating disorders
- music groups
- drug and alcohol abuse
- parenting
- crisis intervention
- budget management
- family systems
- event planning
- correspondence
- first aid
- death and dying
- marriage counseling

. . . and most likely a few other things, but there's only so much space. In a typical week, you as a youth worker may:

- prepare multiple talks.
- return calls to students and their families.
- handwrite notes of encouragement.
- plan upcoming events.
- pray with worried parents.
- wade through tons of junk mail and try to keep up with email.
- attend school events.
- meet with and develop staff.
- desperately look for a fresh new game.
- replace the leg on a table upon which seven freshmen sat (and broke) yesterday.

In light of all these expectations, finding a way to manage your calendar is essential. Blocking out periods of time to focus on important areas is essential. Part of your ministry plan has to be recruiting and developing a team of volunteers to assist you in many of these areas. You can't do it all. And to do this—you have to set aside time. You have to plan. You have to use your time wisely.

Setting Priorities

Be aware of the things that use up your time, seemingly without your permission. You are guaranteed trouble if you come to your office without a plan for the day. (In fact, without a plan it's amazing how much time can be consumed by potential time wasters such as social media, email, etc.). Time just slides by—especially when you're sitting in Starbucks with a great cup of coffee. Ministry, however, is not about putting our time in at the office. It's about being men and women who steward time well. Not that you need to plan every moment of every day, which will only lead to frustration, inflexibility, and the end of students dropping by your office. It means being aware of the ways you spend your time—deliberately choosing the things that you will allow to use your time.

Once you have your planning system in place, **use it**. (Sorry, but it's not enough to just have one.) So here's how to start:

Plan your week before it starts.

Commit to spend the last "work" hour of your current week mapping out the next week. Do this by filling in your schedule with standard weekly responsibilities and priorities first: staff meetings, church services, appointments, study time, taking your day off (really!), personal devotional time, Bible studies, calling new students, whatever. Then fill it in with the more flexible stuff: when you'll return emails and calls, when you'll be on campus, when you'll meet with students, write newsletters, clean up Wednesday night's mess . . .

Do long-range planning.

The goal here is to fill in major dates a minimum of six to 12 months out. (Yes, you heard right.) First, however, you must establish your goals. What are they, anyway? Your calendar should reflect your commitment to your goals. Fill in the following (with the help of your boss, spouse, or whoever else is affected by or helps determine your schedule): important family dates (including regular time with your significant other), vacation, long-range planning days, prep time (it's in the previous section), retreats, camps and mission trips, staff retreats, youth ministry conventions, personal retreat days for your spiritual renewal, continuing education days. Don't forget to fill in standard monthly responsibilities in advance. (See "Activities calendaring and ministry values," Chapter 7, for a more complete list of things to consider in your annual planning.)

Take time to design your annual teaching plan.

Lay out your teaching curriculum a year out. Why that far in advance? Because it relieves the weekly "What am I going to teach this week?" pressure. Because it

---

TECHNOLOGY RESOURCES

- The App stores for Apple and Android
- To Do Apps—Wunderlist, Things, Google Tasks, Reminders, ToodleDo, Omnifocus, Remember the Milk

PUBLISHED RESOURCES

- *First Things First*, Stephen Covey (Simon & Schuster, 1994)
- *The On-Purpose Person: Making Your Life Make Sense*, Kevin McCarthy (Piñon Press, 1992)
- *The Seven Habits of Highly Effective People*, Stephen Covey (Simon & Schuster, 1989)
- *Getting Things Done: The Art of Stress-Free Productivity*, David Allen (Penguin Books, 2001)

FasTrack

Use your last hour each work week to calendar repeating responsibilities and then your to-do list for the next week.

enables you to balance what you teach. Because it allows you to prepare your talks earlier. Your media team can check your teaching schedule and work ahead to support your topic. You can recruit someone to help write great discussion material around your content. Planning ahead gives you time to schedule guest speakers who could do a great job on a certain subject. And last—but certainly not least (because it reinforces that you actually know what you're doing):

Candidates for your regular weekly schedule:

- new student follow-up
- message prep
- Web updates
- staff communication
- check requests
- sharing prayer needs
- personal devotion and prayer
- exercise
- reading
- encouragement-note writing
- relationship-building
- pastor's choice (Ask your pastor what he or she thinks you need to schedule in each week.)

SENSITIZING YOURSELF TO YOUR TIME USE

Be aware of the ways you choose to spend your time. Be aware of the things that use up your time, seemingly without your permission. In youth ministry, we can easily fall into responding to all situations as if they're crises—even when they aren't. To put it plainly, helping a suicidal student would be a crisis; making sure you return every email, respond to every Facebook post, or comment on every Instagram image within an hour isn't.

Time Log
page 311

To take a look at how you use your time, use the following incredibly helpful tool taught by Stephen Covey to evaluate all the things you do during a week. It is based on a famous quote attributed to President Dwight D. Eisenhower:

"What is important is seldom urgent and what is urgent is seldom important."

Use last week as an example, or use the Time Log to track your time use in the coming week. Label each thing you do with one of the four quadrants. Be tough on yourself! Is losing yourself in Twitter updates really "Important and Urgent"? Granted, after seasons in youth ministry where everything is "Urgent and Important," prioritizing things in the "Not Urgent and Not Important" quadrant for a period of time needs to be your first priority. Just don't settle down there.

In reality we spend too little time in the "Not Urgent but Important" quadrant. Yet that's where our creativity is fed, our priorities ordered, and our soul nourished. This quadrant includes spiritual retreats, reading for learning and pleasure, and dreaming and praying over the future of the ministry (further out than tonight's lock-in). If you want to last in a youth ministry career, spend a greater proportion of your time and energy on tasks in the "Not Urgent but Important" quadrant.

This model is available as software and as an app—it's called Priority Matrix and is available at www.appfluence.com. Priority Matrix is simple and effective task management software to help you get the right things done.

	URGENT	NOT URGENT
IMPORTANT	Crises Pressing problems Deadline-driven projects Meetings Preparation	Preparation Prevention Values clarification Planning Relationship building True re-creation Empowerment
NOT IMPORTANT	Interruptions, some phone calls Some email, some reports Some meetings Many proximate, pressing matters Many popular activities	Trivia, busywork Most email Some phone calls Time wasters . . . Escape activities
IMPORTANT	**Quadrant I: Urgent and important.** We experience the activities in Quadrant I as both important and urgent. Our normal day can have its share of unscheduled meetings with parents or students, deadlines for agendas or newsletters, and cries for help from other staff members. This square can get unmanageable, though, if we also fill it with procrastinated tasks that have achieved rush status. Back when we said we'd do these jobs, we had time to do them well and even thought they would be fun to do. But once they make the Quadrant I list, they become unwelcome clutter among the truly important and urgent.	**Quadrant II: Not urgent and important.** Quadrant II represents activities that make for quality ministry: long-range planning, developing interns, professional development, and visioning. Pushing off these kinds of tasks until they're urgent means we're no longer leading; rather we're barely ahead of the pack and maybe just as clueless as they are about where we're headed. "Purpose-driven" describes the results of time spent in this quadrant.
NOT IMPORTANT	**Quadrant III: Urgent and not important.** When we catch ourselves doing Quadrant III activities, we can be sure that other people's priorities and expectations are overshadowing our goals. Like airline passengers at 30,000 feet in a plane that has blown its doors, we're sucked out of our purpose into an unchecked plummet.	**Quadrant IV: Not urgent and not important.** The final square—Covey calls it the Quadrant of Waste—feels like gulping in air after holding our breath too long. But its activities, far from helping us to survive, merely help us deteriorate further. Better to spend time in true re-creation, a Quadrant II energy recharge.

REAL LIFE

I was asked not long ago what it was like to do ministry in the "old days"— you know, before voice mail, smartphones, texting, and email. During the heyday of mimeograph machines and White-Out. When people walked to school barefoot, in the snow, uphill—both ways.

New tools certainly make it easier, faster, and more efficient to communicate with people today, but something tells me it was easier to stay focused then. I'm sure I had more time to think. I could work without hearing "You've got mail" every two minutes.

On the other hand, I can remember frittering away a lot of perfectly good thinking time and visiting around the office, distracting other people. So when we remember the good old days truthfully, we recognize the same saboteurs that derail us in the 21st century— the timeless human traits of restlessness, procrastination, and avoidance in the old days were as prevalent as they are today. It's just that the tools were fewer and simpler.

CHARTING PRIORITIES
Get a Bulletin Board

Create a visual reminder of scheduled appointments, events, and activities by writing the names of projects on index cards and then pinning them on your bulletin board, ordered by project priority. There are several online tools and apps to consider including Trello, Post-it Digital Notes, Stickies, and Evernote.

Don't be afraid to close your door, shut off your phone, and seriously focus on a single task.

Manage Interruptions

We all require slots of uninterrupted time to do tasks that require extended focus. So how do you deal with the inevitable interruptions to your plan for the day? Try these ideas:

If you don't have an office door to close, make a sign: "Revival in progress. Do not disturb."

Work away from your office—a park, restaurant, coffee shop, library. Leave a note on your desk or door or with a receptionist about your return time. Make sure you get approval in advance from your supervisor on this one!

You may want to consider somewhere that DOES NOT provide Wi-Fi if you are looking for time to focus. Or try Freedom, an inexpensive app that locks out the Internet for a set amount of time (http://freedomapp.us).

If someone interrupts, let him know that you must finish what you're working on and suggest another time to get together. Train others to always ask, "Is this a good time for you?" Never assume someone is available just because you are.

Instead of interrupting another person with "just a quick question," write it down so you don't forget. Then when she takes a break, schedule a 10-minute meeting with her.

Send email or text instead of phoning or making face-to-face contact. That way people can respond when it's convenient for them.

Rather than calling or going into someone's office every time you think of something to talk over, make a "People Page" to record thoughts, ideas, conversations, and questions you need to discuss with others.

Interrupting is a bad habit. Interrupting can be as obnoxious as nose picking. Evernote is a great solution for this—create a page for each person you work with and keep your notes and questions for them here.

File questions until you can meet with the person to whom you want to pose them. For example, when you question a receipt, a line item on the budget, or fill out a check request, place the document in a file folder labeled "church treasurer." (Caveat: Never leave checks or cash in a mere file folder or in the back of a desk drawer. Make deposits daily, if necessary. Don't keep money in your office!)

Carry a digital recorder, use an app on your phone, or carry a small notebook in your backpack titled "My Brilliant Thoughts" to capture those big "ah-has" before you forget them five minutes later.

FASTRACK

Schedule regular, interruption-free time for yourself.

When you're on task, give to that task the same consideration you give to students you counsel. Just as those you're helping need 100 percent of your attention (they can always tell when your mind wanders), whatever it is you're working on needs 100 percent of you, too. (By the way, it's probably best to turn your smartphone off while meeting with someone! And ask students to turn off theirs when they're meeting with you.)

Don't read your email while talking on the phone. You listen poorly, and more often than not it's obvious to the person on their other end of the line. Yes, we've all done it—but most of us have also felt it when someone else was doing this to us. So don't do it.

SETTING BOUNDARIES

Part of a youth ministry job description is being available to spontaneously connect with people. All of us face the temptation that we must be all things to all people at all times. That's still a popular myth—many youth workers always have their cell phones on so they can be reached any time, night or day. It's worth stepping back to ask if this is healthy and to explore the potential consequences of this habit. Many smartphones now have a DO NOT DISTURB feature that allows you to set hours when you're not available. Learn how to guard your time so you can stay in ministry for the long haul.

Availability and boundaries

ALWAYS AVAILABLE, ALWAYS ON CALL, ALWAYS WILLING TO LISTEN. Isn't this the youth ministry motto? Isn't this at least what's expected?

Motto or not, this mindset is unhealthy if not impossible and leads to broken lives and broken families. If your church expects your unlimited availability, polish up your résumé. Yes, students must sense your accessibility and feel how deeply you care for them. Yes, we must be available in crises. Yet we must also choose to place appropriate boundaries around our time when there's no legitimate crisis.

Beware of Time Eaters

As a very young child, I was convinced that monsters lived under my bed. Only if my body was between the sheets and all bedding was tucked in tightly around me did I feel safe. If I ever sensed the monsters were about to eat me, I pulled the sheet over my head. No monster ever broke through that protective shield.

SMART TIP

Rotate the on-call responsibility among key leaders (both lay and paid) who then share the responsibility of being Crisis Point-Persons.

Most of us survived childhood monsters, managing to keep them secret from our friends. But as adults we're now terrorized by the monsters of poor time management. Instead of facing them down, many of us pull the sheets over our heads when they threaten to eat up our time.

You can tell the monsters are on the loose in your office if you're:

- distracted by a constant stream of urgent but unimportant email.
- browsing junk mail that cries out "open me now."
- putting out fires (literally and figuratively).
- getting sucked into helping unjam the copy machine . . . for the third time today . . . for the children's ministry volunteer.
- searching YouTube for the latest super funny viral video.
- having multiple unimportant-but-apparently-urgent conversations.
- taking phone calls when you should be writing, studying, or praying.
- rearranging your iTunes library.
- wandering around and calling it a prayer walk.
- not planning your time and working your plan.
- moving piles from your desk to the top of the filing cabinet.
- buying your fourth Mountain Dew (before 11 a.m.).

Multiply Your Time with Time Beaters

A Time Beater is the opposite of a speed bump—it gets you moving faster and more efficiently. People don't plan to fail, it has been said—they simply fail to plan. It can be lots of little things that keep us from planning and thinking clearly and purposefully about the important things. Time Beaters increase the amount of work you can complete in a limited amount of time.

Time Beater #1

Limit the amount of time you spend checking email and social media. Nothing undermines commitment to our priorities more quickly than seeing a new joke that we "just have to read and share." Instant messaging should be renamed instant distraction. The same goes for text messaging.

You're halfway through this week's talk (your self-imposed deadline is one hour away), and you're desperately searching online for the perfect illustration. Accompanied by a custom sound, a messaging window suddenly pops into view. *Hey, it's Julia . . . wonder how she's doing?* Thirty minutes of reliving college life later . . .

If you're online with a mission, mark yourself as not available. Better yet—sign out. Go for finishing your message on time.

Time Beater #2
Schedule a time of day to check and return voice mail messages.

Although it's okay to ignore the message notification on your phone, nothing eats away at your credibility like having a voice mail greeting on your phone that says, "I've just stepped away from my desk, but I'll get right back to you" when the caller knows you're on a missions trip building an orphanage or suspects you're still at home and asleep. A better message (changed daily when appropriate) lets people know when you'll return phone calls: "I'm off-site today doing some retreat prep. I'll be returning phone calls tomorrow morning between 8 and 10. If you need immediate assistance, press 0." This allows you to just say no. Don't worry—if the message is from a kid in a major crisis, someone will figure out how to reach you.

FASTRACK

Use the Touch It Once strategy when a piece of paper first comes across your desk: Read it, respond to it, then file it or toss it. If you don't know how to deal with it today, you probably won't tomorrow, either. Apply the same principle to emails. Read, decide, respond, file.

Time Beater #3
Get out.

Take an occasional day away from the office to plan and reflect. Clear a date with your boss weeks or months in advance. After 20-plus years of ministry, we've found there's never time to take these types of days, but nothing has been more helpful to us. They are especially important when you're faced with significant ministry decisions (including how to tell the pastor about the bus accident, how to reimburse that family for the hole in their living room wall, how to explain to your board about your summer mission trip to Hawaii).

SMART TIP

Intervene for a staff member who may need some quiet time. For instance, give your senior pastor an interruption-free afternoon by covering phone calls and taking messages.

It's amazing what comes to light when you stop to be quiet. Sit down at the beginning of the year with your supervisor and calendar several of these days (or at least half-days). Then no matter what happens when that day arrives—get

FIGHTING YOUTH MINISTRY'S BAD RAP

So let's be honest. Youth workers—we are fun people. People like us. But for some reason, someone got the idea that we are disorganized, don't plan ahead, break things, overspend our budgets, don't return calls or emails, forget to thank people, never tell the church secretary where we went, and don't seem to work very hard . . . say it ain't so!

Take some steps today to. . . .

Get yourself organized—start by bringing some organizers on to your volunteer team.
Develop a plan. Yup—you heard it right.
If you break it—own up to it. Then fix it or replace it.
Go buy some thank-you notes—and then write some thank-you notes.
Share your weekly schedule with people at your church.
Do your part. Work hard. Help others. Initiate.

away. If you take your cell phone, turn it off. Don't call in and check your messages. Be unavailable. Use these days for prayer, journaling, study, reflection, evaluation, planning—and maybe, just maybe—rest. Dare to take a nap. Daydream. Go for a long walk. Who's gonna tell?

THE PRIORITY OF RELATIONSHIPS

Effective time managers value relationships. How is investing in people part of time management? Because the greatest way to spend your time is by developing leaders from among your students and volunteers. While it may be possible within a few years to clone yourself, in the meantime you're charged with the responsibility and privilege of working through others—better known as delegation.

Youth ministry routinely suffers because the youth worker gets caught up in short-term demands and minor duties (Quadrant III activities—see page 75). But it's long-range planning, quality training of volunteer and student leaders, and professional development that produce quality, long-lasting ministry.

To create more time for doing what only you can do, hand off routine work by delegation, even though:

▶ you know you could do it better (and faster) yourself.
▶ you worry that someone else might do it so well it'll make you look bad.
▶ your controlling nature rebels at the thought.
▶ you're too disorganized to have the time and presence of mind to delegate.
▶ _____(Fill in the blank with your personal angst.)

Good delegation is rooted in the soil of good relationships. Good relationships grow when watered with plenty of frank communication and mutual esteem. But this takes time—time that you purposefully calendar into your weekly schedule. Your schedule reflects the things you value. (Remember: You show yourself and others what you value by actually doing it.)

Are you scheduling enough time to effectively delegate significant ministry tasks to paid staff, volunteers, and students? Keep a Time Log for one week. Log in at 15-minute intervals—minimum. At the end of the week classify how you spent your time, using major categories (e.g., appointments, staffing, teaching, planning, studying, email, office stuff). (On-Core Time Master is an inexpensive app that helps you track where you spend your time and generates a variety of reports.) To increase time in key areas for the next week, place those items in your schedule in advance. Then delegate those tasks another person could do, with a few pointers—like purchasing a list of supplies you need for an upcoming trip or retreat. Delegation is an absolutely essential life skill. After successfully delegating simple tasks, you'll gradually learn to trust people to achieve more complex results.

> **HERE'S A SIMPLE PRINCIPLE FOR YOUR LEADERSHIP**—always leave things BETTER than you found them.

Expand Your Network of Relationships

Get to know the principal of the local high school, youth workers from around your city, police (for a real eye-opener, sign up for a ride-along with a cop), a therapist whose specialty is teenagers and parents, sports coaches, and others. Carve out regular time to get to know those who can help you be more effective in your ministry. Some of these people may assist you in a time of need (or you may assist them). Some of these relationships may open up significant doors of ministry in your community. Many of these people will be eager to connect with you—just be sure to give them plenty of lead time when you ask to meet. Most need advance notice to fit you into their schedule.

Be ready for your time with them when they say yes. Think through what you want to ask them. Your goal should be to learn about their worlds. Understand their challenges. Hear their stories. Find out if there are ways your ministry can serve them.

FASTRACK

Make relationship-building a priority when you schedule your week's activities.

For example, some amazing people in San Jose, Calif., decided to serve their community. To simply ask "what do YOU need?" Then they did just that. It has developed into an amazing movement. Learn more at www.beautifulday.org.

Expand your network. Open your eyes. Serve others.

Find ways each week to invest in important relationships. As a people developer (your primary role!), ask yourself questions like these every week:

- ▸ What have I done to encourage others?
- ▸ How am I multiplying my ministry?
- ▸ Who are the different people I (and my ministry) need to relate to: new students, long-time church kids, parents, volunteer staff, troubled teens, the pastor's kids, unchurched kids in the community, others? What about my neighbors? What about the families who live in the neighborhood right next to my church?

▸ Who can help me meet the diverse needs of these groups?

▸ What have I done this week to work my way out of a job? (As crazy as it might sound, delegating and mentoring *build* job security. Yes, it takes time—you could probably do a given job quicker and better by yourself. But by taking the time to train and empower others, you slowly expand and multiply your ministry. A greater number of people have ownership and, ultimately, the opportunity to grow.)

Build relationships by getting to know people and students well. In *Leadership That Works*, Leith Anderson reminds us that everyone needs to be paid—if not with money, then in other ways:

▸ Build a reminder file to help you keep up with their favorite things—foods, music, books, places, and movies.

▸ Mail or email them notes of encouragement.

▸ Remember their birthdays—drop them cards and call them. Family members remember most birthdays. But having non-relatives celebrate birthdays with lunches, calls to wish them a great day, or afternoon snacks help make people feel special. Make a big deal out of that day (unless of course they are trying to forget their age). Business giant Harvey McKay designed his relationship-building strategy around remembering and caring for people on their birthdays.

▸ Request budgeted money to purchase birthday cards, lunches, and other treats for your staff.

▸ Share with them a helpful book or resource.

▸ Send them to a seminar.

▸ Learn to appreciate them in ways that are meaningful to them.

▸ You can do better than wishing them Happy Birthday on Facebook!

Is relationship-building part of your job description? Building relationships is a staple in a youth minister's job description. So, the answer to this question is YES. The only problem is that this task is a "soft" one that defies typical quantification. It's a lot easier to report how many seats were filled in youth group and Sunday school or how many parent complaints you're getting than to describe the states of the several relationships you're cultivating.

Furthermore, just who are you paid (or compelled) to relate to and encourage?

Students? Your adult volunteer staff? Families of your students? Fringe kids? Non-Christians? You'll need to sit down and talk with your pastor or a member of the appropriate board. Ask them point blank, "What do you expect my relationship-building to look like—a soda with a kid at Smash Burger, Sunday school teaching, training a small group of adult volunteers to do youth ministry?" Boldly probe your pastor or board about their expectations until they are articulated to your satisfaction—and preferably in writing.

While it may feel at times that you've been hired to plan lessons and activities, developing people is as important a role—no matter what your ministry title. Calendaring a good chunk of time each week to invest in people helps you keep relationship-building a priority.

Professional Boundaries

Ever wondered how youth workers end up in inappropriate relationships with students? How they end up burned out and angry? How someone who was once so passionate for Christ ends up quitting ministry for something else?

They got confused about their boundaries. Worse yet, they had no boundaries.

As much as technology has helped us increase our impact, it's also underscored our 24/7 availability. It's not uncommon to hear people describe sleeping with their smartphones next to their beds or under their pillows—just to make sure they never miss anything. Social connections allow us to have private conversations with almost anyone at any time. Faced with overwhelming work, pressures, and needs around us, left unchecked we can slowly adopt dangerous relational patterns. We as leaders can begin to look for approval, affirmation, and relationship in the wrong places.

We live in an age of increasingly difficult decisions. How accessible should we be? Who should we be texting? Who should we be friends with on Facebook? How do we practice accountability? Yup—lots of new questions to wrestle with. Questions you as a leader need to take responsibility to discuss with your co-leaders. Questions about texting, Facebook friend decisions, private messaging, what's appropriate to post on social media as a staff person—the list keeps growing.

A growing number of school districts are implementing new policies that govern teachers' social media and texting behavior. A good place to start with your policy development is to check with your local school district. These policies are changing rapidly.

24/7 availability is another significant challenge. There can be subtle pressure

SMART TIP

Role 'em! Is your head spinning with all the roles you must play? No biggie. Write down all your roles. Identify the top six or seven. Number them in order of priority. Use the Priority Scale on page 310 to help you think through what tasks need to happen each week in each of these areas.

Priority Scale
page 310

(or maybe not so subtle . . .) to always be responsive to texts, calls, and emails, especially if the church is providing your phone.

It's just not the case.

We all need down and away time to be healthy. For those with spouses and children, they need focused time with us. For single youth workers, you need undistracted time with friends.

Consider the following boundaries:

> IT'S PROBABLY BEST if you and your student ministry team present your proposed ministry policies to those to whom you're accountable. Many board members and senior leaders in our churches don't understand the social media environment and the potential downfalls. You and your team best know the traps and temptations you each face. Name them, list them, respond to them.

- ▸ Don't bring your cell phone to the dinner table.
- ▸ Have a "no cell phone on date night" rule.
- ▸ If you're single, plan times in the week with friends where you leave your cell phone at home.
- ▸ Use the Do Not Disturb feature on your smartphone.
- ▸ When you're meeting with someone, leave your cell phone in a bag or across the room.
- ▸ Don't bring your cell phone into worship.
- ▸ Turn off your email when you go on vacation.
- ▸ Don't check your messages on your days off—and don't be afraid to use your out-of-office message to let people know whom they can reach in case of an emergency.
- ▸ Share "Pastor on Call" responsibilities with others on staff.
- ▸ Take a break from social media on a regular basis.

In recent conversations, the phrase "smartphones make us dumb" has come up consistently. Carrying on uninterrupted conversations and performing uninterrupted work is nearly nonexistent today. A growing number of studies indicate decreased productivity due to multitasking and frequent social-media distractions. Just Google the phrase "smartphones make us dumb." Happy reading.

Rest and *Sabbath* are expressions that should regularly be a part of all believers' lives, but especially those in ministry. Define your boundaries. Talk about them with your family and friends. Share them with your supervisor. Get serious about being and staying healthy in your relationships.

PLANNING FOR YOUR FUTURE

When faced with exciting ministry opportunities filled with needs from the moment you arrive, it can be difficult to ever stop and think about the long haul. How do we adequately prepare for a lifetime of ministry? Sooner or later, we will all transition out of youth ministry. Will our education, experiences, and personal development path support our next opportunity? By no means am I (Mike) implying that youth ministry is a stepping-stone. In fact, I believe that many youth workers leave youth ministry just as they are reaching their period of greatest impact. Stop and ask yourself: *How old was your favorite high school teacher?* I have found that the answer to this question has generally been teachers who were older—but who still had a deep love for students and the subjects they were teaching. I believe it's the same in ministry with students—it's less about age and more about passion and commitment to students.

MINISTRY FOR THE LONG HAUL

Wherever you are in your ministry journey, finding ways to develop yourself is essential. It begins by knowing yourself, your strengths and weaknesses. Assess areas where you are in need of development. Surround yourself with people who complement you, who fill in for your blind spots. But as you do that, keep growing. Keep developing.

There are a growing number of great tools available to help you know yourself. Search these great options:

▸ Myers-Briggs Personality Test—http://www.myersbriggs.org
▸ DISC Profile—http://www.discprofile.com
▸ StrengthsFinder—http://www.strengthsfinder.com
▸ Predictive Index—http://www.piworldwide.com

While many of these can be taken independently, it's a good idea to consult with someone who has been trained to use and interpret these tools. Career counselors/coaches and many therapists have access to these resources. It's well worth the investment into their work with you.

Education

While opinions vary among churches regarding the importance of education, it seems there are only regrets from people who didn't press themselves forward in this area. While God can and certainly does use people in ministry regardless of education, finishing college and pursuing a graduate degree only increases and expands your opportunities. Theological training is increasingly important as our culture moves further away from any understanding of a biblical framework. The ability to contextualize and discuss practical theology is essential. It's hard to imagine now the doorways that may be opened in the future by the completion of that degree, but just know they are there. They are coming. If all things are equal, your education will give you the advantage over another person with the same experience. And, a growing number of churches and organizations have educational requirements in their hiring.

Many schools have great programs for people currently in ministry. As you're aware, online education has exploded. There are a wide variety of schedules and degree options available. Look, ask, learn.

Personal Development

The GPS has revolutionized how we get places. The fold-up map is a thing of the past. But for the GPS to be useful, we have to enter a destination. Knowing the directions only works when you actually know the final destination. And if you've ever entered an incorrect address on your GPS, you know exactly what we mean.

It's similar with our personal development. We are all headed somewhere in our journey of life. As difficult as it seems, that somewhere extends beyond where you currently are in your journey. Someday you may be called away from your role to be a professor, lead pastor, social worker, missionary, teacher, therapist, multi-site pastor, creative director, writer, cook, or you fill in the blank _____.

Continuing to grow and develop is essential. So look for opportunities to expand your knowledge and be stretched. Some of these experiences include Willow Creek's Leadership Summit, Leadercast, and Catalyst. The National Youth Workers Convention is an annual tradition for many student ministry teams. Coaching groups are another way to learn. An increasing number of leaders are offering coaching groups that meet three to five times a year to discuss important topics and share resources.

Networking

Taking time to develop relationships outside your own ministry is vital. A large number of positions are filled through networking with others. Networking takes intentionality and the investment of time. The tyranny of the urgent often competes with our ability to be involved with others. But you will reap what you sow!

Why network? We reach out to others for a variety of reasons—from the desire to expand friendships, to a place to get fresh ideas, to a group to challenge your thinking, or a place to share and invite others to your ministry idea or event. Sadly, we often shortchange the relationship side of things and rush to the "do this for me" side of things. At its core, good networking involves encouragement, new friendships, shared resources, thought and skill sharpening, and a safe place to share and get support.

Facebook, blogs, and networking organizations provide venues for connections. Can't find a group in your area? Then start your own. Want to host a great network gathering? Look for a central location with good food and a private space that will allow you to help people connect, offer free resources, and create a fast-paced time free of multiple pitches. If you plan ahead (and well), a surprising number of people will want to pay for your gathering. Just be prepared to give them a little time to share about their business, ministry, or organization with you.

RECOMMENDED RESOURCES

▶ *The Plateau Effect: Getting from Stuck to Success*, Bob Sullivan

▶ *The On-Purpose Person: Making Your Life Make Sense*, Kevin McCarthy

▶ *First Things First*, Stephen Covey

▶ *The Seven Habits of Highly Effective People*, Stephen Covey

▶ *The 3 Secrets to Effective Time Investment: Achieve More Success with Less Stress*, by Elizabeth Grace Saunders

▶ *Manage Your Day-to-Day: Build Your Routine, Find Your Focus, and Sharpen Your Creative Mind (The 99U Book Series)* by Jocelyn K. Glei

▶ *Organize Your Mind, Organize Your Life: Train Your Brain to Get More Done in Less Time* by Margaret Moore and Paul Hammerness

▶ *Getting Things Done: The Art of Stress-Free Productivity* by David Allen

FORMS

▶ Priority Scale
▶ Time Log

PART 3

ORGANIZATION AND YOUTH MINISTRY

5 GENERAL OFFICE PROCEDURES

CHAPTER OVERVIEW
▸ Office Setup
▸ Organize the Chaos
▸ Organize the Documents

Organization? Have you tried nailing Jell-O to a tree? The very nature of youth ministry seems to defeat all attempts to organize.

Picture the last time you came into your office early. You are excited to accomplish a bunch of work. Your to-do list includes finishing your next three-month calendar, whipping out a newsletter, stopping by the middle school basketball game, and meeting a volunteer for coffee. As you log on to your email, the church administrator calls to remind you that your budget is due tonight. The phone rings again—a parent wants to know how much money his son has yet to pay for next summer's mission trip. The custodian drops by to ask where the keys to the church van are and how much you spent on gas last week and to remind you to pull the pencils out of the bathroom ceiling.

> **VALID OR NOT,** people will make assumptions about who you are based on the appearance of your office.

By this time, your email has finished synching. Thirty-three new messages? One from the pastor reads, "I've got to make a presentation to the board tonight, and I need some information from you on the last six months in the youth ministry. You know, attendance, finances, event evaluations, etc. I know it's last minute, but I figured you could grab this information quickly. Oh, and a few pictures, and maybe student comments would be a nice touch. And could one of your volunteers come share an inspiring story? Have a blessed day."

So much for an early start. Your task list is overrun by everyone else's crises trying to become your crises. But you are ready for the onslaught because you organize your space, your information, your resources, your paper, and your tasks for days just like this.

> **CREATE A WORK ENVIRONMENT** that helps you be effective, people who work with you find what they need, and students and their parents feel comfortable.

OFFICE SETUP
IF THESE WALLS COULD SPEAK . . .

Like it or not, the condition of your office communicates a lot about your youth ministry and how it runs. What statement does your office make about you—about your approach to ministry? The way you keep your office may communicate that:

- ▸ You are warm and welcoming.
- ▸ You want to get right down to business.
- ▸ Being your friend would be a cozy, comfortable mess.
- ▸ Working with you could be chaotic and life-threatening.
- ▸ Hanging out with you would be hip and cool.

Do you recognize your office among the following examples?

The "Lysol" office looks like it did on the day you started your job—and the way it will look the day after you leave. Nothing's on the desk or bookshelves—no dust, no mission trip memorabilia, no crushed soda cans, and an upright, empty trashcan. It's a germaphobe's dream.

> **REAL LIFE**
> A youth pastor hung on his office wall a photograph of himself sitting in one of the toilet stalls at the church reading the newspaper. He thought it was hilarious. The parents who commandeered his office for a meeting one night, however, were not amused. He didn't quite understand the message he was sending.

The "Hothouse" describes the office in which the Lost and Found box sits on the crumpled sleeping bag that half covers the partially emptied bag of potato chips you cleared out of the rental van from the winter retreat. Is it the mildewed towel that stinks or the coffee cup that has become its own biosphere? The inhabitant of this kind of office takes quiet pride in knowing that a resourceful individual could survive for a week in there with no outside contact.

The "Archeological Dig" has layers of unanswered mail intermingled with new books and magazines to read. On a double dare, this youth worker could uncover checks from last summer's camp (now invalid), urgent memos from the church administrator looking for those checks, and leftover calendars from 2009. Every search yields a new discovery in here.

The "Organized Piler" resents being labeled *disorganized*. This person prefers the term "visual horizontal filing system." Neat stacks throughout the office represent a sophisticated system of organization that, to the uneducated outsider, appears to be merely chaotic piles. This youth worker knows exactly where things are—and only needs a few minutes to find it. The fear is . . . "out of sight, out of mind."

EVALUATE—WHAT IS YOUR OFFICE USED FOR?

- ▶ Studying
- ▶ Meeting students
- ▶ Pastoral care
- ▶ Planning
- ▶ Staff meetings
- ▶ Sunday school classes
- ▶ Confirmation class
- ▶ Staging area for events
- ▶ Equipment storage
- ▶ Storing of curriculum resources
- ▶ Evening committee meetings
- ▶ Other:

How should it be designed for these multiple uses?

ORGANIZING FOR EXPECTATION

Who else sees or uses your office? If your office gets a lot of church staff or parent traffic, then you'll probably want to keep it in corporate shape. If your office is in the basement or a far-flung building that gets visited only by your students, you can stay with something more like mildly chaotic coziness, if that's your style. Generally speaking, the more exposure and use outside of youth ministry that your office receives, the cleaner and more organized you'd better be. Get a sense of the church culture to see what's acceptable for the youth ministry office space. Learn your church's office standards. This is strategic reconnaissance, not brown-nosing: Peek inside your supervisor's

---

CATEGORIES FOR ORGANIZING BOOKS

QUICK-GRAB SHELF
For books within easy reach of where you sit:
Bible
Church directory
Devotional and professional reading
Books you're studying with staff or interns

SHELF SECTIONS
Adolescent development and culture
Biographies
Bible studies, curriculum, commentaries
Church trends
Counseling and adolescent issues
Cross-cultural, multicultural, and missions
Devotional, discipleship, and spiritual formation
Family systems and parenting resources
Games and recreation
History
Leadership and management
Programming
Small groups
Speaking resources
Theology
Volunteer team development
Youth ministry miscellaneous

SMART TIP

Have a section specifically for volunteers to check out books for their own ministry or personal spiritual growth. When someone checks out a book, take a picture of the book and use that for his or her profile picture in your phone until they return it. If someone checks out more than one, add additional titles to the Notes section of his or her contact info.

REAL LIFE

My (Ginny) first church required my desktop to be completely clean at the end of each day. Our office was in a highly trafficked part of the church and used for numerous activities after hours. So how did I manage? I kept one desk drawer empty so that at the end of the day, I could rake everything off my desk and into it.

or senior pastor's door for a glance at his or her desk, for its unspoken guideline for how much or how little clutter will be tolerated in your own office. You could do this during a meeting—maybe even ask your pastor to show you his or her filing system. Whatever gets you some insight into office expectations.

Quiz: Your Organization's Expectations

Ministry environments have differing expectations, different standards. Some expectations are expressed as written rules and some as unstated, assumed rules.

- ▶ What level of orderliness does your organization expect?
- ▶ Can you incur the wrath of some person, institution, or committee for keeping a messy office or using the "pile" system instead of a file system?
- ▶ What are the cultural expectations for a youth worker's office?
- ▶ Can you find what you need quickly? Can you lay your hand on the forms to reserve the church van? Do you know where it is filed online?
- ▶ Do you know where to find out what information to request from event participants so that your insurance will cover accidents? Your insurance company will likely help you develop these forms.
- ▶ Do you even know whether you have a certain piece of information on your server or in your cloud-based system?
- ▶ Could someone else figure out how to find it? Who else knows vital system passwords?
- ▶ If you're not in the office, do other staffers know where to file a brochure about a new camp, how to locate last year's budget figures, where to find student contact information or event details?
- ▶ Is there a common filing system among the staff so that everyone knows where to look for things? Do you file things the same way?

THE WORKING DESK

Your desk should be placed in such a way so it doesn't look like a principal's office. Some prefer to have their desks facing their office doors so they aren't surprised when people walk in. Note: This isn't a great idea if you're easily distracted or an extreme extrovert who wants to say "hi" to anything that walks by. On the other hand, some churches require your computer screen to be immediately visible to anyone who looks inside your office due to concerns about pornography and other inappropriate Web sites. This means your back is to the door. If that's the case in your setting, think about placing a mirror on the wall so the children's pastor can't keep creeping up and scaring you.

The phone should be within easy reach so you can quickly hit the mute button if you're in the midst of a live conversation. Also, think about getting task lighting to help you focus on projects.

This U-shaped work area is functional and easy to set up with inexpensive office furniture. Some youth workers are replacing the "desk for daily projects" with a stand-up desk. Others are replacing the chairs with stability balls.

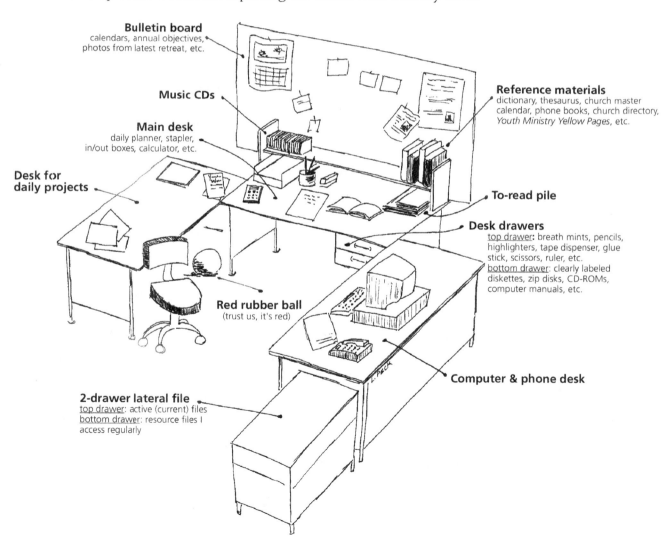

Bulletin board
calendars, annual objectives, photos from latest retreat, etc.

Music CDs

Main desk
daily planner, stapler, in/out boxes, calculator, etc.

Desk for daily projects

Reference materials
dictionary, thesaurus, church master calendar, phone books, church directory, *Youth Ministry Yellow Pages*, etc.

To-read pile

Desk drawers
top drawer: breath mints, pencils, highlighters, tape dispenser, glue stick, scissors, ruler, etc.
bottom drawer: clearly labeled diskettes, zip disks, CD-ROMs, computer manuals, etc.

Red rubber ball
(trust us, it's red)

Computer & phone desk

2-drawer lateral file
top drawer: active (current) files
bottom drawer: resource files I access regularly

We haven't heard of anyone using a treadmill desk yet, but it's only a matter of time.

OFFICE ATMOSPHERE

Even limited or nonexistent budgets can support the creation of the right feel, given your personality and your church's expectations. Before you spend a fortune on decorating, remember your job is to be out with students, so don't make it too comfortable so you don't want to leave. Also, consider if you really need a "whole" office. One youth pastor gave up her office so it could become a prayer/sanctuary space and instead used a built-in desk and wall unit of the storage space in the main youth room as her "office."

GET A DOOR WITH A WINDOW

If you've inherited an office with no windows, ask the facilities board to give you a door with a window in it—or have them sign a statement promising that they will visit you every week in prison. Too much privacy can put us in situations where we are defenseless against accusations. If you conduct one-on-one meetings, you need to have a window in your door—for your protection and for the other person's. Keep the door open until you get that window or meet people in a more public space.

▸ Never underestimate the power of making one of your office walls entirely of whiteboard. You can do that inexpensively by purchasing gloss hardboard wall panel at a hardware store. Mount to the wall using liquid nails on the back to keep the wall from bowing and then wall screws in the four corners. Create a quarterly calendar grid in one section using washi (i.e., designed) tape. Alternatives: a glass board, chalkboard paint, whiteboard paint, static cling sheets.

▸ Bulletin boards protect walls from unsightly nail holes and tape scraps, while earning you points with the facilities committee. Bulletin boards allow you to easily post current calendars, photos from recent events, posters for upcoming events, and student artwork.

▸ Chairs—deny entrance to your office any ancient church chair from the basement. These ergonomic disasters don't exactly exude warmth and welcome. Your four walls may never see a leather club chair, but even a lowly beanbag chair says "Come on in!" better than the folding metal chair.

▸ Fun stuff to do judiciously placed around the office guarantees that students and staff members will want to stop in for an informal visit. A funky gumball machine, a dartboard, Silly Putty (remember that stuff?), fad toys, or even a lava lamp help make your space fun for visitors.

▸ Displaying items that inspire you lets visitors know something of your priorities and your interests. Paintings, carvings, photographs, hobbies, weird lost-and-found junk—all these can express at a glance what it would take an hour for you to explain. (And who would listen anyway?)

- One youth pastor suggests: Have "conversation" art. Something that inspires and is still professional. A print that's been in my office for years shows a busy street as the center aisle of the church with a worship banner hanging near the altar with the great commission written on it. There's also a piranha and a small clay jar labeled "ashes of an obnoxious teenager."

- Ikea is the decorating store of choice for the modern, on-a-budget youth worker. Lacking funds to pull off your vision for your office? Take some simple steps: develop a plan, take some pictures, create a budget, then share the vision and ask your boss or church committee to prayerfully consider upgrading the space where you do vital ministry to students. Think and pray big. Go for it. Don't be afraid to ask. And usually the best time to ask is in your first two months on the job. After that, people assume you can work with what you've inherited.

- Music as ministry or mood setter—you'll never have a shortage of it given today's obsession with sound and rhythm. Invest in secondhand speakers for your computer. There are great sounding Bluetooth-powered speakers for your portable device. There's no shortage of music to buy on iTunes, but you also have a lot of streaming choices (based on the Internet options at your church). So consider a monthly subscription to Pandora or Spotify. You can also get hooked up with great music for your ministry through *www.interlinc-online.com.*

- Posting photos, of course, tells stories about whom you love and what you value. Student pictures (enlarged to poster size if you have room and cash), your spouse, siblings, pets—students and others enjoy viewing these slices of your life when they drop in to see you. If there are lots of pictures to share, consider a high-resolution digital photo frame—get great pricing at *www.Amazon.com* or other online stores, or check out garage sales.

- Consider a student brag board upon which photos of kids and their accomplishments can be displayed. Or a "Come See Me" board (maybe in the youth room?) where kids can post notices of the plays, athletic events, concerts, etc. they're appearing in.

- The types of books on shelves say a lot about the resident of the office. Are you reading the latest trends in adolescent culture or do you prefer the ancient church fathers and mothers? How many you have, what titles you've selected, the systematic (or unsystematic) way you shelve them or loan them out—all of these are clues about you.

> ▸ If the office has a small couch, get a decorative pillow and blanket. They give things a homey feel . . . and double nicely as nap supplies.
> ▸ Get a Distractions basket. If kids are meeting with you, everyone tosses their phones in the basket for the designated meeting time. It's a fun way to tangibly value the face-to-face time and covenant to be present with those in the room.
> ▸ Check out Pinterest for ideas on organizing and decorating your office and the youth room. Start "Youth Ministry Office" and "Youth Room" boards where others can see what you're dreaming of and offer suggestions or donations.

SUPPLIES & EQUIPMENT

New to youth ministry and wondering what to stock in your office? Here's a list generated by veteran youth workers:

A desktop scanner that can quickly scan receipts. Check for one that can handle a lot of receipts (e.g., after a missions trip), exports to Excel or Quicken, and gives you year-end reports.

Use small, clear plastic boxes to store supplies. You can usually get a pack of six for around $5. You can easily see what's in them. You can write on the box with a marker and then erase with acetone nail polish remover. Plus, when you go on trips and retreats, if you purchase some of the rolling storage trunks, you can just stack the plastic supply boxes in them.

Make sure your office has a basic first-aid kit that's always stocked. And a "girls' emergency kit" with a variety of products.

A change of clothing, toothbrush, hair stuff, and deodorant.

A basket of fidget toys (e.g., Koosh or bouncy balls, Rubik's cubes, Slinky, and Tangles) out in the open and a box of "secret weapons" stashed away (e.g., loaded water gun, Silly String, marshmallow shooter and finger rockets).

A basket of snacks. Not just candies but granola bars, pretzels, or chips in single-serving packs along with water bottles or drink pouches. You always have an after-school snack for drop-ins that way.

Tons of postcards, thank-you notes, and encouragement cards. No one seems to get personal snail mail much anymore, yet there are lots of things that can be celebrated. Use these a few times a week as part of a correspondence routine. Put stamps on some for volunteers and student leaders to use.

A small tool chest with basics such as a hammer, pliers, measuring tape, electrical tape, duct tape, screwdriver.

Use the good old-fashioned church bulletin to request supplies that you might not have the budget for or special things you'll need for an event. It gets the congregation to participate and feel connected to your mission. Lilly Lewin, experiential worship designer, suggests this especially if you're starting a multisensory worship service.

Gaffer's tape. It's what you use to secure cords on floors and carpet but won't leave the sticky gunk on flooring or cords. It comes in a variety of colors. Also blue masking or painter's tape will help keep you out of trouble with the building manager.

Command brand hooks and strips. Around Christmastime and back-to-school season, you can find coupons and stores running specials on them to get the most bang for your buck. And get the sturdier heavyweight hooks. They'll hold up better so you can spend less by only needing to buy replacement tape strips.

Breath mints and gum are musts.

"Giveaway" pen cup on top of the desk. Buy the cheap pens at back-to-school time or take a couple of passes through a youth ministry convention exhibit hall to load up on pens that can walk away from your desk.

Always have a box of tissue out and a couple of extra on hand.

ORGANIZE THE CHAOS

From the moment you step into your ministry role, people are lined up to meet with you and already-scheduled events need attention. No wonder office organization is a low (or very low) priority for youth workers. Even so, carving out time to get supplies and clean your office will make your job a lot easier. (Start with at least a half day; those of us with low attention spans can take an hour each day during a week.)

KEEP OR TOSS?

Two basic questions regarding records (e.g., permission slips and medical-release forms):

1. How much should you keep?
2. How long should you keep it?

Find out your church's policy for retaining records and if there are any state or insurance requirements. For legal forms, it's best to consult with your business manager, church board or church lawyer before making a decision on getting rid of old forms and paperwork. If no policy exists, you're at the mercy of your personal preference for either storing everything indefinitely or tossing everything immediately. Think about what should be kept for archival purposes. Scanning makes it possible to archive a significant amount of paperwork with ease (based on your scanner). This is a very good way to securely file records. Work closely with your church administrator regarding where these documents can be securely stored electronically.

For the sake of memorabilia and history, also consider other items you should hang on to. One T-shirt from each retreat. One photo from each confirmation class. One set of fliers, registration materials, and posters from key events over the last five years.

Bible quiz team records from the late '70s should be given either to the church's or denomination's archives or the participants themselves, if they're still around. And there's always the rummage remedy—sell old files, photos, and fliers to sentimental church members at the annual rummage sale. Really, check with others (who, unlike you perhaps, have a long history at that church) before loading all the junk into a dumpster. Your junk may be a prized possession to someone else in the church.

If your office is a contender for an episode of *Hoarders*, here are some quick tactics to get it in order.

Supplies needed for your first-pass office cleaning:

▸ Post-it Notes
▸ 5 cardboard boxes
▸ 2 huge waste cans (for recyclables and unrecyclables)
▸ Shredder

Stage 1: Sort the stuff in your office.

Sort everything into five boxes—quickly! Work around the room in a clockwise fashion. For example, with the door as "12" on a clock, work to the right toward "1 o'clock, 2 o'clock," etc., until you've covered the room. Don't get comfortable. Think "hot potato"—pick up an item and send it to one of the five boxes before it burns your hands:

Label box 1: *File it.* Fill it with forms, old pictures, archive files, anything paper-ish that you need to keep. This also includes things to read such as magazines, brochures, fliers, youth ministry mail.

Label box 2: *Shred it.* This is where you toss documents that contain confidential information for the paper shredder (e.g., notes from the staff meeting where you proposed firing the choir director who keeps scheduling concerts on retreat weekends). But before you shred, make sure you don't need to archive it.

Label box 3: *Donate it.* Fill it with ministry T-shirts (keep one for the archives), free books you'll never read, old books you'll never read again, two-thirds of the pens you've accumulated.

Label box 4: *Toss it.* Fill it with anything not covered by boxes 1 through 3. A deciding question to ask yourself when in doubt: "Can I easily find this information somewhere else if I throw it away (e.g., online, in a book)?" If the answer is yes, toss it.

Label box 5: *Store it.* Parking cones, badminton nets, extra sleeping bags, laminator used only for special events—all goes into one (very large) box. Don't take it to the storage area until you're finished. It's too easy to get distracted and never resume cleaning your office.

Stage 2: Go through the boxes.

The following are activities that could be delegated to a helpful student, intern, or parent EXCEPT the shredding of sensitive documents.

File-It box: Label each item with a sticky note giving the name of the folder in which the item belongs. Then ask an assistant or a volunteer to file each one. Use sticky notes to identify any article you wish to save. Invite an assistant or volunteer to rip out or photocopy necessary articles and file or scan them. Recycle the magazines.

Shred-It box: If you don't have a shredder, check to see if there's a company or organization in town that will do it for free. Some companies periodically offer large quantity shredding but usually have a weight limit.

Donate-It box: Give yourself one week only to find a home for all your "good junk." After that, retire it to the Toss-It box, but NOT the Store-It box.

Toss-It box: Empty it into the dumpster, recycling bin or take it to a thrift store.

Store-It box: Take it to the storage area.

Organize the Documents

In-boxes and out-boxes, a.k.a. "junk stackers." You know how it goes—paperwork comes into your office, overflows the in-basket, and finally guilts you into action. It's really the same with email. You wade through about the top third, throw some pieces away, deal with a few others, and mourn a missed deadline or lost money-saving opportunity. The rest goes back to the in-basket that, within a few days, is overflowing once again.

Just for laughs, see what happens when you apply the following rules:

▶ Use the physical boxes as they were intended—short-term parking for items coming in and going out. Never use them as a long-term, virtual filing cabinet.

▶ Live by the "Touch It Once" strategy. When a piece of paper comes across your desk, read it, respond to it, then file it or throw it away.

▶ Don't open your email for the first hour in the morning. Julie Morgenstern has some great insight into why this is a good idea in her book, *Never Check Email in the Morning.* Writing and responding to emails can eat up your time, and when you're done, you feel like you've done nothing. She suggests immersing yourself into a project first. Doing so helps you feel as though you've been producing from the start of the morning and sets the tone for the rest of the day.

▶ Set up separate email accounts for "read only" emails.

▶ Schedule two to three "meetings" with your inbox every day.

▶ If the email is more than five sentences or deals with a conflict, pick up the phone and talk to the person who sent it instead of replying via email.

▶ Several organizational gurus swear by the "zero email In-box" solution: Organize your emails into three folders:
1. **Archive**: Searchable
2. **Follow-up**: Enter the task on your to-do list
3. **Hold**: You need quick access this week. Clear it out every week as the messages become unnecessary, e.g., UPS delivery, a message from a leader: "I'll get back to you on Tuesday."

Filing System Basics

We've all used filing cabinets to hide things, make messes disappear, store Doritos and Dr. Pepper. More and more these days, those filing cabinets are a thing of the past. A well-organized online or server-based filing system is vital to your ministry. And access to a quality high-speed scanner is essential. Head down to Costco or Sam's Club for combo scanner/printers. They get faster and more affordable by the month.

Here are a few ideas to help you develop your filing system.

▶ **Event files:** Keep one file on every event (Fall Retreat 2015, Project Serve, etc.). At the conclusion of that event, place all the important event documents in that file—e.g., **Planning Worksheets**, **Budget** worksheet, fliers, signup lists, schedules, **Evaluation Worksheets** (filled out!), great pictures, important addresses and phone numbers. If you keep a paper version, staple the event **Notebook Checklist** in front of the file folder. If you keep it as an e-version, store it all in a sub-folder in the broader Events folder. (**Various Event Forms are located in the Forms section**)

▸ **Student files:** Using the **Student Profile** worksheet, start a file on each of your students. Keep anything and everything you come across relating to that student in that file. When they graduate, you'll have some great things to create memory books for them, as well as to track their spiritual progress. You may want to use this as a physical, rather than electronic, file.

▸ **Keep a tickler file in your desk.** A tickler file consists of 12 folders—one for each month of the year. When a piece of paper crosses your desk that's relevant to July and it's only February, place it in the folder named with the month in which you need to take action on it. The key is to review the contents of the folder at the first of each month. For example, you need to order new basketballs in November. Put a note in the November file to order basketballs. When that month rolls around, you'll be reminded (if you open the file, that is).

▸ **Sanity file.** This includes notes of encouragement from students, parents, and others. It also includes anything that inspires you, challenges you, and makes you laugh when you're ready to quit.

Student Profile page 325

Affordable Online Systems

Each ministry is different with regard to its IT approach. If your church is smaller and lacks a server accessible to your ministry, check out a couple of online storage solutions for your ministry. These are just a few that were available when we went to press:

▸ Dropbox: *www.dropbox.com* We love their slogan—"your stuff, anywhere." The downside is you can't collaborate at the same time.

▸ Google Drive & Google Docs: *www.google.com/drive* When you've got multiple people working on a document, presentation, or project, think about using Google Docs on Google Drive. It's a free way to collaborate on documents, presentations, or spreadsheets and have real-time editing capabilities.

▸ Amazon Cloud Drive.

▸ iCloud: If you have a Mac, this is essential.

▸ Egnyte Enterprise File Sharing: *www.egnyte.com*.

What to Keep

Keep only those items that will make your job easier next time. For instance, in a properly labeled folder, place every relevant flier and materials list for the annual "Gut Bomb Strobe Light Pillow Fight." Then ask yourself, "Will what's in this file

help me more easily do the event next time and remind me how to avoid this year's mistakes?" If so, scan it and file it. If not, empty the contents into the trash can and recycle the folder.

FIVE-FILE System

Here's an example of how to coordinate your files. Create five simple categories that encompass your ministry in order to more easily find things (should you forget a name of a file). You can easily expand certain sections. Also, it allows you to maintain confidential files separately from the file contents that other staff may need to share and access.

If you're using physical files, the following folder-tab guidelines can give your system uniformity that makes it easier to use.

- ▸ Use one color of plastic tabs per drawer.
- ▸ Type all labels in a uniform font and size.
- ▸ Place tabs in a uniform place on the folders (that is, the left side of the folder).
- ▸ Insert folder tabs for hanging folders on the front of the file versus the back.

FILE 1: Events (Red)

File event folders alphabetically by your ministry's name for that event, an abbreviation for the age group, and the year the event occurs. Here's an example: E/ FALL RETREAT—JH—2016.

E/ indicates "EVENTS" category
"FALL RETREAT" is the event name
"JH" represents the age group
    EA early adolescents
    JH junior high or MS for middle school
    SH senior high
    CO college
"2016" is, of course, the year

Once you've planned your year calendar, ask a volunteer (student or adult) to write out a file label and set up a folder for every event on the calendar. Yes, if you're filing electronically—it's much simpler.

FILE 2: People: Confidential (Green)

If you don't have a locking file for your PEOPLE: Confidential files, get one today. If you don't have a secure area on your server or cloud—then secure it. You can be held liable for invasion of privacy unless you protect these files. These files contain confidential information that cannot be available to the general public—even to other members of your volunteer team. This information should be available only on a "need to know" basis. Staff applications, references, background checks, counseling notes, student profiles, and any other forms that have social security numbers or other information of interest to an identity thief are not public documents. It's your responsibility to protect them. This is serious stuff.

FASTRACK

Filing by category allows your physical filing system to expand within sections as the content grows.

You likely work hard to communicate that your door is always open. When students, staff, or volunteers stop by, though, will their trust in you be undermined because they discover confidential counseling notes or an updated résumé with a FedEx envelope (oops!) on your desktop or an open email on your screen? How do you guard confidential files such as leadership applications, medical information forms, and counseling notes? A person inclined to entrust you with personal revelations is forming an opinion about your trustworthiness. Ask yourself—

SMART TIP

As you spend more time online, build an extensive, organized, and helpful bookmark list in your Internet browser for sites related to both drawer-three and drawer-four issues. For visual people, use Pinterest to pin appropriate articles and Web sites (e.g., risk management, youth group games, retreat sites, etc.)

▸ Who else has access to my office? Is it ever open when I'm not in it?
▸ Where can I safely file confidential counseling info? Medical release forms? Staff applications?
▸ Is there a way to lock the file drawers? Who else should have the key?
▸ Have I locked the e-document with a password? Where do I store the password? Who else should have the password?
▸ When people open a desk drawer to look for a pen, envelope, or a flier, will they find confidential materials?

Store the key or the password in a safe place, not in your desk drawer. Let another trusted and vetted staff person know how to access the information, in case they need to in your absence.

Create three distinct filing areas: event forms, staff information, student information. For physical files: Event forms include permission and medical forms filed by specific events. These folders are in the back of the file drawer with tabs on the right side of the folder. Next, in the middle of the drawer, are staff folders with the tabs in the center of the folder. Finally, place student files in the front of the drawer, with the tabs on the left side of the folder. This will keep each grouping together, and the distinct tab placement makes it easy to see the three sections in your drawer.

Contents of Staff Files

Keeping good records on the people on your team is essential. You need to demonstrate that you carefully screen and keep good records on all people who work with minors, including minors who work with minors. Screening involves an application, interview, references, and a background check. You also should keep applications and notes from people who applied but who you didn't accept. Just in case they apply to another ministry and you need to revisit why you turned them away.

> SCREENING AND RECORD KEEPING on adult volunteers is not an option; it's a requirement. (See chapter 13 on Teams.)

Include the following information for each paid or volunteer team member:

- ▸ Staff Orientation Process
- ▸ Staff Application (Keep staff applications for the length of time required by your state—perhaps up to 10 years.)
- ▸ Church membership information
- ▸ Disciplinary discussions (dated and stating action taken)
- ▸ Driver application (if an approved driver)
- ▸ Incident Report forms as needed
- ▸ Staff Reference Check and background check
- ▸ Background check results—STORE confidentially
- ▸ Signed Ministry Covenant
- ▸ Volunteer Staff Evaluation

Again, confidentiality MUST be maintained for these files. You must secure these files. MUST. GOTTA. Not optional. Invite a volunteer to label empty folders with P/ for people, the name of the staff person (last name first), followed by the age group with which they work, and finally the word STAFF: P/OWENS, MARK—JH STAFF.

Eventually you'll need to divide the contents of the drawer into active and inactive staff as people move on from your ministry. Consult an attorney to learn how long after staffers' departures you need to keep their files intact. (In some states it will be at least five years after they leave staff.)

Contents of Student Files

Develop and maintain one file for each student, as they each have unique needs and information to track as your ministry expands. Each student file should contain at least the following:

- ▶ Basic contact information.
- ▶ Copies of relevant Incident Report forms
- ▶ Parent Information
- ▶ Photo
- ▶ Photocopy of student Authorization for Medical Treatment
- ▶ Student Profile form

You can file student folders in one large alphabetical file or group them in the following categories:

- ▶ Inactive students
- ▶ New students
- ▶ Regular students

Invite a volunteer to label empty folders with a "P/" for "People," followed by each student's last name, first name, and their year of high school graduation: P/ SANCHEZ, BRANDON, 2017. This enables you to easily find all the student files for a certain grade and label the folders only once—unless a student flunks a grade. And when groups graduate, you can easily locate those files for archiving.

FILE 3: Resources and Organizations—Blue
In these files you'll store mailers, brochures, curriculum samples, scraps of paper—anything that identifies vendors or organizations you use in youth ministry.

FILE 4: Topical Teaching Resources-Yellow
In these files you'll store illustrations, quotes and funnies, borrowed sermon or lesson outlines, news articles, seminar handouts—anything that you might use in developing talks or curriculum.

FILE 5: Messages, Studies, and Lessons-Orange
This is the place to put those messages you agonize over. You worked hard to prepare them. (Okay, you stole them from your friend. Whatever.) After you go to all of that trouble, place in the folder your outline, your study notes, the feedback you received, and anything else helpful to developing the message. On the inside of the folder, write the date and location of the talk. If you're doing this as an e-version, write it in a footnote or endnote. (When you become a famous speaker, you'll need to remember who's already heard it!)

SMART TIP

Release forms. Group them together by event identification. Plan to archive five years of forms in carefully labeled and sealed envelopes. CONFIRM this is how long you should keep them with your ministry board, insurance agent and or lawyer. Place the envelopes in a hanging folder marked with the event information: P/Fall Retreat Forms 2014 or put in a bankers box with a clear sign that reads, "Do not destroy until after 2019."

RESOURCES

► *Organizing from the Inside Out, Second Edition: The Foolproof System For Organizing Your Home, Your Office and Your Life* by Julie Morgenstern

► *Organizing for Your Brain Type: Finding Your Own Solution to Managing Time, Paper, and Stuff* by Lanna Nakone and Arlene Taylor

FORMS

► File Labels Drawer Three
► File Labels Drawer Four
► Monthly Contact Summary Chart
► Contact Number Worksheet
► Student Profile Worksheet

Guidelines for File Management

Keep your system simple. Categories to avoid: THINGS, STUFF, MISCELLANEOUS. The five-file system is a basic foundation on which to build your information storehouse. When needed, a small, portable file box can keep your system flexible.

—Transport files needed for weekly meetings.
—Store attendance information at special events.
—Bring to events necessary staff information, event fliers, and standard forms.

If you hate filing, enlist a volunteer to come regularly to do it. If you are too lazy or have a hard time with the alphabet, create a TO FILE bin for items to be filed. Ask a volunteer to come in once a week and scan and file the contents. If your filing cabinet overflows, use those uniform-sized, cardboard boxes with lids to store files. Carefully label multiple sides of the box to identify the contents. Better yet, just get a scanner and scan it all away.

6 FINANCES

CHAPTER OVERVIEW

For those of you who live by the motto, "Don't sweat the small stuff," managing finances can seem like a menial chore. That kind of youth worker would rather be off with students at a retreat, blissfully ignorant of the fact that the church accountant is home biting her fingernails and awaiting the bad news about the retreat's financial shortfall. If this sounds like you, then we have good news and bad news.

Good news: You can manage your ministry's financial health successfully! Financial management is largely a matter of training, practice, and systems to get and keep your finances in order.

Bad news: It takes time and diligence to learn how to establish and maintain healthy financial habits.

In this section we'll look at ministry finance philosophies, creating and managing general and special-event budgets, managing cash flow, managing donations, and looking at sure-fire fundraisers.

So—sit yourself down, grab a legal pad or open up a spreadsheet, and let's make a plan to keep your ministry afloat financially.

FOUNDATIONS FOR FINANCIAL HEALTH

Three principles make a solid foundation upon which your ministry can stand:

1. Control your finances, or they will control you.
2. Financial management is one area where not making a decision is making a decision.
3. The longer you wait to get a handle on ministry finances, the harder it will be to recover damage done from neglect.

Finances need to be a high priority, or you will stifle the growth and development of your ministry. Here's the rub: Most of us youth workers want to be making an impact on teens' lives, not sitting in a stuffy office poring over boring numbers that sometimes don't make sense.

Or you can look at it this way—understanding those numbers means you recognize a retreat is too costly (and will exclude some of your students) in time to change the location to an affordable site.

Do you need to beef up your financial skills? A healthy, thriving ministry that's going to last for the long haul must demonstrate successful money management. By diligently managing ministry finances, you set yourself up to affect this generation of students for Christ. Whether you have a large or small budget, careful and consistent money management can make a dramatic difference in your effectiveness.

Take the following quiz to see if you're up for the challenge:

▸ When you come face to face with the church accountant, does she duck into a doorway, snicker as you pass by, or shake her head and mumble, "Too bad, he was such a nice guy"?
▸ When you attend elder meetings, do they laugh out loud when you request a budget increase?
▸ Did the phrase "laundering money" take on new meaning when you discovered you not only washed your jeans after the last retreat but also 10 checks?
▸ Are you surprised when you see how much or how little money you have in your youth ministry account at the end of the month?
▸ Have you ever put your personal money and ministry money in the same pocket and then wondered which was which . . . and never really figured it out?
▸ Have you ever borrowed ministry money for personal expenses?

If you answered yes to any of these questions, you might need some help managing your ministry's finances. Take heart—this section is designed for you. Put its suggestions to work, and your ministry will thank you for it. Even the experienced youth worker will find some tips here for staying healthy and on the right track.

BRING IN (OR KEEP) MORE MONEY THAN YOU SPEND

Again, and a little louder: To get ahead, you need to bring in more money than you spend. (If that's the only idea you internalize and live by, the price of this book has been worth it.) The moment you spend more money than you bring in, you begin a slide from which it's enormously hard to recover. Our country's credit-card debt shows that most Americans overspend—we've honed an instant-gratification society in which we're allowed to have it all right now. Only spend what you've budgeted (and spend less if you can). That gaming system (on sale!) would be great in the youth room,

FASTRACK

A youth ministry won't be successful if the leader doesn't understand and take control of her resources.

but it's not in the budget. Where will the purchasing price come from? Downscaling the mission trip? Skipping the traditional gift of new Bibles to the graduates?

The smallest cost of spending more money than you have is regret. The greatest cost? We've all had nightmares about that, I'm sure. Ministry finances can slide down that same slope, and churches tire of bailing out an overspending ministry.

DO THE WORK

Careful money management means you know how much money your organization has budgeted to the youth ministry and that you spend it realistically. Be able to tell the difference between your personal wish list for ministry and actual ministry needs. Focus budgeted monies on what your ministry truly needs to be effective. That means purchases that best support ministry purposes and goals rather than merely reflect your personal preferences. Keep the greater good of the ministry in mind when making all your financial decisions. What is the focus of your ministry? Where do you touch the lives of students? Are Sunday mornings a big deal for your students? Put a good share of your resources there. If you're involved in campus ministry and forever transporting groups of students, a larger, more reliable vehicle may be the best use

PRACTICAL RESOURCES FOR CHURCH LEADERS

Want to learn more about financial accountability? Check out *www.ecfa.org*.

of your ministry money. (If, on the other hand, you're just looking for an excuse to get a four-wheeler, give it up. Get the picture?) Practically speaking, such an attitude also may mean buying inexpensive office supplies that simply do the job rather than cool-looking stuff.

REAL LIFE

One youth pastor's story: I didn't care at all about numbers until Mark, a business friend of mine, offered me a more supportive perspective over lunch. I was telling him of my woes in my fledgling ministry—how the financial details were driving me crazy. I was fishing for advice on how I could pass the financial management to someone who could do a better job than me. He said that the foundation of successfully managing a small business (or ministry in my case) is for the CEO to get a good grasp of the finances, then personally and watchfully manage them.

I squirmed. "I'm not good with numbers," I whined, "and besides, I would rather be in real ministry with the students."

"If you're managing your ministry finances well," he replied, "you are doing real ministry. Rather than hiding from responsibility, you're taking your rightful role as the ministry leader. God put you in this place at this time, and you need to grow into your leadership role. This doesn't mean that you have to fill out every check requisition or personally keep the books. But it does mean that you need to see, approve, and keep a mental record of every dollar that goes in or out of your ministry. That's the only way you can know that your ministry is on track."

For me, financial leadership means that I double-check and pay close attention to my bookkeeper's work. Yes, it takes time and effort, but it has been worth the work. It means that I take time to review the monthly financial statement and not be afraid to ask questions if I don't understand.

KEEP INTEGRITY FIRST, ALWAYS

Finances can be a spiritual warfare magnet. Financial management, although admittedly only a small part of an effective ministry, is one of the most critical that you'll oversee. Yet when it comes to finances, we often let lapse the moral code to which we hold ourselves in other areas of life and ministry. We put the water park money in the same pocket as our own and don't realize it when we come out with an extra ten at the end of the evening. Or we're short $20 for a date that night and figure the ministry can loan us some. (After all, haven't we been working every night for the past week?) We'll pay it back on Monday—or is that "some day"? Satan would like nothing better than to trip us up in the area of finances. But we snatch away his victory when we stay spiritually and financially strong. So let's roll our sleeves up and get to work.

Here's a simple and very practical suggestion: You as the leader should not touch the money if at all possible. Period. Recruit and empower other trusted *leaders* (and that's intentionally plural) to handle this important area for you. And—incorporate good accountability guidelines such as a two-person rule, etc.

STUDENTS AND FINANCE

Invite selected students to learn about this seldom-seen side of ministry—in a limited way and with close supervision (for their protection, as well as the ministry's). Students who are good with numbers, for instance, might attend finance committee meetings. These students could express to the committee the views of the youth group, as well as informing about the planning done by teen leaders in your ministry.

PERSONAL FINANCES

How are you doing on your personal finances? It's likely that if you're good in this area, you'll be good with your ministry finances, too. But the door swings both ways. If you struggle with personal finances, you'll likely have ministry finance troubles, too. Perhaps it's time to put the spotlight on your personal accounts to see what you need to do to get them in order.

Fred E. Waddell addresses some of the psychological issues underlying a person's handling of finances in *Money Mastery in Just Minutes a Day* (Dearborn Financial Publishing, Inc., 1996). Unlike many cerebral financial manuals that present difficult-to-grasp concepts, Waddell helps readers analyze their own financial baggage and offers practical ways to reprogram their thinking where necessary.

He suggests six simple steps to take control of your personal finances:

- ▸ Track your expenses.
- ▸ Have a written spending plan.
- ▸ Reduce your dependence on credit cards and other credit.
- ▸ Pay off the entire balance of your credit cards each month.
- ▸ Save some money each pay period.
- ▸ Balance your checkbook.

Learning to manage finances is a lifelong journey. It's well worth the effort to follow this plan.

SPENDING POLICY

As ministry leader, you are the financial gatekeeper. If you have a hard time saying no, you'd better start practicing, because the gatekeeper's job includes calling for a temporary spending freeze if your finances get out of control.

The gatekeeper is the one who closes credit-card accounts if they're draining the ministry.

Personally strong enough to keep the ministry's best interests in mind, gatekeepers don't have the luxury of feeling crushed when someone disagrees with them or decides not to like them.

Especially in ministry, you can't please everyone all the time. Satisfy yourself that you've heeded wise counsel from several sources, made a reasonable decision to the best of your experience, and acted on your decision consistently and fairly.

FASTRACK

Overspending is a form of greed; your organization won't tolerate continual disregard for responsible handling of finances. The goal with ministry finances is to balance the inflow and the outflow of money.

ON BATHS & BUCKS

Managing finances is like maintaining the water level in a bathtub. If the drain is open, you can still maintain the water level if you have an equal amount of water flowing in from the faucet. However, if you're losing more water than is coming in, your tub will soon be empty.

FASTRACK

Avoid temptation and suspicion by a) keeping yourself accountable to your ministry's financial officer, b) keeping ministry money separate from personal money, c) maintaining a checks-only policy, d) establishing checks and balances to keep others honest, e) putting someone else in charge of petty cash, and f) putting ministry expenses on a credit card dedicated to ministry use only.

As a leader—stay in touch with your ministry's financial status.

AVOIDING TEMPTATION AND SUSPICION

In a conversation with some veteran youth pastors, one commented that he was more likely to fail because of a financial indiscretion than a moral one.

Not surprising, points out veteran youth worker Tiger McLuen (president of Minnesota-based Youth Leadership). In the first year out of college, more cash will pass through a youth pastor's hands than any other graduate's. Think of collecting money from students paying for retreats, mission trips, camps, and overnighters. And then there are the fundraisers. Handling cash with little accountability can tempt even the most honest. I mean, how wrong can it be to take a short-term loan from the retreat food fund and pay it back next week? Or maybe there's some leftover pizza money, and you've been working a lot of unpaid overtime. How bad can it be to take your family out to lunch? On a grand scale, this is called embezzlement. At the very least, it's sloppy and dangerous financial management practice.

The following simple principles can help you wisely manage your money so you don't end up feeling guilty—or sleeping behind bars.

KEEP YOURSELF ACCOUNTABLE

Make it a priority to inform your church accountant, treasurer, or supervisor about your ministry finances. Youth workers often have little supervisory accountability. Being unsupervised might feel fun for a time, but for those who don't make themselves accountable it can be disastrous. Invite a mentor to train, develop, and challenge you in the area of finances. If you already know you're susceptible to monetary temptation, tell someone that you trust and have him or her keep you accountable—if only to let you know that you forgot to deposit the retreat fee.

DON'T BE IN CHARGE OF THE PETTY CASH

Select a detail-oriented administrative assistant or volunteer to take charge of the petty cash. Keep a set amount of cash on hand—$100 to $200, depending on the size and scope of your ministry. When someone takes cash out for an expense, replace it with a marker that tells who has how much. They need to return receipts and or cash equaling the amount of money that was taken. When the cash gets low, have your assistant or volunteer write all the transactions on one piece of paper and attach all the receipts to it. Turn it in to the accounting department and request that amount in cash to refill the petty cash fund.

SMART TIP

"Never use a ten-dollar bill as a torch to find nickels in the snow." —Leo B. Helzel, *A Goal Is a Dream with a Deadline*

BEFORE YOU BUY A BIG TICKET ITEM

Let several people know what you are looking for and ask them to pray with you about acquiring this for your ministry. If they agree the ministry needs the item, then fortify yourself for wisely acquiring it by asking yourself these questions:

- ▸ Do we really need this item?
- ▸ Is there any way we could locate someone who will donate this item?
- ▸ If not, where can we buy it?
- ▸ How much time is it worth to shop around for the best price?

After investigating, wait 24 hours before making a decision, and ask someone (who knows something about the item) whether you're looking at a good deal.

REAL LIFE

Over the course of several events, we received registration forms but could find no associated money. The students claimed they had left cash with the forms. We never did figure out where the cash was going, but someone's wallet got well padded. When we went to the no-cash policy, the stealing stopped; but we had already lost several hundred dollars.

DON'T MIX PERSONAL MONEY WITH MINISTRY MONEY

Amazingly enough, this no-brainer is usually learned the hard way. One youth worker put his family in debt because he foolishly used his personal credit card for some large ministry purchases, then lost the receipts. He couldn't request reimbursement from the church, and his wife was furious. Not a satisfying way to make a donation.

Keep ministry money totally separate from personal money. Don't borrow from the retreat money to buy lunch for yourself and expect that you'll remember why you're $5.23 short when you turn in the retreat fees. Keep the money in separate, marked envelopes.

Stay Away from Cash

Stay away from cash as much as possible. Cash is not only easily mixed up with personal money, but it's difficult to track.

FasTrack

Three important financial principles: take control of your finances; take in more than you spend; do the work to maintain your financial health.

State on all brochures and fliers your policy of requiring that all event payments or T-shirt purchases, for instance, be made by check (or credit card if your church has that capability). The only time you should see cash is for small events costing less than $10 per person. Wisdom: Just make sure you take the checks out of your pocket before you do your wash. Unlike cash, the ink on checks disappears in the rinse cycle.

For spending purposes, if you don't have a ministry credit card, you may want to get a personal credit card that you use only for ministry expenses—and pay it off monthly. Use it when you need to make large purchases and don't want to carry cash or bother with preauthorizing a check. When the bill comes, attach all receipts and a completed reimbursement form

Check out Square!

Square allows your ministry to quickly and easily receive credit cards. The funds are deposited directly into your church account and receipts are emailed directly to the payor. The fee is a flat percentage (that can be built into the price of your event). Learn more at https://squareup.com.

to a copy of your statement. Turn them in to the bookkeeper. Make sure you maintain proper backup for all your expenditures (i.e., keep your receipts). They will be required for reimbursement. Then, for all meal expenditures, additional information is required. Be sure to list whom you met with and the meeting's ministry purpose. The IRS requires this.

Establish Checks and Balances

Evaluate how the money flows in your ministry and create checks and balances to keep others honest. For example, it's never a good idea to have only one person count the offering. By having two people not related to each other sign off on counting and depositing the money, you've instituted a safety precaution. Checks make it harder for a person to be dishonest, but use two people anyway—a counter to fill out a slip that records income received and a depositor to verify and sign it.

CREATING A PAPER TRAIL

Picture 10 crisp, new, $100 bills. (What? You've never seen one? You must be a youth worker!) Anyway, let's say you're managing your ministry on a strict cash basis, and $1,000 is your budget for the year. You keep those $100 bills in one big envelope in your office safe. (Because you wouldn't leave it in your top, right-hand drawer, would you?)

When you need to purchase something, you grab your big envelope in the safe and place one of the bills in a letter-sized envelope marked "Youth Ministry Cash." After you purchase the item, you replace the cash spent with a store receipt and put the change back into the little envelope. Anyone who wants to find out the financial status of the youth ministry could take out the contents of the envelope, add up the cash and the receipt totals and get a total of exactly $1,000.

Your cash and receipts should always total the amount you start with. That is a paper trail.

Paper trails get complicated when there's too much money to keep in an envelope, so you open a checking account (more paper) or a savings account (still more paper) and pay with checks or a credit card, generating even more paper. But this is good (except for the poor trees, of course) because regardless of how complicated the system, your paper trail always shows where the money comes from and where it goes.

REMEMBER WHERE THE MONEY COMES FROM

Money in ministry is peculiar—the source of the vast majority of it is people who have sacrificially given—relinquishing a better car, a nicer family vacation, or dining out—for a ministry they believe in. You're spending money that was contributed as a sacrifice to God. *Money that isn't yours.* Don't forget that.

REAL LIFE

One youth pastor's story: I got involved with a ministry that owed a lot of money to vendors. Aside from the financial mess the debts created, owing so much to so many was a terrible testimony. Some bills were more than a year past due. One account hadn't been settled in more than five years.

Settling the five-years' overdue account required more than 40 hours of reconciling statements against receipts, and the final cost to the ministry exceeded $4,500. About 15 hours into the process, I closed the delinquent account. By hour 20, I was mentally phrasing a letter requesting a salary increase. After 38 hours of this tedium, I was ready to kick my dog (but didn't). By hour 40 I got on the phone and closed every open account that the ministry had.

We began to operate on a strict cash basis and offer reimbursements only for preauthorized expenses. I was not popular with the staff during that time, but by the end of the season (and in spite of the year's early financial blunders), we came out ahead. (And yes, my popularity ratings soared.)

SMART TIP

If you master these financial skills for your ministry, they'll serve you in your home or in a small business, too.

RESOURCE MANAGEMENT

Successful ministry starts with keeping a close eye on ministry resources and learning to utilize your resources so you don't have to spend money unnecessarily. You have a lot of resources at your fingertips and perhaps don't even know it.

FasTrack
Finances are merely one of the most obvious resources that need management.

Resources come in two major categories: relational and physical. You know the old saying: "Love people, use things." That's also the case with resource management: People are meant to be loved, things are meant to be used.

Relational Resources

Relational resource management includes providing administrative support for your ministry team and encouragement. You support the quality of their assistance by being purposeful about where and when they volunteer. For instance, assigning an accountant to make posters wouldn't make the best use of your resources, unless that's the most pressing need of the hour. We need to be careful to invest in volunteers in ways that honor and energize them. Then balance your use of volunteers, avoiding both overusing and under-using them. Place them where they're needed and where they thrive.

Physical Resources

Funds, equipment, space (buildings, rooms, etc.)—the goal of managing these "things" is to use them to help create a more efficient and effective ministry. If using a thing takes a lot of time and produces few results, change or eliminate it.

For example, computers and software products are meant to make us more productive. For those who are limited when it comes to certain programs, the huge learning curve might scare you. But when you consider how your productivity will skyrocket once you learn basic skills, you may decide it's worth the effort.

On the other hand, if you consistently waste valuable time fixing a physical resource over and over again, you may decide to get rid of it and do your work another way. Or you may push for the purchase of a new piece of equipment. When your photocopy repairman drives up in a new Benz, perhaps it's time to donate the copier.

The point: Analyze each physical resource to see if it still does its job, and if so, how efficient it is. Keep each physical resource in the best shape possible. Consistent maintenance increases the lifespan of equipment and stretches your youth ministry budget. A car is an example of the value of regular maintenance, as well as of the wisdom of getting rid of things that you're investing too much time and money in.

Share resources with other ministries—either in your own church or with other churches in the area. One youth worker said, "Often I purchase a youth ministry need, only to find out later that another ministry in the church already has those supplies or that equipment." With other youth workers in your area, list resources you could share. The list can include everything from the best bus company to use to the best local BBQ caterer for the senior banquet.

FasTrack

Financial management is all about knowledge, creativity, and persistence.

TEST YOUR FINANCIAL SKILLS

1. It's your first year at a new church. You need to manage a budget for a retreat that has been done each year for the last five years. What do you do?
   ❏ Use the same numbers that show up on last year's retreat budget.
   ❏ Study budgets from the past five years and base your event budget on the average expenses in similar categories.
   ❏ Because you're pressed for time, simply pick a number that sounds good for each category.
   ❏ Look at the last two years of retreat budgets. If the event finished in the black, use those numbers for your base budget. Then call the retreat facility, the transportation provider, and other expensive vendors to get current prices. Adjust your budget.

2. You sponsor a concert on campus. Because of high attendance, you finish with a $500 surplus in the event account. What do you do with it?
   ❏ Put it into the ministry's general expense account.
   ❏ Put it into a savings account for future use.
   ❏ Refund the money to your students.
   ❏ Purchase a new computer the ministry has wanted.
   ❏ Take the staff on a weekend retreat.
   ❏ Any of the above—but check with your supervisor or the business administrator first.

3. After a missions trip, you learn that you're $4,500 in the red. Your ministry budget is in its last month, and you have a deficit of $1,500—so there's no reserve to draw on. You are a total of $6,000 behind for the whole year. What do you do?
   ❏ Pack your bags and get out of town.

❏ Put it on your personal credit card and repay it from next year's budget

❏ Write a letter to all your students' parents saying that you were financially short from the mission trip and they need to pay $200 more.

❏ Make an appointment with your church treasurer to bring him up to speed, beg forgiveness, and get suggestions on what you need to do now.

4. Each time you collect money from your students for an event or outing, you come up shorter than your estimations. What should you do?

❏ Take a close look at your collection team to see if anyone is wearing a new Nixon™ 51-30 watch.

❏ Double-check your estimations to see if you're estimating correctly.

❏ Require students to pay with a check instead of cash so you can track the money or to pay with a credit or debit card. (Consider the use of Square to help your ministry receive credit cards (https://squareup.com/).

❏ All of the above.

ANSWERS
1. Look at the last two years
2. Any of the above
3. Make an appointment
4. All of the above

BASIC FINANCE STARTUP TASKS
MAKE AND USE A TAX I.D. CARD.

Not-for-profit, 501(c)(3) organizations are exempt from sales tax on purchases in line with their primary purpose. Tax-exempt purchases can include office supplies, furniture, building materials, automobiles, some restaurants (generally not fast food). Your organization should have a tax I.D. letter, stating its nonprofit status.

This exemption is given to individuals purchasing supplies only if they show a copy of the tax-exempt letter to the vendor. To be sure you always have the letter with you, photocopy and shrink the letter to 4" high by 3" wide. Type or write the tax number in bigger print wherever there's white space so that it is easy to read. Fold the paper in half from top to bottom so the card is 2" high by 3" wide—part of the letter shows on the front and part on the back. After it's folded, laminate it, carry it in your wallet, and use it.

SOME COMPANIES PROVIDE A TAX-EXEMPT "QUICK CARD" to use for purchases (versus carrying around a letter). Check into this if you're a frequent shopper with that company.

Give each of your staff members this card, and mention that your church won't reimburse for tax. One ministry set this policy: If a staff person chooses not to use the card, the ministry reimburses authorized expenses and thanks them for paying the tax. It was only one or two times before everyone got the hang of using the card.

Over the next year, the church saved several thousand dollars. It was exciting to see how one little card could make such a difference. A little bit goes a long way.

STORE ALL YOUR RECEIPTS IN A LABELED CLASP ENVELOPE OR SCAN THEM INTO AN APP.

It's illegal for your church to reimburse you for expenses without a receipt. Asking your church to make an exception for you puts it in a precarious position: If the church is audited, they could receive penalties.

The simplest way to track receipts and petty cash is to have one envelope that contains your cash, your church's tax I.D. card, and your receipts. When you purchase something, write on the receipt the name of the activity for which you purchased the item—fall retreat, mission trip, whatever. Then each week fill out and turn in a reimbursement form attached to your receipts. Use the Reimbursement form if your church doesn't have one. Some church policies state that if a receipt isn't submitted within a month, they won't reimburse you. Check with your church administrator. It's simple if you keep up with it; it's a nightmare if you don't. Bottom line: Keep good records in an organized and logical order. Use a scanner if you're doing it digitally. If you insist on using a shoebox, make sure it's for a big pair of shoes!

For meals, the IRS requires that you list the people involved and the meeting's business-related purpose. This means you need to list who was at the meal and what was discussed. This must be done for EVERY receipt—for every meal out.

Monthly Expense Report page 338

Summary Balance Sheet page 345

Budget & Monthly Report page 332

Profit Loss Statement page 340

Reimbursement page 342

SET UP A SIMPLE REPORTING SYSTEM.

At least monthly you'll need to report your income and expenses to your financial officer. To get yourself started, choose one or two reports from among these—Monthly Expense Report, Summary Balance Sheet, Budget & Monthly Report, Profit & Loss Statement—whichever one captures the information you need right away.

PLAN OUT YOUR FINANCIAL CALENDAR

What's the difference between a physical and fiscal year?

- ▶ The physical year, often called calendar year, runs from January 1 through December 31.
- ▶ The fiscal year varies depending on the decision of the corporation. In some ministries, it parallels a school year, running from August 1 of one year to July 31 of the next year. Check with your church to see how it defines its fiscal year. A typical fiscal year begins July 1.
- ▶ Although you will provide reports to the board based on the church's fiscal year, you may choose to track your income and expenses according to when you mark the beginning of your ministry year.

The simplest way to make sure you don't come up short at the end of the year is to take your total yearly budget and divide it by 12—for each month of the year. This will give you guidelines for where your regular spending needs to stay.

DONATIONS AND INCOME

Whether you receive cash donations, money from fundraising activities, or equipment, make it worth the donors' efforts by helping them see how their gifts enhance the youth ministry.

Donations are for ministry use, usually tax deductible, and require a receipt if the donor requests one. Usually the ministry organization tracks donations and sends out year-end receipts to donors.

Income is paid as a fee-for-service—e.g., retreat registration or a New Year's all-nighter—or money paid to the organization so the youth worker can purchase something like concert tickets or entrance to a water park for a group event. The fee charged to sign up for the event covers (or mostly covers) the expense for the individual attending the event. This type of income is not tax deductible.

Honorariums for speaking or leading workshops are also income—whether the income is yours or should be turned over to the church is a matter of policy. Typically, if you are speaking on church time, you need to pass the honorarium on to the church (otherwise you're double dipping—getting paid twice). If you're speaking on your own time, however, you can keep the money. But when in doubt, ask.

SMART TIP

"In-kind donation" is when an individual or company, in lieu of a cash donation, gives you a "thing" instead—like a computer, for instance. You can provide them with a receipt for the item as a tax write-off.

Donation Basics

There are two major forms of donations: cash and in-kind donations.

Cash donations are the easiest to handle. Cash can come in the form of a check, actual dollars and cents, or a credit card (if your organization is equipped to accept them).

In-kind donations are "things"—equipment, furniture, vehicles. Both in-kind and cash donations have their place in ministry, but they both need to be solicited and tracked differently.

1. Develop a donor database.

Keep your donors informed, interested, and motivated. Avoid badgering potential donors; instead help them see the value of your ministry as evidenced by the results you're getting. People want to give to worthwhile causes. Show them the difference your ministry makes in the community, how their gifts can sustain and expand effective ministry.

2. In-kind donations build your resources and supplement your finances by providing directly an object or service that you would otherwise have purchased.

Some items arrive unsolicited (like the computer a youth worker found on her desk one morning, donated anonymously), but usually you must make your need known to the right people at the right time in hopes that they can use their connections or resources to help you out.

Many people would give in-kind donations if they knew what to give. Giving money is not an option for them, but they happen to have the ability to offer certain goods or services. You'll do best to solicit in-kind donations from your closest donors. It's like letting your family know what you need or want for your birthday; so be specific about acceptable quality and quantity of the items you request. Give specific directions on how and when donors can transfer ownership of items to you. Inspect each item as it comes in, and accept or reject it at that time. (There's nothing worse than being given an item that you'll have to fork over cash to get rid of in the future.) Give the donor a tax-deductible receipt for the item. The donor is responsible to assess the presumed value of the item.

3. Keep a wish list of things your ministry needs.

Send it out to your families occasionally, or just keep it handy in case someone asks. My (Mike) own ministry has a lot of self-employed parents who regularly upgrade their office equipment. Their throwaways are better than anything I have, so I welcome their donations. (Since they have probably already depreciated the item over time, and since the donation becomes a write-off for their company, it's as good a deal for them as for me.)

4. Research your church's accepted way to raise money.

Your church or ministry most likely has guidelines for receiving cash donations. Since you need to follow the

FUNDRAISERS

The key to successful fundraising is to be selective. The reward needs to be worth the work. In other words, don't expend a lot of time and resources on fundraisers that promise minimal returns. Sponsor a few choice, well-done fundraisers a year rather than many mini-fundraisers. Concentrate your effort where you can reap the most rewards.

Enter into the fundraiser wholeheartedly, plan it well, drum up a lot of support among your organization's leadership and extended membership, and motivate the students.

FASTRACK

Donations—whether to the larger ministry or to the youth ministry—fund your budget: So ask for specific amounts with a proposed budget in mind, take what you receive and use it wisely, and always say thank you in a meaningful way.

Donor
Receipts
page 334

DONATION LETTERS THAT GENERATE RESPONSES ...

are free of spelling and grammatical errors.

are not texts.

paint a moving picture of the need.

give a specific vision of how you're going to meet the need.

tell the reader what you want them to do and by when.

are short—no more than one page.

are written with heart and conviction.

possess a personal touch.

look clean and neat.

include a handwritten address on the envelope.

include a self-addressed return envelope (with or without a stamp).

are timed appropriately.

are developed with prayer.

plan, check with the finance office before you hand out any fundraising letters at the Sunday morning service, set up bake sale tables, or schedule a ministry garage sale. The guidelines may vary for your personal fundraising, corporate ministry fundraising, or fundraising for special projects (such as mission trips).

Donation Letters That Work

If you're allowed to solicit donations, the traditional donor letter is a good way to start. The most effective fundraising letters are concise, specific, need-driven, and written from the heart. Your mission is to paint a picture to which readers can relate—and that motivates them to respond by giving to your ministry.

Include a return envelope

It seems to make sense that if you include a return envelope with your letter, you may receive a higher percentage of responses. And if you take it one step further by placing a stamp on the return envelope, your chances will likely increase. (You'll have to experiment to learn if that extra expense of the stamp is offset by increased returns on the mailing.) Another tidbit—handwriting addresses on the envelopes is a sure way to get people to actually open the letter in the first place. People respond more readily and generously to the personal touch. This is sorely missing in today's electronic culture. If they can donate online, make sure to acknowledge their donation with a handwritten thank-you note.

Start off on the right foot with donors by using the following sample letter. The main thing is to write the letter on organization letterhead, include the date of the donation, the donor's name, the amount given, and a word of thanks. The IRS views a letter with the above information as a receipt. You may also include an actual receipt, if your church already has one. Or you can enclose the Donor Receipts form with your letter.

CREATING A BUDGET

A ministry budget is as important as an overall vision for the ministry. The finances are the part of the equation that helps the vision become a reality. A budget is a financial plan. Just as a builder works from a plan to avoid construction chaos, you need to work from a budget to analyze ministry needs, prioritize finances, and manage money. That is the way of financial health for your ministry. One easy way to start creating a budget is to find out what has worked in the past. Get copies of what the financial committee has approved in the past. It will give you an idea of how open it is to new ideas and programs.

Starting a budget from scratch isn't that difficult, as long as you don't leave out significant expenditures. You'll need to monitor fixed, variable, and one-time expenses.

Fixed costs are like a mortgage. You pay about the same amount every month, at the same time, month after month. Other fixed costs include electric, utilities, Internet services, subscriptions, etc. These costs are generally fairly easy to predict and plan for.

Variable costs might include items such as educational materials, which may vary from year to year by type and quantity. Gasoline is another variable cost, depending on gas prices and your level of business-related travel. Estimate variable costs to the best of your ability—it's often no more than a guessing game. The way to play is to always estimate on the high side. If you spend less, you're a hero. If you low-ball your estimate, you may wind up short at year's end.

One-time costs generally cover big-ticket items—e.g., a piece of equipment, computer, copier—that you pay out only once in a great while. Those are referred to as capital expenditures and have to be tracked on your books.

THE LAST WORD

Follow up all donations (no matter how small) with a tax-deductible receipt and a heartfelt thank you. People will only give once if they feel their gift wasn't appreciated. Many organizations request donations from your pool of donors. Thank your donors lavishly and often to keep them coming back.

FASTRACK

Plan your work, work your plan. Manage, manage, manage.

ASKING THE RIGHT QUESTIONS

When you join a new ministry, you'll operate under its current budget system and funding. Briefing yourself on the church's and the youth ministry's budget history lets you know how things worked in the past. By the time the next budget year rolls around, however, you'll have the chance to reevaluate the current budget and make some changes. To do that you need to be aware of the philosophy of financial management for both the youth ministry and the larger organization. The budget should reflect the philosophies, not drive them. Allocation of ministry money is directly linked to your values and goals. If you're handed a budget for which the majority of the money goes toward laser lights and smoke machines, but you value relationships built through small groups over big events, then you'll allocate the money differently than the other youth pastor did.

When you develop the budget, you and your team determine where to allocate money by answering questions like the following:

- What does the church value?
- Where does the church invest its resources? (Find out by browsing the last few annual reports.)
- What is the church's spending philosophy? Does it buy the best of a particular item, knowing that it will last a long time, or does it get the cheapest possible item that will do the job because it doesn't have a lot of cash on hand? Is youth ministry spending in line with the philosophy of the larger organization?
- Is youth ministry a critical part of the church or is it a small part? (Find out by examining the percentage of the total budget dedicated to youth ministry. If it's less than the sandbox allotment for the preschool, you're likely in for a struggle if you want to increase your budget.)
- What has the financial committee approved in the past for youth ministry programs and equipment? You'll get an idea of how flexible it is—how open to ideas new to the church.

THE SHORT STORY ON BUDGETS

- Hire or recruit a competent bookkeeper—or take an accounting course.
- Learn how to use Excel spreadsheets or Quicken books or something similar.
- Evaluate the ministry's financial history.
- Assess the ministry values.
- Project large expenses for the next year.
- Assess the ministry calendar to project financial needs.
- Form ministry activities into broad categories (e.g., operations, staff development, curriculum, miscellaneous expenses).
- Add specific items to each category.
- Assign a projected dollar amount needed for each category.
- Total the numbers to determine if the budget is realistic. Add or subtract to make the budget add up.
- Assign management numbers to each category, if needed.
- Develop simple monthly financial reports.

Ask, "What does the youth ministry value?"

- Of all the good things on which we can spend ministry money, which things, programs, and people do we value most? How will our spending reflect those values?

- How important is environment to your ministry? Do you need to appropriate funds to make your ministry area more student-friendly?
- How important is staff development?
- Do you have experienced staffers, or do they need a lot of training and development?
- Do your staff members need a lot of encouragement? A lot of resources?

Ask, "What is the financial history of the youth ministry?"

- What was the annual budget?
- Where does that money come from?
- Where has the majority of money gone (outreach events, small group materials, van rentals)?
- What brought in the most money (fundraisers, mission trips, service or work projects)?
- Have you inherited any debt? What debt can be carried over and what debt must you immediately clear up?
- What needs to be carried on and what can be disposed of?
- Are there any annual events you need to finance—denominational gatherings, the annual junior high/senior citizen putt-putt golf tournament?

Ask, "What are the mechanics of the financial process?"

- Does your church tell you to get what you need when you need it, or does it require you to work the purchase into next year's budget and to live with with what you have for this year?
- Does your church have predetermined vendors for curriculum, sound equipment, retreat sites? Or do you decide from whom to purchase?
- Do you get parental financial support, or are you solely dependent on money allocated from the church general budget? What role do your ministry fundraisers play?
- When do you need to turn in your budget proposal to the administration?

> **POTENTIAL EXPENSE CATEGORIES**
>
> Salaries, travel, vehicles, gas, maintenance, rental equipment, continuing education, staff development, seminars, conventions, educational materials, supplies, phone, research, administration, promotion, printing, advertisement, brochures, mailings (including stamps and shipping), liability insurance, vehicle insurance, events, food or hospitality, repairs, purchased equipment, music, musical equipment, technology and miscellaneous for those unexpected expenses.

- ▸ When is the budget decided, and are midyear changes allowed? If so, what's the procedure?
- ▸ Can you raise additional funds if needed? Do you need approval for that?

Ask, "What financial standards are in harmony with your community?"

- ▸ In what socioeconomic area is the church located and how is that population reflected in your group? (If your church is primarily populated by upper-middle-class members, you can probably request a bigger budget. If your congregation is financially tight, you will have fewer available resources and ministry finances. Study how your church's socioeconomic makeup affects your ministry finances.)
- ▸ Do you have transportation available for ministry outings, or do you have to rent vehicles?
- ▸ What needs upgrading over the next year—for student safety?
- ▸ What must you purchase to make the ministry more student-friendly?
- ▸ What items must be purchased in order to continue your development ministry? List in order of priority and find out the approximate costs of each item.
- ▸ After you've answered these questions, you'll be able to develop a budget that reflects your values.

THE BOTTOM LINE ON BUDGETS

The goal of a budget is to keep the ministry financially healthy. Developing an accurate budget, managing it well, and maintaining tight controls on spending will help you and your ministry to finish the year strong—maybe even with money left over. If you can pull that off, congratulations—you've finished in the black. (Old adding machines and typewriters had either black or red inked ribbons. Black was used for positive numbers, red for negative numbers. If your ministry overspends—oops! You're in the red.)

If at the end of the year your ministry is in the black, you'll need to do something with the remaining money. Some churches and ministries have strict policies about that. Check with your Chief Financial Officer or treasurer. You may be asked to give back any surplus to the governing body for redistribution. It's hard to give up what you count as your share, though. After being thrifty all year, it's tempting to spend the leftovers during the last two weeks of the fiscal year just because you don't want to give any back. Some ministries let departments carry their surplus over to the next year as an addition to their next year's requested budget. Another likely scenario is working within a budget where your expenses must match your income.

A Sample Budget

Let's say for example your church allocates a blanket $10,000 to spend on youth ministry needs in any way you choose. What do you do?

▸ Answer all the above questions.
▸ Determine your broad income and expense categories.
▸ Determine what percentage of your money to allocate to each category.

A list of categories might include staff development, outreach events, Sunday school, small groups, administrative, summer activities, and miscellaneous. Show on a pie chart, like the one below, how much of your $10,000 you set apart for each category. This will let you see how your spending reflects your priorities.

Here's how you do it. List the percentage allocated to a category, then multiply your total budget by that percentage to translate the percentage to a dollar amount.

Staff development	10%	($10,000 x .1 = $1,000)
Outreach events	40%	($10,000 x .4 = $4,000)
Sunday school	20%	($10,000 x .2 = $2,000)
Small groups	5%	($10,000 x .05 = $ 500)
Administrative	10%	($10,000 x .1 = $1,000)
Summer activities	10%	($10,000 x .1 = $1,000)
Miscellaneous	5%	($10,000 x .05 = $ 500)
	100%	$10,000

You can also draw a wheel that shows desired spending compared with actual spending. You'll plainly see where you need to put more dollars and where you're overspending.

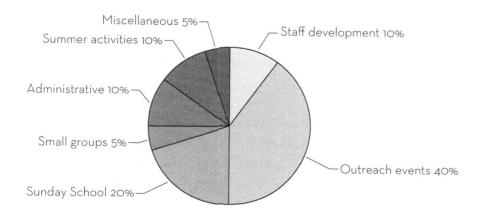

Some ministries, after having their budget approved, receive a lump sum that they use like a savings or checking account. The money isn't designated by line items; rather, spending is at the discretion of the youth pastor. As long as he or she doesn't spend more money than is in the account, it works fine.

On the other hand, some churches can't afford to disburse money in one lump sum. Instead, they approve budgets and then depend on regular giving by their contributors to keep a positive cash flow. Individual ministries within the organization receive small amounts of money as needed (and if there's money available in the bank). In other words, these ministries have both income and expenses throughout the year.

Given a choice, receiving a lump sum is the way to go. On the other hand, living by cash flow requires a special kind of faith. In either case, accurate and consistent tracking of income and expenses is vital. Be sure that there's money in the bank before you spend.

MANAGING A BUDGET

Managing a budget is like taking a shower—if you don't do it every day, people start to notice. Sometimes you can get away with neglecting to shower for a day or two, but when your closest friends start backing away from you, you know there's a problem. Financial tasks (e.g., generating reports, recording receipts, handling income) are also a daily necessity. But stacks of paper, piles of receipts, or months of statements that need balancing are ominous signs of financial mismanagement.

FasTrack

Keep the budget as simple as you can while giving as much detail as you need.

What type of daily (or weekly) management keeps finances manageable?

- ▶ Read your monthly (or weekly) reports as soon as you get them. Be sure you understand what they say. If you don't understand them, ask your accountant or bookkeeper to explain them to you. Use these reports to keep track of where you are in your fiscal year, and how much money you have left to spend.
- ▶ Be willing to say no. Knowing where you are financially—at all times— gives you the freedom to say no to expenditures. Don't shy away from the difficult conversations. Someone should be keeping you accountable, and you should keep your staff and volunteers accountable.
- ▶ Keep the paper flow moving. If you get a check requisition from a staff person, decide within two days whether to okay the expense, and then pass the paper on. If you're keeping up with your monthly statements, you'll know if you can afford the expense or not.

REIMBURSEMENTS

Offer timely reimbursement. Within two days of a reimbursement request, either send it back for more information or sign and give it to the financial officer. (For some reason, volunteers and interns who don't receive timely reimbursements get agitated.)

File your documents. At the end of the paper trail, file each document in the appropriate spot. Keep your files updated, and always add new paperwork to the appropriate file. Add each document to the front of the file—the most recent document will always be on top of the pile.

SMART TIP

If you still don't understand the finances, ask.

Hold your receipts for reimbursement until you have $100 in receipts, or 10 receipts, whichever comes first. Keep all your receipts in one place in your wallet, then one place in your desk. Then, fill out your check requisition form and turn it in to the appropriate staff member. Never hold receipts longer than 30 days unless you have a good reason. Receipts held too long or reimbursement requests that have no proper documentation sometimes don't get paid.

Ask questions. Ask the head of the technology team, "Why do we really need a new video projector right now?" Ask the accountant, "What exactly do you need from me? Do you have a sample format you can show me?" To the pastor say, "Yes, I know I overspent the budget, and we still have two months left, but do you really think it is fair to punish the students for my mistake?" (Well, maybe not the last one!)

QUICK START: MAKING A SIMPLE BUDGET

To create a budget, answer the following questions on one of those columnar accounting pads or spreadsheets:

1. Where does the ministry income currently come from? Make a list of the sources under the column heading "Income."
2. Are there other sources of income you will tap in the coming year? This is a subcategory called "Projected Income" and lists fundraisers you're adding, promised donations, additional funding from the larger organization. Be realistic.
3. Where does the ministry money currently get spent? On another columnar sheet under the heading "Expenses," list all the things ministry money bought in the last year. If you don't have accurate records to guide your list creation, look at what you have in your office or in the youth room. What looks new? Look at old newsletters to discover which activities generated

expenses. A simple budget that does not account for payroll will have at least the following categories:

- administrative and office
- advertisements and mailings
- postage
- travel
- books and materials
- sports and game equipment
- small group materials
- research
- food and hospitality

(If this or any other expense category is large, break it down into subcategories: staff meals, gifts, student meals, pizza socials, etc.).

- janitorial supplies
- utilities—phone, water, heat
- transportation
- fundraising
- miscellaneous

A more complex budget might include:

- payroll expenses (bonuses, employee insurance, dental and health insurance)
- facilities (repairs, contract labor, cleaning, building maintenance)
- mortgage
- utilities (trash, phone, water, sewer)

4. What other areas do you anticipate funding in the next year? This subcategory is "Projected Expenses," and lists anything you believe will be a necessary expense to maintain and improve the youth ministry.

DETERMINING PER-PERSON COST FOR AN EVENT

Finding your stride in creating a budget for an entire year of youth ministry comes after you experience the rhythms unique to your location, kids, and style of ministry. Rather than pulling numbers out of your backpack, you may want to model last year's budget. After working eight to 12 months with an organization, you'll most likely want to make changes.

So for a Quick Start, look ahead on your ministry calendar to an event you'll ask your students to pay for—a weekend retreat, a two-day visit to a theme park

100 miles away, an adventure night with a lock-in. Working from the Budget (or the Trip Budget), the Single-Event Registration, and the Financial Accountability Worksheet, determine the per-person cost of the event and then track your collection and deposits of registration fees.

KEEPING YOUR FINANCIAL PAPERWORK IN ORDER
Monthly Statements
Computer reports are easy and convenient but the notebook method of preserving financial reports can be helpful at keeping important documents easily accessible. They can't be deleted or lost when a hard drive crashes or a back-up fails. Section off a red, two-inch binder based on the kinds of reports and statements that cross your desk each month. Review each month's statement and file it in the notebook with the most recent one at the front of the appropriate section. In the very front of the notebook, place a copy of your annual budget. Create similar binders to store check requisitions (using dividers organized by line-item number) and another for miscellaneous, one-time reports and statements.

Report Formats
Simple and concise reporting is the rule of thumb. Reporting too much information and irrelevant information makes it impossible to determine if the ministry is in debt or just hit the Lotto. Your church might have some standard reports that work for you. If not, try using our Budget & Monthly Report and Profit Loss Statement.

Whichever report form you choose, be certain it effectively communicates where the ministry is financially at any given time. A monthly budget report shows your annual budget allocation and what you spent the previous month in each of your categories. A monthly profit-and-loss statement shows how much money came in within the last month and where it came from—and how much money went out in the last month and where it went. These one-page forms, covering one month, show where you are year-to-date.

Reimbursement Forms
For the sake of whomever writes the checks, reimbursements should be submitted no more than once a week or even once a month (whatever works for your ministry). Reimbursements are made only upon receiving completed documentation. Those submitting receipts must circle the applicable expenditures on the receipts and sign them. They must also complete the reimbursement form so you know the following:

- ▸ How they paid for items
- ▸ What items or types of items they purchased

- ▸ The purpose of the purchase
- ▸ The budget number for their purchases (unless you prefer to assign budget numbers yourself)

SMART TIP

"Year-to-date" describes financial records from the beginning of the budget year (whether calendar or fiscal) to the date the report is printed.

They must attach all receipts to the Reimbursement form and put it in your box.

After your careful review, sign it and put it in the book-keeper's box for a check to be written. Turnaround time for reimbursement should be no more than one to four weeks, depending on when the form is submitted and how often checks are cut. Provide to all those who make purchases the procedures for reimbursement. That ensures properly submitted receipts and timely reimbursements. Remember to give all purchasers a tax-exempt card and remind them of the no-tax-reimbursement policy.

CASE STUDIES

Sit down with your ministry team, supervisor, church finance director and talk through these situations.

They know what they're doing, right?

It's your first week on the job in your first full-time youth ministry position. The ministry is well established, with a good track record. Although you haven't yet seen the budget figures, the ministry seems to be financially sound. A volunteer who's been handling the retreats for the last two years asks you to approve a large expense for the upcoming retreat. What do you do?

Better programming needs better funding.

You've been at a ministry for just under one year. Money is always tight, but some-how you've managed to squeeze by without overspending. You dream of doing so much more, but you feel held back by a lack of money. It's almost time to prepare next year's budget, and you want to recommend budget figures that will support new strategies for building the ministry. What steps do you take to make your dream a reality?

I'm still in control, I'm still in control . . .

You're one week out from an event for which you've planned, budgeted, and already collected student money. You've tracked the finances carefully up to this point, but a whirlwind of last-minute expenses and program additions have thrown you off track. Several staff and volunteers are out making purchases, and you have a feeling they're overspending—but you can't be sure. You really want this event to be great, so you don't want to inhibit their creativity by raising red flags; but you can't overspend either. What immediate steps do you take? How do you handle future events differently?

Uh, honey, about that credit-card bill . . .

You're busy. So busy, in fact, that it's difficult to find time for your husband. At least four nights a week he doesn't even see you before he goes to bed. You're building a volunteer base to take some of the ministry burden off your shoulders, but there just isn't enough time in the day to do everything that needs doing—let alone train and plug in volunteers.

Then, in your rush to get everything done, you can't wait on a check requisition to cover urgently needed supplies. So you decide to charge several hundred dollars to your personal credit card. When you finally get around to requesting reimbursement, you can't find the receipts; and you know the church won't reimburse you without receipts. You're afraid to tell your husband because you know he'll be angry. But he's going to find out soon anyway because he always checks the statements online on Saturdays. What do you do?

CASE STUDY SOLUTIONS

They know what they're doing, right?

Before approving the expense, look at the budget for the past retreat to see if what the volunteer says rings true. Then ask the church treasurer if the youth retreats have paid for themselves in the past. If you sense a go-ahead based on your research, approve the expense. If you find inadequate records or if the records show that retreats usually draw on budgeted money, work with the volunteer to modify the request. With any luck, the volunteer is requesting enough in advance to allow time for your investigation. If, through lack of planning or bad timing of your arrival on staff, you feel pressured to make a snap decision, resist it. Never let someone else's urgency force you to take shortcuts that could cost you in the long run. Always do the homework before approving expenses.

Better programming needs better funding.

- Reevaluate your current budget and spending to determine if it reflects ministry values.
- Decide if you can cut some expenses and put the money saved toward your ministry dreams.
- Meet with the ministry team to brainstorm how you can put feet to your dream.
- Settle on sacrifices you can make up front that will get you closer to your dream.

  ▸ Meet with the treasurer and pastor to describe your vision. They might
    direct you to sources for extra funding or other help.

I'm still in control, I'm still in control . . .

This is a tough case. Whether you track spending on a computer or a yellow pad,
update income and expenses daily. Request purchasers to daily turn in or fax their
receipts. Daily completion of your financial homework is your best bet for staying
in touch with the event balance sheet. Don't let your paperwork start piling up.

Uh, honey, about that credit card bill . . .

Books have been written that offer advice to someone in this position. Any way
you cut it, this one's gonna hurt. Check your health insurance policy and hope it
covers marriage counseling.

TIPS FOR THE NEWCOMER

"It's my first day on the job. What do I do now?"

First week:

  ▸ Request a copy of this year's budget and last year's budget.
  ▸ Schedule a meeting with the person familiar with the youth
    ministry budget.
  ▸ Ask for training on procedures for tracking income
    and expenses.
  ▸ Ask what ways of handling finances have worked in
    the past and what trouble spots you should be aware
    of. (Keep an eye on the trouble spots during the next
    few weeks.)
  ▸ Unless the finances are in crisis, keep to the sys-
    tem that's in place. Change and improvements can
    come when you have more ministry knowledge and
    experience.

First month:

  ▸ Study and understand the budget. Get a feel for how
    it's been used in the past—what worked and what
    didn't.
  ▸ Talk to anyone who's had experience working with
    the youth ministry budget.
  ▸ Talk to the church treasurer to see what has worked
    well with the youth ministry and what hasn't. Also

SPECIAL-EVENT BUDGETS

These contain many of the same
elements as general budgets, but
they focus on specific events.
Very small events, of course,
may be lumped into the general
books, but you'll manage larger
events more effectively if you
track them separately. Larger,
more complex events have
multiple sources of income and
expense details. When the event
is over, transfer to your general
budget one number for income
and one for expenses. (See
Chapter 7 for specific information
on budgeting for events.)

ask if there's anything that can be done differently to help the treasurer.

▶ Work on patching the financial holes. If necessary, call a temporary spending freeze until you get a handle on the finances.

MEET WITH THE PASTOR OR TREASURER TO DISCUSS:

1. The church's philosophy on spending, corporate and personal fundraising, and ministry money management.

2. What things are set in stone and what things are negotiable.

3. The current systems for bill paying and reimbursements, and when you have to submit paperwork to receive timely payment.

4. How youth ministry petty cash, donations, fees, and expense reimbursements are handled. Evaluate if it's successful or not. Try to assign someone else to handle the petty cash (administrative assistant, financial volunteer). If needed, change the system so that every bill, check, donation, petty-cash receipt, and dollar goes across your desk. You need to know how every penny is being collected and spent. That's the only way you'll ever get a handle on the ministry finances.

First six months:

▶ After understanding, observing, and personally monitoring the budget for at least six months, you can delegate to a staff person or trusted (and experienced) volunteer some of the routine procedures. Request weekly or monthly reports from your volunteer so you can monitor any major income or expense (perhaps more than $25 or $100, depending on the size and scope of your ministry).

▶ Reevaluate the budget and adjust it according to your ministry needs.

RESOURCES

▶ *Basic Budgeting for Churches: A Complete Guide*, Jack A. Henry (B&H Academic, 1995)

▶ *Church Administration Handbook*, Bruce P. Powers (B&H Academic, 2008)

▶ *Money Matters in Church*, Aubrey Malphurs and Steve Stroop (Baker Books, 2007)

▶ *Rich Church, Poor Church: Keys to Effective Financial Ministry*, J. Clif Christopher (Abingdon, 2012)

▶ *Church Administration: Creating Efficiency for Effective Ministry*, Robert H. Welch (B&H Academic, 2011)

▶ *The Budget-Building Book for Nonprofits: A Step-by-Step Guide for Managers and Boards*, Murray Dropkin, Jim Halpin, Bill La Touche (Jossey-Bass, 2007)

▶ Training modules for Excel spreadsheets http://office.microsoft.com/

▶ Quicken products: http://quicken.intuit.com/

▶ Search for "budget" in your Apps Store

▶ www.daveramsey.com

▶ www.ecfa.org

FASTRACK

Fundraising and direct-contact requests for donations must follow your organization's protocol.

FORMS

- Budget: Asking the Right Questions
- Budget & Monthly Report Sample
- Budget & Monthly Report
- Budget Categories
- Donor Receipts
- Donor Thank-You Letter Sample
- How to Begin a Budget
- Monthly Expense Report Sample
- Monthly Expense Reports
- Petty Cash Receipt
- Profit Loss Statement
- Profit Loss Statement Sample
- Reimbursement
- Retreat Budget Sample
- Summary Balance Sample
- Summary Balance
- Trip Budget Sample
- Trip Budget
- Tips for the Newcomer
- Youth Ministry Budget Overview

▸ Never assume. Always check and double-check numbers.

▸ If at any time you creep into the financial danger zone—e.g., overspending a monthly budget, losing money on an event, unable to account for some expenses or the reason you're finding checks or cash in your drawer—notify the church's treasurer or CFO and get immediate assistance. CFOs don't like surprises and are more forgiving if you come forward sooner rather than later.

PART 4

PLANS, PROGRAMS, AND RISK

# MAKING PLANS

CHAPTER OVERVIEW
▸ Long-term Planning
▸ Short-term Planning

There's a wide variety of reasons that we all got into this thing called youth ministry. And we all look very different and come from a widening variety of backgrounds: women, men, older, younger, single, married, ordained or not, M.Div. or not, suburban, rural, inner city, international, small or large church, and with or without a budget. We love our Androids or iPhones, use PCs or Macs, prefer backpacks or bags, stream or download our music, love or hate Starbucks, and generally all have a closet full of ministry T-shirts.

Our job involves developing relationships with a ton of people: students, parents, deacons, our volunteer team, the guy who owns the water park, the van rental company owner, the juvenile detention office, a drug and alcohol counselor, several guitar players, a new intern who edits videos, the parent who "needs" to come on your retreat, and a long list of others.

Planning is an integral part of succeeding in your ministry with students and their families. Once again, the well-known quote says it all: "If you fail to plan, you plan to fail." The best way to maximize relationships is to take the time to plan. While it may take you away from hanging with students for a period of time, the investment will be well worth it.

Setting aside time to pray about the planning process is essential. This important area is often an afterthought in our ministries and the planning process. Setting aside specific time for prayer is important and necessary and should be an early part of the planning process. So, where does this fit in your planning? And if there are men and women in your church that consider this their ministry, too, bringing them into your planning will engage them in a deeper way. Ask God to guide you at the start of your planning, in the middle of it, and as you implement it.

LONG-TERM PLANNING

For the sake of this discussion, we're going to use the phrase "long-term planning" to mean planning a minimum of one year ahead. A common framework for this in many student ministry programs is the typical school-year calendar—beginning in August. So this means that by the time August rolls around, you've planned out everything through the end of the following July. Is that your norm? Or did you just fall out of your chair?

A solid discipline to develop in your planning is to begin to think and plan 18 months ahead. A question to ask yourself right now: "Whose help do I need to pull this off?"

As you work to develop your annual plan, you need to work through the following areas:

GOAL SETTING AND EXPECTATIONS

Begin by asking your pastor or direct supervisor to identify any priorities that they are asking you to focus on or address during the upcoming year. Ask them to be specific regarding the intended outcome or specific goal, meaning the money they want you to raise through fundraisers, the number of new small groups to launch, the ratio of staff to students they believe you should attain, or the size they want to see your ministry grow to. Ask directly about these expectations—this is an area where tension can be waiting.

Sometimes church leaders have a hard time articulating their expectations, but be assured, there are expectations. Set up a meeting with the appropriate church leaders to discuss this vital topic. Ask questions such as:

1. What are your expectations for the youth ministry in the upcoming year?
2. Are there any concerns from this past year we need to discuss? Anything you haven't told me?
3. What specific hopes and expectations do you have for our numeric growth, staff development, spiritual development, all-church participation, church calendar, confirmation, membership, baptism, etc. (You make the list that represents your church culture and your vision for the future.)
4. What does a great student ministry look like to you?
5. What do you think I need to know or be aware of?

If this seems intimidating, perhaps it is. If possible, send them your questions in advance so they have time to prepare. Consider taking a trusted team member with you to help you listen, to support you in your ministry, and to give you perspective after the meeting. Misunderstanding about these topics often leads to breakdown in trust between church leaders and youth workers. Don't skip this meeting. It's very important to both you and your ministry.

If you're unable to have this meeting for whatever reason, then present your goals in writing for approval. Ask for written feedback.

Budgeting

Based on your goals, build your budget. If strengthening your volunteer team is a priority, then ask for funds to support that initiative. It likely takes a financial investment of some kind to reach a goal, especially if it's significant. Find some time to sit with trusted members of your team to work this through carefully. A good place to begin to build a future budget is by reviewing previous budgets. Review your actual expenditures for the last three years if possible. Look for overages and ask for funds to help with these areas. Not good with finance and budgeting? Ask your staff and key parents for help. There's certainly someone around with a finance or accounting degree who could help you. (More on this in our chapter on budgeting.)

Planning Meetings

Determine how many staff meetings will be required through the year to accomplish the calendar and events you have developed. An annual planning retreat can be a big help with this. And it leads to better staff buy-in. Then determine how often you need to pull your leadership team together to work through your quarterly calendar. Scheduling these meetings in advance will allow a greater number of your staff to be involved and prepare as needed. In our section on "Short-term planning" we go into more detail on planning meetings.

Calendaring

Don't rush the process of designing an appropriate ministry calendar. And don't take a shortcut by developing the calendar on your own. Planning 12 to 18 months is a significant project. Allow your volunteer leaders, parents, your pastor, and key student leaders to go through this process with you. If you try the shortcuts, you'll likely fill your ministry calendar only with stuff you like to do or that the ministry has always done. And you'll likely miss important considerations such as holidays, community dates, other church-wide commitments, etc.

You have many options to guide your master calendar creation:

▸ Continue doing what the group has always done. Until you really understand the community and ministry, this is not all bad.

▸ Repeat activities you did at another church—which can be good or bad. Ministry must be contextualized.

- ▸ Plan based on your vision, needs, and priorities of your ministry.
- ▸ Adapt calendars from other churches and model your ministry on them.
- ▸ Ask the kids what they want to do; add to the calendar every single idea they give you. Just kidding! Yes, get student input—but be mindful that it's only that: Someone else's opinion.

FASTRACK

Once you have clearly established the vision and purpose of your youth ministry, transfer your vision to reality by planning your master calendar.

- ▸ Find a calendar. Fill up every day with something. Run like crazy. Quit after nine months. Again, yes, get the calendar—then plan wisely.

Okay, kidding aside, let's summarize these:

- ▸ Be mindful of what the church has done historically.
- ▸ Plan based on your vision, needs, and priorities of your ministry.
- ▸ Get input from your students and your volunteer team.
- ▸ Incorporate ideas from previous ministry experience and other churches where it's appropriate.
- ▸ Be careful not to just fill up a calendar with dates. Energy and pacing are important to balance.

Here's an example of a simple calendaring process. First, begin with a blank calendar.

These are out of your control, so place them on the calendar first:

- ▸ church or ministry-mandated dates
- ▸ community or school conflicts to avoid/be aware of
- ▸ significant sporting events, locally and nationally
- ▸ family dates: birthdays, anniversaries, vacations
- ▸ major holidays
- ▸ factor in weather trends for the season you are planning

Examine your mission, values, and goals as created by your ministry team and approved by the church leadership, senior pastor first.

Establish the "why" behind all the events you're considering.

Examine your tentative plan for good balance among the following:

- ▸ outward focused/service projects–
  - • relationship-building, outreach, and evangelistic events
  - • local projects, missions events, and trips
- ▸ opportunities for students to develop relationships and have fun together
- ▸ opportunities for growth (Bible studies, small groups, teaching)
- ▸ leadership development opportunities

- ▸ worship and prayer events
- ▸ staff meetings and training
- ▸ parent meetings

Take time to study your community. How much do you really understand the students in your community who are not a part of your ministry? Meet with a diverse group of representative students. Ask about popular gathering spots, music stations, musical preferences, how they experience peer relationships—including sexual standards, local rites of passage, perceptions of drugs and alcohol—their views of local churches, work, and family relationships. Effective ministry strategy aligns with the needs of your community (see chapter 2 on Strategic Planning).

FasTrack

To be a good planner, you must first become a good student of your church calendar, your various community calendars, and your students' calendars.

Balance of Events
One challenge of building a ministry calendar is providing diverse opportunities in which a variety of kids—in a variety of spiritual growth stages—all can feel excited about being involved. Youth ministries characterized wholly by intense discipleship and seriousness that minimize play or simply coming together for friendship can leave out a large percentage of students. How can you reach and challenge the wide variety of students who have been entrusted to you?

Annual Church Calendar
Most ministries establish significant dates 18 to 24 months in advance as they book speakers, reserve sites, plan community programs, and schedule special guests. Fill in your working ministry calendar with your church's established ministry dates first (senior pastor's birthday party cruise, all-church picnic).

Ask the pastor to be specific regarding his or her expectations of your or students' participation in:

- ▸ Special worship and prayer services
- ▸ Choir and musical performances
- ▸ Easter and Christmas
- ▸ Church membership classes
- ▸ Church staff retreats
- ▸ Holiday services
- ▸ Missions conferences
- ▸ Vacation Bible School
- ▸ All-church picnics
- ▸ Denominational events and retreats

REAL LIFE

Learn about the significant events and holidays in your community. Fishing and hunting dates, fairs, rodeos, music festivals, parades, seasonal farming rhythms, performing arts events. Is there an expected role for your church or youth ministry in any of these events?

The smaller the church, the more closely tied to the community you likely are.

If you're new, sit down with someone from the community who can brief you on the community's traditions and expectations. Subscribe to the local community paper. Contact the mayor's office.

A youth worker in Minnesota learned the hard way the lesson of checking the community calendar before planning a major youth ministry event. He planned a significant special event on a Wednesday night in early March—the week of the state hockey tournament. Two of his major campuses were involved in a final playoff game that very Wednesday night. Needless to say, he couldn't even pay kids to come to his event.

Don't discount traditions your church expects you to be a part of. If you want to change the expectation, first present an alternative (in much the same way we earn the right to be heard with our students). You won't earn this right by planning a major retreat during the annual church missions conference. But you will earn major respect and trust by sitting down with church leaders to discuss these issues before you start your planning.

If you're new, be especially mindful of traditions. They are not automatically bad. Resist the temptation to change these, at least not right away. Take time to listen, try out the event, and learn why it's been important to your ministry. Traditions have their place and when purposefully planned, can have significant impact. If there are none, consider discussing options that your ministry should consider.

Community Schedules

School. Unfortunately, complete school-year calendars often aren't released until August. Ask the school to put you on its mailing list, scour the Web site, or find a parent to be the expert on a certain school. Put the main administrative assistants from your local schools on your "gotta know" list. Buying a cup of coffee for or sending flowers to the main administrative assistant in the school office may reap rewards for months to come. Often an experienced school administrative assistant can share with you subtle scheduling issues before the school calendar is released.

Ask in particular about these important dates:

- school start and end dates
- homecoming
- prom
- fall break (in some areas)
- Christmas break
- spring break
- President's Day and Martin Luther King, Jr. weekend
- state or city holiday
- major testing periods
- SAT, ACT, and PSAT tests
- sports and band schedules (beginning in the summer)

- ▸ major concerts, plays, debates
- ▸ graduations, baccalaureate services
- ▸ captain's practices

Events and concerts. Take advantage of major concerts, Christian music festivals, and citywide Christian events. Bring your staff to the event training offered, encourage your students' parents to hear the speakers, and expose your students to strong events that give them a sense of being part of the broader body of Christ. Seek out the "connected" people in your area who seem to always know about upcoming events. Consult local media Web sites, Facebook pages, or Twitter feeds.

Sports. Are there sporting events that "own" your community? If so, don't plan a retreat on a tournament weekend (unless your team hasn't won a game in the last five years). Check the band and Future Farmers' schedule. Consider both men's and women's recreational or intramural sports schedules.

Sporting events' importance varies by community, so look into the schedule of the following: football, basketball, skiing, baseball, volleyball, swimming, hockey, soccer, lacrosse, track, golf, and tennis.

Also check major dates for college and professional sports (Super Bowl, World Series, Final Four, World Cup, Stanley Cup, NASCAR Racing, X-Games, and the Olympics).

By the way, many of these sporting events provide natural themes for your programming. So instead of avoiding activities on these dates, you might capitalize on them. Ask questions and determine how sporting events can help or hinder your ministry.

Denominational Commitments. If your church is part of a denomination or association, make an appointment for an honest, heart-to-heart talk with your pastor about denominational expectations.

- ▸ What are the expectations regarding denominational events and camps?
- ▸ Is there a denominational network monthly or yearly gathering you are expected to attend?
- ▸ What traditions must be continued and which are up to your discretion? If the choice to attend a denominational event is up to you, ask these questions before making a decision to leave traditions aside:
  - • What was the feedback from the last several denominational events of this kind?
  - • What do the old-timers on your youth team think?
  - • Whom would you offend if you pull out of this event?
  - • What do other youth workers you respect say about it?
  - • How could you and the students benefit from attending the event?

Although creating your own events might make you look better in the eyes of your kids, your denominational event may have a lot more going for it than you realize. If you're new to the denomination, participate in a few events with an open mind. Those events that aren't all they could be might benefit from your contribution to event planning. If your church isn't part of a denomination, a number of quality organizations and even some denominations will invite you to participate with them. Ask other youth workers in your area about upcoming events, retreats, and great camps near you.

Seasonal Schedule. Events may need to be planned around weather and culturally supported seasons.

Does the expected weather support your ministry event? It's hard to play broomball when it's 40 degrees outside, and barbeques are no fun when it's cold and rainy. It's nice to be at the beach or a lake . . . when it's warm. Based on your ministry environment and the culture in which you minister, determine what times of year are best for initiatives in specific areas. August and September and January, for instance, are when students may be more open to new things, fresh starts.

Some churches use the following timeline:

▸ Summer is for relationship building.
▸ Late summer suits volunteer recruitment.
▸ Fall supports reaching out to new students and forming new relationships.
▸ Winter is the season for personal growth, building deeper relationships, and student leadership development.
▸ Spring is a good time for celebration and preparations for summer missions activities.

Develop Balance. Place all your regular weekly and monthly meetings/gatherings on the calendar first. Worship, Sunday school, small groups, service projects, after-school programs, etc. Try to develop some type of basic categories for each of your events. Make it work for you with categories such as outreach, growth, leadership, service, missions, social, etc.

Again this relates to the purpose of all that you do. While planning your year, make sure you always keep in mind your ministry's purpose, which you discovered in chapter 1. If you find yourself getting off track programmatically, pull out the worksheet you wrote it down on, and recommit yourself to that purpose. Then think through each of the groups you work with—students, volunteer staff, parents and church leadership—and take some time to review your overall calendar for balance.

Teaching Calendar. Do you have a plan for how you'll help students learn important biblical topics over their years in your ministry? How age-appropriate are the topics you're looking at with your students?

As challenging as it sounds, taking the time to create an annual teaching calendar is a freeing step. This is generally well-addressed with curriculum. Your denomination may already have curriculum you're expected to follow. If not, several great resources serve your teaching and small groups:

> youthspecialties.com/shop
> youthministry360.com
> downloadyouthministry.com
> davidccook.com
> whatisorange.org/xp3students/about-xp3students/
> http://wearesparkhouse.org/teens/echothestory

Use these as a starting place for content, ideas, and a solid plan. Then customize the material to fit your ministry, staff, and students. As tempted as you may be to write your own material, start by using one of these as a framework. It will save you hours of preparation and research and will likely keep you more balanced.

Approval. A necessary step to ask in every ministry is, "Who needs to review and approve our plans?" Don't find out the hard way that your church has an unspoken policy regarding bake sales that the head deacon shares with you as you lay out all the pies on a Sunday morning. Don't discover that your church leadership has banned trips to Mexico after you've already shared the trip with your students. Get your proposed plans on paper and get them approved. By getting things approved further in advance, if there's an event that needs special consideration or approval, you have time to do that work.

> ▶ *Reserving Space and Signing Contracts.* One important step is making sure you have space for all the events you've planned. Take time to reserve the rooms, vehicles, and resources that need advance scheduling. Again, if you've taken the time to plan out all the details around an event in advance, this step will be simplified as you will already know the required details such as beginning and end time,

---

TAKE TIME TO GET TO KNOW YOUR OPTIONS. Do an Internet search for "David C Cook Scope and Sequence" to get an example of a complete year of content for all age groups.

YM360 youthministry360.com has curriculum called Elements—The Building Blocks of Faith that would be an excellent theology course.

DANGER!

Planning by the old adage "Better to ask forgiveness than permission" can incite a few laughs and actually often works well. But the lifespan of a leader who lives by this rule varies from place to place. If your ministry has a three-strikes policy (that is, mess up three times and you're out), then don't waste a strike by surprising the senior pastor or other church leaders. Ask their permission while you're in the early planning stages.

cost, etc. Secure necessary contracts for camps and retreat centers. Make sure an authorized signer from your church or ministry handles the contracts. Generally, contracts require the signature of your senior pastor, executive pastor, or church administrator. Ask before you sign!

Short-Term Planning. For the sake of this discussion, we'll define "short-term planning" as planning for the next three months. Planning at this level is very important—it's where the detailed communication strategy is developed and specific assignments are handed out. This is where ownership happens—or not. This is where the time adjustments are made based on ministry changes or new developments at the church. It's also where regular planning meetings can really help you.

> **Planning Meetings.** Although it may seem boring or unnecessary, working through each event or ministry activity carefully with your team will lead to amazing results and impact. Create your own planning grid that includes:

Budget development/review
- Event clean-up plan—you really don't want to clean out that van again. Right?
- Food/Meals—people get hungry. Generally three or more times a day. Better have a plan.
- Parent help summary—with enough lead time, you can get plenty of help.
- Payment schedule/Check requests—get your check requests in early. We clear?
- Promotion/Communication—see the entire chapter on this.
- Registration plan—sign them up, receive payment, and collect the forms.
- Review of past evaluations—look back before you look ahead.
- Rooming list(s)—do these as late as possible. Take it from experience.
- Schedule for event—think through every minute. Seriously.
- Set up and tear down—develop a plan and spell out what's needed.
- Staff assignments—develop clear roles and responsibilities.
- Supervision—do you really have enough help?
- Supplies needed—make a list and check it twice.
- Transportation—all we can say is BE SAFE. Think this one through.

Assumptions often get us in trouble. Don't assume the host home is providing snacks. Don't assume that the driver knows what time to arrive if you've disclosed only what time you're leaving. Review and confirm details carefully. Are you not a good detail person? Find a team member to help you in this area. It's essential. Make a checklist to help you remember the final payment check, to pick up the rental van, or have the church unlocked when you return from your event.

Your Calendar. Creating a visual calendar can help get your key leadership team clear on the next 90 days. (Office-supply stores have a variety of options for these types of planning calendars.) Then take time to get all the ministry information into your calendar, whether it's paper or electronic. Establish helpful reminders if there are events in the coming weeks you will struggle to remember. Then make sure all the event details are entered into your main church or Web calendar. We will address organization and calendaring in depth in a later chapter.

Proofreading. Have someone read over all the details once they've been entered. Check times, prices, addresses, and dates for accuracy. Use someone who's one step removed from the work you've been doing and who is extremely thorough.

Getting Ahead with Teaching. Depending on how your ministry is organized, you may have to teach frequently. Planning ahead generally leads to greater creativity, the ability to involve others, and less pressure to find something really good at the last minute. It also helps ensure someone is scheduled in advance when you plan to be away for vacation, conferences, etc. If you already took the step to create an annual teaching calendar, now you can approach how to prepare for the next 90 days. Pull together your teaching team and work through specific assignments and brainstorm creative elements. Do the same with your small-group materials.

> GETTING PARENTS INVOLVED to help behind the scenes is essential. Many have gifts in the area of administration, hospitality, and leadership that could be of significant assistance to you. First, identify the areas where you could use their help. Write out the specific job(s) and expectations. List the time frames. Then start recruiting. Here's a cool Web-based tool that can help you get the slots filled where you need help in your ministry—www.signupgenius.com.

"Teaching team?" you ask. "We're just a small church!" Yes, still develop other volunteers with the gift of teaching to support the ministry. Invest in others. Help them develop. Give them a chance. Later in our book we spend more time discussing volunteers and how to maximize their roles.

Communication. Take some time with your team to work through the best ways and best times to get the word out on what you're doing in the upcoming months. Create a grid that lists all your events/ministries down the left side of the page. Then across the top, list out all the channels for spreading the message. These might include:

- Church calendar
- Web site
- Facebook
- Twitter
- Instagram
- Vine
- Email
- Text blasts
- Announcements
- Small groups
- Calls
- Direct mail

SCANNERS?

There are a growing number of excellent tools to help with your expense tracking. Perhaps one of the best solutions is Expensify (www.expensify.com). Getting your ministry to invest in a high-speed scanner is also a big help in this area. Check out the Neat Scanner.

FORMS

▸ Monthly Planning
▸ Weekly Planning
▸ Calendar Master Checklist

Then determine who's responsible to get those messages written and submitted to the various channels. Recruiting a team member to focus on communications is becoming essential today. Smaller ministry? You can still pull this off by talking with the parents of your students. All the talents hiding out there in your church may surprise you. Consult chapter 8, Communications, for a more in-depth look at communication in your ministry.

Expense Reports and Reimbursements. Sooner or later this topic is going to come up. This is another area that often causes frustration for youth workers because we want to focus on students, not paperwork. Here are some important steps that will help decrease your frustration:

1. Find a safe place to collect all your monthly receipts.
2. Make a note on the receipt at the time you get it of what it is, who was involved, etc.
3. If you have volunteers buy things for the ministry, emphasize that a receipt is required for reimbursement.
4. If you have an event that involved a lot of receipts and expenses, sit down within a couple days of that event and complete your expense report. It's a lot easier when your memory is fresh. And you may have an easier time finding all the necessary receipts and paperwork.
5. Make sure to get all unpaid invoices submitted and coded for payment right away. Most businesses expect payment within seven to 14 days. More on this in our finance chapter.

COMMUNICATIONS

CHAPTER OVERVIEW
▸ Target Your Communication
▸ Tools for Communication
▸ Designing and Prioritizing Communication and Marketing

Communication is an essential component of any organization, and your ministry is no exception. Keeping multiple groups of people informed, in the loop, and current on where things are headed is essential. Too often what is very clear in our heads is very different in the minds and realities of our students, staff, and their parents. What we think we've shared and what has actually been shared can be significantly different. Good communication involves thought, planning, and clarity.

Yes, it requires writing. (Last-minute text blasts are not what we are referring to here.) In fact, many youth workers have found themselves in trouble for simply not communicating.

TARGET YOUR COMMUNICATION
KNOW YOUR AUDIENCE
In ministry, we have four basic groups with whom we need to communicate. Most of us excel with a couple of these groups, but finding a way to communicate with all four of these unique, important groups is essential to your success.

Students: The students we work with are our primary audience. Staying in touch with them continues to be a moving target as technology changes and students become more and more connected. Identify the best method to reach the greatest number of your students. How? Ask! From there, three other vital groups surround you.

Church leadership: This is another big one. They have the power to fund or un-fund your ministry, lay the new carpet or make you use the moldy stuff for another year. Knowing how to get the right information into their hands is essential. You can't afford to assume they understand what your ministry is up to. In fact, it's best you assume they don't. Instead, find ways to share stories of the good things happening in your ministry. When something bad happens, I promise they will find out without your help, so be as quick to share the bad as the good.

Parents: Each of your students has one, two, three, or more parents based on their family situation (or grandparents, aunties, or guardians). Do you have contact information for each caregiver? Do you know who has custody when? Keeping parents informed, in the loop, encouraged, and trusting of you is vital. Most parents are busy, very busy, and too often are reactionary rather than proactive in their communication with you. But you have to communicate with parents—it's essential. Don't treat them like the enemy; they are finding their way along the parenting journey and need all the help they can get.

Staff: Last, but certainly not least, is your staff. Those faithful men and women who stay late with you to clean out the vans, sort through the smelly lost and found, and invest countless hours in the lives of students. You have to keep them in the loop. In fact, you have to try to keep them ahead of things. They do best without surprises.

BE INTENTIONAL

There's no one method to communicate. And your message certainly has to be sent more than once. Here's what we know about communicating today—you have to say things in multiple ways and at multiple times to get your message heard. Remember: "Message sent" certainly is not always equivalent to "message received." Try this next time you're with a group—make some type of simple announcement and then five minutes later, ask people what you said. Don't be discouraged; people have a lot going on inside their heads. They have a lot of messages coming at them.

Start by being clear about the message you are communicating. Do you really understand the purpose and vision behind it? Once your purpose is clear, telling the story becomes easier. Then share the details and make sure they're all there and are correct. Anticipate questions and answer them in advance as part of what you communicate. Then stick to the details you communicate. Last-minute changes can damage the credibility of your communication.

SHARE YOUR VISION

People are drawn to ministries and leaders who are clear about their visions. Vision is the purpose for why you exist. Have you taken the time to write out a short, concise statement that captures the overall vision and mission of your ministry? If not, revisit chapter 2. Vision is inspiring. It calls people to something greater. Repeat it, share it, talk about it. Find ways to share and celebrate your students who live out that vision. Tell their stories. People will rally around a genuine and impactful vision.

TIMING IS EVERYTHING

Finding ways to get your message to your intended audience at the right time is key. Retreat details emailed at the last minute may cause significant frustration and may not even be received by many parents. Messages sent too early, on the other hand, may get lost. Texting a staff person during the workday may result in your message getting missed or forgotten. Discussion questions for group leaders need to arrive in time for them to prepare, not as they're walking in to lead their group.

Schedule your messages. It's that simple. Think through when the mailing, text message, or email should ideally arrive. Then work backward from that. Create a spreadsheet depending on the complexity of messages you need to send to your ministry.

Make sure you leave enough time to help your leaders, students, and their parents as they are planning and budgeting.

SUGGESTED DEADLINE SCHEDULE	
Quarterly Ministry Calendars	due: 1-month ahead minimum
Summer (June-August)	due: April 15
Fall (September-November)	due: Aug 1
Winter (Dec.-Feb.)	due: Nov 1
Spring (March-May)	due: Feb 1
Staff Meeting & Training Schedule	due: Aug 1 (for the upcoming school year)
Annual Teaching Overview	due: Aug 1
Major Date Overview to Parents	due: Aug 15 (for the upcoming school year)
Fall Retreat Brochure	due: Aug 15
Winter Camp Brochure	due: Oct 15
Summer Mission Trip Brochure	due: March 1
Summer Camp Brochure	due: March 1

BE CONCISE

Think about the last really long email you received. Did you read all of it? At what point did you quit or decide to just skim it? It probably depends on whom it's from, how it's written, and how much you care about the message. Shorter messages are more likely to be read. Accurate messages are important—if you send out inaccurate info, your readership will likely decline. So write out your message . . . and then shorten it. Cut nonessential words.

Keep asking yourself, "Who cares?" Be brutally honest in your evaluation. Ask people you trust for feedback on the communication you have in place now. Then listen to what they say to you.

Be Complete

When you share details regarding an upcoming ministry activity or event—answer all these questions:

- ▸ What is the event?
- ▸ What is the purpose of the event?
- ▸ Who is this event for?
- ▸ Where is the event?
- ▸ What time is the event (begin and end times)?
- ▸ How much does it cost and how do people pay?
- ▸ When is the deadline to sign up or register?
- ▸ What do people need to bring?
- ▸ Who is the contact for more information?
- ▸ Is there special information for this event?

Do the hard work to answer all these questions when you plan your event. Resist the temptation to say, "We'll figure that out later . . ." Publish all the details at once. Your staff, students, parents, and church leaders will thank you.

As much as possible, place all these details on your Web site in full, then use other communication channels to highlight various parts of the event. Use email to point people back to your event site.

For example, send an email to parents a week prior to the camp registration deadline with a simple reminder. Send a text blast to your students the evening before you leave on a missions trip with the meeting time reminder for the next morning.

Call People to Action

The purpose of your communication is generally to call people to some type of action. Join a group, give money, serve on your team, sign up, read their Bibles, celebrate something God has done. If your message is passive, don't be surprised when the results are less than inspiring. Be clear when you write your message: What response are you hoping for? What exactly should these people do? What are your expectations?

Ask yourself these questions when thinking about communicating:

What is my audience doing right now? (Facebook and Twitter have researched
    when the best times are to post. Take their advice into account.)
Does my message hit a felt need? If not, how can I reframe the message?
Is my message compelling, clear, and concise?
What day and time is best for my message to be read and acted upon?

TOOLS FOR COMMUNICATION
WEB SITES

Web sites are a vital source of information for your ministry. While good design
is important, accurate information is crucial. A simple, clean design supported by
current, correct information is essential. If you haven't already, recruit a proofer
and fact-checker for your site. Their work is just as impor-
tant as the team doing the planning and writing.

> ### EVENTBRITE
> Check out eventbrite.com if
> you need a great and FREE
> registration solution for your
> free event. If your event
> comes with a cost, it offers an
> affordable solution for collecting
> payments for tickets, retreat
> registration, etc.

    Need a new site? There are a number of Web site solu-
tions available to churches worth investigating. Here are
just a few: www.monkdevelopment.com, www.clover-
sites.com, www.buildachurchwebsite.com, www.share-
faith.com.

    Be sure to investigate how your Web site will perform
on mobile devices. Mobile site use is seeing exponential
growth, and your site must be set up for easy viewing on
a mobile phone.

    You don't have to settle when it comes to your Web site
design. The Internet is filled with examples of great church Web sites (and a ton of
really bad ones!), and companies that can help you create a custom affordable site
of your own. Or better yet, check out wordpress.com for an inexpensive option.
See www.churchmarketingsucks.com for suggestions on what should be included
on a Web site. Highly customizable templates are a great solution for ministries on
a tight budget. You can also check with your own students and leaders as well as
with adults in your church to see who might already be adept in this area. Find
a solution that's easy to update. Keeping your Web site current, accurate, and
updated should be a big priority. If your youth ministry has its own site, make sure
the home page contains basic information including the church address, phone
number, youth ministry meeting times, email addresses, and social media links.

    Then (if it fits your ministry culture) push people to the Web for ministry and
event information, registering for events, and finding updated media. Do what

you can to eliminate printing and mailing forms and brochures—have them available on your Web site for download.

CROWD CONTROL GAMES

Our friends have a great and affordable tool called InstaGrabber that allows you to pick a hashtag and then download to your computer the images it finds. Then, by using their software called Instaplayer, all the images can be easily displayed. A great way to share them from a big event or camp! Visit www.crowdcontrolgames. com to see all their great games.

SOCIAL MEDIA

What began on a college campus after the turn of the 21st century has long since exploded into a time-consuming connector of people. Facebook, as well as Twitter and Instagram, continue to expand usage and popularity.

But don't fall into the trap of seeing these channels simply as ways to get your message out. See them also as avenues for engaging people in relationship and discussion. Ask questions, celebrate victories, tell stories, thank others. No one's responding to or "liking" what you're posting? Time to change something up. Meet needs, make people smile, and find ways to bring others into the story.

Facebook: Facebook has an excellent group and event feature. Create a group for your ministry. This gives you easy feedback on how many are clicking, sharing, and commenting. Consider a private or locked group for your staff. Then create events for your ministry.

Twitter: Create a hashtag for your ministry. Encourage students to use that hashtag when posting pictures or comments from an event, retreat, or trip. Youth Specialties uses #nywc for its National Youth Worker Conventions. Have a look at how it uses this tool to help connect youth workers.

Instagram: Identify a hashtag for your ministry and ask students, staff, and parents to tag their photos so that you can gather everyone's pictures in one place. Because some students are spending more time on Instagram than Facebook or Twitter, youth pastors are trying to reach them by taking Instagrams of announcements.

Tumblr: This site has exploded in its presence and use. It's worth investigating.

A benefit of social media is that you can be intentional about sharing the stories of your ministry's vision being lived out—especially of your students.

EMAIL

Looking for an inexpensive way to get the word out to a lot of people? Email is the answer. That said, keep your audience in mind. Students? No. Parents? Generally yes. Staff? It just depends. Church leaders? Well-written emails and even a letter. Make sure you have permission from people to communicate with them through their emails.

Need to manage a large email list? Check out group-mail solutions such as mailchimp.com and constantcontact.com if you want help with great-looking layouts and the ability to review open and click-through rates. Yes, those things really matter. If people aren't opening what you write, save everyone's time and stop writing.

Here are some thoughts on good emails. They . . .

1. Only get to people whose addresses you have. It begins with the accuracy of your email list.
2. Are opened and read. Help people be motivated to open your email and read it—have something worth reading.
3. Have a growing read list. Give people in your ministry a reason to join your list—an encouraging devotional, a training resource, photos from the latest retreat.
4. Are short. Better to send several short emails leading up to an event than one really long one that no one reads . . .

TEXT MESSAGING

We don't have to tell you—text messaging has exploded. Want to get your message out? Send a text.

Looking for a great way to connect with a small group of your staff? Check out GroupMe—currently a free app. It's like building your own private chat room—it's simple and free. It starts with having an accurate list of the cell numbers of whomever you want to form into a group. This is great for key people you need to reach quickly. Ever forgot to text that "one" student, parent or staff member? It can be haunting.

For larger groups and additional features, group-texting solutions are well worth the investment. Youth Specialties has a product called YS Group Text found at YSgroup-txt.com. Group texting solutions allow you to schedule group text messages in advance, poll people in your ministry, and simultaneously update Facebook and Twitter. Many also have mobile features that allow you to access the group text site from your mobile phone to send those last-minute texts about return times, weather changes, etc. Look at the features carefully before you sign up!

> ### SOCIAL MEDIA POLICY
> Meet with church leaders to discuss your communication policy, especially when it comes to interacting with students over the Internet. Should you be "friends" with students on Facebook? Can you text a student? What about SnapChat, Instagram, Vine, Tumblr? This topic is growing and must be addressed by you and the leaders of your church. Check out the Risk Management section for guidelines on social media policies.

CHURCH SERVICES

Using the announcement time in your church worship service can be a huge credibility builder for your ministry. Rather than viewing this channel as a way to promote future events, view it as a way to share what God is doing in your ministry. Use it as a way to cast vision for ministry to students. You have to assume that the people of your church KNOW NOTHING about your ministry. In fact, if all they ever hear about are future activities, they will likely assume that you are just in the event business. If you want them to know about how a student in your group collected donations for a social justice project instead of receiving birthday presents, you have to tell that story. Do they understand the sacrifices your volunteer staff makes to invest in students—and the difference they're making? Tell others! How about the impact of your recent retreat? Share some stories. Interview a student. Show some pictures. Share more stories and you'll likely spend less time begging for volunteers. In fact, you may end up with a waiting list.

Funding a Scooter

The 5th and 6th graders at a large church learned about an African pastor who was walking between villages to teach a Bible study. He needed a scooter. The 5/6 pastor shared this story and then to his surprise the following week, found that the students had rallied and worked to raise the needed funds. All on their own. Two weeks later the senior pastor invited those students to the front of the church during Sunday worship, shared the story, showed a photo of the new scooter, and the church responded with a standing ovation. The adults were inspired and challenged by the action of these 11-year-olds.

Print Resources

Print has changed drastically in the last 30 years of ministry. Several items that remain relevant and valued are the ministry (quarterly) calendar, event flier, and the event "rave" card or "plugger." In some church communities, print is still the way to go, especially if the community isn't tech savvy. Your ministry needs to evaluate the balance between printed materials that you mail or hand out and the use of your Web site. While the Internet is paperless and certainly more affordable, there may still be a need to make printed materials available. And from time to time, a mailed piece may receive heightened attention.

Quarterly calendars can be used to cover a ministry family's refrigerator with cool reminders. Suggestion: Print up magnets with your ministry Web site, hashtag, texting numbers, etc. and give them to families and staff to use to hang their calendar on the fridge.

Event fliers are essential in communication depending on your ministry preferences. Slowly online solutions are replacing many fliers. But they still have their place in helping you communicate. A mailed flier can actually stand out as a communication tool today in light of the focus on email and Web and social media. Software such as Pages or Publisher can help you make professional-looking brochures for your fundraiser, retreat, or special event.

Rave cards (or "pluggers") are simple event reminders and are great tools for students to use to invite their friends. Generally they are well designed and printed in full color on a high quality glossy stock. Check out OutreachMinistries and Group Imaging to learn more about printed options for your ministry. www.outreach.com www.groupimaging.com

SNAIL MAIL

There are actually a number of ways that regular ol' mail still remains a relevant form of communication. While the use of mail in ministry has greatly decreased in the last few years, there are still times when it's a perfect way to get your message out.

► Quarterly Calendars—want to make sure they get to all the parents of your students? Mail them to their homes.
► Retreat/Camp Brochures—getting these out early is essential in light of parents blocking out those weekends and setting money aside for their students.
► Event Postcards—a simple, colorful card is a great tool to call attention to an upcoming parent meeting, training event, or special activity.
► Postcards—take a few minutes each week to write a handful of postcard notes to students. Someone missing for a couple of weeks? Shoot a note to let the person know he or she is missed. They so rarely get physical mail that you're sure to get their attention.
► Thank-you cards—a handwritten card is a powerful tool. Take the time to make this a habit. People volunteer to help? Write them a note. Use someone's home for a study? Thank them with a note. Borrow a van? Gas it, wash it, vacuum it, and then write a note. Affordable cards can be printed up with your ministry logo.
► Birthday cards—a big deal. Take a few minutes to work ahead on birthday cards and mail them to all of your staff, your students, and key leaders in your ministry. Handwritten, hand addressed and stamped with a real stamp. They will stand out. Again, you can buy these cards or print up your own.

> ### SURVEYS
> A communication survey is a good way to learn about how best to get your message to your church. Find out the ways your students, their parents, your staff, and church leadership prefer to be communicated with: text, phone call, email, Instagram, snail mail. A great tool to survey them is called surveymonkey.com.

PHONE CALLS

Talking with someone directly can be a powerful (and faster) way to encourage, seek clarification, make an invitation, or resolve a conflict. A video call can be even more helpful. Skype is a great (and free) tool for connecting with individuals, as is Google Hangout. A premium version of Skype is also available for connecting groups on video chat.

Pick up the phone when . . .

► A message you receive from someone doesn't make sense.
► Someone is upset with you.
► You need to resolve a conflict.
► You need to personally encourage someone to get involved with something.
► Someone asks you to call.

DESIGNING AND PRIORITIZING COMMUNICATION AND MARKETING

Taking the time to develop a look and "brand" for your ministry is important. You and your church need to sort out the issue of the name of the ministry. A growing number of churches are moving back toward a simple naming and branding structure around the name of the church itself. It keeps communication simpler and cleaner and increases the strength of the overall brand. So rather than Impact High School Ministry, simply calling it First Church SH is a strong option.

Investing in a graphic artist isn't out of the question. First, search to see if any professionals in your church might be willing to donate their time or help you at a reduced rate. Be sure to check with adults or students in your church in case there's someone with strong artistic or graphic design skills. There is probably talent surrounding you that you're not aware of, and they may be eager to volunteer. Regardless, and even if you have to pay full price, it's worth the investment of money and time to get this right. Look through portfolios to determine if design work is a match for your ministry. Visit Web sites. Once you have an artist, have him or her create general design pieces to use regularly in your ministry. By creating these all at once, generally you save money and time and have greater consistency.

► A ministry logo
► Social media landing page templates—Facebook and Twitter
► E-news template
► Basic flier templates for camps, retreats, and other annual events
► Web banners—think through your upcoming year
► Event logos for annual ministry events
► Note cards, birthday cards, postcards

- Signage and backdrops (see Group Imaging for ideas)
- Email signature template

Have them help you create a simple style guide—a simple overview of how you design and write about your ministry. They'll know what this means, and it will help you create a consistent look and feel for your ministry.

Here are a few sites you need to visit to help you in your communication journey:

http://churchbrandingsucks.org
http://www.cfcclabs.org/

RESOURCES

- *Less Clutter. Less Noise. Beyond Bulletins, Brochures, and Bake Sales*. Kem Meyer (31 Press and Wired Churches.com)
- *Good Idea. Now What?* Charles Lee (Wiley)
- *Brand Against the Machine: How to Build Your Brand, Cut Through the Marketing Noise, and Stand Out from the Competition* John Morgan
- *Purple Cow*, Seth Godin (Penguin Group)
- *The Starbucks Experience*, Joseph Michelli (McGraw-Hill)
- *All Marketers Are Liars*, Seth Godin (Penguin Group)

FORMS

- Annual Communication Schedule
- Jr High Calendar Example

9 RISK MANAGEMENT

CHAPTER OVERVIEW

▶ Foundations of Risk Management
▶ Risk Management Process
▶ Events and Forms
▶ Travel Safety
▶ Social Media Policies
▶ Insurance
▶ When Accidents Happen

R isk management identifies and assesses threats, prioritizes and controls risks, and creates a culture of safety for the purpose of ministry.

We should emphasize at the outset:

*This chapter is **not** intended to replace professional legal advice or consultation with your ministry's insurance agent. You must understand and comply with the laws where you live. Laws change and are different from state to state, even city to city. What you read here is only a start—a good start, but a start nonetheless. When you're finished reading here, get legal advice appropriate to your state and city.*

What is risk? According to Nonprofit Risk Management (a leader in the risk field), "Risk is any uncertainty about a future event that threatens your organization's ability to accomplish its mission." As you look around your ministry, what could possibly happen that would stop the ministry or render it ineffective? That's risk. Risk management is a critical and essential part of youth

MISTAKES HAVE COSTS

"We had played the game a month ago with no injuries. This time, though, because of the number of students playing, we adjusted the rules just a bit—and we didn't foresee that those slight modifications would make a huge difference in the safety factor of the game.

Within 15 minutes, three students injured their legs and one received a head injury. And because there were several game stations, the danger wasn't apparent until after the game was over. Too little knowledge, too late in the game.

Our mistake cost us. Of the four students, one ended up having knee surgery that took over a year to heal. Bad? Yes. But it could have been much worse. Needless to say, we didn't play that game again. The fun wasn't worth the risk."

ministry. Unfortunately, no matter how well you manage risks throughout your career, sooner or later every youth pastor has to deal with tragic or unfortunate situations. Perhaps it will be a freak accident and no amount of safeguards and preparations will have helped you avoid it. More likely, it will be an incident whose consequences can be less drastic with adequate planning and preparation. In any case, as the responsible adult, you're obliged to manage potential risk and be prepared for both the avoidable and the unavoidable.

FOUNDATIONS OF RISK MANAGEMENT

If you've spent any time in youth ministry, you know of youth workers who've dealt with disasters. Real-life tragedies happen. Sadly, ministries today must be prepared to deal with—

- ▶ a student's murder
- ▶ random or targeted shootings
- ▶ climbing accidents
- ▶ beach drownings caused by strong currents
- ▶ domestic violence situations
- ▶ rafting accidents
- ▶ bus, van, and other vehicular accidents

For the one chance that these tragic disasters could have been avoided, preparation is priceless.

Youth workers in these cases were sometimes on the sidelines lending support; others were involved in the nitty-gritty details of funeral preparations and legal battles. Although preparation won't make you invulnerable to problems, the tools you find here can prepare you and your ministry for the expected and the unexpected.

Everyone agrees that leaders in ministry have to provide a safe environment for learning and growth. However, people have different interpretations of the meaning of "safe." Youth workers who are risk takers have exciting, charismatic reputations. Their life's motto is "It's flesh; it'll heal." Although they generally bring the group home safely, they may or may not have the actual head count. But they have most of the kids' phone numbers. . . . somewhere. They are, of course, on a first-name basis with the ER personnel. But hey, if it takes kids to the edge of challenge and growth . . .

Other youth workers lean more toward over-protectiveness. An action game for them is Bloody Uno or Four on the Couch. They have notarized release forms for all events, staff-to-student ratio at events is always 1:3, and group members have whistles, laminated "in case of emergency" cards, and snake bite kits slung around their necks. They got an eyeful of whitewater rafting once –at a 3-D IMAX movie theater, which made it pretty exciting.

Of course, the middle ground gets us to our goal: The **maximum amount of adventure for the minimum amount of risk**. Or another way to look at it is, how much risk are you willing to take on and how much risk is your organization willing to take on? Even if the two perspectives are the same, you need to have a conversation with your lead pastor, church chair, or executive director about what is acceptable risk.

In other words, be proactive.

A Risk-Management Process

Risk management provides strategies, techniques, and an approach to recognizing and confronting any change or threat faced by an organization in fulfilling its mission. Whereas insurance covers you after a loss, risk management deals with *anticipating or avoiding* problems or losses and being prepared to deal with them when they do happen.

Your organization, church, or denomination may already have a risk management policies manual; be sure to read policies with which you're expected to comply.

Here's a four-step management process that will help your ministry better protect itself:

1. Assess the context

Our goal for many youth ministry events is a maximum amount of adventure for the minimum amount of risk. Whether your adventure is a high-ropes course,

Taking Risks

Jesus employed risk throughout his ministry on earth. Whether it was walking on water or dealing with hostile crowds, he knew that change comes about when you create an atmosphere of risk. When our status quo is messed with, a.k.a. put at risk, we either rush back to our comfort zones or move forward to something new. When Jesus put the old order at risk, the Pharisees wanted the old status quo. The disciples were ready for something new. We employ this same practice as youth workers; that's why we take students on service projects, retreats, and explorations. When we mess with the students' comfort zones, they're forced to wrestle with whether they want the status quo or life change.

Smart Tip

The legal gloves are off— churches are no longer sanctuaries from lawsuits. Hundreds of lawsuits are brought against churches every year—many of which could have been prevented.

(Adapted from *Business Management in the Local Church*, David R. Pollock, Moody Press, 1995).

gang-intervention program, or a 3-on-3 basketball tournament in the church gym, risk is involved.

You need to ask two questions: 1) "How much risk am I willing to assume?" and 2) "How much risk is my church or organization willing to assume?" Even if the two answers are the same, you need to have a conversation with your lead pastor, church chair, or executive director about what is acceptable risk for your group.

A few questions to ask as you assess the ministry context for risk:

Where are we blind to risk?

This might show up in a leadership attitude of, "We're all family, so why do we need permission slips and background checks?" Or it might be a theology that "God will protect us, so don't worry about it." Or more realistically, there's a culture of "some day we'll get to it," resulting in negligence because of the demands of other parts of the ministry.

Who's advocating for risk management?

If it's just you, you're going to have a difficult job of creating a safe culture. Try to get other advocates on board: the children's pastor, teachers, school administrators, insurance agents, or therapists. All of these people will be familiar with risks in serving vulnerable populations and can help you make your case.

Who will carry out the risk management strategy?

A lot of time can be spent putting together a great set of policies that sit on a shelf or hard drive. All leaders are responsible for carrying out the risk management strategy. This includes high school helpers in the nursery, middle school small group leaders, college interns, and parent chaperones.

2. Identify the risks

Realize that there are risks in any ministry. Even sitting around a table in the church basement: a kid can tip over a chair, fall on the linoleum floor, and suffer a brutal cut on his head. Look around the ministry for the risks that are present or could emerge, such as:

- Loss of ministry capability due to adults forming inappropriate, enmeshed, or abusive relationships with youth (or any vulnerable person).
- Physical injury to leaders or students under normal operating conditions or during special events—like whitewater rafting, mission trips, service projects, retreats, construction projects, and/or higher risk sports.
- Damage to assets such as vehicles, buildings, office equipment.
- Inadequate or nonexistent permission slips and health forms.
- Lack of policies on technology usage.

▶ Loss of goodwill from the community due to inappropriate behavior of staff members or adult volunteers.

▶ Loss of funds due to embezzlement or robbery by staff or students.

—from *Risk facts #2* (Nonprofit Risk Management Center).

3. Evaluate and prioritize risk.

Determine how vulnerable you or your ministry are, then outline appropriate cautions to implement. Consider how likely the accident or incident is to happen and how much it will cost if it does. "Cost" means not just dollars, but harm to a student or leader, loss of goodwill, and other assets.

4. Decide how to manage your risks.

Determine what needs to be done and document it. The plan should include four basic strategies for controlling risk:

▶ *Avoidance.* Don't offer that activity as an option. (No more indoor water parks in the sanctuary.)

▶ *Modification.* Change the activity to minimize the chance of harm. (Give students better padding when playing a physical contact game.)

▶ *Retention.* Accept all or a portion of the risk, then prepare for the consequences if the worst happens. (If you play Capture the Flag on asphalt, for instance, have Band-Aids and Bactine on hand for the inevitable scrapes.)

▶ *Sharing the risk.* Along with the general liability insurance that covers your organization, purchase event-specific insurance that will cover you for higher-risk activities. Contract with another organization to provide leadership for the risky activities, like rock climbing, high ropes challenge courses, or whitewater rafting.

EVENTS AND FORMS

Youth leaders need to demonstrate to parents, leaders, and students that you've planned and prepared for a safe event and are consistently executing that plan. That means you have chosen to be the adult.

Welcome to the real world of youth ministry—the one where you have to make the tough choices and provide the voice of reason.

A youth worker was in the midst of a heated discussion with three high school seniors and not at all appreciating that she had to put the lid on their makeshift indoor water park. Actually, she would much rather have joined them in their only slightly destructive merrymaking. Instead, all she could think of was,

"Who's going to clean up this mess?"

"Am I ever in trouble with the janitor!"

"How long until the running, slipping, and sliding students hurt themselves?"

She had joined the ranks of responsible adults. You're the adult in charge, you're the youth worker—and the one whose task it is to think through possible contingencies, weigh the problems versus the benefits, and decide whether an activity is worth the risk. That's because *you* are the one who must live with the consequences of your decision—right or wrong—before the ministry staff, the students, the board, the pastor, the parents, and perhaps even the community and media.

The church and the minister are not immune from legal responsibility for their actions because they are in the religion business. Anyone related to the activities of the church is responsible for the care and protection of people. Forgetting to have permission slips or laughing off having too many kids in a car isn't something that can be chalked up to an easygoing personality. It's seen as "negligence," a phrase that should be known to, and avoided by, every youth pastor. Negligence can be a career-changer; one that moves you from ministry to prison. It's that serious.

A church may be called upon to provide compensation for anyone—members, visitors, employees, or others outside the church—when there is negligence resulting in any loss or damage. The act of negligence may result from doing or not doing something that a reasonable person would do or not do in a similar situation. Permission slips are a basic requirement in youth ministry, but they cannot be used as an excuse for negligence. The church should make every effort to keep from being negligent by implementing safe policies as well as providing adequate insurance coverage for protection from unforeseen situations. For example, maintain workers' compensation insurance coverage for employees and public liability insurance coverage for property and vehicles in significant amounts. As always, consult with your church board, lawyer and insurance company on these matters.[1]

As you assess the level of risk for a new event or idea, test it through a safety grid. Use the following questions and talk it through with a partner before trying it out.

- ▸ What can go wrong?
- ▸ If something does go wrong, what would we do?
- ▸ How much could a mistake cost?
- ▸ What is the worst thing that could happen if this doesn't work?
- ▸ Who has done this before, and what was their experience like?
- ▸ What do parents (who know all the details) think of this idea?

---

1.   Adapted from *Church Administration Handbook* by Bruce P. Powers (Broadman & Holman), page 209.

▶ Would parents let their kids do this if they were here?

▶ Does this activity need the permission of our pastor or board of directors?

▶ Are the people we're hiring to take or lead our group really qualified to do this? What about their safety record? Who regulates them?

Don't forget parents in the risk management plan. Parents will be your best supporters—until you put their children at risk through unwise choices. You will create and keep the trust and respect of parents by carefully thinking through the risks you face with students. Use the following safety check to evaluate activities:

▶ Do your staff members understand their overall roles and responsibilities?

▶ Do you have enough adult leaders for this activity?

▶ Do they understand their roles for this event? Have you given them clear assignments? Rule of thumb: the younger the kids, the more adults you'll need.

▶ For junior highers or middle schoolers, you'll want one sponsor for every eight students; senior highers require a one-to-10 ratio. The type of activity also influences the number of needed sponsors.

▶ Have you clearly spelled out to both adult leaders and students the guidelines for student behavior for each event?

Forms

When you do any event, either on-site or off-site, where a student could potentially be harmed, you should have two essential forms:

1. Permission slip or consent form

This is a document that outlines the nature of the event, including the types of activities (e.g., sleeping over, basketball tournament, scavenger hunt in cars) and requests that the parent or guardian consents to the student's participation. This form also includes basic contact information and a waiver of liability. For ongoing weekly activities—e.g., Bible study, tutoring, and small groups—there can be a consent form that's good up to one year. Any student who participates in a ministry's activities should have a completed consent form. If the student is a regular participant, some ministries have parents or guardians fill out an annual consent or permission form. These are sometimes notarized. For occasional students, there is the single-event permission slip. The annual permission slip includes such information as:

▶ A description of the type of events students will participate in. For an event outside of this parameter, have a single-use permission slip.

▶ Emergency contact information

- ▸ Health insurance carrier and policy number
- ▸ Permission for low-risk trips (e.g., less than one hour away, not more than six hours, don't engage in high-risk activities, etc.)
- ▸ Permission for emergency medical treatment
- ▸ Special medical instructions
- ▸ Permission to use photographic image for the ministry's use (e.g., publicity materials, retreat recaps, etc.)
- ▸ Custodial permission if there's more than one custodial parent

Single-use event medical-release forms contain similar information but are for one-time events such as retreats, camps, mission trips, one-day excursions as well as higher-risk activities, and/or students who don't come on a regular basis.

2. Medical release forms

This accompanies the permission slip and includes instructions about a student's special medical or physical needs, such as:

- ▸ Health history
- ▸ Allergies and treatment
- ▸ Special medical needs
- ▸ Current medications and dosages
- ▸ Cognitive or behavioral concerns
- ▸ Last tetanus shot
- ▸ Swimming or activity restrictions

Include statements that let medical personnel start helping the student right away.

Both forms should be signed and dated. A parent or *legal* guardian must sign permission and medical forms. Babysitters, sisters, and grandparents don't count. Some churches combine both medical and permission slips into one form. All forms should be reviewed before an event and if there is anything listed on the medical form, you or a trusted leader should follow up with the parent to clarify the concern and treatment.

Ask a legal professional to check out any legal document—including the ones offered in this book. Some ministries request every student to submit a signed medical release at the start of every year. Staff members bring copies of those forms to all ministry events throughout the year. Yes, it's a lot of work, but we can tell you from experience that it's worth it when you face the inevitable emergencies.

Make at least two copies of every form you collect. One stays at the church in the ministry file and the other goes with the leader on the event. You may need more copies so that each vehicle has forms for each of its passengers. These forms should be saved anywhere from one to five years after the event, depending on your state's laws. Talk to your insurance agent to find out specific requirements for your organization and state.

Remember:

▸ If you are transporting students off-site for anything, you need permission slips.

▸ If you conduct an overnight at your church building, you need permission slips.

▸ If a small group of students goes with a youth group leader *anywhere*, you need permission slips. (Gone are the days that the youth worker can pick up a group of students at school and go out for soda without getting permission from parents. Plan ahead and make sure you have, at the very least, verbal permission from a parent directly to you—not through the student. *Never assume.*)

Leaders

Rare is the lone youth worker. These days churches realize that it takes a team to run a ministry, especially when it comes to events. Not only does it lighten the load, but also it creates a safety net for students and for other leaders. There are some risk-management policies you need to put in place with your leaders. (This is also repeated in the team section.)

▸ *Screen all staff members* who are interested in working with students. This screening process involves a written application that grants permission for a background check, references, and a face-to-face interview. References must be checked. Save the applications, references, and interview notes, even of those you turn down. That way you have a record if they apply for another ministry. If you have minors volunteering with younger students or any other vulnerable population, they need to be screened as well.

▸ *Conduct background checks* on all applicants. It's an expense and investment that your ministry MUST make. Talk to your insurance agent about what level of background check your church needs. They should have several companies they can recommend. A free background check is not complete enough for someone who will work with a vulnerable population.

▸ *Lead child abuse training.* Clearly communicate your policies and expectations in this area. Take leaders through this training annually.

▸ *Have proper supervision.* Clear guidelines that prevent an adult from being alone with a student must be in place. That means sleepovers are done only in approved settings with two or more ministry-approved adults present. They are not to be done in homes where there may be other adults who have not been screened and medications and other chemicals easily accessible or weapons that are unsecured. This also means that one adult cannot drive one student home, no matter if they're the same gender or not. Pastoral counseling of students must be done where they are visible at all times, not in a room with a closed, solid door.

The following are samples of risk management checklists for various events. As with any risky endeavor, do due diligence and consult with your insurance agent and church lawyer.

Sample Checklist for a Camping Event

- Bring staff experienced in outdoor camping.
- Require a member of your camp staff to be trained in advanced first aid and CPR.
- Find out how to get help when you're at your destination campsite.
- Obtain current road and trail maps.
- Bring supplies necessary for the kind of camping—tent, cabin, wilderness.
- Try to find out in advance if you will have cell service where you are headed.
- File a plan with two or more people who are not going on the trip that spells out where you are headed, who is going, and when you will return. Also clarify at what point they should contact emergency personnel if they don't hear from you after your anticipated return time.
- On any **Medical Release** form, specifically ask about special medical needs and/or limitations of students relevant to camping: allergies (including food allergies), hay fever, bee stings, seizures, etc. Think about what needs they have that might affect their level of participation in selected activities. Be especially aware of students with asthma and diabetes. Always ask for at least two contact numbers for a parent or guardian, in case of an emergency.

Tips and Reminders:
- Ask a professional outfitter to review your route, supplies, and meal plans.
- Bring a weather radio to warn you of significant weather threats, such as flash floods, thunderstorms, and tornadoes. Do not rely on a smart phone.
- Well ahead of the event, provide a training program for adult leaders for maintaining healthy boundaries and preventing sexual abuse.
- May seem obvious—but no use of the ropes course without trained staff supervising.

- No mixed-gender sharing of sleeping facilities.
- Youth will not share tents with an adult other than their own parent.
- Coed overnight activities require both male and female leadership from qualified members of your staff over 21 years of age.
- Be clear about your expectations related to substances permitted or not permitted.
- Set a curfew—all campers in their sleeping quarters by what time.
- Preview the camping facility to be sure you planned for adequate supervision. Note places and situations where supervision is difficult, and prep your staff.
- Provide the camp director with a list of students participating in an event, accompanied by copies of their **Medical Release** forms. Be certain that the form tells you whom to contact in case of an emergency. It must contain all important medical information about the student.
- Only those adult leaders who have completed the driver screening process may provide transportation to the event.

Sample Checklist for Water Events
Swimming

- Is there at least one certified lifeguard watching your group? What is your plan to give him or her adequate rest breaks?
- Is the diving area deep enough?
- How will you alert the swimmers to get out of the water?
- How do you plan to keep track of all swimmers?
- Are there strong currents present?
- What are the safety procedures for things such as rope swings, diving rafts, and large inflatable water toys like a Waterblob™?

Boating
For a more detailed list, check out the U.S. Coast Guard's Boating Safety Resource Center: http://www.uscgboating.org/regulations/federal_requirements_brochure.aspx.

- Are there enough Coast Guard-approved life preservers?
- Is the boat driver qualified to drive the boat? To haul skiers?
- Have you limited the number of boat riders to what the boat safely holds?
- Have you confirmed that the weather is safe for boating?
- Have you informed your contact person onshore where you're going and when you'll return?

- ▸ Have you confirmed that the boat is equipped with other safety measures?
  - • Whistle or other sound-producing device
  - • Visual distress signals
  - • Drinking water
  - • Paddles
  - • Fire extinguisher
  - • Two-way radio (there may not be cell coverage)
  - • First-Aid kit

Sample Checklist for Retreat Sites

When using a retreat facility or hotel, do you know:

- ▸ Where everyone is staying (room or cabin assignments)?
- ▸ How to evacuate everyone safely in the event of a fire?
- ▸ How to make sure everyone is accounted for in the event of an emergency?
- ▸ How to summon medical or police help, how long it will take for them to arrive, and where the retreat facility is located?
- ▸ The name of the facility's contact person in case of a late-night emergency?
- ▸ How the beachfront or pool is secured after-hours?
- ▸ What First-Aid or medical equipment they have on-site?

SMART TIP

If kids have access to your ministry computers, install a firewall or whatever controls, filters, or safeguards your Internet browser offers. Be sure students can't access inappropriate sites such as those involving gambling, violence, and pornography. Make a policy about computer usage and post it where it can easily be seen.

TRAVEL SAFETY

According to the National Highway Traffic Safety Administration, every 13 minutes someone dies in a traffic accident. Until we experience an accident firsthand, we often don't take precautions to protect our group and ourselves.

Select your drivers carefully. Screen them with the *Driver Application*. Make sure they have received the necessary training and have experience with the type of vehicle you're asking them to drive.

Use a maintenance routine before heading out on any trip. If you're driving a church-owned vehicle, make sure a professional mechanic is maintaining it regularly. It should have thorough, semiannual inspections. Check the file yourself.

Always inspect the vehicle(s) your group uses prior to leaving. Walk around the vehicle to check tires (pressure and tread wear), all lights, and any sign of leakage under the vehicle. Check fluid levels, brakes, wiper operation, and fuel level.

Providing Safe Transportation

- Don't assume your insurance coverage is adequate or in effect. Check with your church business administrator and your insurance agent.
- Check out the driving records of your staff. Don't skip this step. Use the *Driver Application* form to screen potential drivers.
- Don't let students drive. Period. Adult leaders should be at least 21 years old to drive.
- Tell your staff drivers that you expect them to obey all traffic laws. (Seriously!)
- Don't put more people in the car or van than it is designed to handle. Counting seatbelts generally lets you know how many you can legally transport. Don't exceed that number—ever. Then require the use of those seatbelts.
- Check with your insurance agent regarding insurance coverage. Your church can be held liable for the damage and injuries caused by its employees or volunteers using their own vehicles or vehicles that the church rents or borrows for its operations. If your church uses vehicles owned by staff or volunteers, you should consider purchasing non-owned or hired auto liability coverage.
- When you leave for an event, make sure someone knows who went, where you are going, how you're getting there, and when to expect your return. Leave trip details and a list of participants and staff at the church office.
- It's generally safer to rent or lease a vehicle than to borrow. Any problems with the vehicle are the responsibility of the rental company. Plus, insurance coverage is more clearly defined.
- Don't allow the driver to deal with discipline. Appoint a staff member to handle discipline.
- Keep doors closed when moving.
- Never lock the emergency door when passengers are onboard a bus.
- Never transport more than the posted number of passengers.
- Keep students out of the back row of seats, except when the bus is filled, to protect against injury in case the bus is rear-ended.
- Make smooth starts and stops.
- Because of fire hazard, fill the fuel tank only when there are no passengers on the bus. *Never* travel with a gas can or other flammables. Never.
- Keep packages, coats, and other objects out of the aisle.
- Watch for clearances (bridges, overpasses, etc.).
- Pick up and drop off students in such a manner that they are not required to cross streets.

Sample Checklist for Safe Group Travel

- ▶ Do you know how to provide safe food and water for your group?
- ▶ What is the location, phone number, and directions to the closest emergency medical facility?
- ▶ What dangers may you face in a given location (e.g., flash flooding, animals, insects)?
- ▶ How do you contact family members in case of emergency or delay?
- ▶ Can you facilitate an emergency medical evacuation?
- ▶ Do you have an accurate bus or van list for which vehicles students and staff are in and where their medical and permission forms are located? (The forms should be in the vehicle with them.)
- ▶ Are the vehicles you're driving really safe? Who says? Before any road trip, have a mechanic run a safety check on the vehicle for such things as tire pressure, worn tread, various fluids, etc.
- ▶ Do you have a back-up plan for dealing with worst-case scenarios?
- ▶ Have you enlisted a staff person to handle issues such as kids who come late, get sick, or have discipline issues?
- ▶ Do you have a vehicle to transport your group in case of a sudden need? Who has the keys? If you only have the church bus or van, your options are limited.
- ▶ Do you have access to a cell phone or radio for communication?
- ▶ Does the area you're in have a 911 system? If not, what's the emergency number?
- ▶ Have you trained your staff how to respond in the event of an emergency? What if you are injured?

Sample Passenger Rules
(Check out the National Highway Traffic Safety Administration's Web site for detailed and up-to-date guidelines: http://www.safercar.gov)

- ▶ No standing while the vehicle is in motion.
- ▶ Keep arms, feet, and hands inside the vehicle.
- ▶ No throwing things while in the vehicle.
- ▶ Seatbelts are required. One person per seatbelt.

REAL LIFE

One youth pastor's story: We stopped for lunch on our way to a week of ministry in Mexico. For some reason, I walked around inspecting the van and trailer while everyone was eating. I noticed that the back bumper was precariously hanging off. "Hmm, this doesn't look right," I thought. (I have a keen grasp of the obvious.) Taking a closer look, I noticed that the trailer hitch had been welded to the bumper. We were only one weld away from losing our supplies and clothes for the entire trip and from setting a vehicle loose to potentially strike and kill someone else.

Other Safety Rules

Along with regularly inspecting and maintaining vehicles, write up your own travel emergency procedure and distribute it at the organizational meetings for all church activities. Place a copy of the procedure in the first-aid kit that travels with you. That way everyone knows what to do in case of an accident or injury, and the victim will receive help as quickly as possible. In case of serious accidents, even a few minutes can be critical.

Practice Defensive Driving

- Keep your eyes moving.
- Be rested.
- Keep your focus on the road.
- Be courteous to other drivers.
- Use caution.
- Plan ahead.
- Maintain proper following distances.
- Be prepared for the unexpected.
- DON'T text and drive. You've heard about the risks.

Think through carefully the wisdom of driving your group all night:

- Illness or fatigue, highway hypnosis, anger or preoccupied thoughts, effects of alcohol or other drugs affect reaction time.
- Set a maximum time for driving—no more than eight hours per 24-hour day.
- Have a number of qualified drivers for longer trips.
- Respect visibility issues.
- Acknowledge wet pavement.
- Be extra careful in ice and snow.

SOCIAL MEDIA POLICIES

As youth workers, we're acutely aware this area changes monthly. The reality is that students will figure out a way to connect with each other via technology no matter what

REAL LIFE

One youth pastor's story: A person volunteered to drive her van with a load of people for a leadership retreat.

"We better drive carefully," she said offhandedly, "because I don't have any vehicle insurance."

I chuckled. Nice joke, I thought. Later I found out she really didn't have coverage. It could have been disastrous if we'd experienced an accident. Next time, here's what I'll do differently:

Check the driver's insurance coverage before counting on her to drive. No coverage, no driving.

Check the driver's previous accidents or violations. More than two accidents or moving violations within the last two years disqualifies a person.

Check the driver's health for obvious problems. The same driver who had no vehicle insurance is diabetic and had fallen into diabetic convulsions recently, so she shouldn't have been driving anyway. Because of my neglect, I put everyone at risk. Fortunately, there will be a next time—but not for this driver.

IT'S TIME TO SELL THE CHURCH BUS WHEN . . .

Another youth pastor's story: Fifty junior highers packed into our church's 20-year-old bus and headed to the fall retreat. Just over halfway to the camp, the steering mechanism dropped out of the bottom of the bus. Literally. Our driver somehow safely pulled over to the side of the road. Thankfully, no one was injured.

"I don't care how much we save in the future," the shaken driver muttered as he stepped off the bus. "Risking injuries or killing kids is never worth it."

latest app we acquire. Youth ministries need to realize that—and have nimble policies in place that protect both students and leaders.

In developing your social media policies here are some areas to consider addressing:

- ▸ Online communication:
  - What are the guidelines for communicating with students? Other leaders? Encourage leaders to keep copies of all email and texts with students.
  - How should leaders conduct themselves when interacting with other people in the church? For example, if a conflict arises, always seek to resolve it via a face-to-face or voice-to-voice conversation.
  - Do not use ministry email lists for outside endeavors.
  - Do not give the ministry email list to anyone, or any other group or organization, even another ministry.
  - Point out the importance of confidentiality and protecting sensitive information. Do not pass on confidential communications beyond the intended recipients.

- ▸ Leadership disclosure policy:
  - Discuss what leaders can and can't talk about on their blogs, Facebook, Twitter, etc., when it comes to the ministry.
  - Off-limits: any student conversations or quotations without their and their parents' written permission.

- ▸ Facebook usage policy:
  - Discuss with leaders their responsibilities when it comes to Facebook. In other words, they're no longer free to post anything that violates ministry standards. Even if they aren't friends with students, they still may be able to access leaders' timelines.
  - Talk about what constitutes appropriate comments.
  - Discuss power differences between leaders and adolescents. Leaders are not to request that students be friends.

- ▸ Photography & video: with every phone having a camera and every student having a phone, it's difficult to monitor this. Brotherhood Mutual has developed a set of communication conditions as part of their "youth ministry participants' consent form," found at brotherhoodmutual.com:

"You aren't to make comments or share images that are sexually suggestive, disrespectful, or insensitive. Harassment and bullying are strictly forbidden. You must obtain permission from an authorized youth ministry leader before posting photos or personal information about others involved in ministry activities on any Web site or social media site the ministry controls. All information, images, or videos shared electronically through public ministry communication channels aren't considered confidential. Those who violate this policy may lose electronic communication privileges within the ministry or be removed from the youth ministry program. Parents will be notified immediately of any violation."

INSURANCE

FasTrack

Know what your insurance covers—and what it doesn't cover. Ignorance is not bliss—it's stupidity. And then know how to report an incident.

One of your priorities when starting at a new church is to meet with the church's insurance agent as soon as possible. It can be costly to assume you or the ministry has adequate coverage. Don't assume your church administrator completely understands all the issues. Go to the insurance source. Ask questions. Protect yourself, your staff, your students, and your church.

- ▸ Whom do I ask when I have questions about our church's insurance coverage?
- ▸ Who is the insurer?
- ▸ Who is covered by our insurance?
- ▸ What crisis procedures does our insurance company use?
- ▸ What insurance coverage do we need for events?
- ▸ What insurance coverage do we need when we rent a facility?
- ▸ What should our policy(s) be in regard to students and medications?
- ▸ What should our policy(s) be in regard to having medically trained staff on-site for an event?
- ▸ What kind of background checks should we conduct on all leaders? Your insurance agent should know the different levels and price points as well as several reputable services. Running background checks on all people who work with a vulnerable population should be a standard practice for the church.

FasTrack

Ask yourself what would be considered "reasonable" planning and protection in a court of law. Picture yourself standing before the jury and saying, "Yes, I was the only leader on the bus with the 25 kids, and it was my decision to let 17-year-old Eric drive."

Also ask: *How much insurance is enough?* This is something only your insurance agent knows for sure. Check with your church or ministry business administrator to see what kind of insurance you have and what it covers. Then after talking to a good insurance agent (and an attorney), you can determine if your ministry needs any additional coverage.

Remember that insurance is only a safety net. It doesn't remove your responsibility to do what is "reasonable" under the law. If you ever have a situation in which the law could cast doubt on the reasonable safety you provided, you're already in trouble. If you err on the side of doing more to promote safety than what is considered "reasonable," you don't have to worry.

Don't forget to ask about insurance and your volunteer team. What coverage does your ministry provide to those who volunteer? Before you skip over this, realize that volunteers are increasingly being named in lawsuits. Make a note to talk to your church's insurance agent to see what insurance you need to provide for volunteer protection and ask the agent these questions:

▶ What insurance coverage does our organization offer to volunteers?
▶ Does our policy include medical reimbursement, personal liability insurance, or excess automobile insurance?
▶ Do we have a commercial general liability (CGL) policy? If so, can we add volunteers as additional insureds?
▶ Does the CGL include or exclude travel between their home and the church or event?
▶ Do we have accident insurance, and what does it cover? (In case a volunteer is injured during the course of a ministry event.)
▶ Do we have volunteer liability? (If volunteers cause damage or are negligent, they may be sued. This protection helps if financial judgments are rendered.)
▶ Do we have excess auto liability? (This is coverage over and above the volunteers' own coverage as required by state law. See page 177 or 336 for more on vehicle safety and insurance.)
▶ Do we have coverage for volunteer/employee dishonesty? (To protect the ministry in case a volunteer steals money or destroys property.)

HIGH-RISK EVENTS

Does your church allow—and your insurance company cover—the activities listed below? (Your insurance policy generally spells out exclusions. Read the policy carefully.) If you're free to choose the following types of activities, carefully evaluate the fun in context with the accompanying risks. Also provide qualified adults to supervise your group's event. Consult with your supervisor and insurance agent first. Safety is the #1 priority.

Bungee jumping
Skateboarding
Trampolines
Spelunking
Scuba diving
Boating events
Rock climbing
Parasailing
Skiing and snowboarding
Hayrides
Snowmobiling
ATVing or dirt biking
Whitewater rafting
Drag racing in the church parking lot

This isn't a complete list, so you need to meet with your church's insurance agent—and your senior pastor or church administrator, and church lawyer—to discuss this further. Do not assume that it's being taken care of by another staff person at the church. Don't stop asking until you have an answer.

When Accidents Happen

Be prepared to deal with accidents and injuries at your event—and hope they're not headline disasters. They'll change your life forever—and no amount of preparation helps that.

Write up your own travel emergency procedure and distribute it at the organizational meetings for all church activities. Place a copy of the procedure in the first-aid kit that travels with you. That way everyone knows what to do in case of an accident or injury, and the victim will receive help as quickly as possible. In case of serious accidents, even a few minutes can be critical.

Here's a sample of an emergency procedure:

▸ Make the injured person as comfortable as possible. *Do not attempt to move him or her.* Keep him or her warm. Administer first aid *only* if you are certified to do so.
▸ Without leaving the injured person unattended, send someone to call for help.
▸ Call 911 or ask a bystander to call. Give your location clearly and distinctly.
▸ Move uninjured passengers to a safe area away from danger. Get them away from the highway.
▸ Get the names and telephone numbers of any witnesses.
▸ The driver involved in the accident may be, understandably, upset. Don't ask the driver to call the families of the injured. To avoid undue panic, call the pastor (or another designated person) and allow him or her to explain the status of the situation to the injured person's family. Do this as soon as appropriate. With cell phones, it's possible that they can find out from another, less informed, less pastoral party.

> ► Cooperate with police and fire department investigators. If you are a witness, you can answer questions about the accident. Provide investigators with your list of witnesses.

> ► As soon as possible after the injured person has been helped and a preliminary investigation has been made, inform your insurance agent of the accident. Tell what happened, simply and factually. Provide the names of any witnesses. This will facilitate fast, equitable settlement of claims for those injured.

Establish Emergency Procedures

Every youth leader should have a *written* emergency procedure policy for all general ministry activities.

> ► Provide each staff member a written manual, including emergency procedures.

> ► Verbally explain procedures at new-leader orientation.

> ► At each event, assign an emergency or crisis manager (you or another staff person) who knows procedures. Talk to your insurance agent about the pros and cons of having a designated nurse or EMT serve at an event. Sometimes it's better to have them serving in another, non-medical position.

> ► Staff and leadership need to specifically know who is the crisis manager on duty (sometimes called the Event Safety Coordinator, In Case of Emergency (ICE) or point person). In an emergency, speed is important, clarity is critical, and teamwork is essential.

> ► Make sure that several members of your staff have taken basic CPR and first-aid training courses. Clear thinking in a medical crisis comes with proper medical training.

> ► Keep a well-stocked medical kit easily accessible.

> ► Have some staff get advanced first-aid training, if possible.

> ► Get to know doctors, nurses, certified first responders, and EMTs in your ministry. In case you have an emergency, however, do not rely on them as a substitute for calling 911. Instead, rely on them to provide assistance until help arrives. Make yourself aware of liability related to using off-duty medical personnel.

> ► Your church leadership must establish a comprehensive crisis plan to deal with a number of emergency situations your church could face. Resist the temptation to come up with this plan alone. Ask for help. Some experts in this area may already attend your church.

▶ First, good communication can defuse a crisis—cell phones and radios are an asset (especially in the case of large events where your staff are spread out). Before the event starts, decide on a central meeting place in case of a crisis where staff can learn pertinent information. Assign a point person. Store emergency supplies in an accessible but secure place. Keep a procedure notebook with the supplies that spells out what to do in case of an emergency. Create an e-version of this doc and store it on your smartphone.

Depending on your geographic location, you'll need to prepare for specific emergencies:

▶ *Fires.* How quickly can you evacuate your building? Do you have a way to account for everyone? Identify a meeting place if ever you're forced to evacuate.
▶ *Earthquakes.* Where is the safest place to go?
▶ *Tornadoes.* When a warning siren goes off, where is the safe room?
▶ *Missing students.* If you discover a student missing from an event, what steps should you follow?
▶ *Acts of violence.* If one of your students were assaulted at a ministry event, what would you do?
▶ *Suicide.* If you learned of a suicide in your community or group, what should you do?

THE WELL-SUPPLIED MEDICAL KIT

Assuming you call an EMT immediately when you have a serious injury—and a hospital is readily accessible—your medical kit should be filled with these medical supplies:

- bandages
- instant ice packs
- hydrogen peroxide
- rubbing alcohol
- tweezers
- aspirin or non-aspirin medication such as Tylenol (for you and other adults—don't give to students).
- surgical non-latex gloves
- thermometer (the small, plastic disposable ones are handy)
- antibiotic ointment or cream (e.g., Neosporin)
- antibacterial or antiseptic spray (e.g., Bactine)
- bug-bite cream or lotion (e.g., Cortaid or Cortizone 10)
- gauze
- medical tape

Some insurance agencies are suggesting that you don't give out anything to students, including bandages. Please check with your agent to see what the guidelines are for your organization. In any emergency, you should call 911.

You should also keep a biohazard kit on hand in case of bleeding (available in janitorial supply catalogs or visit safetyonline.com for links to suppliers). In addition to surgical gloves and medical supplies, you'll need a chemical that absorbs blood spills and sanitizes the area. If you need a more extensive medical kit (e.g., remote location, international travel, special-needs kids), consult with trained medical personnel.

REAL LIFE

Mike: In the middle of the service on a normal Sunday morning at church, the fire alarm went off. One usher ran to the back of the building and said to me, "How do we shut this thing off? It's disturbing the service!" Another staff member countered, "We've got to get everyone out of the building. I think something is wrong."

The person in the pulpit said, "Let's pray."

For a moment, no one took charge.

Several of us knew the alarm system well. We instructed the ushers that the alarm must be treated as signaling a real emergency until we could determine otherwise. The children's ministry had rehearsed this scene many times and was already evacuating kids. All totaled, 1,600 people lined up outside the building. Was there a fire? Was the evacuation really necessary?

We checked out the alarm system and learned that a sensor had malfunctioned; there was no fire. We gave the all-clear, and everyone came back into the building. We learned several things that day:

In an emergency, people need direction from leaders.

Plans developed in advance remove pressure.

When in doubt, respond to the alarm as if a real emergency is occurring. In a real fire, seconds matter.

- *Bomb threats.* If a caller threatened to bomb your church, how would you handle it?
- *Active shooters.* If there is an immediate threat, should students stay where they are? How will you notify emergency personnel? How will you notify the rest of the group, if they are spread out over an area?
- *Floods.* Is your church, camp, or event location in a flood zone? If so, what are the evacuation routes?

Designate a Crisis Manager: The Event Safety Coordinator

In the event of a crisis, every ministry leader needs to know his or her role—as well as others' roles. We recommend having one crisis manager—one event safety coordinator (or ICE—"In Case of Emergency" person, chief, captain, head honcho, director, bigwig, protector, "the person in charge in case of emergencies").

Realistically you'll need to equip several people to act as event safety coordinators, as well as to handle other more specific tasks. The main caveat regarding the ESCs' "other tasks"—it's best if they're the kind that can be dropped and picked up later if the ESCs are called to manage a crisis (e.g., the ESC shouldn't be the only judge at a sporting event; if the ESC is needed for an emergency, the whole event will come to a halt). Parents are often qualified to play ESC roles and are happy to help.

Qualities of an Event Safety Coordinator
- *Experience in successful crisis managing.* The event safety coordinator needs to be a trained and accomplished leader who's shown the ability to act when a crisis arises. Use a trainee ESC in an apprentice role with a current ESC. Only after proving themselves should trainees be appointed sole event safety coordinator.

Although the job is a "hurry up and wait" type position, when they are needed, event safety coordinators must always be at their best. It's a bummer to find out in the middle of a problem that the adult in charge doesn't handle crisis well.

▸ *Equipped with basic medical training.* ESCs need at least a certification in first aid and CPR—not that the job of the ESC is to diagnose or treat the injured, but rather to assess what the next course of action should be and to lead the team in that direction.

▸ *Calm and cool-headed.* Even though most injuries are minor and only minimal treatment is necessary, the ESC needs to be able to remain calm under pressure.

▸ *Available.* The ESC must be accessible and available. On a retreat or extended event, several people may act as the ESC at different times. That way your crisis manager is always ready and refreshed. You may equip the ESC with a communication tool to make the ESC more accessible. At a retreat use a walkie-talkie, a pager, or an air horn. Try different things to see what works.

▸ *Supported by the rest of the leadership team.* Once the ESC determines the course of action, the staff needs to support the decision. A crisis is not the time to debate issues; it's the time for the leader to lead and the followers to follow. If the stakes are high, the lines of authority must be clear, and everyone has to do his or her job.

▸ The ESC shouldn't accompany the injured to the hospital, if hospitalization is required. The ESC needs to stay with the group in case there are other incidents. The ESC should pick a staff person or two to accompany the injured to the hospital until parents arrive. The accompanying staffers should be responsible people, preferably of the same gender, and with whom the student feels comfortable.

FASTRACK

Prepare for emergencies by writing out procedures—for general as well as specific emergency situations.

EMERGENCY TOOLS

The most valuable emergency tools today are:

- a cell phone (with a charged battery)
- an emergency plan and training
- a first-aid kit.

KIDS ARE KIDS

Teenagers tend to play down their physical ailments in front of their peers. "I'm okay—really! I was only out for a few seconds. I feel fine." Don't be fooled. Do you really want to take responsibility for that student when she collapses 20 minutes later because her brain is bleeding? Leave accident assessment to medical professionals. For clearly minor injuries—or injuries that could escalate to serious—contact the parents and transfer the care responsibility to them. If parents leave it up to you, seek medical attention.

FasTrack

The Event Safety Coordinator manages crises by providing leadership for other staff, being trained in basic medical emergency response, and following your written emergency procedures.

Accompanying a Student to Medical Facilities

The staff person assigned to the student by the ESC should have the Medical Release form, which contains emergency contact numbers, all medical conditions, allergies, and medications. The staff person assigned is the parent's representative and should remain with the student at all times, if possible. Without being in the way, this staffer should persistently request to be included in the decision-making process for treatment.

Once the parents arrive, the staff member brings them up to speed on what has occurred so far, and then slides into a support role for the parents. Once the crisis is over, or when the parents no longer require assistance, the staff person reports to the ESC about events at the medical facility and fills out an Incident Report.

▶ *Good adult communicator.* The ESC discusses the incident with the staff member who accompanied the injured person and reviews the person's written incident report.

Emergency procedures for the ESC

1. One staff person attends to the injured party's needs.
2. Another staff person immediately contacts the ESC. (In a dire emergency, if the ESC can't be located expediently, the staff in charge proceeds with the next steps while sending someone to find the ESC.)
3. ESC assesses the situation.
4. ESC determines if the individual can be assisted locally. If so, the ESC assigns an appropriate adult to assist the injured. The ESC also determines at this point whether to notify the parents or apply a Band-Aid and call it good.
5. If the situation requires trained medical assistance or transportation to the hospital, ESC asks a leader to call 911 to request paramedics and an ambulance. The caller needs to know the status of the injured person and the specific street address or location of the injured. The caller needs to remain on the phone to assist the dispatcher as long as necessary.
6. ESC sends a staff member to the entrance to guide the paramedics.
7. ESC assigns another *calm* staff person to contact the individual's parents and advise them of the situation. If the person is being transported to the hospital, the parents should meet them at the hospital.
8. The ESC and any other needed staff members stay with the injured individual. All other staff members assist the ESC by keeping students and other onlookers away from the victim and out of the emergency team's way.
9. A staff member brings the student's *Medical Release* form to the ESC.
10. The ESC appoints a staff member to accompany the student to the hospital and gives her the form.

11. After the student is transported, the ESC assigns someone to clean up the accident site. If there is blood involved, use a biohazard kit for cleanup.

12. The ESC determines what, if any, explanation needs to be given to the remaining students or if the scheduled activities need to be adjusted or canceled.

13. The staff person who accompanies the student to the hospital checks in with the ESC once they arrive at the medical facilities, and again when there is any news.

14. The ESC and the leaders involved fill out an *Incident Report* and, if necessary, a *Damage Report*.

15. The following day, or as soon as possible, the ESC distributes copies of the reports to the appropriate recipients.

Follow Up Accidents and Injuries

An incident report is written documentation of incidents, accidents, or mishaps involving people in your ministry. Injuries *will* happen. Giving careful thought to the process of crisis managing before it happens protects staff and students, saves precious time in a crisis, and avoids confusion.

Submit copies of the *Incident Report* to the various individuals who need to know what happened. Record in your emergency procedure manual the pastors or ministry supervisors who should receive an incident report. Contact your insurance company. Deal with the incident report in an objective manner. State the facts as completely as possible. It's not your responsibility to assess blame but to collect and record the facts as accurately as possible. Your report should include what you and other witnesses heard and observed. Given today's legal environment, if a student is injured, assume you will be sued. Document everything. Be proactive in following up with the parents.

WHAT AN EVENT SAFETY COORDINATOR MUST KNOW

Location of phone(s) and how to dial out.

How and where to find trained medical help (especially if the group is in a remote location).

Address, directions, and phone number of the nearest medical center.

Location of the first-aid kit.

Where staff and students are rooming (not generally, but specifically where each person is staying).

How to reach the facility director (camp, hotel, retreat center).

Location of medical release forms.

Where a designated emergency vehicle is parked and who has the keys.

Special medical or physical conditions of the participants as recorded on the medical release forms. ESC must communicate these special needs to the rest of the staff.

How to speak calmly with parents.

FASTRACK

For liability purposes, if at all possible send an injured student to the hospital by ambulance. Call 911 first.

TRANSPORTING THE INJURED

If students need transportation to a hospital, rather than take them by car, call an ambulance.

Transportation by ambulance offers consistent, quality care for the injured person and more protection for you from lawsuits. It's cheaper to take responsibility for the cost of the ambulance trip than to assume liability in the event something goes terribly wrong. You also may be unaware of additional, unseen injuries that may cause greater damage if you try to transport the person yourself. Let trained medical professionals take the responsibility.

Claim Management

Once an injury has occurred, someone must follow through with the management of the case. Check with your pastor or ministry supervisor to learn who manages the paperwork and claims. A file should be started. It is impossible to overemphasize how important accurate and detailed records of incidents and damages are. Accurate documentation by numerous parties is critical to legal treatment of a case. You can jeopardize yourself and your ministry with sloppy documentation.

If a student is filing a claim through her own insurance company (sometimes damage to property is covered on personal homeowner's policies—again, check with your agent), all she might need is a copy of your incident report. If there is an investigation on behalf of the insurance company, you or your staff may be interviewed. Attend the interview knowing that it is not the job of you or your staff to analyze the situation; you must objectively state what happened. Offering your opinions or conclusions about the diagnosis or case is inappropriate at this time. The insurance investigator will check with the medical records for the diagnosis.

When the Worst Happens

It's wise to be prepared for the worst. No one knows when a tragedy will strike. The responsible leader prepares the youth ministry staff and the youth of the church for fatalities—not only accidental deaths, but also suicides and disabling injuries.

REAL LIFE

One youth pastor's story: My friend and I were galloping on horseback when I was awkwardly thrown. I was badly injured and in severe pain. Although I've known my friend my whole life, this was the first time we had to endure a physical crisis together. She is good at many things; I learned that day that she is not good in a crisis. There I was, rolling around on the ground in pain, and all she could do was sit on her horse and laugh. "You looked so funny flying off the horse," she explained.

Next time I'm near death I'm going to call 911. Although I love my friend, I would never place her in the role of [ESC]. Some people just aren't made to be an ESC. Be sure to pick one who is.

Jack Crabtree, in *Better Safe Than Sued*, tells a chilling story of an accident on a youth group trip resulting in the death of a student. Although no preparation is honestly adequate to equip someone to deal with that magnitude of disaster, Crabtree suggests ways to recover from such a trauma.

Help the family and friends emotionally by listening, being supportive, spending time with them, being patient with them, and by asking what they need you to do for them.

Help your group process the tragedy. Take time to process the recent events. Provide counselors who will meet with those students who are deeply affected by the event. Don't expect people to recover at your speed— some require less time, some more.

Take care of yourself. You need rest, friendships, and time to deal with such a life-altering event. Cling to a trusted friend or partner. Restore your personal balance by putting yourself in a healing place: the mountains, the ocean, a garden, among friends, alone. Whatever works for you.

CASE STUDIES

Case studies aren't meant to have right or wrong answers. As you read through these, consider the pros and cons your responses might elicit. Develop potential plans of action. These hypothetical situations are good to go over with your supervisor. It will help you understand their expectations when these circumstances arise. Run them by the ministry's volunteers, some parents, your church's insurance agent, and even some students to see what they'd say.

Busted

You are returning from a great service trip week. As you get to the exit ramp for the church and line up at the traffic light, one of your vans goes speeding by when the light turns green. A second later another van passes you, then a third. Two minutes later the involved vans are pulled over by a local police officer. What do you do?

WHAT TO INCLUDE ON AN INCIDENT REPORT?

All vital information needs to be documented:

Who was hurt, who else was involved, and who was in charge at the time of the injury?

What happened to whom, what exactly was the injury (not the diagnosis but the symptoms)?

When did the incident occur? Include the date and time.

Where was the group? Where was the injured person?

How did the injury occur?

Additional comments. Also include names and contact information of eyewitnesses. Record the specific diagnosis if professional, medical personnel label the injury. Who stayed with the student? Was an ambulance called? Or was the student driven to the hospital in a private vehicle? Who drove? If property was damaged in the incident, attach a copy of the Damage Report.

SMART TIP

Seek counsel from your ministry's attorney prior to facing an accident. Do not use the information in this book as the replacement for professional legal advice. In fact, call and set up that appointment today!

LEGAL COUNSEL

Go to the senior pastor regarding legal issues.

When he or she says, "We're fine and need no help from a lawyer—God can take care of us," write back something like this:

Dear Pastor,
Thanks for speaking with me today. From our conversation I understand that you don't want me to seek legal counsel regarding our current youth ministry situation. I am concerned and disappointed. I feel that this decision is not in the best interests of our students, leaders, and church as a whole. (Name the specifics of the incident—include an incident report.) My primary concern is for the safety of our students. A copy of this letter will be in my permanent file in light of my expressed concerns.

Sincerely,
Susan
Your dedicated youth pastor

Photo Oops

You've just come off a weekend retreat, and the volunteers decide to go out for pizza to celebrate and tell stories. As they're passing around their phones with retreat photos, you notice that a couple of them contain photos of rooms containing students in the background who are in various stages of dressing. How do you handle it?

Climb, Climb Up Sunshine Mountain

Your new middle school staff person (who won't have any idea that Sunshine Mountain is a children's Sunday school chorus) wants to take a small group of students on an overnight, rock-climbing trip. Although he has climbed before, he's never taken students before. What do you do?

School Crisis

It's Thursday morning and you're in your office streaming music on your computer while you prepare your Sunday morning talk. You have a full agenda, with several meetings scheduled throughout the day. Suddenly a student texts you that a bus from her high school has been in an accident. There are serious injuries and some fatalities. Several of your students attend that school. You hope none of them were on the bus. You pray for the injured. You go to the local news Web site and it lists the hospitals to which the injured students are being taken. What do you do?

Game Dilemma

One of your staff wants to lead a game that you're not familiar with at youth group. After listening to him describe the game, you have some reservations about it. What do you do?

And Your Name Is . . . ?

A parent calls four days after your youth meeting to report that her son was injured at your church and request that the church pay his medical bills. The mother also says it's possible that her son will need ongoing treatment. You don't know the student or the parent and assume he may have been a visitor. What do you do?

No kidding—this one really happened.

A youth group was doing a scavenger hunt at a local mall. (You can already see where this is headed . . .)

Carrying a list of things and people that they had to find, the students scattered into the mall. One of their tasks was to find their disguised youth pastor. He had dressed as an old woman being pushed in a wheelchair by a staff person dressed as an older man. Trying very hard to look like an old woman and not succeeding, the youth pastor was stopped by the mall security and questioned. When he said that the group was doing a scavenger hunt, the officers told him that was illegal and they arrested him. After cuffing him, they escorted him out of the mall and drove him to the police station. Unfortunately, he had the van keys in his backpack. The stranded students began calling home for help.

We must carefully think through the activities we lead our students into. Take time to run events by trusted advisors in advance. While this mall game certainly may have sounded fun at one point, wisdom could have prevented the arrest and the obvious concern caused to many families.

Okay, we'll give you the answer to this one: Call your insurance company right away. Ask for their guidance in walking through this situation. Inform your pastor/church administrator. Don't delay—take immediate action. If there was an incident report—pull it out and review the details and submit it to your insurance company.

Document and place in the file every step that you or your staff members take during and after the crisis.

Choose Your Own Ending—Car Trouble

You are beginning a two-week summer trip and retreat that has you driving more than 1,000 miles with 27 students and five leaders. Of your three large, borrowed vans, one is eight years old. On a two-lane rural highway the older van starts to overheat. No gas stations, no McDonald's, and no convenience store for 20 miles in either direction. What do you do?

1. Leave all the students, take two leaders, and go to get help.
2. Take as many students as you can fit in the other vans, leave a few students and leaders with the old van, and go to the nearest gas station.
3. Go to the nearest farm and ask for help.
4. Use your cell phone to call for a tow truck and wait in a safe place with everyone until help comes.
5. Use your cell phone to call for a tow truck, take all the students you can fit in the vans, and go to the nearest town where there is fast food. Wait there.

RESOURCES

For more on insurance, see:

▶ The CIMA Companies www.cimaworld.com A great help putting this section together.
▶ Brotherhood Mutual www.brotherhoodmutual. com They have resources and webinars for youth pastors.
▶ Church Mutual www.churchmutual.com

Check out the Red Cross at redcross.org for resources and local training in:

▶ First aid and CPR
▶ HIV and AIDS awareness
▶ Disaster services
▶ Baby sitter training

For the larger event you might want to get some additional coverage besides the standard church coverage. Check with your church's insurance agent.

FORMS

▶ Church Incident Report
▶ Emergency Procedures
▶ Participation Survey - Adult
▶ Participation Survey - Minor
▶ Risk Event Manager Qualifications & Tasks
▶ Risk Guidelines: Safe Group Travel
▶ Incident Report
▶ Insurance Coverage Worksheet
▶ Copyright Laws for Digital Content
▶ Damage Report
▶ Medical Kit
▶ Questions to Ask Your Insurance Agent
▶ Safety Grid Questions
▶ Sexual Abuse Screening Checklist
▶ Travel Guidelines
▶ Safety & Accident Policies & Procedures
▶ Safety Guidelines for Various Activities - Sample

Tired of Waiting

Only one student remains to be picked up after an event ends. The other staff already went home. It's just you and the student at the church. What do you do?

We'll give you the answer to this one as well, since it seems every youth pastor has to face this situation: Don't get caught in this situation. Always have two staff (preferably one male and one female) stay until all students are picked up. Ask the student to call his parents—even if he's called before—and leave a message stating that he is the only student left, that the youth worker is waiting with them, and where he is to be picked up.

If possible, wait outdoors or in the entrance hall with the student until the parents come. If it's a chronic problem, be prepared to talk with the parent about their punctuality. Delegate the job of waiting on late parents to parents. Recruit a married couple with kids in your program to handle these situations.

10 EVENTS

CHAPTER OVERVIEW
- ▶ What Is an Event?
- ▶ Five Essentials for Planning a Purposeful Event
- ▶ Tools for Event Management
- ▶ Small On-Site Events
- ▶ Small Off-Site Events
- ▶ Evaluating Your Event

Youth ministry, by its nature, cycles all year through the stages of event management. You're always planning an event, in the middle of one, completing it, or evaluating it.

This chapter coaches both the detail-conscious and the organizationally challenged to:

Acquire basic skills for planning events.
- ▶ Discover five ways to build success into every event.
- ▶ Master tools that help you coordinate and manage events, retreats, camps, or mission projects.
- ▶ Get a handle on what tasks you personally need to do and be responsible for, and what tasks you can delegate.

Although event managing is hard work, it gets easier with practice. Living the event in your head several times over before you ever get in the van, for instance, prepares you to create a purposeful event that will impact students for the right reasons. (Forgetting a student at a rest stop is not a memory you want people to talk about. And running out of gas in the middle of the desert with 12 junior highers is not as cool a time as your anecdote cracks it up to be.) Your goal through the process is to repeat successes and avoid pitfalls. Putting time and effort into planning and executing a well-run event saves money and time, and produces impact.

WHAT IS AN EVENT?

For youth ministry purposes, an event is a gathering of people who have a common goal or who unite around a common theme, often with activities containing the elements of connecting, learning, engaging, serving, and fun!

EVENT LOCATIONS

Youth ministry events occur in the following event locations:

- The church building
- Homes of students/church families
- A rented meeting venue
- An activity location (bowling alley, water park, etc.)
- Camps or retreat centers
- Service/mission project locations

Each of these locations comes with a set of planning needs. And each of these locations is best suited for certain types of events and activities.

EVENT TYPES

Youth ministry events typically fall into the following categories:

- Weekly youth group gatherings/meetings
- Small group studies
- Fundraisers
- Social activities
- Outreach activities
- Service/justice projects
- Staff meetings
- Family/parents
- Volunteer development and training
- Spiritual formation activities
- Trips/retreats

FIVE ESSENTIALS FOR PLANNING

Events thrive when you apply the five essentials. The trick is to keep the big picture in mind while you focus on the details that will make your event a reality. As you prepare for an event, keep in mind the following: determining goals (purposeful planning), designing details (coordinated details), preparing purpose-driven content (focused programming), getting the word out (directed promotion), praying (trust in God.)

1. Purposeful Planning

The detail work invested in the event-planning stage sets apart the novice from the professional youth worker. As you begin to plan an event, ask yourself the following questions:

- ▶ What outcome do you want?
- ▶ Are your ministry goals in harmony with this event?
- ▶ Who will participate? How many?
- ▶ How long will it last?
- ▶ Where is the best place to meet?
- ▶ When is the best time for this event (based on above answers)?
- ▶ Do you need to receive anything from the participants (either before or during the event)?

Now is a good time to pull out our Meeting Planning Worksheet. It will help you carefully work through all the key elements in your meeting preparation. Take some time to write a brief overview of the event that paints a picture of what you hope to accomplish so your team can begin to visualize the event with you.

2. Coordinated Details

There's no shortcut through the planning of a successful event. Although many youth workers see tracking details as grueling punishment, in reality this pre-work makes your event smoother and more enjoyable for all concerned—especially you. You'll be much further ahead, if you begin by:

- ▶ Describing how your purpose is best accomplished.
- ▶ Outlining the event schedule.
- ▶ Determining the budget.
- ▶ Determining the needs regarding facility, transportation, housing, food, meeting space, contracts, and printed materials.

After sketching out your event, sit down with a yellow pad and list all the steps needed to make the event a reality. Yes, every step. Again, consider the location of your event in the planning. Ask these questions:

- ▶ Who will be responsible for this element?
- ▶ What setup will be required?
- ▶ How much time will this actually take?
- ▶ What supplies are needed?
- ▶ What advance communication is required?

If the complexity of the event takes more time and skills than you have, be sure to involve others and delegate to staff and volunteers.

IS IT WORTH IT?

Saves Money. If events are driven over budget, it's typically because of crisis management or mismanagement. Overlooking needed materials or services means you acquire them at the last minute. You can forget price checking or shopping for the best deal. Last-minute decisions can be expensive.

Saves Time. Close your eyes and roughly calculate the time you've spent scrambling to save an event that's falling apart at the last minute. Now tack about half that amount onto the beginning of the planning process, and you'll save yourself the rest of the time and all the associated stress. As they say, if it's worth doing, it's worth doing right the first time.

Gives Impact. Well-run events are more likely to equip students to grow up in their faith—or to find faith. Last-minute events generally don't motivate teens, no matter how good we are at flying by the seats of our pants. In fact, the larger and more complex the event, the more likely our short-changing the planning process will produce mistakes that negatively affect the event's overall impact and everyone's experience.

Successful delegation begins by thoughtfully matching the right staff person or volunteer with the right task:

▶ The next step is to clearly communicate instructions, expectations, and deadlines.

▶ Once they understand what has to be done, support them while they do the job. Providing support to a volunteer, or even a staff member, is essential until you know the person is able to complete the task. Following up with volunteers can be trickier than with staff since they are not on-site, and they may be scheduling your tasks around their work hours and around other projects for which they've volunteered.

▶ Finally, demonstrate to both volunteers and paid staff your appreciation for their efforts. Your support should be heavy on appreciation and making sure they know they are essential parts of the team and that you're counting on them.

Plan a Visit

If you've never been to the location of your event, plan a visit. Make sure you have the chance to see it for yourself. Be sure to take some pictures, make notes regarding special directions, review the upkeep and safety of the property/facility. How are first-aid needs handled? Are they current on special training required? Ask to see certifications and licenses as necessary. In the event planning business, these are called "site visits."

3. FOCUSED PROGRAMMING

Programming is the heart (or content) of an event. For this step you will be fashioning general sessions and small group time, coordinating meals, activities, games, work projects, and so on.

As you prepare for your event, begin to focus your programming by:

▶ focusing your vision and goals into a theme that will attract participants.

- storyboarding the event: playing out event goals through general sessions, small-group times, meals, activities, games, work projects, and so on.
- developing an event timeline.
- developing contingency plans.
- Focused programming means designing each of those components around your event goals.
- Focused programming means describing specific, desired outcomes for each component. Either by yourself or in a planning group, ask questions to help define the theme and general tone for a meeting or event.
- What is the purpose of the event?
- Who is the audience?
- What will participants walk away with after the event?
- What key principles will participants learn?
- What is the best way to communicate this information to them?
- What environment best encourages communication of and receptivity to the information?
- Who would best communicate this information?
- What activities will help accomplish meeting or event goals and objectives?

Planning Worksheet page 395

Site Inspection page 402

Develop Your Theme

After answering these questions, you're prepared to develop your theme. That means you condense your vision and goals into a contemporary theme that students can get excited about. Long before the event, with a handful of creative people, storyboard the event. The person directing the event (probably you) usually leads the meeting of staff and select volunteers who can contribute creative and wacky ideas. The overall time frame for the event is written on colored 3x5 cards pinned (or taped) to the walls or to fabric-covered foam boards. The planning team then walks through the event, coming up with ideas to make it fun and exciting for students. Each suggestion, no matter how crazy, is posted on the storyboard (usually with a point person's name on it). The general sessions are slotted, but the actual moment-by-moment cue sheets can be

FasTrack

Purposeful planning informs your event programming early enough in the process to support unique touches that make for a memorable occasion.

Smart Tip

Think about using old movies for retreat themes. For example: Mission Impossible. Create brochures, promotions, and curriculum around some of the catch phrases and video clips students may, or may not be, familiar with. Mission Impossible: God has a mission for each of us, and it's our job to discover it and take steps toward accomplishing it. Pinterest is a great way to begin to brainstorm about retreat themes. Search for "Youth retreat ideas."

completed at a second meeting dedicated just to general sessions. As the storyboard fills up, your program will start to unfold.

Be Clear on Your Purpose

Before you run over to the storyboard to start filling it up, you and your team need to make sure you're all on the same page by developing a rationale or purpose statement: the why and what for the event. Sometimes the program director comes into the meeting with the rationale. Other times it's developed at the first meeting. Whatever the case, with the rationale clear in everyone's mind, the team maps out the specifics. At this meeting, life is breathed into the theme. The event's environment is carefully constructed to creatively and effectively communicate God's truths to students. Your goal is to influence students with the life-changing message of God through creative communication. Maximize that impact in every moment of the event—in other words, create a purpose-driven event.

FasTrack

Purposeful planning gives you room in an event timeline to equip a staff and delegate tasks to them.

Developing a theme and storyboarding put the content of the event in a context, a form that is easy for students to assimilate into their lives. A memorable theme makes a retreat or event more tangible. Themes inspire sound bites that will stick with the students long after the event is over. It also gives the programming team more to work with. Even a mission trip benefits from a theme by unifying your group—base the theme on a verse or brainstorm with the students for a motto that expresses their hopes or goals for the trip.

Be Prepared

Being prepared for a medical emergency is essential. Study the medical forms of students in advance and be aware of special allergies, medical conditions (e.g., asthma and diabetes). Yes, you should take CPR and Advanced First Aid. Where is the closest medical facility?

List out the details

Following the programming meeting, use the Event Manager to work out more details and assign tasks. Beside each action point, place the name of the person responsible, the date by which the task needs to be done, and a list of all the equipment needed to accomplish the task.

Prepare for the worst

Finally, the team lays out contingency plans for potential problems. It's not a waste of time, either. More often than not, one or more contingency plans have to be implemented at the last minute. With smaller groups it's easier to be flexible and to get away with last-minute changes. The larger the group, however, the more difficult it is to flex with emergencies. Planning alternative options can be a lifesaver.

Ski resorts are screaming for business during their off-seasons (or "shoulder seasons" or "slush seasons"): between fall and winter and between ski season and late spring. If you're flexible with your time schedule and creative with your programming, you might be able to land the deal of the century.

4. DIRECTED PROMOTION

You can read more about methods of communication in the chapter on communication, but for now keep in mind that how you promote an event largely depends on who and how many are coming. The larger the scope of event, the more you and your team need to develop a workable marketing strategy. Be more efficient in your advertising by making sure you're using directed promotion techniques:

SMART TIP

Timing is everything in event planning. Did you know that you save money using a facility during its off-season? During the middle of summer, every good camp near water is packed. But come late fall or early spring, they're usually begging for business.

- ▸ Tailor promotion to group size and makeup as well as to the personality of the occasion.
- ▸ Develop a marketing strategy well in advance of the event: posters, mailings, announcements, video clips, and word-of-mouth invitation.
- ▸ Allow enough time for participants to respond to the promotion.

FASTRACK

Purposeful planning increases the chances for a well-attended event.

The power of personal invitation

Probably the most effective method of promoting an event is a personal invitation from staff and students. The media blitz sets the stage, but the personal invite is what gets students to buy in and decide to attend. The key to getting the leaders and students to buy into the event is to keep them informed and excited. Through spoken and written words we try to give as much information as kids need to catch the vision.

Get the word out early—but not too early

Another key to event promotion is giving students enough time to respond. In mass marketing, statistics show that it takes approximately seven contacts through written or spoken words for a person to take action. You want to give students as much time as possible to get used to the idea of the event and to hear about it in unique and creative ways. Event promotion should reflect the event's personality. As the first snapshot that students see of the event, it should be fun and inviting. It's that picture that creates energy and excitement about the event before it happens. See the communication chapter for more on this topic.

Marketing
Strategy
page 385

5. TRUST IN GOD

Trust in God is essential, and prayer is the power that drives any ministry—

including events. In the ever-changing student world in which we minister, we work hard at staying relevant and on top of our game. Prayer transcends cultures and connects our hearts to students. Here are just a few of the areas where we need to focus our prayers:

Wisdom

From the time that you calendar an event, invite God to be an integral part of it. You and your team need wisdom and discernment to carefully and creatively design an environment where God will be glorified and his principles taught. Pray that God's wisdom will influence your thoughts and ideas. Pray that you and your team will be open to God's leading and direction.

FasTrack

Purposeful planning, energized by prayer, assures leaders that God's presence pervades the event.

Flexibility

When the event occurs, no matter how much planning went into it, unexpected glitches require flexibility among the planners. Pray that people and programs will be able to flex if needed. When a portion of a program gets cut at the last minute, for instance, its contributors can feel frustrated and hurt and lose sight of the fact that the changing or axing of their idea is not an indicator of its quality or value. Pray that God will keep you and your team humble and flexible.

Safety

Never take this for granted. Continually do your part to keep your students safe, and leave the rest up to God. Pray that God will keep your students safe from the time they step onto your campus to the time they open their own front door. You can find excellent safety resources online at www.brotherhoodmutual.com.

Growth

You and your team plan, program, create, and labor to build an environment in which students will grow. No amount of effort on your part will touch the hearts of students, however; that job is God's alone. Pray that God will significantly affect your students' lives, as well as your own.

QUICK START: MAKING A SIMPLE EVENT TIMELINE

Starting with the actual date of the event, live the event through in reverse, making notes as you go. (Leave space between each category to add related items and potential volunteer assistants as they come to mind.) That way you'll consider those non-glamorous issues that are often forgotten until the last moment:

Event cleanup. Do you really want to do that job one more time—alone?

Staff responsibilities the day of event. Staff feel needed and part of the team when you entrust to them real jobs to do in advance, give them staff shirts or cool I.D. tags, or give them a radio.

Transportation. Knowing how you'll get there—plane, train, bus, van, or car. Know where your "there" is—accurate map and directions for all drivers. Know how long travel time will be—including different legs of the trip.

Checks needed for the event. The business office may not have signer(s) on-site to cut you an emergency check on the day (or night) you leave.

Promotion. Fliers, social media, Web site, phone calls, emails, community announcements, word of mouth—leave yourself plenty of time to populate your event with kids who would like to come . . . if only they had known about it.

Staff. It's amazing who offers to lend a hand when you contact people well in advance of the day you need the help—parents (site inspections, sign-up monitors, promotional pieces), the church's women's groups and men's groups (prop making, sewing, food preparation, setup and cleanup), community organizations (see if the Boy Scouts will cook your send-off barbecue), local retailers (sponsor ads, donate goods or services, use of parking lot or warehouse), etc.

Supplies you'll need (and who can get them). List supplies early, and someone else can shop for them.

Reservations at the room or place you're having the event—'nuff said!

For each category on the list you've created, detail the related tasks. Beside each task write two or three names of people who might help complete the task. Assign a date for when the task ought to be completed, based on the date of your event and on how long it takes to complete. Another thing to keep in mind—some tasks can't be started unless a certain other task is completed, or at least begun.

Once you've done all of this pre-thinking, start calling to find those who will form a core event leadership group. Set a first-meeting date, and go for it.

TOOLS FOR EVENT MANAGEMENT

Efficient use of management tools can walk you through the maze of producing a quality event.

PROFESSIONAL EVENT PLANNER

Chances are your ministry doesn't need to hire a professional event planner. Most of our events are much smaller than this. BUT WAIT. Don't be afraid to see if you have people in your church with this type of experience who might be willing to lend a hand.

A professional event planner could come in handy if you're planning a denominational or network event that involves lots of churches and lots of people.

But even for the detail-oriented, event management can seem overwhelming. If your event is large and complex enough that you wish to hire a professional event planner to manage logistical details, then your responsibilities shift from things like facilities, transportation, and food to primarily programming.

Christian meeting planning professionals can help with site selection, contract negotiation, registration, and on-site management. Especially if you select a hotel as your event site, hiring an event professional who is trained and experienced in providing the level of detail hotels require is a good way to go. Many times, the meeting planner negotiates a better fee with the hotel—not only because they do it all the time, but also because they bring the hotel so many other clients that the hotel wants to give them the best deal.

FasTrack

For a particularly complex event, let a professional event planner handle logistics.

Meeting planner fees vary based on the amount of responsibility you delegate to them and on the facility you desire to use. In some cases, hotel facilities work with professional meeting planners on a commission basis. That means the planner won't charge you at all for finding the facility and negotiating the contract. (For more information regarding training or potential meeting planners look at the resources at the back of the chapter.)

Event Manager

The Planning Worksheet (page 395) can guide your preparation for your first team meeting. Use the Event Manager to prompt you to send out assignments to team members after the first meeting. The goal of using this tool is to map out your critical path.

The critical path of an event is the sequence of critical activities that connect the event's start with the event's conclusion. Knowing the critical path of an event helps you prioritize tasks that have no leeway in their timing, letting you see exactly what needs to happen and when to keep your event planning on schedule. Most tasks in event management have some slack, and you can delay them some without affecting the event itself. If you delay critical tasks, however, you jeopardize your event. Some tasks that at first aren't on the critical path move onto the critical path if you procrastinate.

Set the Date

Your first entry on the critical path map is the date your event is to occur. Once you've established that, move backward to assign dates to tasks that must be completed the day before the event begins, the week before, the month before, and so on. This is how it works in simple form:

- On July 10, at 7 p.m., you want to play a game of cards on your back porch with a few friends and serve them ice cream. That means that by—
- July 10 you must have pulled out the cards, put chairs on the deck, set the bowls and spoons on the countertop.
- July 9 you must have cleaned the house.
- July 7 you must have bought the ice cream.
- July 1 you must have invited a few friends to come over.

House cleaning must occur as scheduled—by July 9—or it won't get done in time for the event. It's already a critical task on the path since there's no room for delay. (If you're not a clean freak, of course, you can always skip this step.) You can't have the party without ice cream, though. That means buying it is already a critical task, and you've built in some slack time to cover yourself for emergencies (or procrastination). If the 9th rolls around, and you still haven't bought ice cream, however, that becomes your number-one priority on the critical path.

How the event actually pans out can look very different from your critical path map. Here's one scenario:

- On July 1 you could only reach four of your seven friends. Two were out of town and won't get their messages until after the July 4th holiday, and one must not have been paying attention to her call-waiting feature.
- On July 3 you finally remember to call the one back, and she can't come. You start to think of who can finish out the second foursome.
- By July 8 you've finally got seven yeses and you go buy the ice cream.
- July 9 starts with your car breaking down and ends with you buying paper plates because you still haven't had time to do your dishes, let alone clean the house.
- On July 10 your friends show up at 7:20 and apologize for being late—and for bringing three extra friends. You improvise partners for the card game and everyone gets a little less ice cream, but hey—it turns out to be a fun evening just as you'd hoped when you planned it.

The critical path is your map for event planning. Based on your map, you fill in your Event Manager and start making your to-do lists.

1. Visualize your desired event—how the space will support your goals, what activities will happen and in what order, who will provide leadership for small groups, etc.

2. Describe in a list all the steps you believe are required to make the event happen.

3. Put the steps in order according to which steps need to happen before other steps can happen, and according to which steps take the longest time to accomplish or the longest lead-time to get the desired results.

4. Assign each step a deadline and a person to be responsible for the task.

5. Track your progress, and don't slack on the details that need to be completed early in the process. If you go off schedule early on, you'll be playing catch-up all the way through.

6. Although your critical path map started with the day of the event and worked backward, your timeline should start with today's date and work forward toward the event date.

To-Do List

Generate a Master To-Do List

Include tasks from your Planning Worksheet (page 395), your Task Master (page 419), and action steps brought up at your team meetings. (See Task Master List Sample for an example of what a prepared one looks like.) The master to-do list is a catch-all place for any job, no matter how simple, that you have to do to make the event happen. (You can use the Monthly Planning and Weekly Planning forms on pages 350 and 351.) Instead of naming complex jobs on the list, break them down into parts and list each part. To the left of an item, record the date you entered it; to the right jot down the task's deadline.

FasTrack

Track your event planning progress on a master timeline.

Review Your To-Do's

At least weekly skim your master to-do list for tasks that must be done (and can be done) the next day, or on each day in the next week. Transfer those items to daily to-do lists that you keep in this section of your event notebook. Don't write down more tasks than you can actually do on a given day—and then do them.

Event Notebook/E-File

Tracking event details can swamp even the most organized of leaders if they have no one place to keep all the papers in order. After planning hundreds of events, professional meeting planner and senior partner of Conferences Inc., Linda Daniels, recommends keeping an event notebook—one three-ring binder per event, with at least 12 section markers. An event notebook helps keep your event tracking smooth and organized. (Evernote would be a perfect solution for an electronic notebook for your event management.)

On the cover of your notebook write the event name, your church name, and your name. That way if it's misplaced during the event, it can be returned to you.

Event Forms
page 379 to 421

Notebook Contents

The notebook or e-file holds all your ideas, logistical information, maps, original copies, etc.—a one-stop-shop for everything you need to manage your event. Keep a three-hole punch handy so you can add fliers and other written materials, or these documents can easily be scanned for electronic storage. Insert some blank pages for meeting notes and clear-pocket page holders for originals, room keys, and miscellaneous items. When a piece of paper, idea, or detail comes your way, immediately file it in the proper section of the notebook. That way, things will always be at your fingertips. The notebook will evolve into a tool that you can't live without:

SMART TIP

When you negotiate the facility contract, bring in a similar schedule from a prior event. The camp director or retreat center manager will get a better idea of the type of space you need and of your program requirements.

Event File Checklist

▸ Timeline: Keep a current copy of your Master Timeline (page 388), with its adjusted dates and assignments, at the front of the file.

▸ To-do list: Build a list based on your timeline that tells you what needs to be done today or in the next few days.

▸ Meeting notes: Keep a copy of all meeting notes, including your Planning Worksheet (page 395). Record assignment changes, action items, and other vital information to the appropriate sections of your notebook as well. Choose one team member to take notes during your planning meetings, then type them up and email them to all the team members or put them onto a file sharing site such as Google Docs or Dropbox. Your copy can make its home in your event file.

FASTRACK

Browse your master to-do list at the end of each week to set up daily tasks for the next week.

▸ Event schedule: Make up two event schedules—one that gives details necessary for planning (primarily for parents and students), and the other a Simplified Timeline (page 401) for staff use. On your final, detailed schedule, show meeting room assignments beside each entry.

▸ Budget: Keep a copy of the general budget. The Financial Accountability Worksheet (page 384) and the Budget (page 379) would go here. If you do your books manually, keep your expense sheet in this section as well. Place unprocessed receipts in a clear sheet-holder within this section.

CONTRACTS

Read and understand every word of the contract before you sign it. A contract serves two purposes: clarification and instructions. Find out if you have the authority to sign the contract. Many churches require the senior pastor or executive pastor to sign all contracts. Ask another person to read a contract before you sign it—the fine print can be devastating. Depending on the complexity, have a lawyer review the contract.

A contract can be changed... until both parties sign it. Before you sign, let the service provider know if you're uncomfortable about something in the contract. After the contract is signed, you have to live with it.

A contract often bounces back and forth several times before it's usable. Make sure that you sign only the edited and clean copy of the contract. You will be referring to the contract several times throughout your event and need to be able to read and understand it.

Be prepared to live and die by the contract. Don't assume anything. Put it in writing. If they say they can do this or that, ask them to write it into the contract. If it's not in writing, it's considered hearsay and not legally binding. Food services can say that you'll have 14 meals a day per person, but if the contract says you'll get only one meal, you'll go hungry.

It's best to have another folder and envelope for processed receipts, or the event notebook gets too bulky.

- ▶ Facility: Once you have the big picture of the kind of event you want to do, record in your event notebook specific details of the kind of facility you need to accomplish your goals. Once you've inspected the site, the Site Inspection form (page 402) would go here as well. The facility category in event planning includes maps, rules and regulations, general facility schedule, snack bar hours, lake front/pool hours, etc. Place at the front of the section a list of the phone numbers or extension numbers of individuals on-site who work with you: site director, program director, meeting planner, facilities manager, banquet manager.

- ▶ Transportation. Pull from your office filing system information on transportation companies in your area. Start calling. Keep notes from your phone calls in this section, including whom you spoke to and the date and time. When you select the company to use, scan their flier or brochure or print out their Web site and place the copy in your event file (just in case the Web site goes down). You can file a copy of the contract with your selected company in this section as well.

- ▶ Housing. The more people attending your event, the more housing concerns can make or break your event. The facility generally provides a grounds map or hotel floor plan that specifically shows sleeping rooms. From a camp/retreat center, ask for an overview of all the sleeping areas. Request a sales packet with housing-specific information from a hotel. Find out the type of bed setup in each room: king, queen, double/double (two double beds), or two singles. Hotels also list what amenities each room offers.

▸ Food. Your food service choices depend on the type of facility you select. Some retreat centers offer a fixed menu or may allow you to request special menus. Just ask. Upscale retreat centers and hotels give you lots of choices, and only your budget limits your cuisine. In this section you can put menus, lists of meals needed, and any choices that you're offered. Be sure to be mindful of special dietary requirements, including food allergies, diabetic menus, vegan, and gluten-free requirements.

▸ Meeting space. Keep in your event notebook floor plans of the meeting spaces you've reserved on your Meeting Space Setup Worksheet (page 392). Facility-provided diagrams generally show room footage and possible room arrangements. Your staging plans affect the number of seats you can set up. Since you might use one room in several ways, sketch out the details of your set-up needs—along with the dates and times for each set-up. They like to have your exact schedule two to four weeks in advance.

▸ Contracts: You make several contracts as you progress with your event: facility, speaker, transportation (if you use buses), and perhaps a meeting planner. Keep the clean, signed original in your notebook and a copy in your office file drawer. During an event, you will refer to the contracts several times, especially if there are issues that need clarifying.

▸ Programming: Programming is an expanded version of the event schedule. It encompasses general sessions, small group time, meals, activities, games, work projects, and so on. From another perspective, the schedule is the synopsis of the program.

SMART TIP

If another group uses your chosen facility at the same time, place a copy of their schedule in your notebook so you plan with the other group in mind.

▸ Printed materials: Keep with you in a clear page holder any originals of schedules, discussion questions, PR and registration brochures, logo, etc. You never know when you'll need to make just one more copy of whatever. Put a Post-it Note on each sheet saying "Original."

▸ Miscellaneous: As you live out the event, note things that work and things that don't. Write out what you would change if you could and what you would never do again or note it on your phone to print/save for later. In a clear sheet-holder, collect any incident reports or other items that don't fit any notebook category.

Once your notebook is organized, so are you. And when the event is over, scan the complete contents of your notebook and file it away for future planning reference. It will be well worth the time you spend setting it up and keeping it up.

The next time someone asks you a tough question about the event, you can turn to your file and give the right answer in a moment.

Small On-Site Events

On-site events typically are easier, less expensive, and less cumbersome than off-site events. Following a few guidelines will keep you in favor on your home turf.

Be a team player.

Some churches have systems in place for facilities that you need to follow. Be a good team member to the other ministries in the church by sharing the rooms. Working together with other ministries for resources is part of being a good teammate. We work for the same boss, and no one ministry is more important than another.

Be a good neighbor.

Unless your church is located in a remote area, it is likely surrounded by homes and businesses. Be mindful of what it is like to be one of those neighbors as you plan your event. Putting a PA system outside? Think it through . . . Parking cars in the neighborhood or near adjoining businesses? Think it through. And, if an issue ever develops, go directly to the person/organization involved and have a conversation. Seek to be a peacemaker and find a good solution.

Respect and value your facility.

Not only must you treat the facilities respectfully, your staff, volunteers, and students need to be taught the same respect. Waterlogged bathrooms or paint-splattered walls discredit your ministry. Do your best to leave the facility in better shape than you found it. Clean it up, put it away and take out the trash.

Communicate with your custodian(s).

Keep your facility team in the loop on your event and get your set-up requests submitted early. We as youth workers are infamous for waiting until the last minute to make our set-up requests. Review events one month in advance. Suggest monthly meetings to review upcoming needs and evaluate previous events. Bottom line—communicate. Yes, email is good, but face-to-face is best to prevent miscommunication and for the sake of the relationship. Yes, get the details submitted in writing for the sake of clarity—but follow up with face-to-face.

Clean up the kitchen.

Most of our on-site events involve the church kitchen. Keep yourself on the good side of the kitchen committee by taking special care of this area. A few keys: Replenish supplies, wash the dishes, put away the dishes, don't use supplies or food without permission. These small things are a big deal in most churches.

Small Off-Site Events

Some of the greatest events are simple ones where a youth worker and a few volunteers take a van full of students on a weekend retreat at a cabin. Even though most of you may have to sleep on the floor, your time can be rich and memorable. Events don't have to be huge to have impact. Smaller events can effectively build and develop the personal relationships that can drive growth.

Facility

Depending on your group's size, you might use anything from a tent to a cabin in a retreat center. Many retreat centers or camp facilities accommodate small groups. Scheduling facility use for small groups is easier and can be done even at a later date because a small group can often use a facility at the same time as larger, previously scheduled groups. A living room or conference room can serve as your meeting room. Meals can be on campus or at the local McDonald's. Your event can be more spontaneous and flexible, but some planning is likely still required.

Your facility is your home away from home and needs to be comfortable and appropriate for you, as well as for your students. If it's 20 below, and you're staying in a drafty barn, your students won't catch anything but a cold. Conversely, if you're thinking of shutting high-energy kids in with hanging chandeliers at the Hilton, you'll only drive yourself out of ministry.

Sometimes budget determines facility; sometimes facility determines budget. If your group has been using a certain retreat center for the last bazillion years, for example, the facility cost will drive the budget. If on the other hand you're looking for a new facility, check out several to find an affordable one that works for you

Event planning isn't exactly like real estate—location, location, location—but you must use a thoughtful and complete selection process when choosing the appropriate location for your event. And you need to get your feet on the ground and not just look at Web photos of the site. The Site Inspection form (page 402) walks you through: the distance from your home base, facility flexibility, room sizes and usability,

---

SMALL RETREAT PROGRAMMING IDEAS

Use a video series for your program and spend time in discussion.

Choose a small book to work through and have the students read through it before the retreat.

Have everyone share their faith and life journeys in detail with the whole group.

Choose a book of the Bible to work through.

Talk about one or two characters in the Bible and make it relevant to your students' world.

Choose a curriculum and spend time working through it.

Partner with one or two small churches to combine resources.

Have the seniors lead the retreat.

eating area and recreation facilities, and other site issues that affect your event experience.

Before your first event planning meeting, read through the lists of questions. Add in questions about location that relate to the general kind of event you have in mind. Maybe you want to include a sleep-out under the stars one night. Write that criteria, in question form, under "General facility flexibility." Just browsing the list will spark ideas for other inquiries about event facilities and help you to quickly focus your location search.

Record your search results in your notebook with the Site Inspection form.

On first contact with a facility, ask them to check their calendar to see if they have available space on your selected dates. If not, check alternate times that could work for you. If you can plan enough in advance, you can offer several date options to facilities. If they're booked on all the dates you have available, ask them to send you an information packet for future reference—and keep dialing.

Before making your final selection, always conduct site inspections of facilities under serious consideration. (See the Site Inspection form.) Even if you've conducted dozens and dozens of site inspections and feel like you're really good at it—take good notes and answer all the questions on the form. Some facilities wine and dine you, and others merely give you a quick tour. If you fill out the Site Inspection form, your recollection of the facility will be more objective. (Just don't let the T-bone steak with mushroom gravy weigh too heavily in your thinking.) At least tour the sleeping rooms, general session room, and meeting spaces. Take time to envision what the rooms will look like when they're full of your students: Is there enough space in the halls? Will you be staying too close to other guests? What's the worst damage that could occur? What might it cost you? Take pictures or video to refresh your memory when you're back at home.

SMART TIP
Although hotels are generally more work on the front end, it usually pays off with the service on the back end.

Dollars and cents will probably weigh heaviest in choosing your event facility. Be sure you compare apples with apples. Although it's difficult to compare a retreat center to a hotel, in the financial midrange, upscale retreat centers compete with the lower-end hotels. Each kind of facility has its pros and cons. Make sure you know all the costs involved before you choose which way to head.

1. Retreat centers

Typically, camps and retreat centers give you one, all-inclusive price per person for the entire event, and the prices are more affordable than hotels. However, you get what you pay for. You might be expected to do anything from table setup to cleaning your own bathrooms. Some retreat facilities offer administrative and set-up staff only during daytime hours. Double-check to make sure your needs will be met for setup and for emergencies. Check to see if you're sharing the facilities with another group. You may need to make programming adjustments if that's the case. Ask if there's an additional charge for using the waterfront, low or high ropes courses, horseback riding, paint ball, etc.

2. Hotels

In general, hotels cost more. They charge per room (leaving you to decide how to divide the cost per person), and they charge per person for food costs. Hotels vary in service quality, but most are very service-oriented. When they say they'll do something, they do it.

Hotels are often open to negotiating details. For example, the more sleeping rooms you take, the less they charge you for your meeting space. Also, hotels make their gravy on food and beverages. That means, crazy as it sounds, that it's sometimes less expensive to eat more. As your food dollars go up, your meeting space charges go down. In essence, you pay the same dollars but get a meal for it.

Hotels come with three major downsides:

1. They charge you for every add-on—sleeping cots, extra snacks, etc., which can kill your budget.
2. If you break it, you buy it.
3. Student noise and behavior can disturb other hotel guests.

> ### EVENT INSURANCE
> One youth pastor's story: On occasion you may take out an insurance policy in addition to your standard coverage. The additional insurance would cover unavoidable accidents, mishaps, or cancellations. Do a Google search for not-for-profit event insurance. You can check out their policy and coverage options online. Our group once had $1,000 added to our hotel bill due to room damage. On top of that, we ended up paying another $1,000 to pacify unhappy guests in the rooms next door who either had to be moved or had left the facility because of our noise. Ouch. That was expensive.

> ### FASTRACK
> Facility representatives expect you to negotiate every offer they make—don't disappoint them.

Facility Negotiation

The rule of thumb on negotiation is to keep working the numbers until both you and the facility representative are happy. You want to walk away knowing that you received a fair deal and that your needs will be met. A reputable hotel lives to serve their clients and will bend over backward to do so. A non-reputable or lower-end hotel, however, may be a significant challenge to work with as they have limited resources. Choose carefully. Also, be aware that hotels can often feel like they nickel-and-dime you to death. There are hidden costs that can kill your budget—and you won't know about it till the event is over.

THE SAVVY NEGOTIATOR

You never want the facility to give up everything in the first round of negotiations. Going straight to their rock-bottom price won't leave any room for favors. The first time at the table, you may negotiate only until the facility manager gets a little uncomfortable. To know where they draw the line, you might push them until they say no.

But don't push them in every area. You might get a lower sleeping room price but not push them on the food prices. Later—when you recognize you'll need an additional night snack, some vegetarian plates not mentioned in the meal plan, or a change in setup here or there that wasn't originally in the contract—you can ask them if they'll throw it in for you at no additional cost.

If you pull out of them in the beginning what you believe is every little detail you need, they'll end up charging you for every little change that you make after the contract is signed. Believe me, you don't want that.

Retreat and camping facilities vary greatly with respect to fees and in management structures. Investigate the management. Get to know the person who will be assisting your group with logistics. That person can make or break your retreat. Know him by name, and keep in frequent contact with him. Retreat facilities generally negotiate less on the per-person fees than hotels, but offer more flexibility on the programming side. Be very specific about your needs and your expectations so you're not surprised. For example, hotel staff is available 24/7. At a retreat center, the staff members often go home at a certain hour, which may be a few miles away.

The fine art of negotiations is a book of its own. These few tips will be helpful, but not close to thorough. If you are facilitating a large group and are using a hotel property, your best bet is to use a professional meeting planner to do the negotiating for you. With large events (say a denominational gathering) you can save thousands of dollars just because of the professional planner's expertise. In general, the larger the group, the more room for negotiation. The smaller the group, the less flexibility the facility will agree to. Retreat properties negotiate little. It's best to ask them up front what their best price is and then live with it. If the experience is successful and you wish to use the facility again, come back to the table ready to talk about possible cost reduction or extra amenities. Sometimes they'll work with you to get your business back.

Tips for Negotiating
▸ Always come to the table with a kind, friendly attitude.
▸ Act and dress in a professional manner.
▸ Think smart.
▸ If you don't understand, ask.
▸ Come across as the decision-maker, but if you're feeling pressured to sign something, don't hesitate to use your boss as an excuse to buy yourself some processing time. ("It looks good to me, but there are a few things that I would like to run by the senior pastor before I sign." Or say, "I need a few

days to think about it. I'll get back to you then.")
(See "More about Contracts" on page 215.)

▸ You're not ready to finish the deal until you feel good about it.

Housing

Although you secure your facility very early in the planning process, you'll assign rooms or cabins within the week before the event. That way you only do housing assignments once. If you assign housing too early and a few more students join, you end up having to redo the assignments.

Transportation

Small groups can use a van or two, along with some other leaders' vehicles. Remember that transportation is as important to the event as housing, speakers, or breakout sessions. Submit your vehicle requests early. Be mindful of the needs of other ministries and work together with them in your planning. Make sure that you follow the policies your ministry has for providing safe drivers for your students. Your event starts the moment your students show up at the church doors and ends when they step into their parent's car.

A small group traveling a moderate distance can recruit parent drivers and personal vehicles to transport students. Bus and van rental, of course, remains an option. If your group is large enough for several buses and if you're traveling a substantial distance, investigate chartering through a large transportation company. In addition to increased comfort and bathroom facilities, chartered buses offer separate storage for luggage.

Food

No matter what facility you select, you'll have to select menus. If you've purchased a prepackaged meal deal, request complete menus so you're certain the food is appropriate for your group. Simple is best, and large quantity is mandatory. After all, you're bringing in growing kids with healthy appetites. Quality is tricky to judge accurately for a group

---

MORE ABOUT CONTRACTS

While on-site or just prior to the event, state in writing mutually agreed upon additions or changes to the contract and add them to your contract. Keep good notes.

Honor your contract. If it says that you need to pay X amount by Y date, then make sure that you do. Don't jeopardize your event by tardy payments.

Keep the original of each of your contracts in your event notebook for quick reference. Keep a copy in your office.

You must have a contract for any service provider that you pay: facility, speaker(s), musicians, transportation. Spell out in the contract any specifics related to the service—fees, special circumstances, benefits, and anything else you want the service provider to be accountable to fulfill.

Investigate putting in a clause for Christian arbitration in case of a dispute. Seldom, if ever, would you actually need it, but should problems arise, it's a lifesaver.

of students. Request well in advance additions or changes necessary for any student's special dietary needs.

Ask if you can supplement the food offered. Some facilities don't allow you to bring store-bought snacks or to call out for pizza, but you can bring homemade goodies. Others might let you bring packaged snacks, like candy bars or sodas, only if you're selling them at break times. Most facilities let students bring their own snacks for their own rooms.

Meeting Space

Appropriate meeting space for a small event is determined by your programming plans. Are you always going to meet as one big group? Do you need breakout rooms? If so, how many and when? Talk through your schedule with the facility manager, noting group size and kind of activity for each time and room. Hotels require your exact schedule in order to work around the needs of other groups. Retreat settings are usually more flexible. You can even have a 24-hour access to your main meeting space.

Event Sign-Up Sheet

A necessary part of event registration is the pre-event sign-up. Event facilities want to know one or two weeks ahead of time exactly how many are coming to the event. That means you need a list of students, adult leaders, and speakers or entertainers who have committed to be there. For speakers and entertainment you have their contract to assure you. Students need to pay their registration fees before you can count on their participation. So before you give a final count to a facility, use the Single-Event Registration to track attendees and their payments.

Some ministries have several event sign-ups going on at the same time. Use the Multiple-Event Registration form to minimize paper shuffling at the sign-up table. Be sure to note which participants have turned in their medical release and/or permission forms. If you don't have one already, check out the Medical Release and Permission form on page 390.

Registration

From the moment students arrive at the event, they should experience the energy of the planning your team has done. The theme and purpose of the event can begin its trek into their hearts, even during registration. Set the stage for what's ahead by making registration festive and inviting. Easily overlooked as unrelated to the "real" event itself, registration can take an unexpected chunk out of your event time if it's done haphazardly.

Disney World is the master at moving masses of people efficiently. Use that model to lay out registration. Leave open spaces. Spread tables out. Train more leaders than you think you need. Form follows function. Think logically about what needs to happen when, and set up your registration accordingly.

Students arrive to register.

▸ They put down their luggage. (Where?)

▸ They pick up their registration packets. (How will they locate them?)

▸ They turn in their permission forms. (How will your team verify them? Where will you file them?)

▸ When they pick up their packets, they'll find out if they owe money. (What is the process for them to pay off their accounts?)

▸ Students with special medical needs go from registration or finance to the nurse's table to register their meds or discuss their medical needs. (Does this require a private setting? What are your insurance company's recommendations?)

▸ Students return to pick up their luggage and head for the bus that's marked with their corresponding numbers. (When and how do they learn which bus they're on? What if they want to trade buses to ride with friends?)

▸ A couple of students may have made arrangements for a friend to pick them up around the corner of the building to take off for the weekend and

MEETING SPACE SETUP

You'll need to answer these questions for each room you use, both for general sessions and breakouts.

Do you require staging? If so, what size and what height?

Do you want chairs? Tables? How many? Set up in which way?

Theater: chairs in rows, all facing front.

Classroom: narrow tables with chairs behind them, all facing front.

Rounds: round tables for 6-10 people each (good for discussions; bad for lectures).

Cocktail rounds or high tops: tall, round tables for 3-4.

Table square: Four or eight tables set in a square. Participants sit around the outer edge of the table facing each other.

Generally, you are not charged for chairs or tables—but never assume...

How many tables and where?

Do you need numbers on the tables to indicate where students sit?

Do you need information tables?

Do you want the tables skirted?

Do you want water service in the meeting rooms?

What audiovisual equipment do you need?

Is there a Green Room near the staging area for the musicians and speakers?

REGISTRATION TIME SAVERS

Waiting in long lines can leave a bad first impression. Shorten the process by preparing ahead of time as much of the registration process as possible.

Clearly mark the areas where students sign in and strategically place volunteers to assist and direct when needed.

Lay out your floor plan to leave plenty of space for all activities to be done in an orderly fashion. Traffic should always move in one direction when there are multiple stations.

Place trained volunteers at each station for efficiency. Plan for enough staff to handle the most congestion possible, and then you'll be able to meet your time deadlines.

Place in one large envelope completed nametags labeled with group and room (and transportation) assignments. Include curriculum, an event schedule, and any other instructions for participants.

Divide the retreat roster into manageable, alphabetical chunks (2-4 groups). You might end up having three tables labeled A-F, G-L, and M-Z.

Designate one table as a solutions table, where a student can receive help from a trained volunteer without clogging up the system.

At events where registration occurs before travel, number all the vehicles/vans/buses so that students easily recognize which bus they are to ride. Have a roster for each bus leader to verify, both coming and going, that each student is on board.

show up again when you unload the buses. (Will you know that they are gone? What supervision is in place to be sure students actually leave on their bus?)

▶ Parents pick up an information brochure providing the name, address, and phone number of the facility and a map showing how to get there. Include contact information for the leadership team at the event in case of an emergency. (Who is available to answer their questions?)

Handling Copyrighted Materials

Many of our events involve the use of media. We project lyrics, show movies, play music and then create our own videos and media presentations, often setting them to music. Specific laws that affect you govern many of these. Being mindful of keeping yourself legal in this area is important.

An often-overlooked—even intentionally ignored—area is copyright infringement. This is an ethical issue that churches tend to skate over. Although we're sure that section 110 of the Copyright Law of 1976 {17 U.S.C. 110(3)} is on your recreational reading list this year, let us relieve your suspense regarding its content:

Without fear of breaking the law, churches may—

▶ perform nondramatic literary or musical works and religious dramatic and musical works.

▶ display individual works of a nonsequential nature (17 U.S.C. 101).

This means that during worship, you may—

▸ perform contemporary songs, regardless of the owner.
▸ show any still image, regardless of its source. You may even show frames of a film, if they are not in sequence. You may show scanned images of any sort, including newspaper headlines, periodicals, and pictorial books.

Here's what churches may NOT do during worship, according to Section 110(3):

▸ Play any non-live-performed recording of a musical work—whether on CD or any type of recording.
▸ Reproduce lyrics in any fashion from a copyright-protected musical work, including displaying lyrics within projected graphic images and printing the lyrics in bulletins or other handouts. Section 110(1) applies the same rules for media use in nonprofit educational environments, as well.
▸ Outside of worship and classroom, legal use of copyrighted works (including posting works on the Internet and selling works to other churches or individuals) is not as clearly defined. Much is made of the exemption in the copyright law for fair use (NUGGET). As a rule, never make blanket use of fair use.

Keep in mind the following guidelines for claiming fair use of a copyrighted piece:

▸ The more creative the work, the less likely that it's covered by the fair use clause.
▸ Although no specific percentages apply, the more of a work you use, the less likely that your use is covered by fair use.
▸ The more fair use decreases a work's market value, the less likely that you can claim fair use of it.
▸ The only activities qualifying for blanket fair use, according to standard interpretations of the First Amendment, are news reporting, research, and criticism. Evaluate all other uses on a work-by-work basis.

Just in case (hint, hint, hint)

Check with your umbrella organization or your denomination to see what copyright licenses you may already be covered by.

SMART TIP

Give parents a copy of a simple event schedule that includes the event location, address, phone number, and emergency phone numbers. (Obviously this information should also be available in advance on your Web site.) On the back of the schedule, spell out the code of student conduct and draw a map to the event location. That way, if disciplinary action is taken, parents are fully aware of the consequences (like receiving a call in the middle of the night to pick up Johnny because you caught him smoking weed . . .).

That said, check out these licensing resources for your ministry:

- *http://www.ccli.com*—licensing for music in your church
- *http://cvli.com*—licensing for showing movies in your church
- Or simply go to the source—*http://www.copyright.com*

Parodies may violate copyright protection. Fair use of copyrighted works for parodies may allow use of prerecorded music with original dramatics, such as in a skit or video version of a sketch or TV show. To be sure you're not in audio-visual copyright violations, however, check with a copyright lawyer on a case-by-case basis.

Non-home showing of rented videos requires a license. By law, as well as by intent, prerecorded DVDs and Blu-Rays available for rental or purchase are for home use only. You must have a license to show them in any other setting. Rentals or purchases of home movies do not carry with them licenses for non-home showings. Yes, this is a big deal.

These rules are stated in the Federal Copyright Act, Public Law 94-553, Title 17 of the United States Code. Any institution, organization, company, or individual wishing to engage in non-home showings of DVDs and Blu-Ray discs must obtain a special license to show video materials. Among other rights, the Copyright Act grants to the copyright owner the exclusive right "to perform the copyrighted work publicly" (Section 106).

Obtaining a license for non-home use of copyrighted materials. Licenses to show motion pictures at a church meeting and to display song lyrics are available through the following businesses, as well as through other channels:

- Motion Picture Licensing Corporation, P.O. Box 66970, Los Angeles, CA 90066. 800/462-8855. The MPLC offers an umbrella license for a number of studios whose films are already available for rental. They charge an affordable yearly fee. mplc.com.
- Swank Motion Pictures, 201 S. Jefferson Avenue, St. Louis, Missouri 63103-2579. 800/876-5577, swank.com. Swank offers copies with license for public showings of films not yet available for rent.
- Criterion Pictures, www.criterionpic.com
- Christian Copyright Licensing International (CCLI), 17201 N.E. Sacramento St., Portland, OR 97230. 800/234-2446 or ccli.com.

BUDGETING YOUR EVENT

Although sometimes difficult to estimate and time consuming to develop, accurate budgets are essential to a financially successful event.

The estimating process for retreat budgets—or large events where a fee is charged to students—includes many of the same questions that you need to ask regarding a general budget (see the finance chapter on page 109. Basing a budget on specific, accurate prices is critical to the budget's effectiveness. There are a lot of variables to consider.

First, determine your budget criteria. Your socioeconomic area, for example, directly affects how much you can charge your students. Don't make assumptions here. Sometimes students can live in huge homes, but if you go inside, there's no furniture and very little food due to a parent being laid off or deeply in debt. The opposite is also true: a student looks like they come from modest means and yet brings $200 to spend at the camp snack shop.

Determine the most that you can charge the students for the activity and not exclude potential attendees. Also, think about how many kids a family has involved in the youth ministry. This can add up to several hundreds of dollars if they have multiple teenagers who are active in the ministry.

Then ask if you should:

FasTrack

You'll always cover your expenses if you follow this basic formula: Divide all expenses by the lowest number of students that might attend the retreat. That way, if you only meet your minimum student attendance, you'll still make your budget.

- charge your staff to attend the event. If so, how much?
- charge your volunteer staff to attend the event. If so, how much?
- have scholarships for your students. If so, how do you determine need?
- pay your hourly staff when working at an event. If so, how much?
- cut expenses for the event to lower the price. If so, what would you cut out completely?
- What would you trim to save money?

Based on your answers to the budget questions—and keeping in mind your event purpose and group size—you can get a good sense of your budget. Your budget then informs your facility choice. What accommodations can the group afford and still accomplish the event's purpose: tents, rustic camp, retreat center, or hotel?

GETTING AT THE COST

To select categories to include on a retreat budget, think through what will occur during your event. List all the areas, with their associated costs. Some costs start as per-person costs, and some are bulk costs that have to be translated into per-person costs.

Per-Person Costs
- housing (what the location charges for a person to stay there)
- food (what the facility charges per meal, per person)

- ► transportation (tickets or mileage)
- ► materials (what will be provided to each individual)
- ► activities charged per person (any additional entrance fees)

Bulk Costs
- ► meeting space (reserving a camp lodge, another church, or hotel meeting room or other space where the whole group gathers)
- ► sound system (rental or purchase)
- ► staff costs (counselors, speakers, chaperones)
- ► hospitality (snacks, door prizes)
- ► decorations (for tables, walls, stage)
- ► registration
- ► office supplies

After totaling the bulk cost for a given expense, translate your bulk costs to per-person costs by dividing the total cost for one category by the number of attendees. For example, if renting a 50-passenger bus costs $500 and 50 students are signed up, the cost per person is $10 ($500 ÷ 50 = $10). What if only 40 students sign up? Then your cost per person for transportation goes up to $12.50 per person ($500 ÷ 40 = $12.50). The Budget form leads you through the process.

Smart Tip
To avoid pricing your students out of an event, slightly overprice less costly events to make a small percentage of money to subsidize more costly events.

Case Studies
Circle up your leadership team and discuss the following planning situations using the material presented in this chapter.

Mission Trip Mania
It's December and you're starting to make plans for taking 15 students on a mission trip over spring break. Your destination is any distant country where your kids can experience another culture, as well as develop a heart toward service. What are your options for effectively planning, preparing, and executing a mission trip in the next three months?

Making the Most of Little
You lead a small youth ministry with a dozen students and one volunteer. As a part-time youth worker finishing up seminary, you don't have a lot of time to plan an event. Your students don't have much money to put toward an event, either. What events can you do?

Wrestling with Tradition

You're the new kid on the block in a ministry that has been using the same summer camp for the last half century. Parents say things like, "I got saved at that camp back in 1987, and I want my kids to have a good camp experience, too." Although steeped in tradition, the camp is not well maintained. In some cases, it's literally falling apart. During your site inspection you felt compelled to ask, "When was the last time you had the camp inspected by the fire marshal, and did it pass?" You'd like to see your group go to a better facility—one that has flush toilets, say, and lights that are actually attached to the ceiling rather than hanging by the wires. What do you do?

FASTRACK

You want to charge the least amount to your students (so that as many students as possible can participate), but you can't regularly lose money on your event or you jeopardize future ministry or events.

The Best Laid Plans . . .

You're directing a huge, weeklong event that's one week away. It's crunch time. You've signed up 300 students, 50 staff, and a big-time speaker. You've verified the facility, double-checked the transportation. Your staff is trained, and you've even completed your housing lists. Then, you receive a phone call that no leader ever wants to receive—your speaker slipped a disk in her back and must cancel. What do you do?

Snow Im-mobile

It's 5 p.m. on a Friday—exactly one hour from the departure time for the winter retreat. You've already paid a nonrefundable $1,000 deposit for the facility and a bus fee of $400. At one end of the parking lot, the bus is warming up its engines for the 150-mile trip. At the other end, 45 students are eagerly lining up to complete registration. You've been listening to the weather report all day, and six to eight inches of snow have been predicted for this evening. Anxious parents are now hovering around you as the first snowflakes begin to fall. What do you do?

FASTRACK

Evaluate the total event—neither berate nor congratulate your event-site management on the basis of one or two of its pieces.

- ▶ Cancel the trip and send the students home.
- ▶ Keep on schedule and pray that the snow doesn't affect the trip.
- ▶ Cancel the trip and have an overnight lock-in instead.
- ▶ Having prepared for such a contingency, forge ahead with your original plan.

RECOMMENDED RESOURCES

▸ Christian Camp and Conference Association: www.ccca.org
▸ Christian Conference Centers: www.christianconferencecenters.com
▸ International Conference Center Association (ICCA): http://www.iacconline.org
▸ Religious Conference Management Association (RCMA): rcmaweb.org (member benefits, training conferences)

Portions of this chapter are printed with permission from the event chapter of *Camping and Retreating*, Bo Boshers, Zondervan.

FORMS

▸ Medical Release and Permission form
▸ Meeting Space Setup Worksheet
▸ Planning Worksheet
▸ Task Master
▸ Monthly Planning and Weekly Planning forms
▸ Marketing Strategy
▸ Master Timeline
▸ Planning Worksheet
▸ Simplified Timeline page
▸ Financial Accountability Worksheet
▸ Budget
▸ Site Inspection
▸ Checklist for Staff Assignments
▸ Evaluation Feedback Memo Sample
▸ Evaluation Worksheet
▸ Financial Accountability Worksheet
▸ Marketing Strategy
▸ Master Timeline
▸ Medical Release and Permission Form
▸ Meeting Space Setup
▸ Ministry Event Form

▸ Notebook Checklist
▸ Sample Confirmation Letter
▸ Sample Schedule
▸ Simplified Timeline
▸ Site Inspection
▸ Staff Director
▸ Staff Meeting Planner
▸ Staff Sound Engineer
▸ Staff Speakers/Artists Rep
▸ Staff Steer Chairperson
▸ Staff Steering Committee
▸ Staff Steering Committee - Sample
▸ Staff Steering Committee Program Coordinator
▸ Staff Steering Committee Registration Coordinator
▸ Staff Steering Committee Secretary
▸ Staff Steering Committee Volunteer Coordinator
▸ Task Master List/ Large Event - Sample
▸ Task Master List/ Large Event
▸ Marketing Press Release Packet

EVALUATING YOUR EVENT

You've invested a significant amount of time in your ministry event. Resist the temptation to skip the evaluation component of the planning process.

Participants

Be intentional to secure feedback from the people who participated in your event with a written evaluation if at all possible. Make it simple, brief, and use a scoring guide of 1 to 10 when possible. You never know what you don't know – so ask. Take some time during your event to get these completed – this will allow a much higher response. Online surveys are a good tool following your event to get feedback as well. Again – keep them short.

Leadership Team

Find a time very soon after your event to sit down with your leaders and secure thorough, honest, and thoughtful feedback. Begin by celebrating the victories and things that went well. As you work through the entire event, take notes and highlight things that need to be remembered, especially if this is an annual event.

Format

While the form in this book covers a broad list of evaluation topics, don't forget to review people and team members who need to be thanked or deserve special recognition, list any outstanding issues to be resolved, file pictures electronically from the event for reference and promotion in the future, and finally be sure to take time to file away all helpful planning notes, schedules, promotional materials, and anything that might serve the future of your ministry.

THE MEASURE OF SUCCESS

We've looked at what it takes to program and execute an event. These three questions can help you to measure its success.

- ▶ Did students and leaders show any movement of growth toward God?
- ▶ Did you meet your event goals and did it measure up to your expectations?
- ▶ From a logistical standpoint, did you create a God-honoring event that you're proud to identify with?

Base your evaluation on the totality of the event—in particular, how effectively students' hearts turned toward God as a result of your efforts. If you can look back over your event and answer yes, you've had a successful event. Every event has potholes and bumps along the way. If you see marks of spiritual growth, if you met your goals, if no logistical difficulties overshadowed it, then you have hit the mark. Well done.

PART 5

PEOPLE
AND
YOUTH MINISTRY

WORKING WITH BOARDS AND COMMITTEES

CHAPTER OVERVIEW
► Boards, Committees, and Task Forces
► Conducting a Successful Meeting

BOARDS, COMMITTEES, AND TASK FORCES

Depending on your church structure, these can either be the holy trinity of organization or an unholy headache. Each of these varies based on the way the church is set up and how they view the organizational hierarchy. For the sake of our discussion, here's how we'll describe them:

BOARD

A group of elected or appointed people who represent the larger organization. They should be members of the church in good standing, wise people marked by integrity and prayer, representative of a variety of perspectives present in the community, committed to the mission of the organization and ready to serve. The board has both the responsibility and the authority of making decisions in the area(s) they oversee. Their focus should be **on** the organization, not **in** the organization. In other words, they have the macro picture in mind but leave the micro picture—the day-to-day operations—to the staff. They may have the power to hire or fire a staff member, as well as the responsibility to advocate for them (e.g., in conflict, when pay raises are being negotiated, etc.). They should meet regularly and communicate often with the lead staff person. They determine the long-term strategy and policies of the ministry and should be an advocate for the youth ministry to the congregation.

An advisory board has neither authority nor responsibility. Their role is to give guidance and to make recommendations to the staff on major issues or concerns.

BOARDS
Christian education board, advisory board, denominational youth ministry board, board of elders, board of directors.

COMMITTEES
Some churches and organizations barely have any committees, while others create committees for choosing toilet paper and coffee urns. If you're one of the latter, there's an art to making committees work for you, rather than against you. So what exactly is a committee? A committee is a more formal working group (as opposed to a task force) and has a designated chairperson or head. The organization's by-laws may designate the different committees and their terms and scope of service.

If you're new to a church, find out what the committee process was before you came. If the church operates by committee, find an in-house mentor to coach you on the committee culture. How much authority do they have? Are they responsible for generating ideas? Approving ideas? Are they responsible for the completion of tasks? Do committees overlap responsibilities? If so, do some need to be put to rest?

Whenever possible, if a committee influences your area of ministry, make sure you have a voice in how the committee is formed and how it runs. For productivity's sake, committees should be between three and twelve people and be made up of members who have a variety of perspectives.

There are several types of committees:

▸ Standing committees are usually established by the board, and carry out the actions of the board. The board usually appoints a chair and allows the chair to recruit the rest of the committee.

▸ An advisory committee is made up of people who have wisdom and knowledge about the ministry or about what the ministry is trying to accomplish. They exist to give the ministry leader input and help guide him or her in making key decisions. For example, the ministry is developing a college preparatory ministry. People on the advisory committee might include educators, college admission personnel, a financial aid consultant and a tutor. This group may never meet together, but the ministry leader can run ideas and decisions by them either individually or as a group.

▶ Ad hoc committees: These are short-term committees with a deadline. They come about because of a need: create risk management policies, review confirmation curriculum, etc.

TASK FORCES

A task force is a short-term group that comes together to focus on a particular task or problem. In youth ministry, the youth pastor might put together a group with expertise to focus on a specific project. Once the project is completed, the group disbands. For example: You have to design, implement, and evaluate the annual fall catfish and spaghetti fundraiser. This group needs to be made up of action-oriented people and strategic thinkers. You might pull a task force together if you're redoing the youth room or if you need to organize a large fundraiser. This group creates and implements a plan and evaluates it when it's over.

If you oversee a board, committee, or task force, be honest and up-front when you recruit new members. Make sure they have a clear understanding of what the role entails and that they have the time and desire to work toward the mission of the ministry. Once they agree to come aboard, make sure to orient them to policies and procedures. Perhaps have a veteran member (who had a positive experience serving) mentor the newcomers for the first few meetings.

As a ministry leader, it's important that you keep committee members informed about the areas they oversee. If they have decision-making power over an area, invite them to visit that part of the ministry so they are making informed decisions. For example, if they oversee the youth ministry budget, they need to come on a retreat to see not just how the money is spent . . . but why. Help them become advocates of the youth ministry.

CONDUCTING A SUCCESSFUL MEETING

Whether it's holding a meeting to discuss the feeding of 5000 on a hillside or evaluating the summer ministry program, there's an art to planning a good meeting that doesn't waste people's time but is effective and productive. Rather than dreading them, view meetings as a chance to gather people together to accomplish the ministry's mission.

It takes practice, skill, patience, self-confidence, and flexibility. Meetings don't often turn out exactly as you expect. We've all been in meetings (and led some) that never should have been. Unclear roles and undefined outcomes promise nothing but bumpy, frustrating, and unproductive meetings. Even well-planned meetings take unexpected turns—simply because they're all about people, different personalities, and uniqueness. A well-prepared leader can guide those unexpected turns back to the task at hand.

Here are some questions to consider as you put meetings together:

1. WHAT'S THE PURPOSE?

Every meeting should have a clear purpose that can be stated in one or two sentences. Otherwise, you're wasting people's time. Take a few minutes to clearly identify why you are having this meeting.

Here are some purpose statements. Notice the different types of meetings that are present here.

We are meeting to:

- ▸ Evaluate the denomination's confirmation curriculum.
- ▸ Brainstorm the theme of this fall's lock-in.
- ▸ Review the last three years of budgets and to propose next year's budget.
- ▸ Inform parents about the summer's mission trip.
- ▸ Have a discussion on moving toward intergenerational worship.
- ▸ Create an action plan for recruiting new small group leaders.
- ▸ Get approval to hire a new intern.
- ▸ Discuss the theology behind family-based youth ministry and how it impacts our program.
- ▸ Play in order to build team morale and cohesiveness.
- ▸ Coordinate the after-school program.
- ▸ Celebrate the ministry's accomplishments this season.

2. WHO ARE THE PARTICIPANTS?

As you think through the agenda of the meeting, carefully consider who needs to be in attendance. Every person should have a reason for being there and should be able to clearly state it. Either they are there to contribute to a task or project or they are there because they will be impacted by the information being presented. Make sure the audience you're discussing is represented in the meeting. For example, if you're talking about designing a middle school after-school program, have two middle school students present. Before the meeting even begins, remind them that they are an important part of the meeting and need to speak up on behalf of those they are representing. If you're planning a parents' meeting, have two or more parents present to remind you what questions they might ask and what issues are important to them.

FasTrack

If people can't physically be there, consider having a virtual meeting using Skype, Google Hangout, or another virtual meeting app.

Examples of why people are at the table:

▸ "I'm at this meeting because I have the creative ideas that can help as we create a fundraiser for our fall youth retreat."
▸ "I'm at this meeting because of my expertise in curriculum writing."
▸ "I'm at this meeting because I need to know how to get my child involved in the youth ministry this summer."
▸ "I'm at this meeting because I'm a student who has been active and invested in the ministry for two years, and I desire to see us build a student leadership team."

3. WHAT'S THE AGENDA?

Each meeting should have some type of written agenda to help people track the flow of what's going on in the meeting. Ideally, an abbreviated version should be sent to participants a few days ahead of time, asking them for input. It should either be posted so it's easily visible to participants, or each member should have a printed or electronic version. The agenda should include:

A meeting agenda template is located in Forms page 428

▸ The purpose of this meeting.
▸ The mission of the ministry to remind people to what you're moving toward. (It may be included as a footer on the meeting agenda.)
▸ If it's a small group, the names of the expected participants.
▸ Updates on previous meetings. This should be short, informative, and only include what's necessary to move this meeting's agenda forward.
▸ The topics with action steps and time allotments.

"A meeting without an objective is a meeting to cancel." Jim Rapp, *Successful Sales Meetings*

For example, a meeting to discuss a fall retreat might include the following agenda items:

Agenda item #1—Participant check in. 14 minutes
Action step: Participants have two minutes to mention the highlight of their day.

Agenda item #2—Retreat theme. 20 minutes
Action step: Brainstorm themes and choose one.

Agenda item #3—Retreat location. 15 minutes
Action step: Examine the pros and cons of four sites and choose one.

Agenda item #4—Retreat speaker. 20 minutes
Action step: Watch three YouTube clips of potential speakers and decide on one.

On the agenda, designate who is responsible for each item. For example, if you're discussing curriculum for Vacation Bible School, in the weeks leading up to the meeting assign a curriculum to each person so they can examine it and come prepared to explain it to the others in the group. Another example: You're working on a retreat for youth pastors in the community. Have one person come prepared to discuss the various site options. Another one comes prepared to present three possible speakers. And yet another comes prepared to present two schedule options.

4. WHERE AND WHEN IS THE MEETING?

Communicate where you're meeting, when the meeting starts, and how long it will last. If you're new to a church or organization, ask about their meeting culture. Some cultures start right on the minute; with others, it's important to allow a few minutes for people to arrive and socialize. Some cultures meet around food and conversation. Others want to get to the task and get out.

People are extremely busy and/or are traveling from a distance or through heavy traffic. Think about "crossroads" meetings: meetings attached to other events at the church. This reduces people's travel times and allows for greater participation.

Consider if the location of the meeting is conducive to what you want to accomplish. The room should be well lit and comfortable. If you're in someone's home, make sure the pets are put away and phones are on silent. If you're running a longer meeting where creativity is crucial, consider going to a camp or a cabin or a high floor of a skyscraper, somewhere where the context is conducive to generating creative ideas.

TYPES OF MEETINGS

In *To Do . . . Doing . . . Done: A Creative Approach to Managing Projects & Effectively Finishing What Matters Most*[2], authors Snead and Wycoff describe several types of meetings. We've adapted them to a youth ministry setting.

---

2   Snead, G.L. & Wycoff, J. (1997). *To Do . . . Doing . . . Done: A Creative Approach to Managing Projects & Effectively Finishing What Matters Most*. New York, NY: Simon & Schuster.

TYPES OF MEETINGS	IN YOUTH MINISTRY, THESE ARE:
Establishing goals and objectives	Useful when planning the vision and/or mission of the ministry, when figuring out the "scope & sequence" of curriculum for the ministry, when making changes in programming.
Gathering information	Useful when new to a ministry or when considering making a major change in the ministry.
Planning	Useful in planning the year or a specific event. By having others involved, you increase ownership. Brainstorming fits in this type.
Making decisions	Useful when you need ownership and/or approval by others. This may be a Youth Ministry Committee or a Student Leadership Committee.
Coordinating	Useful when implementing the results of the planning meeting.
Evaluating	Useful after a season of ministry or after a major event (e.g., a fundraiser).

RUNNING A MEETING

Before it begins:

A good meeting takes preparation. Here are a few things to either do or assemble ahead of time to help the meeting run smoothly.

- ▶ Write a few rules on butcher paper and keep them visible. Rules such as: "Listen for understanding. Respect the speaker. Have fun." These help everyone to operate on the same page.
- ▶ If people don't know each other—make nameplates. Take an 8.5 x 11 piece of cardstock and fold it in half. Have people's names on both sides so that people across the room and on either side can easily see their names.
- ▶ Have a plan to deal with people who dominate and those who are quiet.
- ▶ Bring plenty of toys like clay squeeze balls and fuzzy sticks (a.k.a. pipe cleaners) if it's a brainstorming or creative meeting.
- ▶ Set out munchies like M&Ms™, Starbursts™, grapes, etc. to keep hunger pangs at bay.
- ▶ Bring lots of giant sticky notes or butcher paper with wall-friendly tape to record ideas.
- ▶ Have plenty of non-bleed markers.
- ▶ Start on time. Sound like a no-brainer? It's not. If you set a precedent of starting 15 minutes late, committee members will learn to come 20 minutes

late. Set the example you want your team to follow. Arrive a little early so that you have time to say hello to people as they arrive. Come to the meeting prepared—make sure the room and any props, handouts, or equipment are ready to go. Start on time, and don't interrupt the meeting to brief latecomers on what they missed. They'll learn to be on time or miss out on important information. All you owe them is a quick "thanks for coming, this is where we are now," 15-second intro—and keep moving.

As it begins:
- Make sure you reiterate the purpose, introduce new participants, walk through the schedule, let people know when there will be breaks, and where the bathrooms are if they are new to the meeting space.
- If you're facilitating the meeting, have someone else record the notes.
- Have people go around the room and introduce themselves. It may be helpful to have them say why they think they're there.
- Define meeting etiquette or protocol. Defining protocol by Robert's Rules of Order (a detailed summary with downloads can be found at http://www.robertsrules.org) is appropriate for ministries that want to be corporate. Even if you don't follow RRO, you'll still need to define some simple rules prior to leading a meeting, or you may lead the members to come up with a set of rules at the beginning of the meeting. Rules may relate to confidentiality, respecting one another, no negativity or inappropriate sarcasm, etc. You know your group. Do what you need to do to keep it on the topic and productive.

As it gets rolling:
- Schedule the questions. Dedicate a time for questions and answers. This avoids interruptions by those who may not be taking notes and assists them in focusing on the business at hand.
- Keep things moving. Before discussions bog down, call for a time by which you will bring an issue's discussion to an end. Acknowledge that the group might not be able to resolve the issue in that time frame, and place the topic on the agenda for the next meeting. Or if you anticipate that a particular issue could monopolize the meeting, write into the agenda a time limit for discussion of it. Some issues are better resolved after a curing time, anyway.
- Designate a Parking Lot. Have one sheet of paper on the wall marked, "Parking Lot." This is where you put all ideas/issues/questions that don't deal directly with the topic at hand and will take the group off track if discussed. Example: In a retreat theme-planning meeting, someone asks about transportation. It doesn't deal with the purpose of the meeting but is worthwhile. Ask the group if they need to address it now or can it be

put in the Parking Lot for later. At the end of the meeting, go through the items listed on the Parking Lot sheet. It's surprising how many of the items will be dealt with during the course of the meeting without ever taking the conversation down rabbit trails.

▶ Sometimes it's a person, not an issue, who bogs down the discussion. Avert that danger by letting the group know at the start of the meeting that there are only 10 minutes (or 30, or 60) for discussion on any given topic. If someone goes on and on, give him a three-minute warning before you request him to stop speaking. If you have to, gently intervene with a request for others to share their opinions. If people regularly disrupt meetings in this way, talk to them afterward, and individually. Let them know their input is important, but ask that they respect others' needs to offer input as well.

▶ Who's Doing What: As you work through the agenda, determine who will be responsible for carrying out the decisions made. Write down deadlines when necessary.

▶ End on time. If you say your meeting will end at 8 p.m., end at 8 p.m. No exceptions. Like a good counselor, keep track of the time so the end of the meeting won't surprise anyone. At 7:55 p.m., for instance, say something like, "It looks like our time is almost over. Let's wrap up with . . ." or "We can pick up here next time." If you don't end on time, people won't want to come. Let the group know the meeting is officially finished when you reach the predetermined time. Assure them they can stay on and chat or finish off the snacks, but that the meeting is officially ended. People then understand that their obligation is complete, and they won't feel imposed upon.

▶ Plan a follow-up meeting to tie up loose ends. This is especially important if it's a planning or coordinating meeting.

After it's over:
▶ Provide follow-up notes. After the meeting, email notes and decisions within two days. This helps people follow up on what they agreed to do.

▶ Follow up with attendees who have tasks to complete before the next meeting. Help them be successful committee members. Be clear about action steps required prior to the next meeting.

BRAINSTORMING MEETINGS

Because youth ministries are often creating new programs and events, brainstorming meetings especially can be very helpful. The goal of a brainstorming meeting is creativity. If you're trying to come up with a new ministry, new theme, or a new

YOUTH MINISTRY MANAGEMENT TOOLS 2.0

model of ministry, consider using the discussion technique of brainstorming. In a lively group it can feel like a party. Here are few rules for fruitful brainstorming:

- There are no bad ideas. Ideas shouldn't be evaluated during a brainstorming session—that's why it's called *brainstorming*.
- Be kind when someone comes up with a really bad idea. Assure them you're not laughing at them; you're laughing with them. Sometimes what seems like a really bad idea can lead to a great idea (this is why there are no bad ideas).
- Keep the brainstorming session long enough to get good ideas, but short enough to maintain energy.

FORMS
- Conflict of Interest Disclosure Form
- Meeting Planning Worksheet
- Meeting Agenda Worksheet

To kick off a brainstorming session, gather a group of creative, free thinkers around a table for a specified amount of time. They may be a mix of leaders, students, and even some artistic folks who aren't part of your ministry (yet). Before your group arrives, tape plenty of newsprint to the walls and place colorful markers (that won't bleed through to the wall) on the table. Spread across the center of the table small toys like Slinkys, Koosh balls, Silly Putty, Legos, and Play-Doh. Giving people something to occupy their hands frees their minds for creative thinking. Offer snacks and drinks if you can. Have high energy music playing.

1. Begin by thanking the attendees for coming. Invite them to play and eat.
2. Restate the focus for the meeting. (Since you've sent the agenda in advance, this will be old news to some—unfortunately, not the majority.)
3. Precede the brainstorming session with an activity or question that catches the group off guard. For instance, if your focus is the theme for a retreat, ask them to draw a picture of what a retreat looks like to them. Laughing at each other's pictures breaks the ice and readies the planners to think outside of traditional lines.
4. Shift gears into actual brainstorming by writing on the newsprint some of the crazy ideas that surfaced from the opening activity. Assure everyone that no idea is too bizarre to be recorded on the newsprint. You never know when a ridiculous idea becomes the gateway to a great idea. Like the time in one ministry when a comment about pirates and Peter Pan led to planning a retreat that was a weekend-long scavenger/adventure hunt for cabin groups. They exchanged the pirate part for more of an Indiana Jones feel. The kids loved getting close with their small groups, felt challenged by thinking through clues, and enjoyed competing. All this from a comment about Peter Pan.

FIVE ESSENTIALS FOR LEADERSHIP MEETINGS

What sets the novice youth worker apart from the veteran? Paying attention to five essential planning ingredients as you put together meetings, and answering the questions or completing the tasks related to each ingredient. Quickly answering the questions listed can put you well on your way to a successful meeting. [See Form: Quick Start Meeting Guide]

Meeting Planning Worksheet page 426

Leadership Meetings

DETERMINING GOALS	
Purposeful planning	• What is the goal of the meeting? • What is the desired outcome? • Who will participate? How many? • How long does it need to last? • Where is the best place to meet? • When is the best time for this meeting (based on above answers)? • What resources will I contribute to the meeting? • Do I need to receive anything from the participants (either before or during the meeting)?
DESIGNING DETAILS	
Coordinated details	• How are my goals best accomplished? • When and how do I deliver the meeting agenda to participants? • Will there be any costs? • What do I need to do ahead of time to secure and make the most of the location? • What food shall I offer to attendees? • What materials do I need to prepare ahead to bring?
GETTING OUT THE WORD—INFORM AND ENERGIZE PARTICIPANTS (Tailor promotion to the group size, makeup, and the personality of the occasion.)	
Directed promotion	• Use one or all of the regular avenues of communication in your church: phone calls, group texts, memos, email or snail-mail invitations, announcements, one-on-one invitations, etc.
PURPOSE-DRIVEN CONTENT	
Focused programming	• Provide the agenda in advance. • Start on time. • Define meeting etiquette or protocol. • Keep things moving. • Use creativity to make meetings fun. • Define action points. • End on time. • Provide follow-up notes.
PRAYER	
Trust in God	Ask for wisdom, flexibility, and growth. Pray about issues raised during the meeting.

12 INTERNS

CHAPTER OVERVIEW

You've just come off your sixth all-day event this year, and it's only February. You did everything—designed the fliers, collected the permission slips and the money, drove the van, and cleaned up the mess. The volunteer team was great during the event, but they all left two minutes after it was over. As you're sitting around waiting for the senior pastor's daughter to be picked up (again), you think to yourself, "It would be nice to have some help I could count on, some kind of partner in this craziness. Someone to mentor and coach." Then, in your semi-slumbering state, you have an epiphany. *Intern* blazes across your mind. You vow to pursue this as soon as you're fully awake, along with confronting the pastor about consistently forgetting what time events end.

As you begin this process, ask yourself these questions:

▶ Do I have enough experience to develop another youth worker? What will an aspiring youth worker learn from spending time with this ministry and with me?

▶ Do I have the time to develop and guide another youth worker? In the beginning, supervising an intern will take more of your time than doing it yourself. You have to be committed to the process and not see this as hiring grunt labor.

▶ Is the church or organization supportive of an intern? And, is it willing to take on the accompanying risks?

▶ Is the church willing to provide financial compensation to the intern? (This can be housing/meals and a small stipend, tuition credit to a college or a seminary, or a salary.)

▶ Does it believe in developing future leaders for ministry; is it willing to invest in someone who will go and serve somewhere else?

▶ Do I have a clear job description with measurable goals?

▶ Does the church staff understand the job description of a youth ministry intern? Or, does the church staff assign miscellaneous tasks to the intern – helping in the office, setting up chairs, etc.?

▶ Is my church willing to let this person fail as well as succeed? Interns are rookies. As they learn and grow, there are bound to be mistakes and messes as well as successes. Is the church willing to extend grace?

GETTING THE CHURCH ON BOARD

In youth ministry an internship means introducing someone to ministry by exposing this person to short-term, real-life experiences and then helping them constructively reflect on those experiences. It's a season of guided supervision, where interns can learn from both their successes and failures. It's a time to discern whether full-time youth ministry is the path the intern should follow. All of this is done with a supervisor and a church committed to the internship process.

If internships are a new idea to your organization, you'll need to do some preliminary work before you bring an intern on board. When you meet with the decision-making body of your organization, have the following prepared:

▶ A narrative of how internships serve the larger Church. If the church is focused only on their local congregation, an internship might be a tough sell. You'll need to help them to think more broadly about the Church with a capital "C." They may not see the direct, long-term benefits of investing in an intern who will eventually serve elsewhere, but the Church will be stronger because of their investment.

▶ An explanation of how the supervising relationship works between you and the intern.

▶ A description of the type of internship and the various experiences the intern will receive during his or her term.

▶ A budget that clarifies the cost of an intern (depending on the type): stipend, housing, tuition reimbursement, transportation, conferences, etc.

If your church had an awful experience with interns in the past, you may need to do some repair work first. Explore what went wrong and how you will address that this time around. It might be a better screening process, clarifying the job description, strengthening the supervision, or helping the rest of the church leadership understand the intern's role.

[In the forms section: See Internships: Assessing Organizational Readiness]

PREPARING FOR THE INTERNSHIP

An *internship* is a process of preparation and discernment before someone enters youth ministry as a professional. An *internship* is *not* a source of cheap labor, a chance to give the pastor's kid a summer job, a way to get a substitute so you can have the summer to travel and speak and have time off.

> The word internship usually refers to real-world work experience where students take on temporary roles as workers in an organization and reflect on these experiences in an academic setting.
>
> *Internship Success*, Marianne Ehrlich Green (VGM Career Horizons 1997)

An undefined internship can force you to wrestle with the VBS director or any number of other staff members and volunteers to win your intern's time. Like the punch line of a bad Dilbert cartoon, people remark, "After all, you are the *intern*. What else are you doing with your time?"

STEP 1: DETERMINE THE TYPE OF INTERNSHIP

If you're working with a university or seminary, you need to determine what their internship expectations are: how many hours do they expect, what kind of experiences do they require, and what percentage of the student's time is dedicated to the internship? Schools offer two types of internships:

Concurrent

The student is taking classes while interning. This can work if the school is nearby or offers online courses. If the school is more than 30 minutes from the site, it takes a major commitment from the intern to make sure the internship is a priority.

Full Time

The student is dedicated fully to the ministry. A full-time internship usually occurs during the summer or over a semester. This type is helpful if your site is located quite a distance from a school or if their complete attention is needed for the position, e.g., a camp internship. In cases where the church cannot afford a large stipend, interns may pick up a part-time job in the community to help cover expenses.

In addition to timing, internships can differ by format and structure. Here are some different ways internships can be structured:

Shadow internship

The intern follows the supervisor around and watches what life is like in that profession or role. This type emphasizes observing and assessing. There's very little hands-on participation and, thus, should be a short-term internship. Constant debriefing of every major experience exposes the intern to the supervisor's motives for making choices, the rationale for handling a situation in a certain way, and other available options and why they weren't used.

A shadow internship might be appropriate when:

▸ A high school junior feels a call into youth ministry. She also thinks that you have the easiest job in the world—give a talk on the weekend and spend the rest of the time hanging out at Chipotle with students. She needs to see behind the curtain.

▸ A younger high school student wants to be a counselor-in-training at your camp. He's not old enough nor does he have enough experience to handle the job. Capitalize on his eagerness by inviting him to "shadow" a veteran counselor for a week or two.

▸ A seminary student is taking a pastoral care and counseling course and would like to observe several sessions of family counseling. (Participants must grant permission.)

Project internship

This focuses on a special project that the youth pastor is eager to get going but for which he or she just doesn't have the time. Voilà! The intern takes it on. The project can be anything from jump-starting a middle school program to reworking the confirmation curriculum to starting a drama team. Interns can experience a lot of pride in taking an idea from creation to implementation. The danger is that when they become the sole youth pastor they quickly realize that although they know how to design a great after-school program, they have no idea how to run a parents' meeting or how to counsel a kid in crisis.

Situations where a project internship is appropriate:

▸ A college student who's grown up in the church and is now double-majoring in youth ministry and theater. He'll be home for the summer and would love to help you fulfill your dream of having a college and high school drama team that would perform both in the youth ministry and the larger church.

▸ You're looking at your twelfth annual week at camp at the end of July, and you have no energy or creativity to put toward it. You recall that as you interviewed one of the interns, she said that one of her dreams is to design a camp. Too good to be true.

▸ The church is drawing families with adolescents who are on the autism spectrum. Your team has limited knowledge and experience in this area, but desire to serve these families. A project intern can research what other youth ministries and nonprofits have developed and propose several models, along with action steps.

Associate internship

With this type, interns explore all the areas of youth ministry—a final step before heading into full-time ministry. Along with overseeing a wide variety of tasks and challenges, they're exposed to staff meetings, church leader meetings, budget development, crisis counseling with students (when appropriate), and conflict resolution. There are high expectations, increasing levels of challenge, and regular, constructive feedback. It is expected that this intern will be seen as vital to the mission of the church.

Situations where this internship would be appropriate:

▸ A youth ministry student at a university or seminary.

▸ A volunteer from the team who's taking steps toward a midlife career change into ministry.

STEP 2: CREATE THE POSITION DESCRIPTION

Once you know the type of internship you desire, you're ready to develop the position description. This will eventually be supplemented by a learning contract with the actual intern. Before you pull out a job description to erase *volunteer* and replace it with *intern,* sit down and begin answering these questions:

▸ Who will be the intern's supervisor?

▸ How long does the internship last?
  • Is it full time during the summer? Part time for a year? Does it run concurrently with school, or does the intern commit a block of time (e.g., one year before starting seminary)?

▸ How many hours per week will he or she be working?
  • Does the internship pay enough to live on, or will the intern need a part-time job to supplement income?
  • If the internship runs concurrently with school, how many hours a week is it feasible for the intern to work? Is the church willing to be flexible when finals roll around?

▸ What age group will the intern work with and why?
  • Tweens? Middle school? High school? College?

- What program(s) will the intern work with?
  - Vacation Bible School, day camp, small groups, worship ministry, dance team?
- Will there be some sort of payment?
  - Is there a salary or stipend?
  - Will room and board be provided? If so, with whom will the intern live?
  - Will the intern need a car? If not, will he or she be reimbursed for mileage?
  - Will there be reimbursement for travel and entertainment expenses?
  - Will he or she be covered by the church's insurance or is the intern covered by school insurance? Can the intern be added to the church's insurance plan? Will Workers' Compensation cover any injuries that may occur?

As part of the position description, identify clear objectives that will be focused on during the internship. These will eventually be part of the learning contract between you as the supervisor and the intern. Note that all are measurable objectives.

By the end of this internship, the intern should be able to:

- Articulate a philosophy of youth ministry.
- Identify the key characteristics of adolescence, as well as the impact of family, society, and church on adolescents.
- Explain the rationale behind the model of youth ministry the church employs.
- Articulate the demographics of the community and the services available through the local community.
- Describe the importance of the youth minister, whether professional or volunteer, in effective leadership of adolescents and their families.
- Write and lead an hour-long Bible study appropriate for senior high students.
- Initiate exploratory conversations with parents and with several subcultures of adolescents.
- Develop and produce a worship experience.
- Put together a three-month program that includes a variety of events and topics geared toward adolescents' felt and real needs. It may include Sunday school, confirmation, and weekly activities.
- Develop and manage a youth ministry budget.
- Run an effective meeting.

- Recruit and interview potential volunteers.
- Conduct a conflict resolution session with an adolescent and his or her parents.

By the end of this internship, the intern will have experienced:

- Weekly church staff meetings in order to better understand how the whole church operates.
- A weekly Bible study as both an observer and a leader.
- Participating in the organization and leadership of a weeklong missions trip.
- Producing or utilizing a variety of communication tools: fliers, church and youth ministry announcements on the Web site, calendars, permission slips, group text messaging service.
- Participating in strategy and evaluation meetings.

> A SUCCESSFUL INTERNSHIP requires clear definition—identifying a specific type of intern and specific tasks to achieve.

During this internship, the intern can expect:

- Weekly or biweekly meetings with the supervisor, which will include constructive feedback.
- Monthly meetings with the senior pastor or executive director.
- Exposure to the full scope of the ministry, including administrative areas (budget development, fundraising, communication), the recruiting and development of volunteer staff, church staff meetings, congregational meetings, and counseling appointments (when appropriate).
- Timely payment of a salary or stipend.

During this internship, the church or organization can expect that the intern will:

- Show up on time to all meetings or responsibilities and be appropriately dressed.
- Prepare appropriately for the ministry situation.
- Maintain an exemplary lifestyle during the internship.
- Immediately inform the supervisor of any areas of concern or conflict.

STEP 3: RECRUIT AND SCREEN THE INTERN

There are several ways to recruit potential interns:

- ▸ *Look within.* Is there a student or young adult who is trying to discern his or her interest and passion for student ministry?
- ▸ *Look at local universities and seminaries.* Christian universities with youth ministry majors or minors usually post job openings. Send yours to the chairs of the departments, as well as to the career counseling offices. (Sometimes students interested in going into youth ministry will major in another field.) Also, post your internship with local community colleges or universities.
- ▸ *Look at your denominational seminary.* If you have a strong denominational affiliation and are looking for several interns, sometimes it helps to actually recruit live on a campus. "Cold call" students are more likely to consider your ministry's internship if they have a conversation with you. This also helps the seminary field supervision/internship supervisors to get to know you and keep an eye out for potential interns who would be a good fit.
- ▸ *Look at other youth ministries.* Are there colleagues who have students who might be potential interns in your ministry? This is somewhat controversial, but many schools won't let students who have grown up at a church return to do their internships at that same church — because it's difficult for these interns to be seen as emerging professionals in their field. Rather, they are often seen as "so and so's child." Plus, it's good for these interns to have a church experience outside of what they were raised in. Perhaps some intern-swapping might work in your local network.

Interviewing Prospective Interns

Letter of
Reference
for Applicant
page 437

Thoroughly interview prospective interns (i.e., hire in haste, repent in leisure). Check all references. (See **Letter of Reference for Applicant**.) This is critical and could save you from legal trouble should you hire someone who ends up making poor choices. You need to be able to show that you properly vetted this person. Be aware of your predisposition as you interview them. You may think this person's incredible based on his or her résumé and youth pastor's recommendation, so you don't really pay attention to the Resident Assistant's comment that he or she has been involved in some questionable behavior. You imagine that merely means college pranks. Ignoring that reference means you fail to find out that he or she has been found guilty of stealing money from other rooms in the hall. You realize that you should have paid better attention after he or she is discovered pocketing $75 from the car-wash fundraiser.

For best results, have the intern interview with several people in the church—several parents (who can be a promoter of the intern and help break the ice with others in the church), the senior pastor (so he or she not only remembers that you're bringing on an intern this summer, but can advocate for them), and some of the students (so they're familiar with the intern before he or she arrives).

SUPERVISING AN INTERN

Supervising an intern involves a lot of time and intentionality on your part. First-time supervisors are often surprised that it often increases their workload, rather than reduces it, at least at the beginning of the internship. At the beginning, you will need to have the intern shadow you, then observe him or her as the intern tries out leading different elements of the ministry, and then debrief the experiences, all of which are time intensive. Realize that the time you're investing now will have an impact on how this intern ministers in the future.

STEP 1: DEVELOP GOALS

Stephen Covey says, "Begin with the end in mind." Revisit the position description with the intern and talk about what he or she wants to accomplish or experience by the end of the internship. Talk about what you would like to see accomplished in the ministry. How will both parties be different because of this experience? Write it all down. Ministry memories are short, especially when it comes to measurable objectives. If the intern is a student, many schools will require a learning covenant between the site supervisor, the field education supervisor (at the school) and the intern, which includes goals (along with work expectations, financial arrangements, supervision—who and when, and ministry hours, including time off).

Consider grouping goals in the following categories:

▶ Knowledge: this includes theological reflection, reading, conferences, webinars, etc.
▶ Skills: writing Bible studies, leading small groups, preaching, teaching, strategic planning, etc.
▶ Character qualities: patience, control of temper, integrity, trustworthiness, faithfulness, etc.

Develop the goals in collaboration with the intern. Make sure you look at his or her time, abilities, motivations, strengths, resources available, and so on.

STEP 2: CLARIFY EXPECTATIONS

Clarify at the beginning, and then several times throughout the internship:

▶ Is church attendance an expectation, beyond youth ministry responsibilities?
▶ What meetings and gatherings must interns attend on a regular basis?

- What meetings should interns attend once or twice for the experience?
- When do you expect interns to be in the office? What about days off? Compensation time for long events like camp or a service trip?
- What is acceptable dress in the church? What about when interns are with students?
- What are relational expectations for the intern? What do relationships with students look like? Parents? Volunteers?
- Are there social media guidelines?
- Who has a say regarding the intern's time, e.g., can the church administrator, custodian, or children's minister give him or her assignments?
- How does the intern gain access to resources—administrative help, church vehicles?
- How does the intern pay for meetings with students or leaders?
- How will you deal with conflict? (It's always better to be proactive than reactive on this one.)
- How will the relationship be terminated if things don't work out as planned?

STEP 3: SET UP AN ONGOING FEEDBACK PROCESS

The best internships are when the intern and supervisor meet regularly and often, and when constructive feedback is given immediately. If you have difficulty delivering tough feedback, then don't supervise an intern. Would you want to be operated on by a surgeon who only received "encouragement" during his or her residency and not coaching? You need to be comfortable calling out the good things an intern is doing and helping him or her address growth areas. The evaluation should be both results-oriented (what happened?) and learning-oriented (why did it happen?). The intern should also have the freedom to give feedback to you, the supervisor. Is there something he or she needs, or would like, from you? More time? More assistance? More responsibility?

> BUILD INTO YOUR INTERNSHIP clear goals, expectations, an evaluation process, and a grace-full way to conclude an internship.

Besides giving feedback, your regular meetings should help interns integrate what they're learning (or learned) in school and what they're experiencing on the job. Sometimes an internship can reinforce what they've learned. Other times, there's a conflict between theory and practice that can cause angst for an intern and he or she needs some help working through it.

These meetings, whether formal or informal, can be a helpful time for an intern to work through a call to ministry. It's possible that the internship helps clarify that he or she is not cut out for ministry, or at least ministry in this form. It's also possible that he or she falls in love with ministry and doesn't want to go back to school. As tempting as it is to have the intern stay involved in the ministry, encourage him or her to finish an education.

ENDING AN INTERNSHIP

Officially conclude an internship through evaluation and celebration. Even if the person stays on, acknowledge the transition into another capacity.

MEET TO DEBRIEF THE INTERNSHIP.

▸ Discuss the objectives set at the beginning of the internship. (This should be the conclusion of an ongoing discussion and shouldn't have any surprises.)

▸ Talk about what the intern's relationships with students should look like, e.g., can they continue to connect with them via text or Facebook? If the intern does, remind him or her to keep you in the loop with emerging areas of concern.

▸ Ask what suggestions the intern has for future interns.

▸ Fill out any paperwork required by the academic institution evaluating the intern, as well as the church. Often, the school's field education supervisor will be part of this, either physically or virtually.

▸ In this final evaluation, note the progress the intern has made, his or her success in facing increasingly complicated tasks and experiences, and some particular challenge he or she either did well at or learned from.

> FORMS
> ▸ Intern Application
> ▸ Developing an Intern Job Description – Worksheet
> ▸ Letter of Reference for Intern Applicant
> ▸ Self Evaluation
> ▸ Intern Supervisor Evaluation
> ▸ Internships: Assessing Organizational Readiness

(See Intern Self-Evaluation and Intern Supervisor Evaluation.)

CELEBRATE

Let the ministry and the church celebrate this person's season with you through a party or through special acknowledgment at a church service. Launch a formal commissioning tradition if this fits with the philosophy and theology of your church. This helps the congregation understand that they are part of the broader Church and are sending out youth pastors to serve throughout the world.

13 TEAMS

CHAPTER OVERVIEW
- ▶ Building a Healthy Team
- ▶ Recruiting Volunteers
- ▶ Life-Cycle of Team Members

Sometimes it seems youth workers use the revolving door of the church more than any other staff person. What we can't understand is why youth workers burn out when they get to lead exhausting lock-ins with really bad pizza and generic soda, sing never-ending choruses, and play a hundred games of Uno during *loooong* bus rides, sleep on dirt floors during weeklong mission trips, and run poorly attended fundraisers. (Then again, maybe we *can* understand why.)

Perhaps youth ministers can survive five and ten and fifteen years in the same church when they experience a synergy of:

- ▶ team support among staff, church leaders, and parents;
- ▶ personal maturity that affects how they manage the risks inherent to youth ministry;
- ▶ practical preparation to pursue their calling.

> TWO STONECUTTERS WERE ASKED what they were doing.
>
> The first said, "I'm cutting this stone into blocks."
>
> The second replied, "I'm on a team that's building a cathedral."

A **strong team** doesn't happen by accident. It takes intentional recruitment, careful screening, discernment of when to say no to certain people and yes to others, and lots of prayer. It takes knowing when it's time to bring on an intern. It takes being committed to investing in others. It takes determination to share visibility, praises, and even the credit. Yes—share the credit. In fact, give it away.

> "A TEAM IS a small number of people with complementary skills who are committed to a common purpose, performance goals, and approach for which they are mutually accountable."
> Katzenbach and Smith, *The Wisdom of Teams: Creating the High Performance Organization*

BUILDING A HEALTHY TEAM

It's 3 p.m. on a Sunday afternoon. You're standing in the church parking lot with a smelly sleeping bag, a half-empty bag of Doritos, and the insides of a couple of cans of shaving cream.

You've just sent the last student home from the retreat, and you look around at an exhausted group of volunteers. Somebody suggests heading out for burgers and you think, "Bed or burgers?" You know in a second what your decision will be—as bone tired as you are, you want to spend just a little more time with this group of people to hear their stories and to celebrate the weekend.

Because that's what it means to be part of a team with members who are committed to each other.

> "IT'S DIFFICULT TO WORK IN A GROUP when you're omnipotent."
> —Q, "Star Trek: The Next Generation"

Being a team member is about standing up at each other's weddings. It's about getting up before sunrise in order to get to the hospital to pray together before a member of your team has surgery. It's about bringing over lasagna to a home whose cook is down with a broken leg, or a big green supper salad with homemade bread and apple crisp when a baby is born. (In fact, you may want to make cooking a qualification for being on your team.) It's about helping them move, again!

Team building is about creating community together. It's about doing ministry together.

WHY YOU NEED A TEAM

The needs of adolescents and the adults who work with them make team ministry essential.

THE NEED OF THIS GENERATION

Whereas adolescents used to have all sorts of adults with whom to connect—parents, grandparents, Scout leaders, teachers, coaches, Sunday school teachers—these days those connections are fewer and seem to be more challenging. Students have much more coming at them, but they have fewer places to talk about what's going on in their lives.

THE NEED FOR MULTIPLICATION

Experience shows that a person can develop only a limited number of relationships in the limited amount of time available. That means you have a choice—you can pour your life into 15 kids, and at the end of the year you'll have affected 15 kids. Or you can spend your time developing five or 10 volunteers (and five kids on the side because that's why you're doing this in the first place), and those 10 volunteers in turn nurture five or 10 kids each. At the end of the year you'll have reached anywhere from 30 to 105 kids and five to 10 adults.

FASTRACK

Unless our youth ministries are going to remain very small, we're going to need some help.

THE NEED TO USE OUR GIFTS

Youth workers do everything from designing brochures to reserving buses to counseling kids in crisis. In other words, we spend a lot of energy doing things that pull us away from what we're good at because of what Charles Hummel calls the "tyranny of the urgent." Volunteers can help out by bringing their gifts and passions to the team. If one of your weak areas is graphic design, for instance, and yet you find yourself spending hours designing camp graphics, pray and search for someone in your church who has a background in design. He may never have thought about volunteering with the youth ministry because he's scared to death of having a conversation with a high school student. But he'd love to help out using his gift in design (and maybe you'll even end up with a T-shirt everyone really likes). The task gets done faster and the result is professional. You're freed up to prepare the messages, and he's using his gifts for the kingdom in a way he hadn't realized he could.

THE NEED TO USE COMMON SENSE

Wherever two or more are gathered, there is more protection than if there was just one. Youth ministry tends to be both relational and risky. No youth worker these days should lead an overnighter with students without another ministry-approved adult. No new volunteer should lead a group without first shadowing a veteran to watch and learn. No veteran volunteer should squeeze 10 kids into her five-seat car. The wise youth worker—and the youth worker determined to stay at one job more than two years—thinks beforehand about the consequences of scenarios like these. Risk is real. Accidents happen. We are working with a generation that shirks risk and can push you if you are not careful into placing them into harm's way. Think twice. Pray hard. Surround yourself with wise staff.

FASTRACK

Your requirements for a volunteer's weekly time commitment must be long enough to form relationships with students and yet reasonable to appeal to volunteers.

CREATIVE ARTS TEAM POSITION DESCRIPTION

Worship team leader. Gives direction to the team, both on a personal and a performance ministry level. 5 hours a week

Band members. Guitar, drums, keyboard, etc. 4 hours a week, includes rehearsal time

Drama leader. Develops a team of students to perform once a month. 3 hours a week

Media Coordinator. Guides students and adults who develop media for youth ministry projects. 4 hours a week

Tech Coordinator. Students and adults who manage all the AV and support all ministry gatherings. 4 hours a week

Director of a student arts festival. An entrepreneurial type who understands the importance of the arts in communicating the gospel to this generation, who knows how to organize and promote a festival, and who can coach a team of volunteers to assist in the development. Varying time commitment

SMALL GROUPS

Adult leaders. Adults who meet with a group of three to eight students on a weekly basis for Bible study, prayer, discussion, and application. 4 hours a week

Student leaders. Current members of the high school ministry who desire to develop their leadership skills by leading a small group of their peers. 4 hours a week

Coach. An adult volunteer who helps shepherd the student small group leaders. 4 hours a week

MAKE WAY FOR VOLUNTEERS

Before recruiting volunteers, take time to lay the groundwork. A strong foundation minimizes future errors. Granted, not many people ever see the foundation, but they can sure tell whether or not you had one as soon as the first major storm hits (and the storms will hit).

Laying the groundwork involves CLEARLY . . .

DESCRIBING THE ROLES

List all the roles (both existing and potential) for volunteers in the youth ministry. Let your imagination run wild. What have you been dying to see happen in the ministry but don't have the time or perhaps the ability to pull off? Jog your vision by thinking in categories, such as area of service or time required to do the service. People seeking to volunteer need (and deserve) to know what they are getting into.

DEFINING THE EXPECTATIONS FOR VOLUNTEERS

Set your phone to DO NOT DISTURB, and head out to Starbucks, Caribou or your favorite local coffee shop with your iPad, scratch pad, or your favorite new gadget. However you choose to do it, get some uninterrupted

HANDS-ON TEAM

Greeters. Volunteers who make new students feel welcome, gather permission slips, and hand out fliers. They also connect with adults or students who may have questions. 2 hours a week

Hosts. Parents who provide both food and a place for small groups to meet, either on a regular basis or for special occasions. Variable time commitment

Drivers. Parents who chauffeur the middle schoolers to various ministry events. 4 hours a month (requires pre-screening and driver safety education)

Office help. Adults with an administrative bent who can organize and maintain a student database, send out mailings, call on event details, follow up on explanations on medical release forms, and assist with other office-based administrative tasks. Variable time commitment

SPECIALTY TEAMS

Light and sound. A team of students who run the sound and media on retreats and special occasions.

Technology. Includes an adult or student who can put your messages on Keynote, PowerPoint, ProPresenter or other presentation software.

Photography. Adults and students who take pictures of ministry events to be used in social media, Web sites and other special presentations. (Hint: Dropbox is a great tool for organizing and sharing the pictures you take for your ministry.)

Graphic design. Either a student or an adult with a strong graphic design bent who can put together e-newsletters, ministry brochures, Web graphics, fliers, posters, banners, birthday cards, welcome cards, and so on.

Games. Adults or students who run weekly competitions or monthly events, like three-on-three basketball tournaments for outreach, the Valentine's Day parent-student 10K run, or the annual senior-citizens-versus-the-senior-highers sand volleyball competition.

Fundraising. Adults with marketing, accounting, and entrepreneurial experience to run several fundraisers—or one large fundraiser—each year. Make sure they work with your church treasurer to stay within the policies and procedures your ministry needs to have in place for fundraising.

Special events and projects. Adults and students who develop service projects, missions trips, special events, or parent-student events.

Driving. Adults who help transport students. To screen drivers use the Driver Application (page 454)

Driver
Application
page 454

time to write out your expectations for volunteers in youth ministry—expectations for spiritual maturity, lifestyle, student investment, and participation.

RELATIONAL EXPECTATIONS

Support your volunteers by clearly describing what kind of relationship you expect them to have with students. Without guidance the extroverts will try to build a life-changing relationship with every kid in the group, and the introverts will merely show up and sit in the back. Okay, that's an overgeneralization—but volunteers do want to know if they're to meet with students only during the scheduled meeting times, or if you expect them to contact students outside those gatherings. Are weekly phone calls an expectation? What about texting? What about social media interaction? Do you want your small group leaders to get the students together for an activity once a month? Or would you be thrilled if a leader does it once a year? If initiating extra activities with students is among your expectations for volunteers, consider offering a small stipend to cover expenses—fast food, gas, etc.

What expectations do you have of a volunteer's relationship to you? Do they need to meet with you on a regular basis? It's important that volunteers can regularly have access to you, one-on-one, to share their joys as well as their frustrations. Set up regular evaluations where they can evaluate both you and the ministry. Remember, you're there to serve them as they serve God through ministering to kids.

SPIRITUAL MATURITY EXPECTATIONS

What level of spiritual maturity are you looking for in volunteers? Is it okay for some of the volunteers to be new believers? Seekers? Or do they need to have major portions of Scripture tattooed to their forearms before you'll even consider them?

A good rule of thumb: Volunteers who have direct and regular contact with students (e.g., a small-group leader) need a fairly well-developed faith that they can easily share. A behind-the-scenes volunteer who does data entry or serves as the media technician can be a new or young believer, or still searching, depending on your ministry philosophy. The

SMART TIP—KEEP THE CULTURE IN MIND

For volunteers who believe that spending time together is more important than starting on schedule, a 6 p.m. meeting won't start till everyone has informally traded news and enjoyed a few munchies. For volunteers who live by their smartphone schedule, a 6 p.m. meeting that doesn't get rolling until 6:15 p.m. frustrates and discourages them. By placing on the agenda crucial, relationship-building activities like eating and socializing, you honor both styles . . . and even keep to the schedule. But—be sure to be ready and start on time. We youth leaders often have the reputation of being late and unprepared for most things in our life. OUCH.

main objective of your youth ministry is probably not evangelization of adult volunteers, though. Make sure you keep your main thing the main thing.

LIFESTYLE EXPECTATIONS

Think through the following lifestyle concerns. What is your personal view on each one? What are your church's expectations regarding each lifestyle for its staff and volunteers?

Alcohol
▸ What is the view of your church or organization about alcohol? What is your view?
▸ Can someone attending a 12-step program for alcohol issues also work with your students?
▸ Does your church have a policy about alcohol being served at church events?
▸ If volunteers must sign a ministry covenant of any sort, does it include a statement regarding alcohol?

Drug Use
▸ How long does someone need to be "clean" before they can work with students?
▸ Can someone attending a 12-step program be involved with your students?

Sexuality
▸ What's your ministry's sexual ethic?
▸ What is the view of your church or organization about sexual identity? What is your view? Do people's views on this affect their ability to be in leadership positions?
▸ What is the view of your church or organization about premarital or extramarital relations? Do people's views on this affect their ability to be in leadership positions?
▸ What's your policy on potential leaders who aren't married living together?

> WE LIKE TO MAKE A DISTINCTION between our private and public lives and say, "Whatever I do in my private life is nobody else's business." But anyone trying to live a spiritual life will soon discover that the most personal is the most universal, the most hidden is the most public, and the most solitary is the most communal.
> —Henri Nouwen, *Bread for the Journey*

IDENTIFY SPIRITUAL GIFTS AND AREAS OF INTEREST

Many tools for discerning spiritual gifts are currently in use in churches. Find out right away if your church offers workshops or adult classes on spiritual gifts.

Prospective volunteers who have taken the classes may already know that youth ministry suits their interests and abilities.

You can use the following questions to help volunteers identify their areas of interest and discern the most appropriate area in which they might serve.

AREA OF SERVICE

Find out what triggers a person to dream and plan and take action. That arena is where she'll find most satisfaction and where you'll get her best work.

- What keeps you awake at night (beside too much coffee)?
- What do you find yourself pounding the table over?
- What would your friends say is a recurring theme in your conversations?
- What topics do you find yourself drawn to read about?
- What Web trail do you find yourself following—music, movies, youth culture, counseling?

SPIRITUAL GIFTS AND NATURAL ABILITIES

Sometimes these overlap . . .

- What activities brought you joy, energy, or success in early childhood? In grade school? Middle school? High school? College? As a young adult?
- What are the recurring themes of your memories?
- What verbs do you find yourself using—organizing, creating, discussing, building, performing, writing, talking, thinking, listening, writing, drawing?
- What patterns do you discern?
- What insights have you gained in spiritual gifts surveys or from sermons or Christian teaching?
- From the following list, choose those spiritual gifts you feel you already use. (Some of these gifts are alluded to rather than named in the Bible.)

  - Administration
  - Creative communication
  - Counseling
  - Discernment
  - Encouragement
  - Evangelism
  - Helping
  - Hospitality
  - Leadership
  - Listening
  - Mediation
  - Mercy
  - Shepherding
  - Teaching

In what way have those close to you (who are honest with you) affirmed those gifts?

STAFF REQUIREMENTS AND EXPECTATIONS

- ▶ What level of participation do you expect from team members?
- ▶ Do you require church membership and worship attendance? Can leaders worship at another church?
- ▶ Do all ministry roles carry the same expectations for participation?
- ▶ Do they need to attend weekly staff meetings? Quarterly volunteer training events?
- ▶ Do they need to attend retreats, mission trips, and camps?
- ▶ How often do you expect them to meet one-on-one with you?
- ▶ How long do you expect them to serve?

EXPECTATIONS ON LENGTH OF SERVICE

Many people hesitate to volunteer for fear they're signing up for an unending commitment. Write into the job description how long you're asking them to serve. Some ministries require commitment for one school year: leadership training and development in mid-August, ministry kick-off in early September, and ministry closeout in early June. You'll get more people willing to volunteer if they know it's not for the rest of their lives. (Little do they know that it is.) It's hard because it's likely you'll never have enough volunteers, but give them a chance to periodically evaluate their role and either step aside or re-up. You'll have a much healthier team.

A summer team of interns comes in from June through August to allow the regular leaders to take the summer off to relax. One ministry that used the school-year commitment had leaders who stayed an average of three years. The leaders started with a group of sixth graders and stayed with them until they went to high school. The summers off allowed them to recuperate and come back eager to serve.

It's a good idea to add up the amount of time you expect volunteers to give each week. Also chart how many ongoing meetings they need to attend. You may begin to see why you have difficulty recruiting people. Adults generally won't give up two nights a week to be at church.

Schedule as many "crossroads" meetings as possible. If the team is going to be at church on Sunday morning anyway, for instance, can you provide early morning donuts and good coffee and have your weekly prep or check an hour before church starts? Can team members come an hour before the Bible study starts on Wednesday night for training, rather than making a special trip on Saturday?

SMART TIP

The Importance of Food...

In case you haven't figured it out yet, food always helps motivate people to get to a meeting. Besides that, people tend to talk more freely when they have food or a drink in their hand. No wonder eating and parties show up so often in the Bible.

RECRUITING VOLUNTEERS

Make it a priority to meet the new people who are looking to get involved in your church. Request copies of the interest form new members fill out during their new member class. There's usually a question like "Do you have any interest or experience in these areas: media development, music, graphic design, education, social media/Web development?" (If there's not, request that it be added.) Use the information to recruit for specific roles in your ministry.

Here's a very good idea: Ask your students for the names of adults in the church they'd like to see volunteering in the ministry. Don't be surprised when they suggest a vibrant woman in her 70s.

Check out who's worked with the current students in their younger years. Sometimes a fifth-grade Sunday school teacher really connects with a group and would like to continue into middle school with them. You'll never know unless you ask.

Invite potential volunteers to a certain event or regular meeting to check out things and see how they might fit in. Let a few students and leaders know about the visit, and encourage them to introduce themselves and converse with these potential volunteers. Schedule time afterward for visitors to ask questions of you, other volunteers, and a few key students.

FASTRACK

Because recruiting volunteers is typically difficult, we tend to lower our standards and allow people who aren't qualified or who have significant issues to help out. Don't do this. It's better to have a few healthy leaders than many who need care themselves.

During weekend worship, hold a church-wide ministry fair that highlights opportunities for adults to help out the youth ministry. Serve lots of food.

Ask for the opportunity for students and leaders to speak about their youth ministry experiences during all church worship as often as possible. Share and celebrate what God is doing in the ministry. Let the church hear your vision, heart, and passion for ministry with students. Stories from retreats, missions trips, service projects, or small groups are great ways to pass along where God is at work. Help the speakers plan what they'll say. Listen to them rehearse—in the worship space, using the microphone, when possible.

Include stories from students about how their leader made a difference and from parents about how a leader went out of his way to reach their student. Throw in pictures or video clips, too. Stories can be the best motivators of all.

Let volunteers know and feel that they will be shepherded, cared for, built into, developed.

JOB DESCRIPTIONS

SMART TIP

Different people respond to different challenges. For some it's "Make a difference in a teenager's life." For others, it's more like, "I believe that God has gifted you to work with students, and I want to help you succeed."

Once you've determined the roles you need filled and your expectations for those different roles, you're ready to create job descriptions. A person who doesn't know his purpose for being there won't stick around. Worse yet, it will be next to impossible to ever get him to consider coming back to the youth ministry. So before you challenge people to consider being a part of the team, know what you're going to ask them to do.

Another reason for a job description is to help you screen applicants. By clearly articulating what you expect from a volunteer, you establish clear qualifications. In case an applicant wants to take legal action against you or the ministry because of the information you're requesting for screening, the qualifications help protect you. They help ensure that you are not arbitrarily asking questions or discriminating. For example, if a volunteer will work with young children, you have a legitimate reason to inquire about his or her history in working with minors. (*RiskFacts: Screening Staff and Volunteers: A Guide for Action and Caution*, Nonprofit Risk Management Center, Washington D.C.)

COMPONENTS OF A JOB DESCRIPTION

Job title. Head the job descriptions with a one-to-three-word phrase that sums up the role and describes the job focus—Small Group Leader, College-Prep Tutor, Program Team Member, Mentor, Social Coordinator, Social Justice Coordinator, E-News Designer.

FASTRACK

One of the quickest ways to de-motivate people is to inspire them to volunteer and then neglect to tell them what to do.

Ministry mission statement. Write the one- or two-sentence description of the ultimate purpose of the youth ministry—"To glorify God and enjoy him fully through serving middle school students and serving the team that works with them . . . To assist students in the development of their Christian faith . . . To challenge the students at Hope Church to seriously consider the claims of Christ and to act on those claims." (See chapter 2 for more information on writing a mission statement.)

Mission statement for that role. Write a short description of the purpose of the job—"The sound and lights team does our job with excellence so that the gospel can clearly be understood . . . A small group leader challenges high school students to grow closer to Christ through conversations and relationship building."

Job essentials. List essential tasks for a given role— "Small group leaders build caring and supportive relationships with students, lead group discussions, develop the group's identity, support the students' families, guide students, and help build the larger ministry team through encouraging other leaders, supporting ministry efforts, and networking to recruit new leaders."

Gift areas. Name spiritual gifts or natural abilities essential to handling this role—"A small group leader is gifted to teach or to shepherd teens . . . An office team leader is a gifted administrator . . . The game director is gifted in teaching and leadership (is there a spiritual gift of "fun"?). The artistic director is able to bring creative ideas to fruition.

Support system. Describe the number of people they'll be responsible for. Tell whether they'll be responsible for students or adults. Who will support this volunteer—you or someone else? If it's someone else, make that clear. Their desire in joining the team may be to spend time with you. If the interview is the only conversation they ever have with you, they'll feel disappointed— and disappointed volunteers can infect others with their frustration.

Weekly responsibilities. Describe what they would do in a given week. A small group leader, for instance, needs to be at all weekly prep meetings (1 hour), as well as at the small group (90 minutes). They also must contact all the regularly attending students in their group by phone, email or other social interactions (1 hour). One hour of personal preparation for the small group study is also expected. Total hours: 4.5. Yes—that's a significant commitment. Be clear up front.

Other responsibilities. Let volunteers know the other activities, besides regular meetings, that they will be required to attend. Do they need to be at all retreats? Do they need to attend the quarterly staff training days? What is their role at the annual missions trip fundraiser?

Costs. Also, let them know what it will cost them to attend required events. Are they expected to pay for their ticket to the water park? Do they have to pay the same amount to go on the winter retreat as the students do?

FasTrack

People want to be wanted. Qualified individuals may not be ready to say yes the first time you explain to them why you think they would be assets to the youth ministry; but when they are ready to make a move, they'll remember your conversation. Check in periodically to see how they're doing.

Budget Planning

Typically the ministry pays for a good portion of the event fees, and those leaders who are financially able chip in extra or insist on paying their own way. Think about it: You're asking them to give up a weekend with their family and pay $120 for the privilege. Raising the student fee by $10 helps you offset the leaders' fees.

LEADERSHIP DEVELOPMENT

What can volunteers expect to receive from the ministry? If you want a team that stays around for a long time, make them feel as if they're getting as much as they're giving. When you support them and help them develop their leadership abilities, they have more to give to their students, their families, and their jobs. Schedule periodic training (beginning of the school year, a midseason retreat, a six-week Sunday school session), and bring in experts to talk about a variety of topics: a panel of social workers, police, and other youth workers to talk about local gang issues; a counselor who specializes in teens with eating disorders, kids who deal with attention deficit hyperactivity disorder, or are on the autism spectrum.

SMART TIP

Be proactive—go after those who are qualified and would be an asset to youth ministry. Over coffee describe your passion and vision for youth ministry and explain how you see them making significant contributions to the ministry.

DEVELOP AN APPLICATION

You *must* have a written application on file for *everyone* who volunteers with the youth ministry, including lifelong volunteers who helped build the church with their own hands. We'll say it again: *Everyone needs to fill out an application.* Keep applications in a locked file, along with notes from the interview and any notes dealing with disciplinary action. Better yet—save them all electronically on your ministry server in a password-protected file.

You may find the **Staff Application** covers all the information you require to start an applicant into the process. These categories and fields must show up in some form on a ministry application:

Identification—name, address, phone numbers (home, work, cell—which number would they prefer and when is the best time to reach them?). Ask for their social media information.

Qualifications—education, training, licenses (including driver's license).

Job experience—positions held, current workplace name and address, years they've been at their jobs.

Ministry experience—current and past positions, along with the name of the ministry, dates of service, names and phone numbers of supervisors.

Asking about ministry experience gives you a feel for an applicant's readiness and suitability for serving in your youth ministry. You learn about their previous youth ministry experience, if any. Based on your knowledge of their tenure in past ministry jobs, you can discern their level of perseverance. If they've jumped from ministry to ministry after only a short tenure in each, find out why during the interview.

You receive contact information for previous ministries. It's worth checking to see if the applicant's story of why he left is congruent with the ministry's story. You learn whether she is currently working with other ministries. If your calls reveal the applicant's former church heavily relies on her, you may want to recommend that the applicant and her previous supervisor talk before you consider her application. This prevents conflict between ministries.

Family—On the application make it clear to applicants that their response to this section is optional (this lets you avoid charges of discrimination): marital status (single, married, separated, divorced, or widowed). If married, spouse's name. If children, names and ages. (A quick question for you—-why are you really asking these questions? Does it matter to your ministry? Is there a chance you will discriminate based on their answer?)

Honor an applicant's desire to leave these questions unanswered. Yet they're still worth asking, if only for getting a feel for the applicant's season of life. Those with small children who need a lot of hands-on attention may have limited time to give to the ministry, so they might be looking for ways to stay connected that are less time intensive or are flexible, like stuffing envelopes, working on the Web site, tackling fundraising or graphic-design projects. Someone who's recently separated may be in an emotionally intense season of life, and may be better served by focusing on their personal growth for a season before checking out the youth ministry.

Information considered private—Don't include questions about age, height, weight, or personal physical information other than necessary medical questions. Don't ask about race, ethnicity, or ethnic association. Don't request a personal photo. These are not acceptable practices in the marketplace and will send up yellow flags for some people filling out the form.

Faith and accountability—Childhood church denomination (if any); year they became a Christian; years they were discipled; current small group involvement; name and phone number of current small group leader or mentor. (Discussing their responses is a good way to start the interview).

Church involvement—What church do they attend and are they a member or regular attendee? (Decide whether it's vital that they're members of your church.) What's their level of involvement in adult Sunday school, Bible study, or small groups? (You'll confirm whether they're receiving spiritual encouragement elsewhere. Although spiritual growth occurs among active youth leaders, they must not look to the youth ministry as their primary source of spiritual challenge.)

Self-description—In this section an applicant describes how she sees herself. It's a convenient checking tool to use with the references: Does the reference describe the person in the same way? You can design this section as short essay questions, as a "word salad," or any other creative way to assist the applicant to talk about herself.

Short-answer essay questions—What are your strengths? What are your shadows? How would your closest friends respond if we asked them the same questions about you?

A word salad—Ask the applicant to circle words that best describe him and to cross out words that least describe him:

> **FASTRACK**
>
> Honor other ministries in the church by not stealing volunteers. Communicate with leaders of other ministries to make sure you have the green light to pursue a possible new team member.

trustworthy, dependable, active, compassionate, reliable, self-starter, punctual, laid-back, flexible, quick thinker, spontaneous, decisive, night owl, teachable, team player, big tipper, humorous, thoughtful, solitary, leader, cautious, risk taker, patient, reflective, quick tempered, organized, creative, disciplined

A spiritual gifts assessment—If a potential volunteer has taken part in your church's gifts identification program, ask what they discovered about their spiritual gifts and passions. Invite them to identify the areas in which they are currently growing and how that could affect their ministry to students.

Background—Are there any accusations of child abuse or neglect, convictions for serious criminal activity or any major motor vehicle violations. (As with any legal area, check with your ministry lawyer to be sure you don't overstep your bounds in any questions you ask or background checks you request.)

References—Ask applicants to list three non-related people who can identify their character weaknesses and strengths and who can speak to their ability to work with adolescents. Is there someone you can talk to from their last church? For each reference, request an address, work or home phone number, and relationship to the applicant. You can fax or email copies of the **Volunteer Letter of Reference** to each reference. (See how to follow up reference checks on page 271.)

> **ITEMS TO INCLUDE IN AN APPLICATION PACKET:**
>
> (see **Staff Application Checklist, page 466**)
>
> - Introductory letter explaining the process
> - Staff Application Process Letter page 470
> - Staff Application (1 or 2) page 461
> - Staff Expectations page 467
> - Church's statement of faith
> - **Reducing the Risk of Physical and Sexual Abuse page 449**
> - Health form
> - Permission for background check and possibly fingerprinting

GRACE (i.e., Godly Response to Abuse in the Christian Environment) is an organization designed to empower the Christian community through education and training to recognize and respond to the sin of child abuse. Visit the Web site to learn more: http://netgrace.org.

Waiver or consent—Include on the application a line where the potential volunteer signs indicating the information given is accurate and true, and authorizing the ministry to confirm any information given. Also include a statement for signing that the applicant waives rights to confidentiality and authorizes the ministry to perform criminal background checks, reference checks, and employment or education verification. Have your church's attorney okay the waiver/release form for your use. Seriously—you need to do this.

SCREENING VOLUNTEERS

If a new youth pastor makes any mistake, it'll likely be in volunteer screening—specifically, not doing a thorough job of it, in our passion to create programs that have an impact on teens, in our need to simply get the bases covered. We may bring on a volunteer after having little more than a casual conversation with them and an usher's assurance that they are in church every week.

Think about these recruiting realities:

Adults who want to harm children and students attend your church. These adults really do target youth ministries. We're sticking our heads in the sand if we don't believe it.

Sexual abuse is real. Protecting students and our volunteers from abuse is our job. Take allegations seriously.

REAL LIFE
A youth worker who started her own ministry: My assistant (nonpaid volunteer) was the organizational brains of the outfit. She kept my creative craziness in check. Also, find volunteers who have the gift of acquisition. Those who enjoy shopping at Costco and garage sales or simply like sales in general who can help you get supplies.

High standards are attractive. People are drawn to serve where high standards characterize the ministry and where being involved carries a certain distinction.

It's far more difficult to remove volunteers once you bring them on board. Once relationships begin to be established, it becomes far more challenging to remove someone with whom you have concerns. Saying no right up front is easier by far.

HOW TO PROTECT YOUR STUDENTS

Screen everybody interested in working with your students. This involves a written application, references, and an interview. You need to check the references. Save the applications, references, and interview notes of those you turn down. That way you have a record if they apply for another ministry.

Conduct background checks on all applicants. It's an expense and investment that your ministry MUST make.

Lead child-abuse training. Clearly communicate your policies and expectations in this area.

Have proper supervision. Clear guidelines that prevent an adult from being alone with a student must be in place. (See below for a more expanded explanation.)

The screening process is meant to screen out those who are not a fit, either because of a mismatch in mission, personality, giftedness, season of life, or because they pose a possible threat. Once you have an applicant who makes it through the screening process, ask yourself these questions:

Would I want my children to be in this person's small group? Would I feel comfortable letting them be alone with him or her? If the answer to either of these is no, don't bring the person on board.

Am I bringing this person on because I see latent potential instead of actual skills? If the answer is yes, am I willing to take the time and energy to develop this person, or might he be better developed in a less kid-intensive ministry?

Are there any lingering questions that won't go away no matter how much I probe? Pay attention to your intuition. In all my years of interviewing volunteers, I have never regretted paying attention to that still, small, doubting voice. When I've ignored it, however, I've deeply regretted it.

Quick Start: Plugging In a Volunteer
- Identify the need.
- Get to know potential volunteers—their stories, their journeys, their availability.
- Once a person shows interest in working with the youth ministry, start a **Volunteer Staff Orientation Process** form for him or her.
- Cast the vision—including specifics of the job you have in mind for them.

VOLUNTEER ROLES

Here are several ways interested people can support your ministry:

Find a person in your church with the gift of helping. These people love to assist you and the ministry with overseeing simple tasks, requiring little more than time, that would make for smoother ministry—tasks that when tacked on to your to-do list either never get done or are just more pressure points in an already demanding schedule.

Compile a master vendor list
Create a list of emergency phone numbers.
Organize permission forms.
Manage your ministry database.
Buy event supplies.
Label file folders (see pages 312 to 319 for a system).
Select cards for special events—birthdays, get well, graduation, thank you.
Come in weekly to file everything in your in-basket.
Clip and scan magazine articles you've flagged.
Send ministry books home with a volunteer to skim the contents and write up quick summaries for the rest of the leadership team.

▸ Screen them—interview, do reference and background checks.

▸ Involve them—train, support, encourage, excite.

▸ Develop them—give evaluative feedback, both encouraging and constructive. Challenge them to explore new areas of ministry and personal growth. When they achieve mastery in some area, help them learn to develop other workers.

▸ Appreciate them—find out what says "I appreciate you" in their love languages. Is it gifts, time, recognition, greater opportunities?

Staff Orientation
Process
page 469

LIFE-CYCLE OF TEAM MEMBERS

Proceed in the application process only with qualified candidates whose applications you've thoroughly reviewed.

PHASE 1: THE APPLICATION PROCESS

Schedule interviews only with applicants who have:

1. observed the ministry in action,
2. filled out a Staff Application, and
3. read all the written information distributed. Additionally,
4. interview only those qualified candidates whose applications you've thoroughly reviewed, and
5. whose references you've checked.

Observing the ministry in action informs potential volunteers. Some people expect youth ministry to look like it did 20 years ago when they were in high school. Finding out that you don't bob for leeches anymore may drive them out of the process right away.

Rule of thumb: Assign observers to veteran volunteers who're doing what they are interested in doing. Don't leave any observer unescorted in the ministry. Would you let a stranger roam freely around your home? Then don't allow it at church.

Staff Application
page 461

A completed staff application answers questions about ministry experience and faith that help you plan more effective interviews.

The written material should be read before candidates turn in their applications. What they learn from their reading may end the process before they go to the trouble to apply. (The readings include **Reducing the Risk of Physical and Sexual Abuse**, church and ministry statements of belief, **Staff Expectations**, your philosophy of the youth ministry, etc.)

Review the applications. This potential stopping point can clue you in to unqualified applicants before it costs you too much time.

Wait until you receive their references before setting dates for the interviews. Information you learn from applicants' experience of observing the group and from these documents may stop the application process or help redirect applicants. For example, you'll find out if they regularly attend your church, and if so, for how long. If they're applying to be small group leaders or cabin counselors at camp, for instance, and have only been attending the church for two months, they wouldn't be good candidates. Potential volunteers need to become more familiar with the church and better known to the church community before they actively lead in a ministry.

FASTRACK

A staff application process protects you from inviting unqualified or potentially dangerous volunteers into your ministry setting.

PHASE 2: REFERENCE CHECKS

A non-negotiable element of the screening process, the reference check needs to be done thoroughly and done for each applicant consistently. (See **Volunteer Letter of Reference**.) If you check one person's references, you must check everyone's. Make sure you insert a sentence in your reference letter that gives the reference an opportunity to request a phone call from you. (For example, "If you are uncomfortable answering any of these questions in writing, or if you wish to discuss an issue over the phone, check this box and write in your phone number and the best time to reach you.") People appreciate the option of expanding on the referral, even if they rarely use it. Remember to keep notes on all your references: date sent out, date returned, date and essence of any follow-up phone calls.

Volunteer Letter of Reference page 456

Staff Orientation Process page 269

Use the **Volunteer Staff Orientation Process** form to track your steps in bringing in new volunteers. Put all the information you gather in the applicants' file folders.

You want to know about the applicant's:

FASTRACK

A thorough staff application process assures families and team members that you have in mind the safety of the students and the best interests of the volunteers.

▶ expectations of the ministry
▶ reasons for wanting to be involved
▶ attitude toward students and families
▶ ability to handle crisis and conflict
▶ special abilities and gifts
▶ legal or criminal history
▶ areas of growth
▶ spiritual commitment to Christ

Remember to take notes, date them, and keep them on file. You may think you have a great memory. You don't. Especially after the third interview that day.

PHASE 3: INTERVIEW

If you're new to a youth ministry position, practice interviewing by using the **Prospective Staff Interview Worksheet** (page 457) and asking questions of those who have been holding down the fort until you got there. You could ask them in the past tense—"Why were you interested in working with the youth ministry?" Or you could phrase them with the future in mind—"Are you interested in continuing to work in your current role?" (The **Prospective Staff Interview Worksheet with Rationale** on page 459 includes the commentary for these questions.)

The environment. Meet in a place with minimal distractions, private enough to discuss personal issues. Avoid inadvertently putting the applicant at a perceived disadvantage, like sitting in the taller chair, facing the applicant into the sun—in other words, you want a comfortable and confidential setting.

Ideally, two people interview an applicant—you and someone who doesn't know the candidate well. It's easier for a stranger to ask the difficult questions. Select a perceptive interview partner who can keep the interview confidential. Furthermore, the burden of evaluating the candidate rests on more than your opinion (an especially good idea if the candidate is married to the head of the elder board).

Offer coffee or water to help set a relaxed tone.

The preparation. When you make the interview appointment, let the applicant know who will be present, where it will take place, and why it's important. Ask him to set aside about an hour, and let him know that you'll ask some intense and possibly very personal questions. That gives the applicant a heads-up and, if he's uncomfortable with that, the chance to pull out of the process.

Be familiar with the role the candidate's applying for. Bring to the interview the candidate's application, as well as a notepad or tablet for taking notes.

The interview. Help the applicant feel at ease by introducing other interviewers and explaining why they are there. Then explain the interview process: getting to know each other, discussing how the ministry works, responding to the applicant's questions.

You'll ask questions about the applicant and then answer questions from the applicant.

If after this first part you're satisfied that the applicant may be a good fit with the ministry, take time to describe in some detail . . .

▸ your philosophy of ministry
▸ what it's like to work with adolescents in your ministry

- the details of the candidate's desired role
- what you expect of volunteers (read **Staff Expectations** so there are no surprises)

Placing ministry descriptions after the discussion of the application avoids influencing the applicant's responses to the interview questions and possibly providing an inaccurate picture of the person. Plus, if he's plainly not a good fit, you can end the interview at this point.

FasTrack

Flow with give and take in an interview—help everyone present feel comfortable both asking and answering questions.

At the conclusion of the interview, if you've discerned reasons for stopping the process, let them know that and explain why. If you believe they are a good fit, let them know what happens next—a background check, an interview with the rest of the team, an assignment for ministry, any training required, follow-up appointments, and so on.

What does the applicant want to know from you? It is likely the applicant will have several questions for you, including:

How confidential will this interview be? Only those present at the interview will know what is said, unless you ask permission to share the information with another person or board. For example, say in an interview you learn that the applicant was convicted of drunken driving charges four years ago, before she became a Christian. Since that time she's been active in a 12-step program and has had no recurrences. You ask her permission to talk this over with your supervisor. If she doesn't give you permission, you will tell no one—and, depending on how significant it is that you discuss this with your supervisor, she may have chosen to not be part of the youth ministry.

How did you end up in youth ministry? Especially in a larger church, the applicant may be unfamiliar with your journey into youth ministry. Briefly tell him your story—why you're involved and what you do. Hearing your anecdotes can help put him at ease before he starts answering questions.

INTERVIEW ROLE-PLAYS

To train those who help you interview and to sharpen your skills, role-play the following situations with an interviewer and an "applicant." Give the applicant a piece of paper describing her situation. It's up to her to reveal as much or as little as she wants to. If you're doing this in a group setting, the interviewer can say "pause" and get advice from others in the audience or pass to someone else if they get stuck.

A single parent exploring Christianity. You're a divorced dad or mom who has custody on weekends of your seventh-grade son. You want to spend some more time with him, so you thought you'd volunteer for his Saturday night youth group. You've been going to the church for two months, since the time your divorce was final. You're in the process of exploring Christianity, but you haven't made a commitment to Christ yet.

A schoolteacher in love. You're a 24-year-old schoolteacher who's engaged to be married this summer. You've been a Christian for six months and are excited to work with senior high students. You just bought a townhouse with your fiancé and since you're getting married in a few months, you decided to move in together to save money and get ready for the wedding. He sleeps on the hide-a-bed in the living room.

An architect with a past. You're a single architect in your early 30s. You've been a Christian for more than five years and have spent the last three years in a spiritually intense, coed group. One of the group members is getting married and another is moving out of state, so your group is disbanding. You thought you'd try youth ministry to keep the small group accountability. You had some significant same-sex relationships as a college student but have not pursued anything since then.

Do as I say, not as I did. You're a recent college graduate who grew up at the church. Your high school and college years were marked by heavy partying, but in recent months you've turned your life back over to God. You want to work with students so that you can stop them from making the same mistakes you did.

Good intentions. Good idea? You're in your mid-thirties, and you're chairing the church board that oversees the youth ministry. You think that it would be a good idea to volunteer in the youth ministry so that you can have a better idea of what's going on in the ministry. You've never worked with kids before in your life.

Following the role-plays, use these questions to debrief the group:

For the interviewer:
    Where did you find yourself getting stuck?
    Was there any time when you felt uncomfortable? Why do you think that was?
    What do you wish you would've done differently?
    What lingering questions or doubts do you have?

For the applicant:
    Was there any time when you felt uncomfortable? Why was that?
    What questions do you wish you had asked that you didn't?
    What advice do you have for someone who's performing an interview?

PHASE 4: BACKGROUND CHECKS

The law requires that you exercise "reasonable care" in selecting staff (*RiskFacts:*

Screening Staff and Volunteers. Nonprofit Risk Management Center, Washington, D.C.) How detailed your check is depends on the guidelines your ministry has adopted. When in doubt, do a more thorough background check, especially if the person has lived in multiple states. There are companies that will do the checks for you at a reasonable rate. Partner with other ministries in the church who minister to vulnerable populations (children, elderly, those with disabilities) so you're all using the same company.

Decide on how you will screen minors who work with vulnerable populations (e.g., the nursery or Vacation Bible School). You will need the permission of a parent or guardian to do a background check and even then, you will only be able to access their motor vehicle records, and verify their work history and educational history. It is recommended that you do reference checks and have interviews with all minors and have them supervised by a ministry-approved adult.

How often do you need to repeat background checks? Talk with your insurance agent about this. There doesn't appear to be any laws in this regard, but some organizations do so every two to five years . . . while others repeat them annually. It's recommended that you repeat a background check when a volunteer returns to the ministry after a break in serving. A background check service can check the following and more:

- Social security number trace
- Department of Motor Vehicles check
- Address history
- Criminal report
- National Sex Offender Search
- Single County Criminal Search
- All County Criminal Search
- Education verification
- Employment verification
- Alias search
- Credit history
- Civil court actions
- Military history
- Drug and alcohol test results

Make sure to put any information you receive in the applicant's file (which is kept in a locked drawer). Remember that these are not fail-safe tools. You still need to check references and perform an interview. To learn more about other excellent resources, visit: *http://www.nonprofitrisk.org.*

INTERVIEW TECHNIQUE

Order the questions to go with the flow of the conversation.

Supplement them with any of your questions raised by their application.

Help the applicant articulate how he will deal with conflict by using situational questions (e.g., "What will you do if a student in your group consistently disrupts the discussion?" or "How will you handle a parent who comes up to you right before an event begins with concerns about her student?")

Stay away from questions that can be answered with a simple yes or no.

Remember to listen. Don't get so excited to talk about ministry issues that you lose track that this is an interview. Get them to tell their story. It's about them—not you.

FASTRACK

Background and reference checks benefit all parties—even the prospective volunteer; it's not too much to ask of someone into whose care you're entrusting your kids and your reputation.

PHASE 5: OBSERVATION

Invite potential volunteers to observe the ministry for one to three months. Pair them up with veterans with the gift of discernment. What you may miss in a one-hour interview they may pick up during the one-month observation. When you have high ministry standards, you'll find that the other volunteers get pretty protective about who comes near the students. They want to uphold the reputation and level of care as much as you do.

At any point during this time, either side can pull out of the process. Make sure you do not assign them any responsibilities dealing directly with students—that's a sure way to create difficulty if the process ends in a no. Also make sure that the team and the students know this person is merely observing and that he or she is not an official team member.

PHASE 6: THE DECISION

Okay, you and the applicant have completed steps one through five: They've filled out the forms, you've checked all their references and done a background check, they've spent a month observing, and you've checked in with them and their host during that span. Now, it's decision time.

If you both decide to say yes:

▶ Welcome them to the team by officially introducing them to leaders and students, as well as sending them a letter.

▶ Keep a high level of contact with them the first few weeks. Be available to answer any questions and help them get their feet on the ground.

▶ Follow through on your orientation process—set them up to succeed.

If your answer is no:

▶ Be as specific as possible about why they're not a fit with the ministry at this time. Give them constructive criticism only if they request it.

▸ Don't back down from your decision. If necessary, discuss it ahead of time with your supervisor and request her support.

▸ Suggest other avenues of service if you've truthfully observed that their gifts may be better used in another ministry. However, do not try to push unhealthy people into another ministry just because you don't want to deal with the situation.

▸ If this is not a permanent no, suggest ways for them to develop in the areas that will bring them up to your standard for volunteers—e.g., getting into a small group or seeking counseling. Let them know that you will be willing to consider them again in the future.

No more solo volunteers. No adult in your ministry should ever be alone with a student. Period. As team leader, you always need to have access to observe any group. That means that the Bible study that meets in the janitor's closet needs to have the door left open if there's not a window in the door. That means that if there's a sleepover, there are two ministry-approved adults participating and it's not held in a home where there might be adults who haven't been screened and where there might be medications and other risk items that are easily accessible. That means anyone who refuses to partner with others in ministry cannot be part of this youth ministry.

Phase 7: Developing the Team

Once you have a team in place, spend time developing them. Invite brand-new volunteers to "shadow" either you or a veteran so they can get a feel for the ministry, and so you can get a feel for how they operate. As they meet the challenges you give them, you can ease back on direct supervision and coach them more from the sidelines—asking them questions, posing case studies.

Constantly offer feedback. When they do something well, tell them in detail why it was effective. When they find themselves at a loss in a given situation, offer constructive comments—or ask them to critique themselves as you discuss the experience. Eventually, they'll need less direction from you, but every volunteer always needs feedback. Even if you delegate projects with complete confidence (and very little direction) to team members, they still need to receive both encouragement and feedback from you.

Here are some topics you can cover as part of your team development:

ENCOURAGEMENT CARDS

In these days of fast Facebook messages and quick texts, people appreciate a handwritten note. By making the process easy, you're more likely to do it.

Purchase a three- to-six-month supply of cards appropriate for various people: staff, parents, students, others. Or print up your own cards. (Several software packages and many printers come with card-making software and samples.) However you acquire them, have cards on hand.

Find a volunteer to help you organize the cards. Find another volunteer to handwrite the addresses on a month's worth of envelopes and then bring them to you to sign and send in the office mail. (This works great for students' birthdays as well. In the corner of the envelope where the stamp goes, ask the volunteer to write the number of the birthdate so you know when in the month to mail the cards.)

Make your cards feel more personal by:
    writing the names/addresses on the envelopes by hand—never use mailing labels.
    sticking real stamps on envelopes instead of running them through the postage meter.
    spelling names correctly.

Block out a few hours and write a month's worth of cards.

Seal the envelopes and, if it's a birthday card, put a sticky note on the outside showing when it should be mailed (ideally four days prior to the date).

How-To Skills
    Leading small groups
    Building relationships
    Talking about Christianity
    Speaking to students
    Leading discussions
    Creating community
    Developing creativity
    Responding to students in crisis
    Training on prevention of sexual abuse
    Working with parents

Ministry Behavior and Expectations
    Cover the ministry's policy on sexual abuse or molestation.
    Go over appropriate touch boundaries (for your students and staff).
    Never be alone with or give a student a ride home alone (key word is *alone*).
    There always must be two adults at any event—period.
    Don't give piggyback rides.
    Don't let students sit on your lap.
    Review appropriate discipline boundaries with adolescents.
    Never use physical punishment.
    Never withhold food or sleep as punishment.
    Never shame students in front of their peers.
    Always contact the parent immediately if a student has been asked to leave the ministry for any length of time.

Philosophy: The Whys Behind the How-Tos
    The importance of youth ministry
    A philosophy of youth ministry
    The basics of adolescent development
    Understanding and analyzing adolescent culture

Personal Needs
  Characteristics of an effective youth worker
  Time management
  Prayer and spiritual journey
  Getting into the Bible
  Family
  Self-image

PHASE 8: SAYING GOODBYE

Leaders naturally cycle in and out of ministry. When it's a positive parting of ways, create an environment where the leader is honored for their service and students, parents, and other leaders have a chance to voice their thanks. Make this a consistent ritual for all positive departures. It's a great way to respect someone's legacy, to help students understand that they're not being abandoned, and to communicate to the larger church body that all people are valued in the youth ministry. Have a time of prayer and blessing for the leader and perhaps gift them with something that will help them in their next stage of life or ministry. If they're moving to a different ministry, have a leader from that ministry be in attendance so there's a healthy passing of the baton.

When a team member isn't working out in a ministry, typically we defer to mercy or grace—"They just need a little more time." Or "We all make mistakes." In reality, you need to let them go. Or as a colleague puts it, "Free them up to succeed elsewhere." Before you let someone go, however, you need to make sure you've done three things:

1) Consistently given feedback. Part of your team development is observing team members in action and talking with them about what you observe. If someone isn't working out, he or she should be aware of it well before it's time to part ways. Ask yourself: Is this a ministry issue, an attitude issue, or a moral boundary issue? If it's one (or both) of the first two, you can take some time to work with him or her on the difficulty. If it's a moral boundary issue, investigate further if confirmed, then think about if an immediate release is needed. Then be sure to let your senior pastor or ministry

FASTRACK

Release volunteers who don't develop themselves in team ministry by acting on feedback, learning from experience, having a teachable disposition, or maintaining moral integrity.

PAY VOLUNTEERS

Not, of course, with money. People eagerly participate in a ministry that gives back to them with training that they can use in their daily lives, challenges and encouragement that push them to grow, and opportunities to make a significant difference in someone else's life. And never forget the simple power of a thank you and proper recognition.

supervisor know as soon as possible so he or she can advocate for you should there be any repercussions.

2. *Made sure that their failure is not related merely to job position.* Sometimes, if someone's not working out in the position they volunteered for, the position itself might be wrong for the person. Think about moving them to another position.

3. *Documented the conversations leading up to dismissal.* Note the date, the person, and the gist of any disciplinary conversation that you have with a team member. Also record any steps recommended for change and whether or not he or she followed those steps.

If you address the behavior or attitude and see no change in the volunteer's performance, you need to release that volunteer. If you don't, you drain the morale of the team, the ministry, and yourself.

Here's how to release a volunteer:

- ► Pray for wisdom.
- ► Get your facts straight. Go over your notes.
- ► Think through all the consequences carefully before you take action. Don't give a knee-jerk reaction. Sleep on it. When in doubt, call a trusted ministry friend, therapist, or talk it over with another youth pastor. Maintain confidentiality.
- ► Get wise, confidential counsel from someone who can help you sort out the issues from the emotions.
- ► Dismiss a person face-to-face, not over the phone or via email—certainly not a text. Find a quiet location where you won't be disturbed.
- ► Do it with a loving and caring attitude.
- ► Be clear and honest without being mean. Bill Hybels has a saying: "Have the courage to say the last 10 percent." By that he means that too many of us shy away from saying what really needs to be said. We'll say the 90 percent that's easy. But it's usually the last 10 percent that's the most powerful and important information for the person.
- ► Point out positive contributions as well as reasons for dismissal.
- ► Suggest alternative places of ministry (if appropriate).
- ► Don't ask them to stay on until a replacement is found.
- ► Talk about a plan of action to tell the other volunteers or students.
- ► Keep confidentiality even if the other party doesn't.
- ► Remember that most volunteers will be relieved. They generally know at a gut level when it's not working.

Once you've let someone go, check in with the person a few days later to see how he or she is doing or to see if anything needs to be clarified. Also let your supervisor know about the decision and the process; he or she needs to be your advocate.

Consider the following Team Case Study. What would you do?

CASE STUDY

Julia, hired to oversee junior high and senior high ministries, set as her first priority getting to know those already working with the students. She learned that one of the seventh-grade small group leaders was a nonbeliever. It had happened this way: During the past few years, this woman's husband and child had become Christians. She was curious about what they believed and decided to check out the church and Christianity. The pastor's messages were over her head, she told Julia, and she didn't quite follow what went on in the Bible study her husband attended. She did understand the material in the junior high ministry, however; so she started to help out there. She ended up teaching.

Question: Should Julia let her stay or ask her to stop teaching? Why or why not?

One Solution: Julia made the call to let her stay—contingent upon her service in an assisting capacity. The other leader in the group understood the situation and accepted the woman in the role of assisting. Two years later the woman was baptized after becoming a believer.

What would you do?

A youth pastor was interviewing a woman to be a small group leader. She had been a Christian less than a year, but was actively pursuing her faith. Everything seemed to be a fit. At the end of the interview, the youth pastor asked her if there was anything else she needed to know. After a pause she said, "I'm living with my fiancé right now. I moved in for financial reasons. We're not having sex. I'd make sure he'd never

RECOMMENDED RESOURCES

To develop your team, consider inviting these groups in for short training segments with your staff:

▸ **Your Local Police:** Local police can help you with issues of crisis management, gang issues, personal safety, violence in the community, and substance abuse issues.

▸ **Social Work Agencies:** Social workers can inform you and your team about current family trends, dealing with families on welfare, and abuse issues.

▸ **Therapists/Counselors:** Counselors can help train you on dealing with crisis situations, working with kids who have ADD/ADHD, and identifying students in pain.

▸ **Park District Workers:** They can be a great resource for learning about recreation options in your area, and in some cases, developing a philosophy of play.

▸ **Teachers/School Administrators:** Teachers and administrators may be willing to talk about adolescent development, and you can invite them to share trends, challenges, and explore opportunities for partnership.

▸ **Events:** It's a huge perk for a youth ministry team when the church pays their way to training seminars or conventions. Youth Specialties has a number of annual national and regional training events.

▸ **Denominational Resources:** There are many, many low- or no-cost trainings available in the form of video rentals or seminars on tape, special speakers, leader retreats, and books.

FORMS

- Abuse and Harassment Policies and Guidelines
- Reducing the Risk of Physical and Sexual Abuse
- Staff Guidelines- Sample
- Team Staff Contact Monthly
- Volunteer Applicant Checklist
- Driver Application
- Volunteer Letter of Reference
- Prospective Staff Interview Worksheet
- Prospective Staff Interview Worksheet with Rationale
- Staff Application
- Staff Application Checklist
- Volunteer Staff Expectations
- Volunteer Staff Orientation Process
- Volunteer Staff Application Process Letter
- Spiritual Gifts

answer the phone, so if students were to call me, they would never know. Could this be a problem?"

You're thinking, "I'm desperate for volunteers. Do I trust that she's not sleeping with him and say yes? Do I say that it's okay because they're getting married anyway (even though no date has been set)?"

One Response: "When you're a small group leader in our ministry, you're modeling the Christian life, not just by what you say but by what you do. Let me ask you a question. Are you modeling the kind of decision that you would want a student to imitate?"

That question put the applicant's choices into perspective. As a result, she and her fiancé did some serious thinking and praying. Their deepening faith led them to get separate living situations until they were married and pursue pre-marital counseling through the church.

CONCLUSION: STAYING ORGANIZED

Organizing a ministry is an ongoing process. Our desire is that you'll come back to this book time after time, eventually wearing it out. And each time you pick it up, you'll learn different things as you face new situations, you'll scribble new ideas in the margins, and write your own case studies as you use it to develop other leaders. Our deep hope is that by utilizing this book, you will indeed do ministry for the long haul and that you will do it well, and with others, and with the guidance of God.

By no means do we imply that organization is itself the goal. Jesus didn't call us to go into the world and ORGANIZE students. He called us to love them, invest in them, and help them know and love him. But—this is where organization comes in. We have to have a process and plan for how all these things happen. Especially if we hope to invest in and multiply ourselves through others. And that is why we spent time developing this book on management tools.

Your understanding and application of this book will deepen and even change as you live youth ministry up close and personal. You know—it's called *experience*. Your experiences as a leader shape you. Trust us: Stay around ministry with students long enough, and you too will have first-hand experience with most of this book. This book is meant to help provide a framework and structure for guiding, developing, protecting, and releasing students as they graduate from your ministry. Our prayer for you as a youth worker is that you succeed in your ministry with students, that you spread the Good News, and that you and your ministry are sustained over the long haul due to good planning and management.

In the final section of this book, you will find copies of the forms referred to throughout this book. Feel free to photocopy these, or, if you prefer to utilize electronic copies, you can download copies from http://downloads.zondervan.com/ymmtools2.

Feel free to edit, revise, and personalize these forms to fit your ministry needs.

Finally, have fun. Know that the work you do makes a real, eternal difference in the lives of students. Stay organized, work hard, and enjoy what God has called you to do.

—Ginny Olson & Mike Work

PART 6

FORMS

MAKING PLANS

COMMUNICATIONS

RISK MANAGEMENT

Teams

BUILDING A FOUNDATION
PHILOSOPHY OF YOUTH MINISTRY WORKSHEET

COMPONENT #1 – PRIMARY PURPOSE

What is the primary purpose of youth ministry?

Why is youth ministry important to the church?

Why is youth ministry important to the local community?

Why do I want to invest in youth ministry at this point in my life?

Why do I want to invest in adolescents?

Why do I want to invest in volunteers?

COMPONENT #2 – PERCEPTIONS OF PEOPLE

Do I believe adolescents are basically good or basically evil?

What are the ministry implications for my view?

What are the cultural and moral trends affecting adolescents? Adult leaders? Families?

What is the impact of these trends on those in our community?

If I were to describe adolescents in our community, I would say they're . . .

COMPONENT #3 – FOCUS

If the local news were to do a story profiling our ministry, how would they describe us?

What do we want our youth ministry to be known for?

What should we be focusing on in this season of ministry?

What are some good ideas that we might need to say "no" to in order to stay focused?

COMPONENT #4 – PRACTICES

Based on 1, 2, and 3: what practices do we want to implement in our ministry?

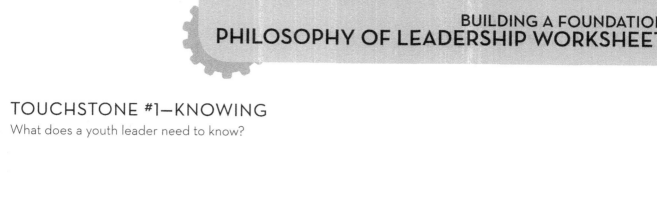

TOUCHSTONE #1—KNOWING

What does a youth leader need to know?

TOUCHSTONE #2—BEING

What character qualities or values does a youth leader need to possess?

TOUCHSTONE #3—DOING

What are the practices or behaviors a leader in youth ministry needs to embody?

BASED ON MY THREE TOUCHSTONES, MY PHILOSOPHY OF LEADERSHIP IS:

I believe leaders should know...

I believe leaders should have these qualities...

I believe leaders should be able to do...

WHAT ARE OUR STRENGTHS?

WHAT ARE OUR WEAKNESSES?

WHAT ARE THE OPPORTUNITIES?

WHAT ARE THE THREATS?

WHAT SHOULD WE **KEEP**?	WHAT SHOULD WE **TOSS**?

WHAT SHOULD WE **ADD**?	WHAT SHOULD WE **TWEAK**?

Prayerfully consider the descriptions that you hope characterize the ministry or the students in the next three years. Write down standout goals. In the appropriate columns list action steps that will move your group toward each goal, sketch a potential timeline for taking the steps, name barriers you'll likely need to overcome to reach the goal, and identify people to involve in the process.

Vision / Goal	Action Steps	Dates	Potential Barriers	Potential Partners

Prayerfully consider the descriptions of yourself and your ministry that you hope to grow into in the next three years. Dream about

- **What you would like to be.** Patient under stress, valuing solitude, a licensed social worker.
- **What you would like to do.** Administrate a recovery camp, work on a master's degree, write an article.
- **What you would like to have.** Control of your schedule, a home of your own, a reliable car.

Write down your standout goals. In the appropriate columns, list action steps to move yourself toward each goal, then prioritize them and attach a goal date. Name barriers you'll likely need to overcome, and identify people to involve in the process of achieving your goals. Work a little bit each week on one or two goals at a time.

Vision / Goal	Action Steps	Dates	Potential Barriers	Potential Partners

You need to get clear answers to the following questions before you ever agree to take a position:

- **How are raises determined?** You'll find out if you'll be locked into your starting salary for the rest of your tenure or if you can negotiate a raise. Are raises based on merit or on life circumstances (someone gets married, has kids, buys a house)? Are raises based on gender or marital status? (If so, warning flags should go off.) **Veteran advice:** Negotiate the salary you want up front; don't plan on making up the difference in a raise. If the church starts you at a certain amount but promises to raise you to a higher amount within the first two years, *get it in writing.* Promises fade quickly once you're hired.

- **If the ministry is to be considered successful in three months, what will that look like? In six months? In one year?** This tells you more about their philosophy of ministry than any Web site ever will. They may deny being about numbers, but if they describe a successful ministry as being "packed out," "crammed with kids," or language like that, you know immediately what you'll be evaluated on.

- **Why did the last youth pastor leave?** If this raises the least bit of suspicion, reframe this question and ask it again. For example: **Who have been some staff who didn't make it here and why?** or **Tell me who has been a staff hero in the past and why?"** (Is the former youth pastor one of them? Why or why not?)

- **Are you hiring me to be the pastor to every kid or to train and equip the adults?** In other words, will your primary focus be building relationships with students or building a team of adults? The answer you seek will be different based on what season of life you're in.

- **What has been the budget for youth ministry? How do you see that changing in the future? Is the youth pastor's salary included in that?** Listen for what percentage it gets out of the total budget and listen for the reasoning. It may be that there were no adolescents up until a year ago when the church experienced a huge growth surge. It may also be that the increase in budget is due to the youth pastor's proposed salary. You may take the job, but have only $800 a year to work with.

- **What are the church's expectations for numerical and spiritual growth?** Listen for which piece they focus on. Which seems to be a priority and why?

- How often are job reviews done? Who does them? What happens to the results of them?

- **Who am I going to report to, and how much time per week will I spend with them?** This is especially important if you are expecting to be mentored by the senior pastor or someone else. You may be interested in the position because it would mean being able to spend time with them. They may only expect to see you on the platform Sunday morning and at church meetings.

- **If someone were to ask you about me one year from now and you would respond that I have exceeded expectations, what would I be doing?**

- **If someone were to ask you about me one year from now and you would respond that I am barely surviving, what would I have done or not done?** This question may be the way to get at the heart of why the last youth pastor left.

- **What's the process for determining and approving what the youth ministry does?** a) Does everything get approved by a youth committee? b) Does the senior pastor approve everything? c) Do I have sole authority to decide what we do?

- **What other expectations are there for me outside of youth ministry?** Does the church expect you to preach on a regular basis? Do nursing home visits? Perform weddings and funerals? Fill in when the nursery hits overload?

- **Has the staff ever had a paycheck withheld because the church was short of money?** If so, when was that and how was that communicated to the church?

- **What happens when the church is behind budget?** Again, how is that communicated to the congregation?

- **What does a typical week look like?** If you're expecting to work 45 hours a week and they're expecting 60, you're headed for a major confrontation. Get it out in the open before you start.

- **What about outside speaking engagements?** Find out their policy for staff speaking to groups and camps outside the church. Are you allowed a certain number of days per year for that? Is there a ministry leave? Does it come out of your vacation time? What about honorariums—can you keep them or do you need to turn them over to the church?

- **Where will my office be located?** This isn't about having a corner office with huge windows. It's about having a place that is easily accessible to the public and that does not isolate you from people. Because of the amount of pastoral counseling that goes on, your office should be in a central location with a window in the door, not tucked under the basement stairs where people need a map to find it.

- **What computer equipment and technology will I have?** Now is the time to ask for what you want. If possible, choose what you prefer using. Also inquire about software and Internet usage. What about a cell phone?

- **Will I have access to an administrative assistant?** How many hours a week? With whom are you sharing his or her time? Who has priority on their time? What is their base of computer knowledge?

- **What are the three most important qualities for a staff member at this church to possess?**

- **What does this church do well?**

- **What is this church known for in the community?**

- **In five years, what will the church look like?**

- **In five years, what do you hope the youth ministry looks like? What is our reputation in the community? In the congregation?**

- **What is this church really about? What is important here?**

POSITION:_____ Date: _____

MISSION STATEMENT FOR THE MINISTRY

MISSION STATEMENT FOR THIS POSITION

JOB SUMMARY

JOB DUTIES

WORKING RELATIONSHIPS

Responsible for:

Responsible to:

Works closely with:

GIFTS REQUIRED

SKILLS REQUIRED

TIME REQUIRED

LENGTH OF SERVICE

TRAINING AND DEVELOPMENT

COMMENTS

Prepare yourself for your job interview.

FAMILIARIZE YOURSELF WITH THAT PARTICULAR CHURCH OR ORGANIZATION.

- Find out as much as you can about the ministry with which you're interviewing. That way, you walk in primed to ask key questions and to explore the significant issues.

  ❏ Request annual reports, denominational information, mission statements, and informational brochures.

  ❏ Check out their Web site, if they have one. Look not only for what they say, but what they omit. How often does the youth ministry get mentioned? What percentage of the whole church budget is dedicated to the youth ministry?

  ❏ Use your discretion to determine how best to talk with former youth pastors, counselors, the church secretary (a gold mine of information), or students in the group. Ask, What is this youth ministry known for? What are its strengths? What areas need growth?

  ❏ Call other churches in the area to get their perspective. You may want to ask, "When you think of First Church, what comes to mind? How is First Church perceived by members in the community?"

- Based on what you learn, prepare a list of questions to put to your interviewer.

FAMILIARIZE YOURSELF WITH THE COMMUNITY.

  ❏ Browse local newspapers on the Internet.

  ❏ Check out housing costs.

  ❏ Look up Web sites of the local schools.

  ❏ Look up the city's Web site to learn about recreational opportunities, cultural offerings, the crime rate.

  ❏ If you're married, is this a place where your family will feel comfortable?

  ❏ If you're single, is this a place where you'll find like-minded / similar age people?

PREPARE YOURSELF.

- Ask a friend to rehearse with you answers to possible interview questions. (See **Job-Interview Questions You May Be Asked** and **Critical Questions You Need to Ask in the Interview**)

- Ask what dress code you should follow for the meetings you'll attend—then, dress a step above. (If this is one of your first two jobs, compensate for your youth and inexperience by dressing up, business casual would be a minimum. Look at your purchases as an investment in your career wardrobe.)

- If you're candidating over a weekend, ask what activities you'll observe or participate in and bring appropriate clothing.

- Bring a prepared message with you. As one youth pastor advises, "Always be ready to preach, pray, and die."

- Bring breath mints. Stick a couple loose ones in your pockets so they're easy to reach for.

- Be careful what you eat before you interview. Butterflies don't mix with nachos. Let's just leave it at that.

- How and when did you become a Christian?

- Why do you feel called to youth ministry?

- What is your philosophy of youth ministry?

- Why do you feel called to this church/ministry?

- What do you know about our church? (Note: in the corporate world, this question is a test to see if you've done your homework. It's the same way in the ministry world. At one church I know of, this is the defining question. If you don't have something to say, the interview is over—no matter how strong your résumé is. No church wants someone who's just looking for a job. They want someone who can be as committed to the place as they are.)

- What are your strengths?

- In what areas do you need to grow?

- What would you do in this situation—(fill in the blank)? (BTW, this question provides a huge clue to what has been an issue in the past. If they ask you questions about discipline or punctuality or communication, odds are, that was a problem for the previous youth pastor.)

- What are your views on (fill in the blank)? (This could be anything from world affairs and politics to the Pepsi vs. Coke conflict. It all depends on the church and the agenda of the interviewers.)

- Where do you see youth ministry going in the future?

- What does a successful youth ministry look like?

- What would you do in your first three months at our church?

- What is your style of teaching?

- What is your current salary package / what are your financial expectations?

- What is your view on mission trips, retreats, camps?

- Why do you want to leave your current situation? (By the way, when you're asked about your present or past employer, say only positive things. The interviewers don't want to know the dirt, and if you're too negative, they'll begin to wonder if they'd be hiring someone divisive, angry, deeply hurt, etc.)

CHRIS SMITH
1234 Third Ave.
Second City, SD 60625
123/555-5555
CSmith@freemail.com

Ministry address (if appropriate)
Second Church
2323 Second Ave.
Second City, SD 60625
123/ 555-5555

MISSION STATEMENT

To help adolescents and their families become committed followers of Christ and empower them how to minister to others.

**LEADERSHIP /
MANAGEMENT
POSITIONS**

SECOND CHURCH, Second City, SD
Director, High School Ministry, 2008 - present
Responsible for selecting, developing, and evaluating volunteer leaders in a high school ministry that serves over 75 adolescent students and their families. Coordinate idea development, planning efforts, and leadership training. Develop ongoing youth development experiences such as student leadership teams, outreach events, retreats, service projects, and camps and missions trips. Other responsibilities also include: creating and maintaining the youth ministry budget, some individual and family counseling, speaking in the public schools, overseeing a part-time administrator, and curriculum development for confirmation and Wednesday night Bible studies.

SECOND CITY COMMUNITY SERVICE BUREAU, Second City, SD
Consultant, 2009 - present
Perform workshops and consultations that assist churches, schools, and community groups in building relationships with adolescents and their families. Some crisis counseling and intervention work as well. Currently, developing a team of consultants for neighboring towns.

THIRD CHURCH, Third Town , NJ
Middle School Director, 2002 - 2008
Organized and carried out a variety of events, including retreats, camps, training conferences, and service projects for middle school adolescents and their families. Selected and developed a team of adult volunteers. Public speaking opportunities included public and private schools as well as church functions.

**VOLUNTEER LEADERSHIP
POSITIONS**

SECOND CITY NETWORK OF YOUTH WORKERS, Second City, SD
Network coordinator, 2009 - present
Coordinate monthly meetings for a group of local youth workers. Provide training, support, and community events to supplement individual ministries.

**PRESENTATIONS AND
SEMINARS**

SECOND CHURCH'S YOUTH WORKERS FORUM, 2010 & 2011
Various seminars on the topics of middle school ministry, community ministry, and team building.

FORMAL EDUCATION

SECOND SEMINARY, Second City, SD
Master of Divinity degree with an emphasis in Youth Ministries, 2014

SECOND COLLEGE, Second City, SD
Bachelor of Arts, May, 2004
Major: Youth Ministry. Minors: Biology and Philosophy.

ADDITIONAL EDUCATION

• *Youth Specialties Youth Workers' Convention*, Fall, 2010
• *Youth Specialties One day Resource Seminars*, 2009 – 2011

CHRIS SMITH

ADDRESS

1234 Third Ave.
Second City, SD 60625

PHONE

123/555-5555

EMAIL

CSmith@internet.com

WEB

www.csmithdoesnotexist.com

AREAS OF INTEREST

Seminar speaker: adolescent issues, worship and youth ministry, parents and social media, ministry and community partnerships

Board member: Big City Community Youth Bureau

PROFILE

I am a Christ-follower, youth pastor, and blogger. I am passionate about leadership and empowering adults to love and serve adolescents.

DIRECTOR, HIGH SCHOOL MINISTRY, 2010 – present
Second Church, Big City, SD

I have the privilege of selecting, developing, and evaluating volunteer leaders in a high school ministry that serves over 75 adolescent students and their families. Responsibilities include coordinating idea development, planning efforts, and leadership training, developing ongoing youth development experiences such as student leadership teams, outreach events, retreats, service projects, and camps and missions trips.

CONSULTANT, 2010-present
Big City Community Youth Bureau, Big City, SD

MIDDLE SCHOOL DIRECTOR, 2002-2009
Third Church, Third Town, NJ

YOUTH MINISTRY INTERN, 2000-2002
Little City Church, Little City, NJ

WORSHIP INTERN, 1999-2000
Little City Church, Little City, NJ

EDUCATION

MASTER OF DIVINITY with an emphasis in youth ministries
Big Seminary, Big City, SD

BACHELOR OF ARTS with an emphasis in theology
Little City University, Little City, NJ

SKILLS & STRENGTHS

Myers-Briggs: ESFJ

Strengths Finders: Achiever, Connectedness, Woo

DISC Profile: Strong D with a high I

Web design

Social media savvy

Vision developer

Strategic planner

BETH SMITH
1234 Third Ave.
Second City, SD 60625
123/555-5555
CSmith@freemail.com

School address (from September to May)
Second College
2323 Second Ave.
Second City, SD 60625
123/ 555-5555

VOCATIONAL OBJECTIVE

To find a full-time ministry position ministering with high school students in a church or parachurch setting.

FORMAL EDUCATION

SECOND COLLEGE, Second City, SD
Bachelor of Arts candidate, May, 2015
Major: Youth Ministry. Minors: Biology and Philosophy.
Courses include: Leadership and Management in Youth Ministry, Child and Adolescent Psychology, Philosophy, Curriculum Development, and Creative Teaching.

LEADERSHIP / MANAGEMENT POSITIONS

SECOND CAMP, Second City, SD
Program Director, Summers, 2013 –2014
Oversaw the summer camp program for age groups ranging from grade school through college-age, and including one week of family camp. Responsibilities included: creating and developing the theme for the summer, directing staff meetings, overseeing summer staff, organizing various special events and games, maintaining the morale and the safety of the camp, and leading daily staff devotions.

SECOND COLLEGE, Second City, SD
Resident Assistant, 2012-2014
Leader of 24 college students in the Second Memorial Dormitory. Responsibilities included: building relationships with every resident on the floor, developing community-building programs, implementing disciplinary procedures, facilitating weekly Bible studies, counseling residents as needed, and working with other Resident Assistants, the Resident Director, the Campus Counseling Center and the college administration.

SECOND GROCERY STORE, Second City, SD
Head Grocery Bagger, 2007-2011
Responsible for accurately and carefully bagging customers' groceries, greeting customers, and initiating community-building activities among other baggers, as well as leading a bagger Bible study.

VOLUNTEER LEADERSHIP POSITIONS

SECOND CHURCH, Second City, SD
Bible Study Leader, 2013 – present
Organized a Bible study for a group of high school students that met weekly throughout the school year. Responsibilities included: creating new curriculum, coordinating social activities, developing individual and community relationships.

HONORS AND OTHER SEMINARS

• Winner of the National Grocery Bag Scholarship, 2011.
• Contributing writer, National Grocery Bag Newsletter, 2009-2010
• Campus Bible study leader at Second City High School, 2009

REFERENCES

Available upon request

Negotiate your job offer very carefully. As uncomfortable as it feels to talk about money and ministry in the same breath, you live with the reality of paying for a roof and food and utilities, among other necessities. Negotiate for what you want at the beginning—once you've taken the position, you can't go back and ask for more.

Try not to sell yourself too high or too low. And spend some time clarifying your expectations of the job and putting it in writing before you sit down to negotiate. If your requests are acceptable to the hiring board, have them write it into your contract—*if you don't have it in writing, you don't have it.*

SALARY EXPECTATIONS

- **If the church contacts you,** during the initial contact, ask these three questions: What's the greatest strength of the church? Where do you see it going in the future? Can you tell me the salary range?

- **If you contact the church,** don't bring up salary. You may end up wasting some time, but that's better than being perceived as only interested in the money.

- **Your base salary** will be affected by

  Your education. If you have a M.Div., your salary should be higher than an employee with only a Bachelor of Arts or an Associate of Arts. If it's not, it tells you that the church doesn't value educational experience. Is that a warning for you? The reality of increased student loans to repay goes with the increased degree.

  Your experience. If you come with only a B.A., but you bring the benefit of eight years of experience, negotiate a salary that compensates for experience. Other professions do; so should the church. Consider negotiating for tuition-assistance for further education.

  Community cost-of-living. How much will it cost to live in this community? Renting a house in Red Oak, Iowa, for instance, costs less than renting an apartment in the Silicon Valley. Too often, youth pastors eager to get a job underestimate how much it will cost to live in a given area. They end up working extra jobs just to pay the bills. Several Web sites can do a cost-of-living analysis for you: http://www.bestplaces.net/cost-of-living, http://money.cnn.com/calculator/pf/cost-of-living, http://www.bankrate.com/calculators/savings/moving-cost-of-living-calculator.aspx or www.monster.com

  Comparable salaries. It's helpful to put your position into perspective by comparing it with other professions with similar job requirements. A rule of thumb for recent college graduates is to find out what the area's first year high school teachers are paid. The school system knows the cost of living for the community. If you have an advanced degree and experience, find out what counselors, principals, and medical personnel in the area are paid. You may also want to call your denominational offices to request salary guidance.

- **Find out if the package includes housing. If so—**
  - Is this considered non-taxable income?
  - How does the fact that you are (or are not) licensed impact your taxes in this sphere? (You need to discuss this with your tax advisor.)
  - What costs of housing does the church pay for, and what are you responsible for? You may need to pay the utility bills, which sounds like a great deal until you see that it costs $350 a month to heat the bargain house.
  - Who is responsible for the upkeep? Usually, it will be you. Do you have time to spend repaving driveways, painting shutters, and fixing screens and leaky pipes on a 75-year-old house? And who pays for the repairs?
  - Does the church offer the option of home ownership with a housing allowance or a parsonage with an equity allowance? Again, talk over these issues with your tax advisor.

- Ask if your compensation includes cost-of-living increases and bonuses.
  - How much of an increase does the staff receive each year? (If they don't give cost-of-living increases, you are, in effect, losing money each year.)
  - Are bonuses given if ministry goals are exceeded?
  - Are merit-based raises given? (If so, how often and how are they determined?)
- Find out what employee benefits come with your package.

  Retirement. Some churches have mandatory pension plans if you are licensed and/or ordained. Others have matching plans—they will match your retirement contributions up to, say, 5 percent of your salary.

  Insurance. Which insurance, among all the different types, is covered by the church's plan?

  Medical. If you have a family, are they covered? Do you need to pay any extra for their coverage? Is dental included? What about ---

  Disability insurance.

  Life insurance.

  Liability insurance.

  Accidental death and dismemberment.

TAXES AND DAYS OFF

- **FICA.** If you are considered self-employed, it is *your* responsibility to make quarterly tax payments to the government (both state and federal). Some churches pay the employer's share of the youth pastor's social security payments. Check to see your church's policy.

- **Time off.**

  Days off. Expect a minimum of one full day off a week—the norm is two. Don't accept partial days off— like having Friday afternoon and Tuesday morning off. A person needs a full day to be able to disengage and relax.

  Vacation. The length of your first year's vacation depends on when you start. If you start in June, you usually get half the number of days written into your contract. A piece of advice—don't even touch a position that offers less than two weeks of vacation. Ministry is such a time- and energy-intensive profession that you need that time to recuperate. Find out when your vacation is increased. An example is receiving an additional week of vacation, up to 5 weeks a year, for every three years on staff. For an experienced youth pastor, four paid weeks a year is appropriate. Sometimes, churches that can't afford a large base salary offer more vacation time. If that seems to be the case of the interviewing church, you may negotiate more vacation time in lieu of the higher salary.

  Compensation time. Ask what the church's policy is on giving you time off after a time-intensive event, such as a mission trip or weekend retreat. If they blink rapidly and mumble, "Whazzat?" run... fast. Some churches expect you to show up at the 8:00 a.m. staff meeting despite the fact you were gone all weekend with the senior highers. They usually don't keep a youth pastor for long.

  Reasonable comp time would be one extra day off (not to be confused with your regular days off) for every weekend retreat, and three extra days off for every weeklong event. You also need to ask if you can store up comp time and use it later in the year, or if they expect you to use that time the week after you get back.

Holidays. Typically, holidays are some of the most heavily scheduled times of the year in youth ministry. Is holiday time off for the staff scheduled in light of this? Many churches require pastoral staff to be there for Christmas services. Is this acceptable to you and your family?

Sabbatical. What is the church's policy on staff sabbaticals? Do pastors get a three-month sabbatical every five years? Do they ever get a longer sabbatical? Does it have to be used for a certain purpose (for example, study, continuing education), or can it be used for a special project (for example, spending time with missionaries overseas, pursuing your desire to be a NASCAR driver)?

Sick days. Can these be stored up for future use or do they get "erased" at the end of the year?

Continuing education. Anywhere from 3 days to two weeks is appropriate for study leave. This allows you to attend a conference or take an intensive course at a local seminary.

PROFESSIONAL EXPENSES THAT ARE PAID FOR BY THE ORGANIZATION, BUT NOT FACTORED INTO YOUR COMPENSATION PACKAGE

Car allowance. You should be reimbursed for the use of your car for ministry purposes. This can come as a monthly sum or as a per mile reimbursement. If it's the latter, retain all receipts as well and keep a mileage log that includes date, destination, miles driven, and purpose of trip. Any drug store or discount store will have a small notebook for this purpose in their stationery section.

Continuing education. One way a church can honor its staff is to encourage them to continually sharpen their professional skills. They should offer enough money to cover at least a weeklong conference (registration, airfare, and food and lodging). They may offer tuition and textbook reimbursement. If the church expects you to get a seminary degree, will they cover those expenses (either partially or totally)? Will you still have money to attend youth worker conferences?

Subscriptions. This can be used for books or magazine subscriptions to help you in ministry.

Hospitality. There's a certain expectation that you will entertain people involved in your ministry, or even just the larger church, in your home or meet them at restaurants. Will the church reimburse you for these expenses?

Denominational gatherings. If you are at a denominationally affiliated church, you may be expected to attend certain denominational events. The church should pick up those related expenses.

Counseling stipend. Ministry is one of the most stressful careers you can enter. More and more churches understand the importance of regular counseling for its pastoral staff. They view it as part of overall health care. Does the church provide an annual stipend for counseling? Do they provide a special fund? Do they have a relationship with a local therapist who provides counseling on a sliding fee scale to the church?

MANAGING YOUR LIFE IN MINISTRY
PRIORITY SCALE

| Step one | Write your to-do list for a given day, week, or month. |

TO-DO LIST

1.
2.
3.
4.
5.
6.
7.
8.
9.

| Step two | Using the numbers in column 1, compare item 1 with item 2 in your to-do list. Next compare 1 with 3; 1 with 4, et cetera, all the way through item 9. With each comparison, circle the number of the item that is the highest priority. Then do the same to columns 2-8. |

COLUMN	1	2	3	4	5	6	7	8
	1							
	2							
	1	2						
	3	3						
	1	2	3					
	4	4	4					
	1	2	3	4				
	5	5	5	5				
	1	2	3	4	5			
	6	6	6	6	6			
	1	2	3	4	5	6		
	7	7	7	7	7	7		
	1	2	3	4	5	6	7	
	8	8	8	8	8	8	8	
	1	2	3	4	5	6	7	8
	9	9	9	9	9	9	9	9

| Step three | Total the times each number is circled and record here. |

1's	2's	3's	4's	5's	6's	7's	8's	9's

| Step four | Based on the totals from step three, reorder your to-do list. |

TOP PRIORITIES

1.
2.
3.
4.
5.
6.
7.
8.
9.

| Step five | Complete your top priorities one after the other. What you don't finish on one day becomes the first item on your list for the next day. |

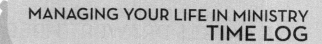
Day of the week _____ Date _____

W here does the time go? Here's your chance to find out. Log activities at 30-minute intervals.
    As inconvenient as it may be to note what you're doing every 30 minutes, what you find out about how you use your time is worth the effort. The clock notations will give you a sense of what you're most likely to be doing at different times of the day and on different days of the week. The Quadrant notations help you evaluate your use of working hours. (See chapter 14 of *Youth Ministry Management Tools 2.0* for a refresher on Stephen Covey's time-management quadrants.) Armed with the knowledge you gather, you can plan ahead more effectively.

Activity	Clock Start	Clock Stop	Time Spent	Quadrant

Resources and organizations—catalogs, brochures on organizations (blue)

ABSTINENCE TRAINING	**CRISIS**	**CRISIS:** Violence
BIBLE STUDIES	**CRISIS:** Substance Abuse	**CRISIS: PREGNANCY CENTERS**
CAMPS	**CRISIS:** Addictions	**CURRICULUM & PUBLISHERS**
CAMPUS MINISTRY	**CRISIS:** Depression	**CURRICULUM & PUBLISHERS:** Youth Specialties
CHOIR MUSIC	**CRISIS:** Eating disorders	**CURRICULUM & PUBLISHERS:** Simply
COLLEGE	**CRISIS:** Family issues	**CURRICULUM & PUBLISHERS:** Orange
COMPUTER	**CRISIS:** Runaways	**CURRICULUM & PUBLISHERS:** re:form
CONFIRMATION	**CRISIS:** Suicide	**CURRICULUM & PUBLISHERS:** YouthMinistry360

Resources and organizations—catalogs, brochures on organizations (blue)

CURRICULUM & PUBLISHERS: DYM	**LEADERSHIP:** Committees / Teams	**MISCELLANEOUS**
ICE BREAKERS	**LEADERSHIP:** Staff training	**OUTREACH**
DISCIPLESHIP	**LEADERSHIP:** Follow-up materials	**OUTREACH:** Evangelism materials
DRAMA	**LEADERSHIP:** Student	**PARACHURCH MINISTRIES**
EVANGELISM TRAINING ORGANIZATIONS	**MAGAZINES**	**PARACHURCH MINISTRIES:** Fellowship of Christian Athletes
GAMES	**MISSIONS**	**PARACHURCH MINISTRIES:** Other
INTERNET RESOURCES	**MUSIC**	**PARACHURCH MINISTRIES:** Student Venture
LEADERSHIP	**NETWORKING**	**PARACHURCH MINISTRIES:** Young Life

Resources and organizations—catalogs, brochures on organizations (blue)

PARACHURCH MINISTRIES: Youth for Christ	SPECIAL EVENTS	YOUTH-WORKER TRAINING ORGANIZATIONS
PRAYER	STEWARDSHIP	
RENTAL COMPANIES	URBAN MINISTRY	
RETREAT CENTERS	URBAN MINISTRY: Community resources	
RURAL MINISTRY	URBAN MINISTRY: Community partnerships	
SEMINARY	URBAN MINISTRY: Other	
SERVICE ORGANIZATIONS	VIDEO	
SPEAKERS	WORSHIP	

Topical—teaching resources (yellow)

ADOLESCENT DEVELOPMENT	**ADOLESCENT DEVELOPMENT:** Emotional	**ADOLESCENT DEVELOPMENT:** Seminars/Handouts
ADOLESCENT DEVELOPMENT: Mental	**ADOLESCENT DEVELOPMENT:** Social	**MINISTRY SPECIFIC TO GUYS / GIRLS**
ADOLESCENT DEVELOPMENT: ADD / ADHD	**ADOLESCENT DEVELOPMENT:** Peer pressure	**CAMPING**
ADOLESCENT DEVELOPMENT: Physical	**ADOLESCENT DEVELOPMENT:** Spiritual	**COUNSELING**
ADOLESCENT DEVELOPMENT: Eating disorders	**ADOLESCENT DEVELOPMENT:** Moral	**COUNSELING—ABUSE:** Physical, mental, sexual, verbal
ADOLESCENT DEVELOPMENT: Health & body image	**ADOLESCENT DEVELOPMENT:** Seminars	**COUNSELING:** Family
ADOLESCENT DEVELOPMENT: Sexual identity	**ADOLESCENT DEVELOPMENT:** Age group characteristics	**COUNSELING:** Chemical & substance
ADOLESCENT DEVELOPMENT: Gender identity	**ADOLESCENT DEVELOPMENT:** Articles & resources	**COUNSELING:** Depression / suicide

Topical—teaching resources (yellow)

COUNSELING: Eating disorders	COMMUNICATION: Teaching tips	FAMILY-PARENTS: Fliers, calendars, etc.
COUNSELING: Miscellaneous	**DISCIPLESHIP**	FAMILY-PARENTS: Parenting articles
COUNSELING: Peer counseling	**ENCOURAGEMENT**	FAMILY-PARENTS: Parent ministry
COUNSELING: Local contacts & resources	**EVANGELISM**	FAMILY-PARENTS: Seminars & talks
COMMUNICATION	**FAMILY**	**GENERATIONAL RESEARCH**
COMMUNICATION: Styles, tests, & explanations	FAMILY: Blended families	GENERATIONAL RESEARCH: Millennials
COMMUNICATION SEMINARS: Social media	FAMILY: Death & Grief	GENERATIONAL RESEARCH: Seminars
COMMUNICATION: Ways people communicate	FAMILY: Divorce	GENERATIONAL RESEARCH: Emerging generations

Topical—teaching resources (yellow)

JUSTICE SYSTEM & YOUTH	**MISSIONS:** Articles	**RACE, ETHNICITY & CULTURE** Awareness education
LEADERSHIP	**MISSIONS:** Theology	**RELATIONSHIPS**
LEADERSHIP: Articles	**MISSIONS:** Training	**RELATIONSHIPS:** Dating
LEADERSHIP—MINISTRY: Expectations	**MODELS OF YOUTH MINISTRY**	**RELATIONSHIPS:** Divorce
LEADERSHIP—MINISTRY: Mission & vision	**PROGRAMMING**	**RELATIONSHIPS:** Friendships
LEADERSHIP—MINISTRY: Values	**RACE, ETHNICITY, & CULTURE**	**RELATIONSHIPS:** Marriage
MISSIONS	**RACE, ETHNICITY & CULTURE:** Articles & resources	**RELATIONSHIPS:** Miscellaneous
MISSIONS: Activities / simulations	**RACE, ETHNICITY & CULTURE:** Reconciliation	**RELATIONSHIPS:** Singleness

(Topical—teaching resources yellow)

RELATIONSHIPS: Sex / sexuality	**SPIRITUAL ISSUES**	**YOUTH CULTURE:** Articles
SMALL GROUPS	**SPIRITUAL ISSUES:** Fasting	**YOUTH CULTURE:** Drugs
SMALL GROUPS: Activities	**SPIRITUAL ISSUES:** Other disciplines	**YOUTH CULTURE:** Gangs
SMALL GROUPS: Community building	**SPIRITUAL ISSUES:** Prayer	**YOUTH CULTURE:** Media / Music
SMALL GROUPS: Expectations	**SPIRITUAL ISSUES:** Worship	**YOUTH CULTURE:** Violence
SMALL GROUPS: Forms	**SPIRITUAL ISSUES:** Warfare	**YOUTH WORKER: PERSONAL**
SMALL GROUPS: Ideas	**SPIRITUAL ISSUES:** Witchcraft & occult	**YOUTH WORKER—PERSONAL:** Growth plans
SPIRITUAL FORMATION	**YOUTH CULTURE**	**YOUTH WORKER—PERSONAL:** Reviews

(Topical—teaching resources yellow)

YOUTH WORKER: PROFESSIONAL		
YOUTH WORKER—PROF.: Continuing education		
YOUTH WORKER—PROF.: Salary research		
YOUTH WORKER—PROF.: Sample résumés		

GENERAL OFFICE PROCEDURES
MONTHLY CONTACT SUMMARY CHART

Staff member _____ Due _____

Student's name	Phone number	Weekly call						Comments
1.								
2.								
3.								
4.								
5.								
6.								
7.								
8.								
9.								
10.								
11.								
12.								

Special concerns _____

_____

Group activity (1 every month) _____ Date _____

Brief description _____

_____

Is there anything the pastoral staff should be aware of? _____

_____

How can we encourage and pray for youth over the next month? _____

_____

EMERGENCY NUMBERS & WEB SITES

Local schools

Police emergency numbers

Counseling centers – identify counselors in advance by specialty

Depression / Suicide

Eating disorders

Addiction / Chemical dependency

Self-injury

Sexual abuse

Family systems

Crisis pregnancy centers

Crisis referral numbers

Drug rehabilitation centers

Emergency contact numbers for co-workers, staff members, and families active in the ministry

Hospitals (surgery center, emergency room number, as well as the names and numbers of the chaplains)

Church leaders

Board

Staff

SCHOOLS

Booster club

Head of the PTA

Key teachers and coaches

Local schools (and their Web sites)

Principals

School board members

Superintendents

RENTAL COMPANIES

Bus and van rental companies (contact person, great drivers you have used)

Rental centers (large popcorn poppers, carnival games, tents, climbing equipment, folding chairs, etc.)

SERVICES

Bowling alleys (when you've used them, what event)

Coffee shops

Graphic artists (and what projects you used them for)

Insurance agent

Lawyer

Local restaurants (Do they deliver? Can you get a copy of their menu?)

Office supply stores (and Web site)

Party supply stores (and Web site)

Printing companies (and what projects you used them for)

T-shirt companies (and what projects you used them for)

MINISTRIES

Camps you frequently use (and the contact person's name and rates)

Churches in your area

Missions organizations

Music resources / bands

Parachurch ministries

Resource ministries

Speakers

The National Network of Youth Ministries releases the *Youth Ministry Yellow Pages* each year. See them online at www.YouthWorkers.Net.

GENERAL OFFICE PROCEDURES
STUDENT PROFILE WORKSHEET

Page 1 of 3
Page 1 for student to fill out, pages 2 & 3 for office use only.

Confidential

Today's Date

PERSONAL INFORMATION

Student's Name _____ Phone _____

❏ Male ❏ Female Email address _____

Address _____ City _____ State _____ Zip _____

Birthday _____ School _____ Graduation year _____

FAMILY INFORMATION

Father's name_____ phone _____ email _____

Mother's name_____ phone _____ email _____

Other caregivers (relationship)_____ phone _____ email _____

Who do you live with most of the time?_____

Who should we contact about ministry events, updates, and schedule changes?_____

Do parents attend this church? ❏ Yes ❏ No   Do parents attend an adult education class? ❏ Yes ❏ No

If yes, which one? _____

Brothers/Sisters: Name _____ Age/Grade_____

Name _____ Age/Grade_____

Name _____ Age/Grade_____

Name _____ Age/Grade_____

INTERESTS check all that apply

Sports: ❏ Basketball ❏ Baseball ❏ Football ❏ Soccer ❏ Volleyball ❏ Hockey

❏ Golf ❏ Broomball ❏ Snow skiing ❏ Water skiing ❏ Golf ❏ Tennis

❏ Swimming ❏ Gymnastics ❏ Other_____

Music: ❏ Likes to sing! ❏ Instruments _____

Hobbies: ❏ Drama ❏ Computer ❏ Reading ❏ Other_____

GENERAL OFFICE PROCEDURES
STUDENT PROFILE WORKSHEET

Confidential

STUDENT'S NAME

Last _____ First _____ Middle _____

Preferred name or nickname _____ Birthday _____

School _____ Graduation year _____ ❑ Male ❑ Female

Current church _____ Member ❑ Yes ❑ No   Brought by_____

STUDENT'S ADDRESS

Street Address _____ City _____ State _____ Zip _____

Alternate Address _____ City _____ State _____ Zip _____

Home phone _____ Personal / Cell phone _____

Email _____ Other: Twitter, Instagram, etc _____

Emergency contact (parent or guardian _____ Phone_____

Emergency contact (non-parent or guardian)_____ Phone_____

Peer sponsor_____ Sponsor _____

PRIMARY GUARDIAN

Last _____ First _____

Relationship_____

Address _____

City _____ State _____ Zip _____

Home Phone _____ Cell phone_____

Email _____

Employer _____ Phone_____

SECONDARY GUARDIAN

Last _____ First _____

Relationship_____

Address _____

City _____ State _____ Zip _____

Home Phone _____ Cell phone_____

Email _____

Employer _____ Phone_____

School activities (list)

Small groups (list)

Spiritual gifts (list)

Interests

GENERAL OFFICE PROCEDURES
STUDENT PROFILE WORKSHEET

Page 3 of 3
Page 1 for student to fill out, pages 2 & 3 for office use only.

Confidential

MINISTRY INVOLVEMENT

Sunday ❑ New attender ❑ Active ❑ Inactive

Wednesday (or other day) ❑ New attender ❑ Active ❑ Inactive

Retreats attended:

Missions trips attended:

Spiritual gifts:

Church membership ❑ Yes ❑ No

Baptism ❑ Yes ❑ No

Describe this student's faith journey:

Describe any other areas of ministry involvement:

Describe significant conversations or experiences:

It's time to reevaluate the current budget and make some changes. That means you need to articulate the philosophy of financial management for both the youth ministry and the larger organization. The budget should reflect the philosophies, not drive them.

Allocation of ministry money is directly linked to your values and goals. When you develop the budget, you and your team determine where to allocate money by answering questions like the following.

WHAT DOES THE CHURCH VALUE?

• Where does the church invest its resources? (Find out by browsing the last few annual reports.)

• What is the church's spending philosophy? Do they buy the best of a particular item knowing that it will last a long time, or do they get the cheapest possible item that will do the job because they don't have a lot of cash on hand? Is youth ministry spending in line with the philosophy of the larger organization?

• Is youth ministry a critical part of the church or is it a small part? (Find out by examining the percent of the total budget dedicated to youth ministry. If it's less than the sandbox allotment for the preschool, you're likely to be in for a struggle if you wish to increase your budget.)

• What has the financial committee approved in the past for youth ministry programs and equipment? You'll get an idea of how flexible they are—how open to ideas new to the church.

WHAT DOES THE YOUTH MINISTRY VALUE?

• Of all the good things on which we can spend ministry money, which things, programs, and people do we value most? How will our spending reflect those values?

• How important is environment to your ministry? Do you need to appropriate funds to make your ministry area more student-friendly?

• How important is staff and staff development?

• Do you have experienced staff, or do they need a lot of training and development?

• Do your staff members need a lot of encouragement? A lot of resources?

WHAT IS THE FINANCIAL HISTORY OF THE YOUTH MINISTRY?

• What was the annual budget?

• Where does that money come from?

• Where has the majority of money gone (outreach events, small group materials, van rentals)?

• What brought in the most money (fundraisers, mission trips, service or work projects)?

• Have you inherited any debt? What debt can be carried over, and what debt must you immediately clear up?

• What budget items need to be carried on, and what can be disposed of?

• Are there any annual events you need to finance—denominational gatherings, the annual junior high/senior citizen putt-putt golf tournament?

WHAT ARE THE MECHANICS OF THE FINANCIAL PROCESS?

• Does your church tell you to get what you need when you need it, or does it require you to work the purchase into next year's budget and to make do with what you have for this year?

• Are there predetermined vendors for curriculum, sound equipment, retreat sites? Or do you determine from whom to purchase?

- Do you get parental financial support, or are you solely dependent on money allocated from the church general budget? What role do your ministry fundraisers play?

- When do you need to turn in your budget proposal to the administration?

- When is the budget decided, and are midyear changes allowed? If so, what's the procedure?

- Can you raise additional funds if needed? Do you need approval for that?

WHAT FINANCIAL STANDARDS ARE IN HARMONY WITH YOUR COMMUNITY?

- In what socioeconomic area is the church located and in what way is that population reflected in your group? (If upper-middle-class members primarily populate your church, you can probably request a bigger budget. If your congregation is financially strapped, you will have less available financing resources. Study how your church's socioeconomic makeup affects your ministry finances.)

- Do you have transportation available to you for ministry outings, or do you have to rent vehicles?

- What needs upgrading over the course of the next year for student safety?

- What do you need to make the ministry student-friendly?

- What items need to be purchased in order for you to continue the development of your ministry? List in order of priority and find out the approximate cost of each item.

BUDGET: MONTHLY REPORT SAMPLE

Accounts	Category	Budget	Year-to-date actual	Over / under	Aug.	Sep.	Oct.	Nov.	Dec.	Jan.	Feb.	Mar.	Apr.	May	Jun.	Jul.
Income																
	Church support		$10,000.00													
	Donations		$2,000.00													
	Fundraisers		$1,500.00													
	Other income		$600.00													
	Total income		$14,100.00													
Expense																
	Administration		$150.00													
	Advertisement		$75.00													
	Books and materials		$250.00													
	Dues & subscriptions		$25.00													
	Facilities		$2,500.00													
	Finance charges		$15.00													
	Fundraising expenses		$98.00													
	Gifts		$200.00													
	Insurance		$250.00													
	Communications		$350.00													
	Office expenses		$125.00													
	Payroll		$8,000.00													
	Postage		$150.00													
	Transportation		$455.00													
	Travel		$209.00													
	Miscellaneous																
	Total expenses		$12,852.00													
	Net income		$1,248.00	(income - expenses = net income)													

Accounts	Category	Budget	Year-to-date actual	Over / under	Aug.	Sep.	Oct.	Nov.	Dec.	Jan.	Feb.	Mar.	Apr.	May	Jun.	Jul.
Income																
	Church support															
	Donations															
	Fundraisers															
	Other income															
	Total income															
Expense																
	Administration															
	Advertisement															
	Books and materials															
	Dues & subscriptions															
	Facilities															
	Finance charges															
	Fundraising expenses															
	Gifts															
	Insurance															
	Communications															
	Office expenses															
	Payroll															
	Postage															
	Transportation															
	Travel															
	Miscellaneous															
	Total expenses															
	Net income															

(income - expenses = net income)

WHAT TO INCLUDE IN YOUR BUDGET

SALARY AND BENEFITS

YOUTH ADMINISTRATION
- Professional books
- Magazines / periodicals / newsletters
- Continuing education
- Training / seminars / workshops
- Dues
- Office expenses

PROGRAM (listed alphabetically)
- Activities
    - *Fall*
    - *Winter*
    - *Spring*
    - *Summer*
- Banquets
- Camps and retreats
    - *Honorariums*
    - *Programming*
    - *Scholarships*
    - *Miscellaneous*
- Campus ministry
    - *Bible clubs*
    - *"See You at the Pole"*
- Curriculum
- Fundraising
- Gifts
- Honorariums
- Insurance
- Leadership development / discipleship
- Library / resource center
    - *Books*
    - *Magazines*
- Ministry teams
    - *Drama*
    - *Music*
        - Sunday / Wednesday program
        - Choir
        - Groups
        - Worship Band
- Office supplies
- Photography / video / media
- Promotion / publicity / advertising
- Recreation equipment
- Senior recognition
    - *Graduation gifts*
    - *Banquet / reception*
- Special events
- Transportation
- Travel
- Miscellaneous

POSTAGE
- Mass mailings
- Weekly communications / monthly newsletter / personal letters
    - *Students*
    - *Volunteers*
    - *Parents*
- UPS / FedEx / other
- Miscellaneous

PRINTING
- Class notes / lessons
- Calendars
- Fliers
- Class newspaper
- Letters / mass mailings
- Transparencies / overheads
- Daily use
- Other

TRANSPORTATION
- Activities
    - *Fall*
    - *Winter*
    - *Spring*
    - *Summer*
    - *Miscellaneous*
- Camps and retreats
- Youth administration
    - *Visitation*
    - *Hospital visitation*
    - *Miscellaneous*

COMMUNICATIONS
- Web site development
- Facebook development / advertising
- Email blasts
- Group text subscription

Adapted from "What I Include in My Budget" by Kevin Winningham, *Youthworker*, Spring 1994.

Organization name _____

Address _____

City _____ State _____ Zip _____

Phone _____

Received from_____
                          Donor name

Date _____ Donation amount _____

Organization name _____

Address _____

City _____ State _____ Zip _____

Phone _____

Received from_____
                          Donor name

Date _____ Donation amount _____

Organization name _____

Address _____

City _____ State _____ Zip _____

Phone _____

Received from_____
                          Donor name

Date _____ Donation amount _____

Organization name _____

Address _____

City _____ State _____ Zip _____

Phone _____

Received from_____
                          Donor name

Date _____ Donation amount _____

Organization name _____

Address _____

City _____ State _____ Zip _____

Phone _____

Received from_____
                          Donor name

Date _____ Donation amount _____

Organization name _____

Address _____

City _____ State _____ Zip _____

Phone _____

Received from_____
                          Donor name

Date _____ Donation amount _____

(Place on church letterhead)

October 15, 20xx

David Schmidt
6475 Lake Lamont Pass
San Diego, CA 22618

Dear David,

Thank you for your thoughtful gift of [amount of money, description of item, or service given]. Your generosity allows us to continue our mission to [insert your adjusted mission statement here].

May God return to you the blessing you have so generously given to us. We appreciate your continued prayers for our ministry among adolescents. The staff depends on the Lord's strength and provision every day.

Sincerely,

Your name

With this gift, you did not receive any goods or services in exchange for your donation other than religious benefits.

HOW TO BEGIN A BUDGET

STEP 1

See that youth ministry becomes a budget item in the larger church budget.

STEP 2

Check out the budgets of other youth ministries to learn what your budget may need to include. Start with ministries in your own area, then network with other ministries in your region and even across the country. Pay particular attention to budgets of ministries similar in size to yours and in a similar economic situation.

STEP 3

Determine what should and shouldn't be included in your budget, based on last year's check disbursements and purchase orders, this year's check disbursements and purchase orders, and old budgets (if there are any).

STEP 4

Keep a file of your research. Include articles on budgets from youth magazines and denominational and secular publications, as well as actual budgets researched in Steps 1 and 3 above.

STEP 5

Propose a budget. Present yourself as a professional—distribute handouts, use presentation media and respond with detailed rationale for each item you propose. Preface your presentation with a persuasive talk about why youth ministry should be part of the budget. Buttress your requests by sharing information gleaned from networking (in Step 1, above). Conclude your presentation with a brief overview of your proposed youth ministry.

STEP 6

Keep good records for the next year, including income (from activities, camps, retreats, fundraisers) and all expenses.

STEP 7

Be a good steward of your ministry resources. Let your use of resources be guided by prayer and accountability to one or more individuals who support the youth ministry.

Adapted and Reprinted by permission from *Youthworker*, Spring 1994.

Fiscal Year: 2016

Acc. #	Category	Budget	Year-to-date actual	Over / under	Aug.	Sep.	Oct.	Nov.	Dec.	Jan.	Feb.	Mar.	Apr.	May	Jun.	Jul.
1001	Staff Dev.	$125	$100	$25	$10		$10	$10	$10	$10	$50					
1002	Operations	$200	$60	$140		$25		$10		$25						
1003	Materials	$150	$50	$100		$25					$25					
1004	Transportation	$20	$-	$20												
1005	Food	$100	$250	$(150)	$50		$25	$25		$25		$75		$25	$25	
1006	Misc.	$75	$75	$-		$25		$25				$25				
	Total expenses	$670	$535	$135	$60	$75	$35	$70	$10	$60	$75	$100	$-	$25	$25	$-

MONTHLY EXPENSE REPORTS

Fiscal Year: _____

Acc. #	Category	Budget	Year-to-date actual	Over / under	Aug.	Sep.	Oct.	Nov.	Dec.	Jan.	Feb.	Mar.	Apr.	May	Jun.	Jul.
	Total expenses															

PETTY CASH RECEIPT

Date_____ / _____ / _____

To_____
NAME OF RECIPIENT

Amount $ _____

To use for—

Return date—

_____ / _____ / _____

PETTY CASH RECEIPT

Date_____ / _____ / _____

To_____
NAME OF RECIPIENT

Amount $ _____

To use for—

Return date—

_____ / _____ / _____

PETTY CASH RECEIPT

Date_____ / _____ / _____

To_____
NAME OF RECIPIENT

Amount $ _____

To use for—

Return date—

_____ / _____ / _____

PETTY CASH RECEIPT

Date_____ / _____ / _____

To_____
NAME OF RECIPIENT

Amount $ _____

To use for—

Return date—

_____ / _____ / _____

PETTY CASH RECEIPT

Date_____ / _____ / _____

To_____
NAME OF RECIPIENT

Amount $ _____

To use for—

Return date—

_____ / _____ / _____

PETTY CASH RECEIPT

Date_____ / _____ / _____

To_____
NAME OF RECIPIENT

Amount $ _____

To use for—

Return date—

_____ / _____ / _____

PETTY CASH RECEIPT

Date_____ / _____ / _____

To_____
NAME OF RECIPIENT

Amount $ _____

To use for—

Return date—

_____ / _____ / _____

PETTY CASH RECEIPT

Date_____ / _____ / _____

To_____
NAME OF RECIPIENT

Amount $ _____

To use for—

Return date—

_____ / _____ / _____

From _____ to _____
DATE   DATE

INCOME

Church support

Donations

Fundraisers

Other income
_____

Total income

EXPENSE

Administration

Advertisement

Books and materials

Dues & subscriptions

Facilities

Finance charges

Fundraising expenses

Gifts

Insurance

Mailings

Office expense

Payroll

Postage

Transportation

Travel
_____

Total expense
_____

Net income
(Total income minus total expense)

PROFIT LOSS STATEMENT SAMPLE

From _____ to _____
DATE   DATE

INCOME

Church support	$ 10,000
Donations	$ 2,000
Fundraisers	$ 1,500
Other income	$ 600
Total income	$14,100

EXPENSE

Administration	$ 500
Advertisement	$ 75
Books and materials	$ 250
Dues & subscriptions	$ 25
Facilities	$ 2,500
Finance charges	$ 15
Fundraising expenses	$ 98
Gifts	$ 200
Insurance	$ 250
Mailings	$ 350
Office expense	$ 125
Payroll	$ 8,000
Postage	$ 150
Transportation	$ 455
Travel	$ 209
Total expense	$13,202
Net income	$ 898

(Total income minus total expense)

REIMBURSEMENT

Name_____

Whose money _____

Address (optional)_____

_____

Account name _____

Explanation _____

_____

Receipt total

Deduct

Tax & personal expenses

Reimbursement total

Division leader's approval

REIMBURSEMENT

Name_____

Whose money _____

Address (optional)_____

_____

Account name _____

Explanation _____

_____

Receipt total

Deduct

Tax & personal expenses

Reimbursement total

Division leader's approval

REIMBURSEMENT

Name_____

Whose money _____

Address (optional)_____

_____

Account name _____

Explanation _____

_____

Receipt total

Deduct

Tax & personal expenses

Reimbursement total

Division leader's approval

REIMBURSEMENT

Name_____

Whose money _____

Address (optional)_____

_____

Account name _____

Explanation _____

_____

Receipt total

Deduct

Tax & personal expenses

Reimbursement total

Division leader's approval

	Quantity	Cost	Projected	Actual	Projected	Actual
Expenses						
Brochure printing	1	$65	$65	$ -		
Postage	1	$50	$50	$ -		
T-shirts	125	$8	$1,000	$ -		
Student camp fees	100	$49	$4,900	$ -		
Bus rental	2	$200	$400	$ -		
Bus mileage	1	$100	$100	$ -		
Speaker	1	$450	$450	$ -		
Late vehicle	1	$120	$120	$ -		
Fuel	1	$150	$150	$ -		
Band	1	$800	$800	$ -		
Truck rental	1	$200	$200	$ -		
Equipment rental	1	$225	$225	$ -		
Supplies/props	1	$300	$300	$ -		
Dinner	1	$250	$250	$ -		
Program staff	8	$59	$472	$ -		
Staff expense	10	$49	$490	$ -		
Total Expenses			**$9,972**	**$ -**		

Revenue (not including student fees)						
Program budget	1	$1,000	$1,000	$ -		
Staff payment	8	$25	$200	$ -		
Revenue			**$1,200**	**$ -**		
					Projected	**Actual**
Total expenses					$9,972	$ -
Minus total revenue					$1,200	$ -
Equals Net Cost					**$8,772**	**$ -**

Student fees					
Net cost (same as total student fees)		$8,772			
Divided by Number of students attending		$100			
Cost per student		$ 87.72			
				Projected	**Actual**
Revenue				$1,200	
Plus total student fees				$8,772	
					$9,972
Minus total expenses				$9,972	
NET (+\-)					$0

SUMMARY BALANCE SAMPLE

As of July 31, 20XX

ASSETS

Checking / savings	$ 2,000	
Other current assets	$248	(include all assets)
Total current assets	**$ 2,248**	

LIABILITIES AND EQUITY

Current liabilities	$ 1,000	(include all outstanding bills)
Total liabilities	**$ 1,000**	
Net income	**$ 1,248**	

As of _____

ASSETS

Checking / savings $

Other current assets $ (include all assets)

Total current assets $

LIABILITIES AND EQUITY

Current liabilities $ (include all outstanding bills)

Total liabilities $

Net income $

Cedar Pines Retreat - May 20xx

LODGING				
Price of room per night	$	85.95		
Divided by—number of people per room	/	4		
Equals—price per person	$	21.49		
Multiplied by—number of nights	x	3		
	=		**Per-person lodging cost**	**$ 64.49**

TRANSPORTATION				
• Transportation package				
Price of round trip to event	$	400.00		
Divided by—number of participants	/	13		
	=		**Per-person cost with package**	**$ 30.75**
• Vehicle rental and gas				
Miles we're traveling		850		
Miles per gallon in rental vehicle		15	Use only *one* calculation:	
Total gallons needed=		56	Per-person cost with package	
Multiplied by average price per gallon	x $	3.75	**OR**	
Total gas cost=	**$**	**210.00**	Per-person cost with vehicle rental and gas	
Plus—total vehicle rental cost=	**$**	**250.00**		
Total of gas and rental=	**$**	**460.00**		
Divided by—number of riders	/	13		
	=		**Per-person cost with vehicle rental and gas**	**$ 35.38**

FOOD				
Number of breakfasts per person		3		
Multiplied by—average price for breakfast	x	$4.00		
Total for breakfasts (A)	$	12.00		
Number of lunches per person		4		
Multiplied by—average price for lunch	x	$6.00		
Total for lunches (B)	$	24.00		
Number of dinners per person		4		
Multiplied by—average price for dinner	x	$8.00		
Total for dinners (C)	$	32.00		
(A)	$	12.00		
Plus (B)	+ $	24.00	**Per-person cost for lodging**	**$ 64.46**
Plus (C)	+ $	32.00	**Per-person cost for travel**	**$ 30.75**
	=		**Per-person cost for all meals**	**$ 68.00**
			Total per-person cost for trip	**$ 163.21**

Trip _____ Date _____

LODGING

Price of room per night	$	
Divided by—number of people per room	/	
Equals—price per person	$	
Multiplied by—number of nights	x	
	=	Per-person lodging cost $

TRANSPORTATION

• Transportation package		
Price of round trip to event	$	
Divided by—number of participants	/	
	=	Per-person cost with package $
• Vehicle rental and gas		
Miles we're traveling		
Miles per gallon in rental vehicle		Use only *one* calculation:
Total gallons needed=		Per-person cost with package
Multiplied by average price per gallon	x $	**OR**
Total gas cost=	$	Per-person cost with vehicle rental and gas
Plus—total vehicle rental cost=	$	
Total of gas and rental=	$	
Divided by—number of riders	/	
	=	Per-person cost with vehicle rental and gas $

FOOD

Number of breakfasts per person		
Multiplied by—average price for breakfast	x	
Total for breakfasts (A)	$	
Number of lunches per person		
Multiplied by—average price for lunch	x	
Total for lunches (B)	$	
Number of dinners per person		
Multiplied by—average price for dinner	x	
Total for dinners (C)	$	
(A)	$	
Plus (B)	+ $	Per-person cost for lodging $
Plus (C)	+ $	Per-person cost for travel $
	=	Per-person cost for all meals $
		Total per-person cost for trip $

FINANCES
TIPS FOR THE NEWCOMER

"It's my first day on the job. What do I do now when it comes to finances?"

FIRST WEEK:

- Request a copy of the current budget and of last year's budget.
- Schedule a meeting with the person familiar with the youth ministry budget.
- Ask for training on current procedures for tracking income and expenses.
- Ask what ways of handling finances have worked in the past and what trouble spots you should be aware of. (Keep an eye on the trouble spots during the next few weeks.)
- Unless the finances are in crisis, keep to the system currently in place. Change and improvements can come when you have more knowledge of and experience with the ministry.

FIRST MONTH:

- Study and understand the budget. Get a feel for how it's been used in the past—what worked and what didn't.
- Talk to anyone who's had experience working with the youth ministry budget.
- Talk to the current church treasurer to see what has worked well with the youth ministry and what hasn't. Also ask if there's anything that could be done differently to be helpful to the treasurer.
- Work on patching the financial holes. If necessary, call a temporary spending freeze until you get a handle on the finances.
- Meet with the pastor and/or treasurer to discuss

  —the church's philosophy on spending, on corporate and personal fundraising, and on ministry money management.

  —what things are in stone and what things are negotiable.

  —what the current systems are for bill paying and reimbursements, and when you have to submit the paperwork to receive timely payment.
- Investigate how youth ministry petty cash, donations, fees, and expense reimbursement are currently handled and evaluate if it's successful or not. Try to assign someone else to handle the petty cash (administrative assistant, financial volunteer, etc.). If needed, change the system so that every bill, check, donation, petty cash receipt, and dollar go across your desk. You need to know how every penny is being collected and spent. That's the only way that you'll ever get a handle on the ministry finances.

FIRST SIX MONTHS:

- After understanding, observing, and personally monitoring the budget for at least 6 months, you can delegate to a staff person or trusted (experienced) volunteer some of the routine procedures. Request weekly or monthly reports from your volunteer so you can monitor any major income or expenses (perhaps over $25 or $100, depending on the size and scope of your ministry).
- Reevaluate the current budget and adjust it according to your ministry needs.
- Never assume. Always check and double-check numbers.
- If at any time you creep into the financial danger zone—overspending a monthly budget, losing money on an event, unable to account for some expenses or the reason for some checks or cash you find in a drawer—notify the church's treasurer or Business Administrator and get assistance ASAP. Business Administrators don't like surprises and are more forgiving if you come forward sooner rather than later.

PURPOSE

Total Budget Allocated: $ _____

YM100 Events: $ _____

RETREATS, ALL NIGHTERS, STAFF CONFERENCES, LEADER FUNDING

YM200 Youth Equipment: $ _____

SUPPLIES, ROOM DECOR, RECREATIONAL SUPPLIES

YM300 Resources: $ _____

CURRICULUM, TRAINING MATERIALS

YM400 Food: $ _____

YM500 AV Equipment / Music: $ _____

YM600 Communication / Technology: $ _____

YM700 Misc: $ _____

Month of _____

GOALS / PRIORITIES

IDEAS

PHONE CALLS / PEOPLE TO SEE

LETTERS & NOTES TO WRITE

THINGS TO PLAN

OTHER THINGS TO DO

NEW PEOPLE

Week of _____

GOALS / PRIORITIES

IDEAS

PHONE CALLS / PEOPLE TO SEE

LETTERS & NOTES TO WRITE

THINGS TO PLAN

OTHER THINGS TO DO

NEW PEOPLE

One of the challenges of building a ministry calendar is providing diverse opportunities in which a variety of students, ranging in stages of spiritual growth and personal development, can all feel excited about being involved. How can you reach and challenge the wide variety of students that have been entrusted to you?

Don't rush the process of designing an appropriate ministry calendar. And don't try to take a shortcut by developing the calendar on your own. Allow adult leaders, parents, your pastor, and key student leaders to walk through this process with you.

❑ Begin with a blank calendar.

❑ These are out of your control, so place them on the calendar first:

1. **Church/ministry mandated dates**
   Ask your pastor to be specific on his/her expectations regarding the participation of you or students in things like the following:
   • Special worship and prayer services
   • Choir and musical performances (especially Easter and Christmas)
   • Church membership classes
   • Church staff retreats
   • Holiday services
   • Community outreach events
   • Summer VBS
   • All-church picnics
   • Denominational events and retreats

2. **Community/school conflicts to avoid**
   School—ask in particular about these important dates:
   • Captain's practices
   • Homecoming
   • Fall break (in some areas)
   • Christmas break
   • Spring break
   • President's Day and Martin Luther King, Jr. weekend
   • State or city holidays
   • Major testing periods
   • School start and end dates
   • Sports and band schedules (beginning in the summer)
   • Agricultural or livestock events
   • Prom
   • Major concerts, drama performances, debates, band contests
   • Graduations, baccalaureate services
   • SAT, ACT, and PSAT tests

3. **Significant sports or cultural events, in the area and nationally**
   Events and concerts—
   • Christian music festivals
   • Citywide Christian events—including event training for your staff
   Sports—
   • Tournament weekends
   • Men's, women's, and recreational sports schedules

- College and professional sports, like Super Bowl, World Series, Final Four, World Cup, Stanley Cup, NASCAR, Racing, X-Games, and the Olympics
- Hunting or fishing openers
- Use sporting events as gathering places for programming. Instead of avoiding placing activities on these dates, you might capitalize on them.

4. **Family dates: birthdays, anniversaries, vacations, etc.**

5. **Holiday and seasonal considerations**
   Events may need to be planned around weather and culturally supported seasons.
   - Does the expected weather support your ministry event? It's hard to play broomball when it's 40 degrees outside, and picnics are no fun when it's cold and rainy.
   - Based on your ministry environment and the culture in which you minister, determine what times of year are best for initiatives in specific areas. September and January, for instance, are months when students in the United States are more open to new things, fresh starts. Some churches use the following timeline:

     —**Summer** is for relationship building.

     —**Late summer** suits volunteer recruitment.

     —**Fall** supports outreach and making new relationships.

     —**Winter** is the season for personal growth, for building deeper relationships, and for student leadership development.

     —**Spring** is a good time of year for celebration and preparations for summer service and missions activities.

❏ Examine your purpose, values, and goals, as created by your ministry team and approved by the church leadership, senior pastor first.

❏ Establish the *why* behind all the events you're considering doing.

❏ Examine your tentative plan for good balance among the following activities:

   —outreach and evangelistic events

   —service / justice projects (including local tasks, missions events, and trips)

   —opportunities for students to develop relationships and have fun together

   —opportunities for growth (Bible studies, small groups, serving, etc.)

   —leadership development opportunities

   —worship and prayer events

   —staff meetings and training

   —parent meetings

❏ Study your community. Meet with a diverse group of representative students. Ask about popular social hangouts, radio stations, music preferences, the way they experience peer relationships—including sexual standards, local rites of passage, perceptions of illegal substances—their views of local churches, work habits, and family relationships. Effective ministry strategy aligns with the needs of your community.

Quarterly Ministry Calendars –	due: 1-month ahead minimum
Summer (June-August)	due: March 1
Fall (Sept – Nov)	due: July 1
Winter (Dec – Feb)	due: October 1
Spring (Mar – May)	due: January 1
Staff Meeting & Training Schedule	due: July 1 (for the upcoming school year)
Annual Teaching Overview	due: July 1
Major Date Overview to Parents	due: August 1 (for the upcoming school year)
Fall Retreat Brochure	due: August 15
Winter Camp Brochure	due: October 15
Summer Mission Trip Brochure	due: March 1
Summer Camp Brochure	due: March 1

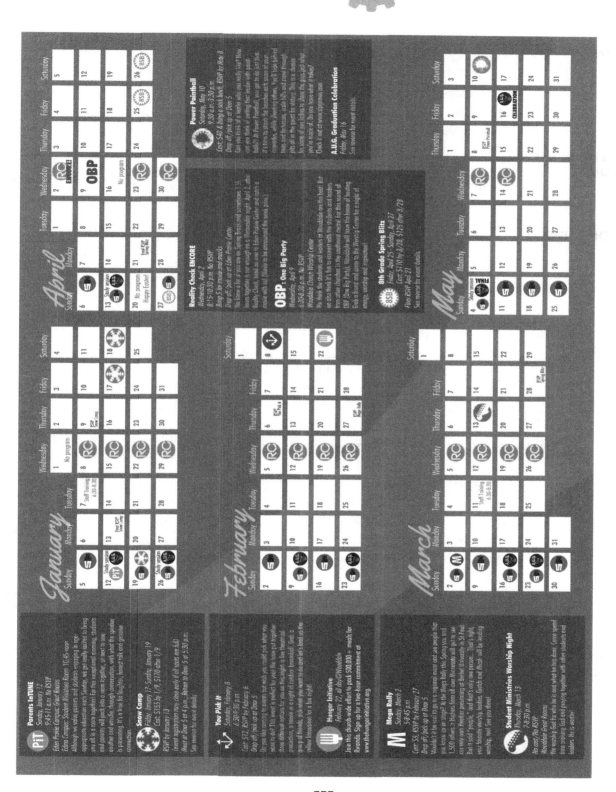

RISK MANAGEMENT
CHURCH INCIDENT REPORT

ORGANIZATION

Church: _____

Address: _____

City, State ZIP: _____

Phone: _____

Web site _____

TIME AND PLACE OF INJURY

Date of Injury: _____ Time: _____ ❑ AM ❑ PM

Where did the injury occur?

PERSON INJURED

Name: _____ Age: _____ Gender: _____

Address: _____ Telephone: _____

Name of parents/guardians (if a minor): _____

Employer: _____

Injuries sustained: _____

Where was injured taken? (hospital/doctor): _____

Relationship to organization: ❑ Member ❑ Visitor ❑ Volunteer
❑ Employee ❑ Student/Camper
❑ Outside Organization using facilities (name): _____

If injury occurred on insured's premises, for what purpose was the injured on the premises?

Who was responsible for supervision at the time of injury?

If injury occurred elsewhere, what connection did it have with the insured's operations or activities?

Does the injured party have personal medical insurance that could apply? ❑ Yes ❑ No

Name & contact information of medical insurance company:

FULL DESCRIPTION OF INCIDENT

(additional space provided on back)

Witnesses

Name: _____   Name: _____

Telephone: _____   Telephone: _____

Address: _____   Address: _____

Every youth leader should have a written emergency procedure policy for all general ministry activities.

• Provide each staff member a *written* manual, including emergency procedures.

• Verbally explain procedures at new staff orientation.

• At each event assign an emergency or crisis manager (you or another staff person) who knows procedures. Larger ministries who retain a doctor, nurse, or emergency medical technician (EMT) may place that professional in the manager position. Check with your insurance agent about the liability of designating this person.

• Staff and leadership need to specifically know who is the crisis manager on duty (sometimes called the Event Manager or point person). In an emergency speed is important, clarity is critical, and teamwork is essential.

• Make sure that several members of your staff have taken basic CPR and first-aid training courses. Clear thinking in a medical crisis comes with proper medical training.

• Keep a well-stocked medical kit easily accessible. Refresh after any incident or every three months.

• Thoroughly review all medical release forms for allergies and special conditions. Be especially mindful of asthma, diabetes, food and bee sting allergies.

• Have additional staff who have received advanced first-aid training, if possible.

• Get to know doctors, nurses, Certified First Responders, and emergency medical technicians (EMTs) in your ministry. In case you have an emergency, however, do not rely on them as a substitute for calling 911. Instead rely on them to provide assistance until help arrives. Make yourself aware of liability related to using off-duty medical personnel.

• Be sure that a certified lifeguard is on duty whenever swimming is part of an activity.

• Know how to give a 911 operator detailed instructions as to how to reach your group.

• Know the location of the closest medical facility.

RISK MANAGEMENT
PARTICIPATION SURVEY – ADULT

BASIC INFORMATION

Name: _____ Birthday: _____ / _____ / _____ ❑ Male ❑ Female

Address: _____ City: _____ State: _____ Zip: _____

Home Phone: (____) - ____ - _____ Household Email: _____

Email: _____ Cell (____) - ____ - _____

SPOUSE INFO:

Name: _____

Email: _____

Address: _____ City: _____ State: _____ Zip: _____

Phone: Home (____) - ____ - _____ Cell (____) - ____ - _____ Work (____) - ____ - _____

ALTERNATE EMERGENCY CONTACT

Name: _____ Relationship: _____

Email: _____

Address: _____ City: _____ State: _____ Zip: _____

Phone: Home (____) - ____ - _____ Cell (____) - ____ - _____ Work (____) - ____ - _____

HEALTH AND INSURANCE AND HEALTH HISTORY

Medical insurance carrier: _____

Policy#: _____ Group#: _____

Carrier address: _____

Name of insured person: _____

Date of birth of insured person: _____

Insured person's place of employment: _____

Name of family physician: _____ Phone: (____) - ____ - _____

Name of dentist/orthodontist: _____ Phone: (____) - ____ - _____

HEALTH HISTORY (CHECK. GIVE APPROXIMATE DATES)

Conditions:
- ❑ Frequent Ear Infections
- ❑ Diabetes
- ❑ Bleeding Disorders
- ❑ Heart Defect/Disease
- ❑ Seizures
- ❑ ADD/ADHD

- ❑ Down syndrome
- ❑ Tourette's syndrome
- ❑ Chicken Pox
- ❑ Measles
- ❑ Mononucleosis
- ❑ Asthma

Allergies:
- ❑ Hay Fever
- ❑ Penicillin
- ❑ Ivy Poisoning, etc.
- ❑ Insect Stings
- ❑ Food (specify) _____
- ❑ Drugs (specify) _____
- ❑ Other _____

Chronic/recurring illness/medical conditions including mental illness: (depression, anxiety, etc.) _____

_____

Dietary restrictions: _____

Current medications: (List both prescription, OTC & herbal)

Medication name: _____ Dosage: _____ Purpose: _____

Medication name: _____ Dosage: _____ Purpose: _____

Any other information you feel the leaders should know in advance about you: _____

Blood type: _____ Are all immunizations current? ❑ Yes ❑ No

Participant signature: _____ Date: _____

WAIVER, RELEASE, AND ASSUMPTION OF THE RISK

I (we) acknowledge that my participation in First Church activities is voluntary and may require traveling or physical exertion. Such activities may include, but are not limited to: outings, athletic games, physical labor, construction projects, local excursions and meetings, and other physically demanding or hazardous activities. I (we) acknowledge that my participation in a First Church activity presents risks that I (we) may suffer including, but not limited to, damage to personal property, financial damage, emotional injury, illness, bodily injury, or death. I (we) hereby assume those risks. And, in consideration of my being allowed to participate in the First Church activity, I (we) agree and take the following actions:

I (we) waive, release, and discharge First Church, its pastors, directors, officers, members, employees, volunteers, representatives, subcontractors, and agents from any and all claims for: (A) Financial losses, including (but not limited to) insurance deductibles and medical expenses, that I (we) must pay as a result of injury or illness arising out of activities sponsored by First Church; (B) Damage, destruction, loss or theft of personal belongings; and (C) Any claims or liabilities that I (we) may assert (directly or as a spouse) for loss of consortium, death or personal injury, which arise out of or relate to my participation in First Church's activities; and, to the extent allowable by law, all similar or identical claims that we may assert. Notwithstanding any of the foregoing, First Church is not released from any claims or liabilities that are caused solely by First Church.

I (we) agree not to sue any of the persons or entities mentioned above for any of the claims or liabilities that I have waived, released, or discharged herein.

I (we) indemnify and hold harmless the person or entities mentioned above from any claims made or liabilities assessed against them as a result of my actions.

I agree to indemnify and hold harmless the person or entities mentioned above for any claims or liabilities assessed against them as a result of any inaccuracy on the *Basic Information* form, the *Health Insurance and Health History* form, or the *Medical Treatment Authorization* form.

Participant signature _____ Date _____

Spouse's signature _____ Date _____

MEDICAL TREATMENT AUTHORIZATION

I am attending and participating in activities with First Church, which will take place on and off of the church campus, and which are described in the *Waiver, Release, and Assumption of the Risk* form and notifications from First Church (each an "Activity").

If, during such an Activity, I, my spouse and/or my alternate emergency contact am unable to consent at the time, due to incapacity, injury, illness or absence, I hereby authorize the Pastor, _____ _ and his designated leaders or volunteers who will be supervising activities at the Activity to consent to medical care or dental care, or both, for me. The authority granted by this authorization includes the authority to consent to any x-ray examination, anesthetic, medical, or surgical diagnosis or treatment, and hospital care under the general or special supervision and upon the advice of, or to be rendered by, a physician and surgeon. This authority also extends to any x-ray examination, anesthetic, dental or surgical diagnosis, or treatment and hospital care by a dentist.

I give this authorization in advance of any special diagnosis, treatment, or hospital care being required, but is given to provide authority and power on the part of the supervisor and his authorized designee to exercise his/her best judgment regarding what is advisable for me upon advice of such physician, dentist, and surgeon.

I certify that I have adequate health insurance or resources to cover the costs of treatment in case of any such injury or illness. I certify that within the past year I have had a physical examination and that I am physically able to participate in all First Church activities.

I give my permission to the staff to use the information provided in this form in connection with my participation in First Church and to disclose it to any health care provider, hospital, or other health care facility in connection with the provision of medical care to me.

I give my permission to the staff to render emergency first aid (including, but not limited to, "Cardiopulmonary Resuscitation" or the "Heimlich Maneuver") if necessary.

Participant signature _____ Date _____

BASIC INFORMATION

Minor Participant Info

Name: _____ Birthday: _____ / _____ / _____ ❏ Male ❏ Female

Address: _____ City: _____ State: _____ Zip: _____

Home Phone: (____) - ____ - _____ Household Email: _____

Student Email: _____ Student Cell (____) - ____ - _____

School Name: _____ Grade: _____

Does student have Facebook? ❏ Yes ❏ No

Parent/Guardian Info

Name: _____ Legal Relationship: ❏ Father ❏ Mother ❏ Legal Guardian

Email: _____

Address: _____ City: _____ State: _____ Zip: _____

Phone: Home (____) - ____ - _____ Cell (____) - ____ - _____ Work (____) - ____ - _____

Name: _____ Legal Relationship: ❏ Father ❏ Mother ❏ Legal Guardian

Email: _____

Address: _____ City: _____ State: _____ Zip: _____

Phone: Home (____) - ____ - _____ Cell (____) - ____ - _____ Work (____) - ____ - _____

Student lives with: Both parents Mother only Father only Shared custody Other: _____

ALTERNATE EMERGENCY CONTACT

Name: _____ Relationship: _____

Email: _____

Address: _____ City: _____ State: _____ Zip: _____

Phone: Home (____) - ____ - _____ Cell (____) - ____ - _____ Work (____) - ____ - _____

HEALTH AND INSURANCE AND HEALTH HISTORY

Medical insurance carrier: _____

Policy#: _____ Group#: _____

Carrier address: _____

Name of insured person: _____

Date of birth of insured person: _____

Insured person's place of employment: _____

Name of family physician: _____ Phone: (____) - ____ - _____

Name of dentist/orthodontist: _____ Phone: (____) - ____ - _____

RISK MANAGEMENT
PARTICIPATION SURVEY—MINOR

Page 2 of 3

HEALTH HISTORY: (CHECK. GIVE APPROXIMATE DATES)

Conditions:
- ❏ Frequent Ear Infections
- ❏ Diabetes
- ❏ Bleeding Disorders
- ❏ Heart Defect/Disease
- ❏ Asthma
- ❏ Mononucleosis

- ❏ Seizures
- ❏ ADD/ADHD
- ❏ Down syndrome
- ❏ Tourette's syndrome
- ❏ Chicken Pox
- ❏ Measles

Allergies:
- ❏ Hay Fever
- ❏ Penicillin
- ❏ Ivy Poisoning, etc.
- ❏ Insect Stings
- ❏ Food (specify) _____
- ❏ Drugs (specify)_____
- ❏ Other_____

Chronic/recurring illness/medical conditions including mental illness: (depression, anxiety, etc.) _____

Dietary restrictions: _____

Current medications: (List both prescription, OTC & herbal)

Medication name: _____ Dosage: _____ Purpose: _____

Medication name: _____ Dosage: _____ Purpose: _____

Any other information you feel the leaders should know in advance about you: _____

Blood type: _____ Are all immunizations current? ❏ Yes ❏ No

Parent(s)/guardian signature: _____ Date: _____

Student's signature: _____ Date: _____

WAIVER, RELEASE, AND ASSUMPTION OF THE RISK

I (We) acknowledge that my child's participation in First Church activities is voluntary and may require traveling or physical exertion. Such activities may include, but are not limited to: outings, athletic games, local excursions and meetings, and other activities in the *Permission Slip and Acknowledgment of Expectations*. I (We) acknowledge that my child's participation in any First Church youth activity presents risks that I or my child may suffer including, but not limited to, damage to personal property, financial damage, emotional injury, illness, bodily injury, or death. I (we) hereby assume those risks. And, in consideration of my child's being allowed to participate in the First Church youth program activities, I (we) agree and take the following actions for me and my child:

I (we) waive, release, and discharge First Church, its pastors, directors, officers, members, employees, volunteers, representatives, subcontractors, and agents from any and all claims for: (A) Financial losses, including (but not limited to) insurance deductibles and medical expenses, that we as parents or guardians must pay as a result of injury or illness arising out of activities sponsored by First Church; (B) Damage, destruction, loss or theft of personal belongings of the minor participant or parents of the same; and (C) Any claims or liabilities that I (we) may assert as parents for loss of consortium, death or personal injury, which arise out of or relate to my child's participation in First Church's youth activities; and, to the extent allowable by law, all similar or identical claims that my child may assert. Notwithstanding any of the foregoing, First Church is not released from any claims or liabilities that are caused solely by First Church.

362

I (we) agree not to sue any of the persons or entities mentioned above for any of the claims or liabilities that I have waived, released, or discharged herein.

I (we) indemnify and hold harmless the person or entities mentioned above from any claims made or liabilities assessed against them as a result of my child's actions.

I agree to indemnify and hold harmless the person or entities mentioned above for any claims or liabilities assessed against them as a result of any inaccuracy on the *Basic Information* form, the *Health Insurance and Health History* form, or the insufficiency of my legal capacity or authority to act for and on behalf of the minor in the execution of the *Waiver, Release, and Assumption of the Risk* form, the *Medical Treatment Authorization* form, or the *Permission Slip and Acknowledgment of Expectations* form.

I hereby execute this document for and on behalf of the minor named herein.

Parent(s)/guardian signature _____ Date _____

Parent(s)/guardian signature _____ Date _____

Student's signature _____ Date _____

PERMISSION SLIP AND ACKNOWLEDGMENT OF EXPECTATIONS

From _____ to _____ , my child has permission to attend all church sponsored youth activities as listed in calendars and/or First Church News, including but not limited to the following: cook-outs, boating, water-skiing, swimming, basketball, roller skating, rollerblading, games in the park, soccer, paintball, broomball, ice-skating, volleyball, softball, baseball, camping, downhill skiing, snow-boarding, hiking, biking, concerts, Bible studies, golfing, miniature golf, hayrides.

I acknowledge these rules of conduct expected from each participant and parent:

- Respect one another, staff, and adult leaders
- Respect property
- No lighters permitted
- No fighting, weapons, fireworks, explosives
- No students permitted to drive for events
- Participation with the group expected
- No offensive or immodest clothing
- No alcohol, drugs, tobacco
- No boys in girls' sleeping quarters & visa versa
- Respect and comply with event schedules

I and my child acknowledge that misconduct may result in transportation home from an activity at the parent's expense. A student dismissed for a disciplinary reason will not receive a refund of ANY activity fee. My child and I agree to follow the instruction of the pastor, leader, or volunteer who has been delegated leadership authority.

I understand and authorize that my child's image may be photographed or filmed and used in First Church video presentations, printed publications, Web site and photo directories.

Parent(s)/guardian signature _____ Date _____

Parent(s)/guardian signature _____ Date _____

Student's signature _____ Date _____

- **Experience in successful crisis management.** The Event Manager (EM) needs to be a trained and accomplished leader that's shown the ability to act when a crisis arises. Use a trainee EM in an apprentice role with a current EM. Only after proving themselves should trainees be appointed sole Event Manager. Although the job is a "hurry up and wait" type position, when they are needed, Event Managers must always be at their best. It's a bummer to find out in the middle of a problem that someone doesn't handle crisis well.

- **Equipped with basic medical training.** EMs need at least a certification in first aid and CPR—not that the job of the EM is to diagnose or treat the injured, but rather to assess what the next course of action should be and to lead the team in that direction.

- **Calm and cool-headed.** Even though most injuries are minor and only minimal treatment is necessary, the EM needs to be able to be calm under pressure.

- **Availability.** The EM needs to be accessible and available. On a retreat or extended event, several people may act as the EM at different times. That way your crisis manager is always ready and refreshed. You may equip the EM with a communication tool to make the EM more accessible. At a retreat use a walkie-talkie, a pager, or an air horn. If all else fails, make them stand under the camp bell at all times waiting for a crisis. Try different things to see what works.

- **Supported by the rest of the leadership team.** Once the EM determines the course of action, the staff needs to support the decision. A crisis is not the time to debate issues; it's the time for the leader to lead and the followers to follow. If the stakes are high, the lines of authority must be clear and everyone has to do their job.

  The EM shouldn't accompany the injured to the hospital, if hospitalization is required. The EM needs to stay with the group in case there are any other incidents. The EM should pick a staff person or two to accompany the student at the hospital until the parents arrive. The accompanying staff should be a responsible person, preferably of the same gender, and with whom the student feels comfortable.

- **Good adult communicator.** The EM discusses the incident with the staff member who accompanied the injured person and reviews their written incident report.

- **Perform appropriate emergency procedures.**
  1. One staff person attends to the injured party's needs.
  2. Another staff person immediately contacts the EM. (In a dire emergency, if the EM can't be located expediently, the staff in charge proceeds with the next steps while sending someone to find the EM.)
  3. EM assesses the situation.
  4. EM determines if the individual can be assisted locally. If so, the EM assigns an appropriate adult to assist the injured. The EM also determines at this point whether to notify the parents, or apply a Band-Aid and call it good.
  5. If the situation requires trained medical assistance or transportation to the hospital, EM asks a leader to call 911 to request paramedics and an ambulance. The caller needs to know the status of the injured person and the specific street address or location of the injured. The caller needs to remain on the phone to assist the dispatcher as long as necessary.
  6. EM sends a staff member to the entrance to guide the paramedics.
  7. EM assigns another, *calm* staff person to contact the individual's parents and advise them of the situation. If the person is being transported to the hospital, the parents should meet them at the hospital.
  8. The EM and any other needed staff member stays with the injured individual. All other staff assists the EM by keeping students and other onlookers away from the victim and out of the emergency team's way.
  9. A staff member brings the student's **Medical Release and Permission Form** to the EM.
  10. The EM appoints a staff member to accompany the student to the hospital, and gives her the form.
  11. After the student is transported, the EM assigns someone to clean up the accident site. If there is blood involved, use a biohazard kit for cleanup.

12. The EM determines what, if any, explanation needs to be given to the remaining students, or if the scheduled activities need to be adjusted or canceled.
13. The staff person that accompanies the student to the hospital checks in with the EM once they arrive at the medical facilities, and again when any news is known.
14. The EM and the leaders involved fill out an **Incident Report** and, if necessary, a **Damage Report**.
15. The following day, or as soon as possible, the EM distributes copies of the reports to the appropriate recipients.

HAVE ACCESS TO THE FOLLOWING INFORMATION

- Location of phone(s) and how to dial out
- How and where to find trained medical help (especially if the group is in a remote location)
- Address, directions, and phone number of the nearest medical center
- Location of the first-aid kit
- Where staff and students are rooming
- How to reach the facility director (camp, hotel, retreat center, etc.)
- Location of medical release forms
- Where a designated emergency vehicle is parked and who has the keys
- Special medical/physical conditions of the participants as recorded on the medical release forms (the EM must communicate these special needs to the rest of the staff)

PASSENGER RULES

- No standing while the vehicle is in motion.
- No smoking inside the bus.
- Keep arms, feet, and hands inside the vehicle.
- No throwing of things while in the vehicle.

OTHER SAFETY RULES

- Don't require the driver to deal with discipline. Appoint a staff member.
- Keep doors closed when moving.
- Never lock the emergency door when passengers are on board a bus.
- Never transport more than the posted number of passengers.
- Keep children out of the back row of seats, except when the bus is filled, to protect against injury in case the bus is rear-ended.
- Make smooth starts and stops.
- Because of fire hazard, fill the fuel tank only when there are no passengers on the bus. Never travel with a gas can or other flammables. *Never.*
- Keep packages, coats, and other objects out of the aisle.
- Watch for clearances (bridges, overpasses, etc.).
- Pick up and drop off students in such a manner that they are not required to cross streets.
- Require the use of seat belts in all vehicles that are equipped.
- Do not exceed the maximum numbers of hours a driver is permitted behind the wheel during any trip.
- Require a review of the driving record of all drivers transporting students / minors.
- Provide and require safe driver training for all church volunteer drivers.
- Drivers should not text or talk on their cell phones when driving. Period. Ever. If they must make a call or send a text, pull in to a rest area or service station.

FURTHER RESOURCES

Visit www.brotherhoodmutual.com for a complete section of resources and forms to assist you in safely transporting students in your ministry. Visit their Resource section and then select "Safety Library" and look for section titled "Vehicles and Drivers."

Visit nonprofitrisk.org and search the word *driving* on their Web site. Again—an amazing resource for ministries!

RISK MANAGEMENT
INCIDENT REPORT

Date of incident _____

Date report filed _____

Person filing report _____

INSTRUCTIONS:

As close as possible to the time the incident occurred, a copy of this report is to be filled out by the person in charge. Other eyewitnesses to the incident (preferably adults) may also fill out additional copies of this form.

YOUR INVOLVEMENT IN THE INCIDENT

DESCRIBE THE INCIDENT

WHERE THE INCIDENT OCCURRED (LOCATION)

INDIVIDUALS WHO WERE INJURED AND A DESCRIPTION OF THE INJURIES

DESCRIBE ACTION TAKEN ON BEHALF OF THE INJURED

NAMES OF OTHERS INVOLVED IN THE INCIDENT

NAME OF THE ADULT IN CHARGE AT TIME OF INCIDENT

NAMES OF OTHER WITNESSES

CAUSE OF INCIDENT (IN YOUR OPINION)

ADDITIONAL COMMENTS

RISK MANAGEMENT
INSURANCE COVERAGE WORKSHEET

What coverage does your ministry provide for those who volunteer? For those participating in events? For automobile accidents? Get answers to these critical volunteer insurance questions from your church's insurance agent.

- Who do I ask when I have questions about our church's insurance coverage?

- Who is the insurer for off-site events, on-site use of facilities, transportation?

- Who is covered by our insurance? What kind and amount of insurance coverage does our organization offer to volunteers?

- Does our policy include medical reimbursement, personal liability insurance, or excess automobile insurance?

- Do we have a commercial general liability (CGL) policy? If so, can we add volunteers as additional insured?

- Does the CGL include or exclude travel between their home and the church or event?

- What level of driver training does our policy require of volunteer drivers?

- Do we have accident insurance and what does it cover (in case a volunteer is injured during the course of a ministry event).

- Do we have volunteer liability? (If a volunteer causes damage or is negligent, he or she may be sued. This protection helps if there is a financial judgment rendered.)

- Do we have excess auto liability? (This is coverage over and above the volunteer's own coverage as required by state law.)

- Do we have coverage for volunteer/employee dishonesty (to protect the ministry in case a volunteer steals money or destroys property)?

- Is it a good idea to include our volunteers in our workers' compensation program?

- What crisis procedures does our insurance company use?

- What kind and amount of insurance is in effect at the facility to which we're going?

- In the event of an incident, who do you contact? What about after hours and on weekends?

This isn't a complete list—so during your conversation find out any other information your agent believes would be helpful to you. Do not assume that insurance questions and needs are being taken care of by another staff person at the church. And don't stop asking until you have an answer.

(For more insurance information, here's just a sampling of insurance companies that specialize in church and/or nonprofits:

Brotherhood Mutual:www.brotherhoodmutual.com

Church Mutual: www.churchmutual.com

CIMA Companies, Inc.: cimaworld.com

Guide One www.guideone.com

An often overlooked—even intentionally ignored—area is copyright infringement. Although it's pretty unlikely that section 110 of the Copyright Law of 1976 (17 U.S.C. 110[3]) is on your recreational reading list this year, here's a quick overview regarding its content. For more information about copyright law in the United States, visit www.copyright.gov.

WITHOUT FEAR OF BREAKING THE LAW, CHURCHES MAY—

Perform non-dramatic literary or musical works and religious dramatic and musical works.
   Display individual works of a non-sequential nature (17 U.S.C. 101).

THIS MEANS THAT DURING WORSHIP, YOU MAY—

Perform contemporary songs, regardless of the owner.
   Show any still image, regardless of its source. You may even show frames of a film, if they are not in sequence. You may show scanned images of any sort, including newspaper headlines, periodicals, and pictorial books.

HERE'S WHAT CHURCHES MAY NOT DO DURING WORSHIP, ACCORDING TO SECTION 110(3):

Play any non-live-performed recording of a musical work—no matter the format.
   Reproduce lyrics in any fashion from a copyright-protected musical work, including displaying lyrics within projected graphic images and printing the lyrics in bulletins or other handouts. Section 110(1) applies the same rules for media use in nonprofit educational environments, as well.
   Outside of worship and classroom, legal use of copyrighted works (including posting works on the Internet and selling works to other churches or individuals) is not as clearly defined. Much is made of the exemption in the copyright law for fair use. As a rule, never make blanket use of fair use.

KEEP IN MIND THE FOLLOWING GUIDELINES FOR CLAIMING FAIR USE OF A COPYRIGHTED PIECE:

- The more creative the work, the less likely it is to be covered by the fair use clause.

- Although no specific percentages apply, the more of a work that you use, the less chance that your use is covered by fair use.

- The more that fair use of a work decreases its market value, the less likely it is that you can claim fair use of it.

   The only activities qualifying for blanket fair use, according to standard interpretations of the First Amendment, are news reporting, research, and criticism. Evaluate all other uses on a work-by-work basis.

PARODIES MAY VIOLATE COPYRIGHT PROTECTION.

Fair use of copyrighted works for parodies *may* allow use of pre-recorded music with original dramatics, such as in a skit or video version of a sketch or TV show. To be sure you're not in audio-visual copyright violations, however, check with a copyright lawyer on a case-by-case basis.

RISK MANAGEMENT
COPYRIGHT LAWS FOR DIGITAL CONTENT

NON-HOME SHOWING OF RENTED VIDEOS REQUIRES A LICENSE.

By law, as well as by intent, pre-recorded DVD and Blu-Ray formatted movies available for rental or purchase are for home use only. You must have a license to show them in any other setting. Rentals or purchases of home DVD / Blu-Ray movies do not carry with them licenses for non-home showings.

These rules are stated in the Federal Copyright Act, Public Law 94-553, Title 17 of the United States Code. Any institution, organization, company, or individual wishing to engage in non-home showings of home video-cassettes *must* obtain a special license to show video materials. Among other rights, the Copyright Act grants to the copyright owner the exclusive right "to perform the copyrighted work publicly" (Section 106).

OBTAINING A LICENSE FOR NON-HOME USE OF COPYRIGHTED MATERIALS.

Licenses to show motion pictures at a church meeting and to display song lyrics are available through the following businesses, as well as through other channels:

- **Motion Picture Licensing Corporation**, P.O. Box 66970, Los Angeles, CA 90066. (800) 462-8855. The MPLC offers an umbrella license for a number of studios whose films are already available for rental. They charge an affordable yearly fee **(mplc.com).**

- Swank Motion Pictures, 201 S. Jefferson Avenue, St. Louis, Missouri 63103-2579. (800) 876-5577. **swank. com** Swank offers copies with license for public showings of films not yet available for rental.

- Criterion Pictures, 800-890-9494

- Christian Copyright Licensing International (CCLI), 17201 N.E. Sacramento St., Portland, OR 97230. 800-234-2446 or **ccli.com**.

Visit http://www.ccli.com to learn about licensing for worship songs, video use in services, worship live-streaming, and for the use of movie clips in your teaching

RISK MANAGEMENT
DAMAGE REPORT

INSTRUCTIONS:

Document all vital information about the damaged items.

Date report is filed?

Date the damage occurred?

Person filing the report?

What was your involvement with the damage?

What happened and how did the damage occur?

Who, if anyone, was involved with the damage?

Where is the damaged item now?

What action was taken?

What do you believe is the reason the damage occurred?

Additional comments?

Assuming you call an EMT immediately when you have a serious injury—and a hospital is readily accessible—your medical kit should be filled with these medical supplies:

- ❏ Band-Aids
- ❏ Instant ice packs
- ❏ Hydrogen peroxide
- ❏ Rubbing alcohol
- ❏ Tweezers
- ❏ Medications, prescription and non-prescription, will be administered to minor participants only with written authorization from a legal guardian/parent. *Consult with your insurance agent about dispensing medications, including aspirin.
- ❏ Surgical (rubber) gloves
- ❏ Thermometer (the small, plastic, disposable ones are handy)
- ❏ Antibiotic ointment or cream (such as Neosporin)
- ❏ Antibacterial or antiseptic spray (such as Bactine)
- ❏ Bug bite cream or lotion (such as Cortaid or Cortizone 10)
- ❏ Various size bandages, butterfly wound closures, etc.
- ❏ Gauze
- ❏ Medical tape

You may also need to stock a biohazard kit in case of bleeding (available in janitorial supply catalogs, or visit www.safetyonline.com for links to suppliers). In addition to surgical gloves and medical supplies, you'll need a chemical that absorbs blood spills and sanitizes the area.

If you need a more extensive medical kit (remote location, international travel, special-needs students, etc.) consult with trained medical personnel.

REGARDING INSURANCE:

Meet with your insurance agent *prior* to having an incident. Seriously. Call your agent and grab coffee. It can be costly to assume you have adequate coverage. And don't assume that your church administrator completely understands all the issues. Go to the insurance source. Ask questions. Protect yourself, your staff, your students, and your church.

- Who do I ask when I have questions about our church's insurance coverage?

- Who is the insurer?

- Who is covered by our insurance?

- Is my vehicle covered if I am required to drive it for the church? What about our volunteer leaders?

- What crisis procedures does our insurance company suggest?

- What insurance coverage is in effect at the facility to which we're going?

- What kind and amount of insurance will protect a volunteer with my group?

- What about accident coverage for special events and camps?

- What level of driver training does our policy require of volunteer drivers?

Don't make the mistake of making assumptions in this area. Ask questions. Ask to see the written policy your church has in effect. Make sure your own personal coverage is adequate as well. Call your own agent and discuss your role at the church and personal risks that you are exposed to.

INSURANCE AND SAFETY GUIDELINES:

Parents can be your best supporters—until you put their child at risk by unwise choices. You will create and keep the trust and respect of parents by carefully thinking through the things you do with students. Use the following safety checkup to evaluate activities sponsored by your ministry:

- Do your staff members understand their overall roles and responsibilities?

- Do you have enough adult leaders for this activity? Do they understand their roles for this event? Have you given them clear assignments? Rule of thumb—the younger the students, the more adults you'll need. For junior highers you'll want one sponsor for every eight students; senior highers require a one-to-ten ratio. The number of sponsors needed is also influenced by the type of activity.

- Have you clearly spelled out, to both adult leaders and students, guidelines for student behavior for each event?

- Do you and your staff have a clear, written plan for responding to and handling incidents that you may face? Parents are counting on the answer to this being YES.

When you're considering doing an activity or event that you haven't done before, run the idea through this set of questions.

1. What could possibly go wrong?

2. If something goes wrong, do I know what to do?
   - Emergency phone numbers for the event site and type of potential emergencies

   - How to get the proper help

   - Directions to closest medical facility

   - Evacuation plan

   - A way to account for every student in case of large-scale emergency

3. How much could this mistake cost (medical bills, repair, liability, legal bills, etc.)?

4. Has someone done this successfully and safely before?

5. What is the safety record of the organization/person you are hiring to lead the event?

6. Are protections in place to lessen the risk to the safety of students? Is the value of the experience worth the risk to students and to your career?

7. If your senior pastor knew you were doing this, what would she think? Would you still be employed?

8. Should an accident policy be purchased for this activity?

9. How many adults will it take to properly supervise this event?

How good are your current screening processes?
Check off the formal employee/volunteer screening programs you have below.

SCREENING AND TRAINING:

❏ Verification of educational background and degree.

❏ Checking at least three past references.

❏ Taking a photo I.D.

❏ Interviews by at least three individuals.

❏ Obtaining a police records check, including fingerprinting and verification on state and national levels.

❏ Maintaining employee/volunteer secure personnel files that document all screening records.

❏ Keeping a checklist for each employee that documents all training.

❏ Guided supervision of new staff members during the first three months on the job.

❏ Orientation of new workers, volunteers, or employees, including a review of the organization's policy on abuse/molestation incidents.

❏ Release form signed by potential volunteers/employees, informing them that there will be extensive screening of applicants through background checks, personal references, and criminal checks specifically geared toward controlling the problem of abuse and molestation.

❏ In-service training for all staff members, including specific information about abuse/molestation and its indications and effects.

❏ Regular written performance appraisals of all staff members.

POLICES AND OBSERVATIONS:

❏ If a student is injured and requires first aid, at least two adults will be present at the examination of the injuries.

❏ At least two staff members are assigned supervisory responsibility over a student.

❏ Students are only released to their legal guardian or someone designated in writing by the guardian.

❏ Students may not be touched on areas of their bodies that would be covered by swimming suits.

❏ Administrators interview students periodically to hear about their experiences in the program.

❏ Staff must immediately report any signs of injury or possible child abuse to the program administrator.

❏ Supervisors make frequent and unannounced visits to observe staff as they work with students, including (for 24-hour programs) late-night visits and shower times.

❏ Staff may not use physical punishment, verbally abusive comments, or denial of necessities of care in dealing with a student.

Adapted with permission from *nonprofitcoverage.com*

Here are a few practical steps to follow as you seek to provide safe transportation for your ministry.

- Have all drivers go through a driving & vehicle safety session. Check with your insurance company for recommendations.

- Don't assume your insurance coverage is adequate or in effect. Check with your church business administrator *and* your insurance agent.

- Check out the driving record of your staff. *Do not skip this step.* Use the Driver Application form to screen potential drivers.

- *Don't let students drive.* Period. Adult leaders should be at least 21 years old to drive.

- Tell your staff drivers that you expect them to obey all traffic laws. Seriously.

- Don't put more people in the car or van than it was designed to handle. Counting seatbelts generally lets you know how many you can legally transport. Don't exceed that number—ever. Then, require the use of these seatbelts.

- Check with your insurance agent regarding insurance coverage. Your church can be held liable for the damage and injuries caused by its employees or volunteers using their own vehicles or vehicles that the church rents or borrows for its operations. If your church uses vehicles owned by staff or volunteers, you should consider purchasing non-owned/hired auto liability coverage.

- When you leave for an event, make sure someone knows who went, where you are going, how you're getting there and when to expect your return. Carry copies of permission slips and medical forms. Leave trip details and a complete list of participants and staff at the church office.

- It's generally safer to rent or lease a vehicle than to borrow. Any problems with the vehicle are the responsibility of the rental company. Plus, insurance coverage is more clearly defined.

- Before driving a vehicle, conduct a safety check including (but not limited to):

  - ❑ Tire tread and pressure

  - ❑ Fluid levels

  - ❑ Lights - working and correctly adjusted

  - ❑ Rearview mirrors in proper position

  - ❑ Brakes have adequate stopping power

  - ❑ Check with your state's safety requirements by searching online for: [State] Vehicle Safety Inspection or Vehicle Safety Check.

SAFETY & ACCIDENT POLICIES & PROCEDURES

SAFETY PROCEDURES

The church expects each of the staff, regardless of his/her position with the church/organization, to cooperate in every respect with our safety program. Some of the major points of our program require that:

All injuries and accidents are reported immediately to the Pastor of Student Ministries or designated leader and to obtain medical aid without delay.

Personal protective equipment, where required, must be worn by all staff. There will be no exceptions to this requirement.

Hazardous conditions and other safety concerns must be reported immediately to the Pastor of Student Ministries.

The staff will follow all safety rules. Failure to follow the rules will result in disciplinary action or removal from staff.

ACCIDENT POLICY

When there is a staff member or a student injured your first priority is for them to receive medical help. Apply immediate first aid and if it is serious call 911 for help or bring the person to the hospital.

Immediately call the parents of the student and let them know about the injury.

Let the Pastor of Student Ministries or designated leader know about the accident and explain the details. Notify other church leaders if appropriate.

Fill out an accident report form and turn in to the Pastor of Student Ministries. Secure witness statements when possible. Include appropriate photographs.

Notify the church / ministry insurance carrier of the accident and open a claim immediately.

ACCIDENT REPORT FORM

Injured's name _____ Age _____

Parent or caregiver's name _____

Contact information _____

Gender _____ Date and time of accident _____

Location _____

Task being performed when accident occurred _____

Date and time accident reported _____ To whom _____

Name(s) of witness(es) _____

Describe how the accident occurred _____

What part of body was injured _____

Describe the injuries in detail _____

Date and time you sought medical attention _____

Name of doctor and/or hospital _____

Could anything be done to prevent accidents of this type? If so, what? _____

Signature of Staff _____ Date _____

Staff Name (please print) _____

Because of who we are in Christ, the organization we represent, and the vulnerable age group we work with, each of us must be willing to pay the price of leadership in every area of our lives.

The following areas are very important if you are to maintain a good reputation. We need your compliance in each of these areas for you to be a staff member.

You must not have a lifestyle that is contrary to clear Bible principles.

Do not plan activities with students or communicate with students without formal parental approval. Activities should also be approved by the youth pastor.

Attend church on a regular basis. Pursue spiritual growth.

Do not form exclusive relationships, e.g., date, with junior high/middle school or senior high youth or any person under your supervision or care.

Do not voice critical opinions about any Christian church, staff, parents, or students in front of students.

Do not use illegal drugs.

Do not get drunk.

When driving students you must obey all laws and use safe driving habits.

Never drive a student home alone.

Male staff are expected to spend time primarily with male students, female staff with female students.

Maintain appropriate physical and emotional boundaries at all times.

TOUCH

Do not initiate or demand touch with any student. Do not force touch upon a student or leader.

Use only appropriate touch. Appropriate touch honors physical and emotional boundaries and communicates encouragement or comfort.

Appropriate touch should take place only when in the presence of two or more leaders.

Counseling and mentoring appointments are confidential so you should not share conversations with any person other than a pastor or supervising staff.

In our setting, we prefer that men build mentoring relationships with young men, women build mentoring relationships with young women.

Always seek to conduct meetings in a visible setting which can be accessed at any time by staff, parents, and/or caregivers.

You **must** report to your supervisor any of the following situations **immediately. Call 911 when appropriate.**

Physical abuse reported to you.

Sexual abuse of any minor reported to you.

When a student tells you he/she is suicidal (take them seriously and report **immediately**).

When a student is in a life-threatening situation.

When the student is threatening someone else.

When a student discloses a pregnancy.

When a student is involved in a runaway situation.

When a student confesses a felony to you.

When you have reason to believe a student is going to commit a crime.

I have read the above and accept the STAFF CONDUCT AND GUIDELINES.

Signature of Staff _____ Date _____

EVENTS BUDGET

Event title _____ Event date _____

Formula: All expenses divided by the *least* number of participating students = the break even point.

Description	Total
STAFF COST	
Number of staff:	
Food:	
Housing:	
Transportation:	
Misc. staff expenses:	
A: Subtotal	
GENERAL EVENT EXPENSES	
Programming:	
Promotional materials:	
Transportation:	
Speaker:	
Teaching materials:	
Sports and activities:	
Rental equipment:	
B: Subtotal	
STUDENTS AND PAYING ADULTS COST FORMULA	
Food:	
Housing:	
Other misc. per-person expenses:	
C: Subtotal	
TOTAL A + B + C = D: TOTAL EVENT COST	
D: Total event cost	
E: Student per-person cost divided by number of students (Round number up to nearest even number or go back and cut expenses.)	
Student per-person price:	

EVENTS
CHECKLIST FOR STAFF ASSIGNMENTS

Event name_____ Dates_____

Time / schedule _____

Location _____ Maximum number of attendees _____

Accounting:

Per-person price for attendees_____ Total anticipated income_____

Total anticipated expenses _____

$ break for early registration?_____ By what date? _____ Refunds given?_____

Deadline for forms or money to be turned in?_____

Other specific rules or regulations?_____

---

* Beside the asterisk, write the name of the individual who's responsible for the listed task.

❑ **Folder setup**   *_____
❑ **Database setup**   *_____
❑ **Special equipment**   *_____
                              *_____
❑ **Room reserved**   *_____
❑ **Promotional materials:**
(Include registration form, permissions, medical releases, emergency #s)
Brochure / invitation / fliers *_____
Postcards or posters   *_____
Need content by? _____ *_____
How many? _____ Mail? _____ Bulk? _____
By what date?_____ Mail to whom?_____
Production: in-house or printer? _____

Advertising media
❑ Posters   *_____
Dates_____
❑ Church news   *_____
Dates_____
❑ Worship folder   *_____
Dates_____
❑ Pulpit announcement   *_____
Dates_____
❑ Church communities   * Which one(s)?
Dates_____
❑ Pastoral staff   *_____
❑ Radio   *_____
❑ Local newspapers   * Which one(s)?
Dates_____
❑ Mail to churches   * Which one(s)?
Dates_____
❑ Emails   * To whom?
❑ Other   * To whom?

❑ **Schedule / booklet**   *_____
How many? _____ Date content needed?_____
❑ **Nametags**   *_____
❑ **What-to-bring list**   *_____
List_____
_____

❑ **Meals or food**   *_____
Menu_____
_____
Budget_____ Cost_____
❑ **Transportation**   *_____
What? _____ Company _____
Budget _____ Cost_____
❑ **Accommodations**   *_____
Where?_____
Budget_____ Cost_____
❑ **Special purchases**   *_____
What?_____
_____ By what date?_____
Budget_____ Cost_____
❑ **Adult chaperones**   *_____
How many? _____ Who?_____
_____
_____ By what date?_____
❑ **Any special forms to fill out?** *_____
If yes, which forms? _____
_____
_____ By what date?_____
❑ **Other**   *_____

EVALUATION FEEDBACK MEMO SAMPLE

To: Team leaders
From: H2O steering committee
RE: Evaluation
Date: October 20, 20xx

Thank you for the awesome job you've done with H2O. We need your help evaluating the effectiveness of H2O, and making suggestions for improving it for next year. Please answer the following questions in detail, and return this feedback to the event director. Thanks.

1. Did you have enough information to effectively lead your team over the course of the event? If not, what more could we have provided for you?

2. Were you clear on why we did this event—event goals, status of pledge achievement, etc.? If not, what other information could we have provided for you?

3. What was your biggest challenge in leading your team?

4. Do you think that the incentives/giveaways motivated the students? Which items got the most enthusiastic response from the students?

5. How did the teams respond to the incentives?

6. On a scale of 1 to 10 (10 being the highest), how would you rate your team's enthusiasm for H2O?

7. How many students did you have on your team? Of that number, how many of the students actually participated in H2O?

8. What could we do to improve student enthusiasm and involvement in H2O?

9. How was your job site (the work, the site contact, etc.)?

10. What one thing about H2O would you change for next year?

EVALUATION WORKSHEET

Event_____ Date _____

Group_____ Leader_____

Purpose

Goals

Attendance
Students_____
Staff_____
Total_____

	Evaluation	Comments or recommended changes or suggestions for improvement:
1	**Promotion:** Was it quality work? Timed appropriately? Did we promote enough? Any changes?	
2	**Staffing:** Did we have enough staff? Any problems? What was their evaluation of the event?	
3	**Budget:** Did the results justify the effort and money spent? Attach completed **Budget**.	
4	**Program:** Describe its effectiveness. Attach an actual schedule.	
5	**Benefits:** What were the PROS for this activity?	

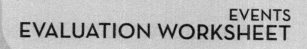

Evaluation	Comments or recommended changes or suggestions for improvement:
Problems: What were the cons for this activity?	
Materials needed: What items, supplies, equipment, et cetera, did we forget that we need to bring next time?	
Repetition: Should we do this activity again? Why or why not?	
Guest performance: Evaluate how well the speaker or musicians related to and connected with our students.	
Contact list: Write out names, phone numbers, addresses, or directions that we need for next time.	
Discipline: Any discipline problems with students? Action taken? Attach any **Incident Report** filed.	
Spiritual results: What difference did this activity make in the lives of our students? Decisions made? Evidence of spiritual growth that occurred?	
Other comments? Next time, make sure...	

EVENTS
FINANCIAL ACCOUNTABILITY WORKSHEET

Event name_____ Event date _____

Cost per student_____

Deposit 1: amount and date _____

Deposit 2: amount and date _____

Deposit 3: amount and date _____

Deposit 4: amount and date _____

Deposit 5: amount and date _____

Student income total   **$**

Attach registration forms with list of students and payment amounts.
Indicate on registration form whether money collected is cash or check.

Student income total divided by total number of students attending should equal cost per student.

_____ divided by _____ = _____
(income)   (students)   (cost / student)

Difference / shortage explanation _____

_____

_____

_____

_____

_____

_____

_____

MINISTRY TARGET MESSAGING

Target messaging is a way to find groups of people who may be interested in your event—groups you wouldn't have thought of otherwise—and then to rate these groups according to how seriously you want to pursue them. The markets on the "A" list are given the most attention. The markets on the "B" and "C" lists receive attention only if resources and time are available.

Define your audience (for example, high school boys who don't regularly attend, but who have shown some interest in spiritual things): _____

_____

_____

With your audience in mind, list all possible advertising options, regardless of expense:

_____

_____

_____

_____

_____

Prioritize your target: Your *A-list groups* are those you most want to come to the event; it's designed for them (for example, middle schoolers at your church who are going into high school and might be a little nervous about it). *B-list groups* are your next target group if you've covered all of A and have more time and resources (for instance, middle schoolers who go to the nearest school). *C-list groups* are of lesser importance. (If you've covered A and B markets and have time and resources left, market your event to middle schoolers who go the three local schools).

A-list groups	B-list groups	C-list groups

SAMPLE TARGET MARKETING FOR AN EVENT

Video promotions—or clips

MP3 downloads sampling the musicians and speakers at an event and/or create iTunes playlists

Social media channels: Facebook, Twitter, Vine, Instagram etc. Create a hashtag for your event and use it leading up to the event.

E-News announcements that build up to the event

Texts and calls to key students (consider how to use group text messaging)

Web presence—on the church site, the youth group page, or a page dedicated solely to the event

Informed and inspired staff who can pump the event (Meet with the staff, send them frequent updates, and call them to keep them energized.)

Create an event on Facebook with all the details and invite everyone in your group

Place a poster at the church information table or lobby bulletin board

Registration brochures at the church information table—make sure new families are aware of your event

Letters to parents and church families

With appropriate permissions, place brochures at other churches

With appropriate permissions, place brochures at the school

Send a postcard

Partner with other youth ministries in the area. Meet with the youth staff to explain the event and to deliver promotional materials—fliers, videotape, brochures, registration forms.

Provide the local radio stations with a press release. See if they can arrange a brief interview with you or the speaker.

Consider a paid Facebook campaign

Take out an advertisement in the local paper, or request they list your event in the religion section of the paper

Invite the local media to come and photograph the event if the event is newsworthy

Promote at local Christian colleges and seminaries when suitable

Promote through local Christian bookstores using posters or brochures

Send press releases to local Christian radio or TV stations. Include a media packet and request a public service announcement; see about advertising on their Web site(s).

TARGET MARKETING WORKSHEET

What groups of people do you want to attract to your event? List them according to how seriously you want to pursue them—

A-list = must attend

B-list = those to whom you market your event if you're confident your A-list will attend, and as long as your time and resources last

C-list = market to these groups if your A- and B-lists are in the bag, and you have time and resources left

A-list

-
-
-
-
-
-
-

B-list

-
-
-
-
-
-
-

C-list

-
-
-
-
-
-
-

SIX MONTHS TO ONE YEAR OUT

- ❏ Start your event project—use a physical notebook, or online Evernote or Basecamp (**Notebook Checklist**)
- ❏ Determine a rough schedule for the event—how many days, arrival, and departure times (**Checklist**) Location size inspection and booking (**Site Inspection**
- ❏ Sign contact for the location size
- ❏ Develop a rough budget and student prices (**Budget**)
- ❏ Develop a rough timeline of what needs to get done by when (**Event Manager's Task Master**)
- ❏ Reserve transportation
- ❏ Determine the event purpose (**Planning Worksheet**)
- ❏ Choose a theme
- ❏ Firm up timeline and assign tasks to individuals in the areas of programming, speaker, games, transportation, promotion, Event Coordinator, and housing and registration.
- ❏ If possible, take staff to the location to assist with planning.
- ❏ Firm up budget and student prices. Make a system for recording all event expenses and income (**Financial Accountability Worksheet: Single-Event Registration**)
- ❏ Start developing the registration brochure and promotional materials, and determine cutoff date. Confirm the date with the facility to make sure there's enough time for the final count. (**Medical Release and Permission**)
- ❏ Develop the promotional strategy (**Marketing Strategy**)
- ❏ Keep in touch with the facility and send them any information they need. Also, plan the meals and reserve all the appropriate meeting spaces.

ONE TO THREE MONTHS OUT

- ❏ Start promoting the event and send out brochures.
- ❏ Meet with the programming team to determine the details of the general sessions and breakout sessions.
- ❏ Determine a detailed schedule, and let all staff and other appropriate individuals know what's expected of them while they're at the event.
- ❏ Develop any handouts that are needed for the event.
- ❏ Meet with each of the committee heads and find out where they are in the planning process. Assist where needed.
- ❏ Outline emergency procedures with Top Dog and come up with any contingency plans needed.
- ❏ Have each committee make a list of all equipment and supplies needed and authorize any purchases.
- ❏ Reserve any rental equipment needed.
- ❏ Secure needed volunteers and assign jobs.

TWO WEEKS OUT

- ❏ Cutoff date for registration is one to two weeks out. (Set a firm date and stick to it!)
- ❏ After the cutoff date, place students and leaders in housing.
- ❏ Meet with staff to go over every aspect of the event, giving enough details so that they are informed: Bible

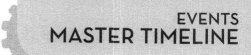

study information, small group questions, detailed schedule, expectations, emergency procedures, driving directions, student policies and rules, etc.

- ❑ Develop a parent handout sheet with retreat address, phone number, contact person, and any other pertinent information
- ❑ Gather any supplies and equipment.
- ❑ Organize the registration process.
- ❑ Make all signs and decorations.
- ❑ Get petty cash, and request financial officer to cut any checks that you'll need.

TWO DAYS OUT

- ❑ Confirm facility, transportation, and any rental equipment.
- ❑ Have all registration forms and permission slips in alphabetical order and available to Top Dog.
- ❑ Check in with all committee leaders to see if they have any needs.
- ❑ Get extra sleep, if possible.

DAY OF EVENT

- ❑ Pack up, load up, get ready to go.
- ❑ Prepare registration area.
- ❑ Instruct any last-minute volunteers.
- ❑ Troubleshoot as different situations arise.
- ❑ Keep your event notebook with you at all times. Try to keep at least one step ahead of the group so that you can make eleventh-hour changes as needed.
- ❑ Encourage where needed.
- ❑ Instruct when necessary.
- ❑ Step in if you have to.
- ❑ Keep on schedule.
- ❑ Implement your plan.
- ❑ See God work.

A SOON AS HUMANLY POSSIBLE AFTER THE EVENT

(within a week before moving on to the next crisis)

- ❑ Finish any paperwork.
- ❑ Pay all your bills.
- ❑ Complete your entries on your budget and see how you did. Panic, if necessary, and make an appointment with the senior pastor to confess.
- ❑ Thank those who need to be thanked.
- ❑ Praise those who deserve to be praised.
- ❑ Fill out **Evaluation.**
- ❑ File any **Incident Reports.**
- ❑ Reorganize your event notebook and put it on the shelf until you start planning next year's event. Archive everything.

389

Please print in ink

Effective dates: _____ to _____

Name _____ Age _____ Birthday _____
LAST   FIRST   MIDDLE

Graduation Year _____ ❑ Male ❑ Female Email_____

Address _____ City _____ State_____ Zip_____

Name of parents/guardians _____

Address _____ Phone _____

Emergency contact_____ Phone: Day_____ Night_____

Medical insurance company_____ Policy # _____

Physician_____ Office phone _____

Dentist _____ Office phone _____

MEDICAL HISTORY

If necessary, describe in detail the nature and severity of any physical and/or psychological ailment, illness, propensity, weakness, limitation, handicap, disability, or condition to which your child is subject and of which the staff should be aware, and what, if any action of protection is required on account thereof. Submit this notification in writing and attach it to this form. Include names of medications and dosages that must be taken.

Check the following areas of concern for this student. If necessary, add another page with details:

1. For your student's safety and our knowledge, is your student a—
   ❑ good swimmer   ❑ fair swimmer   ❑ non-swimmer

2. Does your student have allergies to—
   ❑ pollens   ❑ medications   ❑ food   ❑ insect bites

3. Does your child suffer from, or has ever experienced, or is being treated currently for any of the following:
   ❑ asthma   ❑ epilepsy / seizure disorder   ❑ heart trouble   ❑ diabetes
   ❑ frequently upset stomach   ❑ physical handicap

4. Date of last tetanus shot: _____

5. Does your student wear   ❑ glasses   ❑ contact lenses

6. Please list and explain any major illnesses the student experienced during the past year:

   Additional comments:

   Should this student's activities be restricted for any reason? Please explain:

For your information, we expect each student to conform to these rules of conduct

No possession or use of alcohol, drugs, or tobacco
No students can drive to or from events
No fighting, weapons, fireworks, lighters, or explosives
No offensive or immodest clothing
No boys in girls' sleeping quarters and no girls in boys' sleeping quarters
Participation with the group is expected
Respect property
Respect one another, staff, and adult leaders
Respect and comply with event schedules

Students who fail to comply with these expectations may be sent home at their parents' or guardians' expense.

I, the student, have read the rules of conduct, the above evaluation of my health, and permission to participate in youth group activities. I agree to abide by the stated personal limitations and code of conduct.

Student signature _____ Date _____

Activities may include, but are not limited to: cookouts, boating, bowling, water skiing, swimming, basketball, skate boarding, roller skating, games in the park, soccer, broomball, ice skating, volleyball, softball, baseball, camping, snowboarding, hiking, biking, concerts, Bible studies, golfing, miniature golf, hayrides. *Note: If you desire to limit your child's participation in any event, please submit your wishes in writing to the church youth pastor prior to that event.*

_____ has my permission to attend all
NAME OF STUDENT

youth activities sponsored by _____ (hereinafter the
NAME OF ORGANIZATION

"Church") from _____ to _____.
DATE   DATE

This consent form gives permission to seek whatever medical attention is deemed necessary, and releases the Church and its staff of any liability against personal losses of named child.

I/We the undersigned have legal custody of the student named above, a minor, and have given our consent for him/her to attend events being organized by the Church. I/We understand that there are inherent risks involved in any ministry or athletic event, and I/we hereby release the Church, its pastors, employees, agents, and volunteer workers from any and all liability for any injury, loss, or damage to person or property that may occur during the course of my/our child's involvement. In the event that he/she is injured and requires the attention of a doctor, I/we consent to any reasonable medical treatment as deemed necessary by a licensed physician. In the event treatment is required from a physician and/or hospital personnel designated by the Church, I/we agree to hold such person free and harmless of any claims, demands, or suits for damages arising from the giving of such consent. I/We also acknowledge that we will be ultimately responsible for the cost of any medical care should the cost of that medical care not be reimbursed by the health insurance provider. Further, I/we affirm that the health insurance information provided above is accurate at this date and will, to the best of my/our knowledge, still be in force for the student named above. I/we also agree to bring my/our child home at my/our own expense should they become ill or if deemed necessary by the student ministries staff member.

Parent/guardian signature _____ Date _____

EVENTS
MEETING SPACE SETUP

For each room you use in your church, hotel or retreat center, you'll need to answer these questions—both for general sessions and breakouts.

1. Do you require staging? If so, what size and what height?

2. Do you want chairs? How many? Set up in which way?
   — Theater: chairs in rows, all facing front.
   — Classroom: narrow tables with chairs behind them, all facing front.
   — Rounds: round tables for 6-10 people each (good for discussions; bad for lectures).
   — High-top rounds: taller, small round tables for 3-4.
   — Table square: Four or eight tables set in a square. Participants sit around the outer edge of the table facing each other.
   — Horseshoe: U-shaped setup.

3. How many tables and where? Do you need numbers on the tables to indicate where students sit?

4. Do you need information tables?

5. Do you want the tables skirted?

6. Do you want water/beverage service in the meeting rooms?

7. What audio-visual equipment do you need?
   — Audio needs
   — Video needs
   — Lighting requirements
   — Are you planning to record your sessions?
   — Has your guest speaker or band provided a tech rider? If so, place close attention to specific equipment you have agreed to provide when you signed the agreement.

8. Is there a Green Room off of the staging area for the musicians and speakers? Describe the setup needs. Is refrigeration required?

9. Do they require a certificate of insurance prior to your arrival? You can get this from your ministry insurance company.

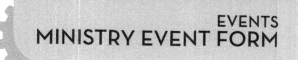

MINISTRY EVENT FORM

This form is to facilitate the process of scheduling, planning, and implementing a church ministry event to ensure that it aligns with our overall purposes and runs as efficiently and effectively as possible. Our goal is to be unified as a church in everything we do.

PLEASE SELECT THE MINISTRY YOU ARE REPRESENTING:

- ❏ Outreach
- ❏ Men
- ❏ Women

- ❏ Missions
- ❏ Adult Education
- ❏ Counseling

- ❏ Music
- ❏ Small Groups
- ❏ Senior Adults

- ❏ Children
- ❏ Jr. High Students
- ❏ Sr. High Students

Name of group: _____

Contact person: (Last) _____ (First) _____ Phone number: _____ Email: _____

Requested event date(s): _____

(Please include day of week and dates of event)

Purpose statement: _____

_____

Alignment with church: How does this event align with our core mission and vision? How can this help us ultimately become Christ-like in our followership?

_____

_____

Budget: _____ Prayer team: ❏ Yes ❏ No

Event agenda: _____

_____

Rooms & facilities needed: _____

_____

Audio/video needs/requests: _____

_____

Refreshments needs/requests: ❏ Yes ❏ No *After event confirmation, a refreshments request form will be sent to you as needed.*

Other special arrangements: _____

_____

_____

_____

When the form is complete, please contact your ministry pastor with the form, so you can discuss the next step. For questions, please call the church office, 555-555-5555.

EVENT APPROVAL

Ministry Pastor: _____ Date: _____

Calendar Coordinator: _____ Date: _____

EVENTS
NOTEBOOK CHECKLIST

PLANNING

- ❏ Event Manager's Master Timeline
- ❏ Planning Worksheet
- ❏ Checklist
- ❏ Agendas and minutes from planning meetings
- ❏ Event Manager's Task Master
- ❏ To-do list

FINANCES

- ❏ Budget
- ❏ Financial Accountability Worksheet
- ❏ Actual event income and expenses

SCHEDULE

- ❏ Projected schedule
- ❏ Actual schedule

PROMOTION

- ❏ Event brochure / registration form
- ❏ Fliers
- ❏ Emails
- ❏ Internet promotion copy
- ❏ Event Marketing Packet

REGISTRATION

- ❏ Student participants
  (copy of information on Single Event Registration Form)
- ❏ Staff
  (names, payment information, other pertinent information)

FACILITY, HOUSING, AND MEALS

- ❏ Signed contract (keep copy in office)
- ❏ General information flier
- ❏ Site Inspection form (filled out)
- ❏ Facility guidelines (rising time, lights out, snack bar hours, lake front hours, etc.)

- ❏ Names and phone extensions for facility staff
  (facilities manager, kitchen manager, etc.)
- ❏ Facility map(s) (of the whole campus, as well as sleeping room floor plans)
- ❏ Certificate of Insurance
- ❏ Menu plan
- ❏ Meeting space
- ❏ Sketch of room layouts
- ❏ Schedule of dates and times for room use and setup types
- ❏ Requests and schedules for AV equipment

TRANSPORTATION

- ❏ Signed contract (keep a copy in your office)
- ❏ Name(s) and phone number(s) of transportation provider(s)
- ❏ Map from church to the facility

PRINTED MATERIALS

- ❏ Simplified event schedules
- ❏ Study notes
- ❏ Brochure, logo, other PR originals

EVALUATION

- ❏ Notes taken during event
- ❏ Any Incident Report that was filed
- ❏ Evaluation

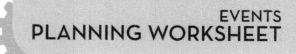

Event name_____ Event date(s) _____

Event manager_____ Event time(s)_____

Audience description

<table>
<tr><td></td><td>**Projected attendance**</td></tr>
</table>

Students_____

Event goals and objectives

Staff_____

Total_____

Weekend event schedule

Hours	Thursday	Friday	Saturday	Sunday	Monday

Facility name_____ Contact person_____

Phone number _____

Housing needs

Meals needed (Including special dietary concerns.)

EVENTS
PLANNING WORKSHEET

General session room

	Setup required	Equipment needs
Session 1		
Session 2		
Session 3		
Session 4		
Session 5		

Breakout rooms: *setup options—theater, classroom, rounds, et cetera*

Date and time	Topic	Teacher	Setup	Equipment needed

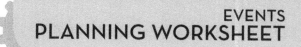

General session speaker name _____ Contact info _____

Date contract signed_____

Topic_____ Equipment needed _____

Program development meetings

Dates	Location	Attendees	Tentative agenda

Publicity and promotion

What type or piece	Who is in charge	Date implemented	Instructions

EVENTS
PLANNING WORKSHEET

Budget: What are your rough budget estimates? Place a copy of the budget with this information. Track expenses on a spreadsheet. (See **Budget** sample.)

Checks needed and when:

Housing needs: How many students and how many staff? What is the facility layout? Where do staff stay if they bring their family? Bedding needs?

Transportation requirements: Distance? Type of vehicles needed? Cost?

Company:

Contact person:

Vehicles reserved:

Office setup: What office and administration items need to be brought to the event site? Computer, printer, paper, stapler, pens, tape, etc.

First-aid requirements: What type of first-aid setup is needed? Who is coordinating the supplies?

Promotion strategy:
    Flier design—due date: _____ Flier mailing date: _____
    Other plans for promotion—
    Church publications
    Community papers
    Posters

Event approval from ministry leadership: Placed on master church / ministry calendar

Program planning: (securing people and resources)
    Speaker
    Musician
    Multimedia
    Miscellaneous needs / equipment

THE CREW RETREAT

Confirmation

You are about to experience a retreat full of challenge and fun that will alter the way you look at God and yourself.

We're excited that you're coming to The Crew retreat Friday through Sunday, September 1-3. Get ready for an incredible weekend of mind-blowing worship, in-your-face talks, small group discussions that will get you out of your comfort zone, lots of laughter, and some new friendships.

RETREAT INFO (READ THIS BEFORE YOU GO!)

Beginning

Meeting at the south door of the church at 6:30 p.m. on Friday night. Check in at registration. Find a seat in our yellow, luxury limo (a.k.a. school bus) for a two-hour drive up to Mission Lodge. *Be sure to eat dinner before you come.*

Ending

We're back at the south door of the church at 2:30 p.m. on Sunday afternoon. Make arrangements here for a ride home *before* you leave home on Friday. The church phone will only be available for emergencies.

Staying

Mission Lodge, nestled in the beautiful mountains of southern Iowa, has log cabins, a sandy lake (bring your swimsuit for our traditional early morning polar-bear swim), trail riding ($10), a small skate park, and two full basketball courts. Each cabin sleeps ten and has its own bathroom. Mission Lodge serves *great* food. We're eating three meals on Saturday and two on Sunday. They also have a snack shop.

Bringing

Sleeping bag, pillow, Bible, pen & notebook, personal stuff (soap, shampoo, towels, toothbrush, change of clothes, shoes, clean socks—you get the picture), flashlight, jacket or rain poncho, spending money, and any medications you might need.

Leaving

Leave these things at home: cell phones, iPads, iPods, etc., weapons, fireworks, alcohol, illegal chemical substances (this means drugs), and matches/lighters.

Office details—We received your ❑ registration ❑ permission slip ❑ medical release

We still need your **balance of payment**. You can bring it with you to registration.

If you have any questions or need assistance, please contact Chris at the church office by phone (555) 555-5555 or email *(Chris@ourchurch.org)*.

We look forward to seeing you!

EVENING OF PRAYER

Setting: Youth Rooms—darkened, candles

6:45	Pre-Service—meditative music; quotes on prayer			
7:00	Opening Prayer			Becca and Zach
7:02	Scriptures on the Promises of Prayer			
			Psalm 34:4-6	Brian
			Jeremiah 33:3	Maggie
			Matthew 7:7-8	Kristina
			Psalm 62:7-8	Heather
7:04	Song:			
7:08	Worship			Worship Team
7:20	Personal Prayer—Confession			
			Luke 18:9-12	Sheree
			Luke 18:13-14	Tyler
	Write out confession	Quiet Music—2 min.	1 John 1:9	Michael
	Kneel to confess	Quiet Music—1 min.		
	Wrap up			Barb
7:30	Verses on Thanksgiving			
			Psalm 34:1-3	Chris
			James 1:17	Kyle
			Colossians 3:15-17	Ken
7:32	Large Group Prayer—Thanksgiving			
	Reading on thankfulness			Heather
	Open mic sentence prayers of thanksgiving			
7:40	Worship			Worship team
7:52	Guided Personal Prayer			
	Major themes			
8:00	Small Group Prayer—groups of 6			
8:15	Closing Verse		Ephesians 3:14-19	CT
	Closing Song			

6 MONTHS TO ONE YEAR AHEAD

Determine event

Seek approval

Reserve location for event

Publish dates (after checking for all possible conflicts)

Get it on master church calendar

Develop budget

3 MONTHS AHEAD

Develop creative for event – Web and print

Reserve transportation

Line up staff and students to help

Determine best promotion strategy

1 MONTH AHEAD

Visit event location (take your digital camera!)

Major announcements and promotion begins

Finalize schedule for event

Determine supplies needed

Begin event sign-up (have system to register and collect money)

ONE WEEK AHEAD

Confirm all event details

Confirm all vendors

Request needed checks

Meet with parents and staff who will be helping

Send emails to all you are inviting

Phone blitz to secure final sign-ups

Recruit people for event cleanup

Final check: think backward through your event—from final cleanup to early planning stages.

FACILITY DISTANCE FROM YOUR CHURCH

- Can you get to it within the time you have for travel?
- What type of transportation will you need to arrange?
- What potential stops are along the way: restrooms, food, etc.?
- Map out the best route to get there

GENERAL FACILITY ACCESSIBILITY

- Is there access for your mode of transportation?
- Where will transporters drop off and pick up students?
- Is there parking to accommodate the vehicles?

GENERAL FACILITY MAINTENANCE

- Is it clean?
- Is it in good repair?
- Is the facility inspected yearly, and when was the last inspection?
- For recommended camps, see Christian Camping International's Web site (www.cci.org.au).

GENERAL FACILITY SAFETY

- Is there anything that might be unsafe for students to be around?
- Are there exposed electrical or other maintenance problems?
- Is there anything that you could not afford to replace if one of your students broke it?
- What injury has occurred most often at the site?

GENERAL FACILITY FLEXIBILITY

- Is the management helpful?
- Does the management seem flexible and able to work with your group's needs?
- Will there be other groups at the facility, or will you be the only group?
  - Is the facility staffed well enough to meet the needs of both groups?
  - Which group has priorities to which area?
  - Will both groups be eating together?
- Is there staff on duty 24/7? If not, what are their hours and in an emergency how can you contact them?
- Is there a certain time for lights out?
- Do you have access to the office area? Phone, fax, Internet? Photocopying?
- Sleeping room size, conditions:
  - Number of beds per room?

– Quality of beds?

– Number of bathrooms?

– Mirrors in the bathrooms?

– Are there areas that can be designated by gender, and how far apart are they?

– What ratio of staff to students can be used in these sleeping areas?

– Are the sleeping rooms in an area that might disturb other guests not in your party?

– Are there rooms available for program staff, speakers, and musicians? Linens available?

GENERAL SESSION ROOM SIZE, CONDITION, AND USABILITY

• What options are there for room setup?

• How many people can fit comfortably in the room?

• Is the room too big or too small?

• Is there permanent staging? What type of staging is available for the room?

• How are the acoustics?

EVENTS
STAFF DIRECTOR

JOB DESCRIPTION

Administrator of the event

RESPONSIBILITIES

General vision execution for the event; location, direction, quality, etc.

Overall finances: budget, accounting, honorariums

Arrange liability, accident, and CCLI licensing if needed.

Assign and follow through with the event logistics.

Quality control manager for the event.

Work in conjunction with the youth pastor for specific site inspection and selection and dates, according to the speaker and program availability.

Collaborate with the youth pastor and facility manager for menus, number of rooms needed, and other logistical details.

Develop Web site, brochures and promotional material with graphic designer.

Coordinate the programming and scheduling with the speaker representative.

Steering committee selection, recruitment, orientation, appointment of a chairperson, and quality control for the committee.

Make sure that the steering committee has the materials needed: media packet, fundraising information, speaker bios, etc.

Negotiate and contract the musicians, performers, sound crew, and tape individuals (from steering committees recommendations).

Make the travel and shuttle arrangements for the speakers.

Prepare final program schedule for the confirmation packets.

Be the on-site representative at the event.

Conduct the final evaluation with the committee and faculty onsite.

Prepare a final evaluation.

Send thank-you notes and gifts to the appropriate individuals.

JOB DESCRIPTION

Work with the Director for the selection of the event site.

Contract and manage the physical facilities for the ministry.

RESPONSIBILITIES

Inspect the site.

Select and contract with the site.

Act as on-site liaison for the director and the site/event location.

Arrange for the physical requirements for the event: meeting space, staging, platforms, podiums, screens, whiteboards, markers, tables, banquet facilities, etc.

Plan menus with the conference director and the steering committee.

Reserve lodging for the speakers and other contracted individuals.

Arrange for a site inspection for the steering committee members.

Review publicity materials.

Manage the event with the conference director and property representative.

Attend the post-event evaluation.

Review all charges posted to the event account.

EVENTS
STAFF SOUND ENGINEER

JOB DESCRIPTION

To equip the event with adequate audio and lighting for the general sessions.

To record all sessions (when needed) and produce good quality, salable MP3 files.

RESPONSIBILITIES

Negotiate and finalize with the director.

Equip the general sessions with sound, lights, microphones, and any other contracted equipment.

Arrive and setup the equipment according to the time schedule determined by the director.

Work with the director to acquire the necessary media files for the event.

While on site, work with the director to meet the audio needs of the performers and speakers.

Arrive 30 minutes before the start of each general session for a sound check with the performers and speakers.

Record all the general sessions and seminar sessions the first time they are given.

Upload recordings for purchase by the event attendees. Reproduce CDs / DVDs if applicable.

Label and prepare the recording resources for sale, available by the end of the event.

Assist the sales volunteers with any recording questions or difficulties.

JOB DESCRIPTION

Represent and be the contact person for an event's speakers, artists, etc. Be the mentor (shepherd), advocate, and team leader for these people.

RESPONSIBILITIES

Work with the speakers/artists and conference director to develop the overall vision for the conference.

Work with the conference director concerning scheduling of the conference and topic and programming coordination.

Contact the speakers for prayer requests, special instructions, biographies, deadlines for notes and special media requirements, and any other special announcements or arrangements.

Organize meals for speakers/artists during the event.

Conduct any meetings or prayer times for speakers/artists during the event.

Relay any messages to the speakers/artists during the event concerning scheduling and announcements.

Debrief with the speakers/artists and steering committee members.

Write evaluation of the overall conference and submit to the conference director.

Send thank-you notes to the speakers/artists.

EVENTS
STAFF STEER CHAIRPERSON

JOB DESCRIPTION

The committee coordinator

The liaison between the director and the committee

RESPONSIBILITIES

Bring enthusiasm, direction, and vision to the committee and volunteers.

Oversee all aspects of the steering committee's involvement with the event, and lead the team.

Meet (communicate) regularly with the director (by phone) or email, keeping him or her apprised of registration numbers, finances, progress on the event, etc.

Brief the director about any peculiarities of the region.

Assign tasks to the committee and check on follow through.

Arrange for the steering committee to visit the event facilities.

Implement the marketing strategy developed by the steering committee.

Raise funds with the assistance of the secretary/treasurer (a minimum of $).

Determine the event schedule with the event director.

Host the visiting faculty and staff with a welcome meal.

Register the committee members with the meeting planner to receive their tuition discount.

Arrange an appropriate individual to be the emcee for the event.

Attend the event evaluation.

Submit a final evaluation and all financial records and other requested materials to the director.

Write thank-you notes to all committee members.

JOB DESCRIPTION

To be the local individuals who attend to the logistics of the event for their areas in conjunction with the director and the meeting planner.

To be the primary marketing agents for the event.

To create a unique environment facilitating growth, warmth, and comfort.

RESPONSIBILITIES

Meet together regularly prior to the event.

Determine each committee member's area of responsibility.

Map out a marketing strategy including letters, phone calling, press releases, Web strategy, social media strategy, advertisements, and radio.

Attend the post-event evaluation.

OFFICES OF THE STEERING COMMITTEE

Chairperson

Registration coordinator

Hospitality coordinator

Volunteer coordinator

Program coordinator

Secretary / treasurer

Marketing coordinator

JOB DESCRIPTION

To develop, implement, and install the decorations at the event.

RESPONSIBILITIES

Develop general session theme / look for staging, table arrangements, signs for seminar rooms, signs for facility, etc.

Work with the committee to establish a decorative theme for the event.

Establish a team of volunteers: designers, artists, and set-up crew.

Work with the volunteer coordinator to develop a cleanup crew for the event.

Submit decorations for the steering committee's approval.

Acquire the necessary materials (with prior financial approval from the chairperson and treasurer).

Develop the products.

Decorate the facility prior to the event in accordance to the schedule.

Arrange to sell the centerpieces / theme pieces and turn in a written report and the funds to the treasurer, if appropriate.

Remove all signs and clean up all decorations after the event.

Attend the event evaluation.

Submit a report to the chairperson.

Write thank-you notes to all the decoration contributors and volunteers.

JOB DESCRIPTION

Develop the special touches to make the program unique and effective.

RESPONSIBILITIES

Create an environment conducive to worship, learning, growth, and warmth.

Nominate and investigate appropriate singers, musicians, song leaders, and performers.

Submit the nominations, *with recordings or Web links* and written material about them, to the director for review.

Communicate any specific needs of the performers to the chairperson who will let the event director know.

Work with the decorations coordinator for the appropriate decorations for the staging.

Work with the committee and the event director for song selection.

Prepare the lyrics for the songs for the general sessions

(a minimum of 50 points depending on the screen size).

Acquire video projectors and sturdy music stands for use in the general sessions and in each of the seminar sessions and have them delivered to each of the rooms during setup time (a small self-standing podium would be helpful for the general sessions, preferably lightweight wood or acrylic).

Arrange time for rehearsals with the performers pre-event if necessary.

Host and assist the performers upon arrival and during setup.

Assist the sound technician and the performers to perform complete sound checks.

Meet performers / speakers 30 minutes before each general session to perform a sound check and to check any other stage props.

Communicate to the sound technician any special needs that the performers might have.

Oversee prop changes and adjustments during the session (adjusting the mic, moving equipment or scenery, keeping in mind that the goal is to help the audience to receive the clearest possible presentation without distraction).

Prepare the stage for the next session after the general session.

Tidy up the general session room and rearrange the chairs if necessary.

Assist the performers with the teardown of their equipment after the event.

Attend the event evaluation.

Write thank-you notes to your volunteers.

STAFF STEERING COMMITTEE REGISTRATION COORDINATOR

JOB DESCRIPTION

To take participants' registrations from the inquiry stage to checking participants in at the event.

RESPONSIBILITIES

Contact individuals from each of the local area churches.

Develop online registration system for the event. Spell out all policies regarding fees, cancellations, and refunds.

Send the information regarding the registration process to involved groups.

Process the registrations as they come in and forward the funds to the treasurer.

Develop a registration confirmation email with all applicable information in it to be sent to each of the registered individuals: location and map, schedule, available local restaurants, hotel arrangement suggestions, etc.

Submit weekly registration summary to the chairperson or directly to the director.

Make nametags for attendees and special nametags with the appropriate designations for speakers, committee members, and other volunteers.

Coordinate the on-site registration with a team of volunteers.

Submit registration funds to the treasurer with written documentation.

Attend the event evaluation.

Work with the treasurer to submit final records and numbers to the event director.

Write thank-you notes to all registration volunteers.

JOB DESCRIPTION

Assist the committee with the secretarial and financial matters of the event.

RESPONSIBILITIES

Take minutes for all steering committee meetings and distribute them within 48 hours.

Assemble a contact list of the committee members for the event director.

Assemble a physical notebook or online Evernote file for the director with all correspondence and minutes taken during the event preparation.

Submit a copy of all outgoing correspondence for final approval to the director before distribution (allow enough time for the director to respond).

Make supplemental marketing tools such as a brochure, fliers, etc.

Keep all the financial records, including all expenses (and the book and resource table).

Work within the predetermined budget for the finances.

Open a checking account if necessary.

Make weekly deposits as registrations start arriving.

Write checks when necessary with approval of the chairperson.

Give weekly financial updates to the chairperson.

Assist the chairperson with the fundraising.

Distribute the evaluation forms and the faculty notes to the appropriate individuals (faculty assistants, ushers, etc.).

Count the offering and fill out appropriate forms (store in a safe place).

Collect and recount the funds from the resources and book tables, initial the appropriate form.

Attend the event evaluation and take notes.

Arrange for the extra books and resource's to be shipped.

Distribute a list of the names and addresses of all event volunteers and steering committee members to the director at the evaluation.

Make the final deposit of all the funds received at the event.

Reimburse outstanding bills to committee members.

Write a final check to the event manager with a full accounting of the financial records after the final accounting.

Close the checking account.

JOB DESCRIPTION

To enthusiastically recruit, equip, and instruct volunteers to fill the assigned positions (possibly drawing from a variety of churches in the area).

RESPONSIBILITIES

The key responsibility is to see that each of the volunteer teams have a *clear* understanding of their positions and their responsibilities, and to monitor each of the teams on site—which may include meeting with them prior to the event

The teams / individuals needed are as follows:

1. Speaker assistant: One for each speaker

Job description

Contact speakers prior to the event to pray together.
Communicate any regional information appropriate for the speakers' presentation.
Meet the speakers at the beginning of the event.
Provide guides for the speakers at the facility.
Provide escorts for the speakers to their seminar room to help arrange the room as needed.
Be available if any errands need to be run (snacks, drinks, etc.) and submit receipts for reimbursement to the treasurer.
Escort the speaker to the reception if needed and introduce to others.
Check in on speaker occasionally to make sure that they are comfortable.
Get the speaker's handouts from the chairperson and put them in the speaker's seminar room.
Introduce the speaker in her seminar (then you can go to another seminar if you wish).
Help the speaker to gather supplies and prepare the room for the next seminar.
Assist the speaker when needed.
Escort the speaker to his or her next scheduled event if needed.
Be sensitive to the speaker to allow them to meet the needs of those asking questions after the seminar.

2. Resource sales: Two volunteers to set up and manage the resource table

Job description

Develop and set up an attractive table display for resource sales.
Work with the sound engineer to bring resources from the audio room to the sales table.
Assist customers in resource selection.

Fill out the appropriate forms.

Take the money for the resources: cash or check (with phone number) or credit card.

Give all the receipts, funds, and a completed report to the treasurer at completion of event.

At the end, box extra resources and bring them to the registration table.

Disassemble table display.

---

3. Assistants: for the meeting planner, director, the chairperson, and steering committee

Job description:

Be available to the individuals to be helpful with any logistical details that are necessary throughout the duration of the event. Specific instructions will be given by each individual.

---

4. Ushers for the general session

Job includes

Head usher arranges for the appropriate containers for the offering and assigns stations for other ushers.

Arrive 15 minutes prior to each general session.

Know the locations of emergency exits, telephones, restrooms, and lost and found (generally located at the registration table).

Keep the doors closed during the sound check until the head usher says that the doors can be opened to let attendees in.

Assist individuals with seat selection, filling in seats from the front.

Do not let individuals block the doorways.

Be attentive to any individuals needing special attention.

Distribute handouts when necessary.

Deliver messages to the general session performers and speakers as necessary.

Close the doors five minutes after the session starts and have latecomers remain in the back of the room until appropriate time to be seated.

Manage the doors to the room so they are closed quietly and minimize hallway noise when people come and go.

Do not seat attendees during special music, drama, or prayers.

Take the offering and bring the funds to the head usher, who counts the money with the treasurer in a private place.

Collect the evaluation forms from the event participants.

Deliver the evaluation forms to the head usher, then to the registration table.

5. Room hosts for the seminar sessions

Job includes

Arrive 15 minutes early to the seminar room.

Make sure that there is a bottle of water for the speaker in the front of the room.

Assist speaker with technology setup.

Welcome the participants into the seminar room and ask them to fill the seats in the front of the room first, filling in all the empty seats.

Distribute any handouts.

Turn on the audio recorder just *before* the speaker assistant introduces the speaker, if requested by the sound engineer.

Stay in the back of the room during the session and assist anyone needing to go in or out.

Cue the speaker five minutes before the session is over.

Stop the recording when the session is finished.

Collect the evaluation forms and bring to the registration table after the session.

Straighten the room and pick up any leftover handouts.

Prepare the room for the next session.

Return leftover handouts to the speakers or to the registration table after the session.

---

6. Photographer of the event

Job includes

Provide your own digital camera; ideally with a zoom lens.

Take multiple photographs during each phase of the event.

Take mostly *close-ups* of small groups of people (2-3 people at a time); also photograph individual participants, the speakers, and the steering committee members.

Seek to take photos that represent the diversity of the audience.

Leave the file of digital pictures at the registration desk when finished / or upload to the appropriate shared file location.

Sample for a large event that takes place in June
Progress keys—Not started (leave blank), In **P**rocess, **N**ear Completion, **C**ompleted, Needs **H**elp

NOVEMBER/DECEMBER
Housing—Laura

Task	Start	Due	Whom	Progress
Camp/retreat/hotel site inspections	Sept.	Dec.	Laura +	C
Camp/retreat/hotel contract negotiation	Nov.	Dec.	Laura +	C
Contracts signed	Dec.	Jan.	Pastor/Laura +	C
Speaker / performers selected and contracted	Sept.	Jan.	Pastor/Dawn	P

JANUARY / FEBRUARY
Event management—Dawn

Task	Start	Due	Whom	Progress
Preliminary calendar / timeline	Feb.	March	Dawn	C
Theme chosen	Feb.	March	Team	C
Mission statement defined	Feb.	March	Team	
Team leader job descriptions developed	Feb.	March	Dawn	C
Team leaders recruited and assigned tasks	Feb.	March	Dawn	P
Organizational flow chart developed	Feb.	March	Dawn	C
Budget developed	Feb.	March	Dawn	C
Take leaders and select staff to event location	Feb.	June	Dawn	P

Programming—Aidan

Task	Start	Due	Whom	Progress
Program team leader job descriptions developed	Feb.	March	Aidan	C
Organizational flow chart developed	Feb.	March		P
Budget developed	Feb.	March		C
Take programming staff to event location	Feb.	May		P

Housing—Laura

Task	Start	Due	Whom	Progress
Ministry staff housing assignments	Feb.			C
Site host's job description	March			C

MARCH
Event management—Dawn

Task	Start	Due	Whom	Progress
Team leaders meetings scheduled	March		John	
Detailed timeline	March	April	Dawn	C
Key leaders to event location	March	April	By Req	C

Child care strategy developed	March	April	Dawn	**C**
Team chosen and assigned tasks	March	April	Dawn	**N**
Logo developed	March	June	Dawn	**P**
Giveaways chosen	March	June	Dawn	**P**

Communications—Jorden & Tari

Task	Start	Due	Whom	Progress
Determine needed communication & written materials	March		Team	**C**
Develop marketing plan	March	April	Tari	**P**
Develop schedule of materials and sign-off procedure	April		Dawn	**P**

Registration/data processing—TBD

Task	Start	Due	Whom	Progress
Scholarship management—detailed	March	May		
• Policies and procedures				
• Determine the ministry needs				
• Track appropriated scholarships				
• Coordinate with registration to document scholarships				
• Contingency plan for on-site troubleshooting of scholarships				

Residence Hall/Hotel/Cabin—Paul

Task	Start	Due	Whom	Progress
Determine space usage, room setups and room assignments for the following:	March	June	Dawn/Paul	**P**
• Registration				
• Operations				
• Equipment storage				
• Communion preparation				
• Counting the offering				
• Volunteer Central and hospitality				
• Registrations solutions				
• Lunch				
• Exhibits				
• Production / Green Room				

Housing—Laura

Task	Start	Due	Whom	Progress
Site host recruited	March			**C**

Key meetings—

Task	Start	Due	Whom	Progress
Executive committee	March	Weekly	Marni	**P**
Area leaders	March	Weekly	John	**C/P**

Progress keys—Not started (leave blank), In **P**rocess, **N**ear Completion, **C**ompleted, Needs **H**elp

6-12 MONTHS IN ADVANCE
Housing—

Task	Start	Due	Whom	Progress
Camp/retreat/hotel site inspections				
Camp/retreat/hotel contract negotiation				
Contracts signed				
Speaker / performers selected and contracted				

5-6 MONTHS IN ADVANCE
Event management—

Task	Start	Due	Whom	Progress
Preliminary calendar / timeline				
Theme chosen				
Mission statement defined				
Team leader job descriptions developed				
Team leaders recruited and assigned tasks				
Organizational flow chart developed				
Budget developed				
Take leaders and select staff to event location				

Programming—

Task	Start	Due	Whom	Progress
Program team leader job descriptions developed				
Organizational flow chart developed				
Budget developed				
Take programming staff to event location				

Housing—

Task	Start	Due	Whom	Progress
Ministry staff housing assignments				
Site host's job description				

3-4 MONTHS IN ADVANCE
Event management—

Task	Start	Due	Whom	Progress
Team leaders meetings scheduled				
Detailed timeline				
Key leaders to event location				

Child care strategy developed
Team chosen and assigned tasks
Logo developed
Giveaways chosen

Communications—

Task	Start	Due	Whom	Progress
Determine needed communication & written materials				
Develop marketing plan				
Develop schedule of materials and sign-off procedure				

Registration/data processing—

Task	Start	Due	Whom	Progress
Scholarship management—detailed				
• Policies and procedures				
• Determine the ministry needs				
• Track appropriated scholarships				
• Coordinate with registration to document scholarships				
• Contingency plan for on-site troubleshooting of scholarships				

Residence Hall/Hotel/Cabin—

Task	Start	Due	Whom	Progress
Determine space usage, room setups and room assignments for the following:				
• Registration				
• Operations				
• Equipment storage				
• Communion preparation				
• Counting the offering				
• Volunteer Central and hospitality				
• Registrations solutions				
• Lunch				
• Exhibits				
• Production / Green Room				

Housing—

Task	Start	Due	Whom	Progress
Site host recruited				C

Key meetings—

Task	Start	Due	Whom	Progress
Executive committee				
Area leaders				

EVENT MARKETING PACKET

In an attractive folder or a 9" x 12" envelope, send advertising information announcing an event that is open to the public. Distribute press packets primarily to your C markets and media outlets, such as the local paper, radio stations, and maybe even television. Free public service announcements for local events are common. The media may even be interested in interviewing participants or performers at your event. Your job is to convince the media through written and oral presentations, that your event is worth talking about to viewers and listeners.

Remember—

- Professional-looking and official press packets should be sent at least four to six weeks prior to the event. One or two weeks after sending the packet, follow up with a personal phone call to the organization.

- Network to find a personal contact within the radio or TV station. You don't want to be merely one of the many requests for airtime. If you can't uncover a personal contact, find out the name of the individual in charge of public service announcements and ask to speak to her. Let her know your packet is coming in the mail, or ask if you can deliver it in person. Without the personal contact, your press packet will likely be thrown away without a second look. Then follow up the press packet with another contact. The main ingredient of marketing success is follow-up, follow-up, follow-up (a perfect job for a motivated and articulate volunteer).

A press packet should include—

- Personal cover letter from the event director

- Event brochure

- List of notable achievements (in résumé style) of your group (social service projects make the most impact)

- Press releases - include two versions: a short paragraph and a longer one of no more than 500 words (one page)

- A short classified advertisement

The following are examples of a press release and a classified ad in the appropriate format.

Press Release
For immediate release
End Date: April 5, 20xx
Contact: Chris Pattersby
Phone: (312) 555-0000

Teens Spend Summer Serving Seniors

The Crew, 23 teenagers from Murray Hill Presbyterian Church, are paying money to spend six weeks of their summer renovating the local senior citizens' center. "Senior Summer" is their motto, and youth leader Chris Pattersby has helped them convince building supply and paint stores near their church to donate lumber, drywall, paint, and other supplies to put a new face on the building where senior citizens gather in the summer to stay cool, play bingo, talk, have a nourishing lunch, get regular medical assistance, and learn how to use the Internet.

Center manager Alex Stuart invited The Crew to make plans with the seniors who use the center. The church's youth staff and the center's staff are working with some of the seniors to repair walls---inside and out---and paint murals representing intergenerational relationships. Contractor Bill Hamaan is donating the time of one of his crew members each of the two weeks of work to supervise the project. "I've seen The Crew in action refurbishing the youth room at our church," Hamaan says. "They're hard workers, but there are building codes to follow and permits to get from the city, et cetera."

The efforts of The Crew and the transformation of the Senior Center will pop up in the pre-show slides at local movie theaters, and a local printer has donated the printing of paper bags for local merchants. Shoppers will carry home the message "Senior Summer: A neighborhood project of The Crew, Murray Hill Presbyterian Church, 2134 SW Franklin Rd. We care, but Jesus cared first! Call 223-0110 to find out about God's TLC for you."

The Senior Center has served residents of the surrounding neighborhoods for 42 years. "Seventy or 80 seniors find their way here every day," Stuart said. "The fix-up and murals these kids are planning will draw even more." If it does, an ad hoc citizens' group will approach the mayor to purchase the empty building next door for a full-fledged medical center that focuses on senior health care. "These seniors have given a lot to our community," said Ellen Davies, a Hillview Community College professor who tutors computer learning at the center once a week. "It's time we serve them. And it's good to see kids investing in another generation. We have to work at building bridges between the generations. We hope the kids will get as much out of this as our seniors will."

If you have professional skills, time, or money to donate, or a relative who uses the center, come to the renovation planning meeting on May 3, 7:30 p.m., at the Senior Center, 8475 First St. For more information, contact Chris Pattersby at 555-0000.

The Crew
2134 SW Franklin Rd.
Chicago, IL 07324
(218) 223-0110

April 15, 20xx

Record Eagle
ATT: Maria Lopez
101 Sonport Express
Chicago, IL 07324

Dear Ms. Lopez:

The Crew, the high school-age youth at Murray Hill Presbyterian Church, want to make a difference for the elderly by renovating the nearby Senior Citizens' Center.

Staff from our church and the center, building contractors, and donations are making it possible for us to repair walls, replace broken fixtures, and paint positive, intergenerationally oriented murals. The folks who use the center are providing artistic talent and volunteering their wisdom, expertise, and even their labor to improve the place where they spend their free time.

We need your help to get the word out to businesses and families who can attend a meeting to list the tasks that need to be done and help us get the remaining supplies. We request that you put out a press release or advertisement in your paper sometime during the weeks of April 20 to May 3. Also, we would like to invite you to come and join us for this kickoff event on May 3 at 7:30 p.m.

Sincerely,

The Crew
Murray Hill Presbyterian Church

Classified advertisement 30 words
For immediate release
Contact:
Phone:

Be part of renovating the Senior Citizens' Center with teens and adults from the Murray Hill Presbyterian Church. Saturday, May 3, at 7:30 p.m. at the Senior Center, 8475 First St. For more information, contact Chris Pattersby at (312) 555-0000.

The Crew
2134 SW Franklin Rd.
Chicago, IL 07324
(218) 225-0072

Mission Statement: The Crew is part of the youth ministry of Murray Hill Presbyterian Church. We are dedicated to making a difference in our community. Every year we research ways to use part of our summer to make something better for others.

Vision: The Crew is a model for Christian outreach that is used in seven churches in the Chicago area. We teach church youth groups, and now non-church youth groups, how to get kids excited about making a difference. We talk to the kids themselves about how to solicit donations and supplies, and how to find professionals to oversee whatever jobs they want to do.

Projects:

- Painted playground equipment at a preschool.

- Developed donors for supplies and professional skills to repair a home with Habitat for Humanity.

- Wrote our plan for another church to use in starting up its own Crew. Helped them scrape and paint two halfway houses where young offenders get a fresh start.

- Presented workshops for six churches and worked a little on each of their sites.

Board of Directors: The committee that oversees the ministry of The Crew is made up of the youth pastor, six adult church members, and three members of the youth group. Every year different teens make up the The Crew, but some stay with it all through high school.

FIRST CHURCH

Date: _____

Name: _____

Position (employee/volunteer/board member):_____

Please describe below any relationships, transactions, positions you hold (volunteer or otherwise), or circumstances that you believe could contribute to a conflict of interest between First Church and your personal interests, financial or otherwise:

❑   I have no conflict of interest to report.

❑   I have the following conflict of interest to report (please specify other nonprofit and for-profit boards you (and your spouse) sit on, any for-profit businesses for which you or an immediate family member are an officer or director, or a majority shareholder, and the name of your employer and any businesses you or a family member own):

1. _____

2. _____

3. _____

I hereby certify that the information set forth above is true and complete to the best of my knowledge. I have reviewed, and agree to abide by, the Policy of Conflict of Interest of First Church. I will inform First Church immediately if any information changes.

Signature: _____

Date: _____

Using these questions, tune up your next meeting a step or two above the last couple meetings you've led. With each meeting, add extra elements of purpose, design, participation, and prayer. And have some fun, while you're all at it.

DETERMINING GOALS-PURPOSEFUL PLANNING

What is the goal of the meeting? *(example—to brainstorm a theme for the winter retreat)*

What is the desired meeting outcome? *(That we come away with the theme for the retreat, Bible passages that illuminate the theme, ideas for games and speakers.)*

Who will participate? How many?

How long does it need to last? *(Remember, all meetings don't have to end on the half hour. Keep people only as long as needed.)*

Where is the best place to meet? *(Is there room to work? To gather in breakout groups? To write on butcher paper or a whiteboard?)*

When is the best time for this meeting *(based on above answers)*

What resources will I contribute to the meeting?

Do I need to receive anything from the participants *(either before or during the meeting)*? What information would be helpful for attendees to receive in advance from you?

DESIGNING DETAILS-COORDINATED DETAILS

How are my goals best accomplished? *(example—brainstorming, feedback groups, surveys, discussion, a potluck for parents)*

When and how do I deliver the meeting agenda to participants?

Will there be any costs?

What do I need to do ahead of time to secure and make the most of the location of the meeting?

What food do I need to prepare for attendees?

What materials do I need to prepare ahead to bring to the meeting? *(handouts, posters, get-acquainted game, etc.)*

GETTING OUT THE WORD—INFORM AND ENERGIZE PARTICIPANTS

(Tailor promotion to the group size and makeup and the personality of the occasion.)

- Phone calls
- Group texts
- Email or snail mail invitations
- Pulpit announcements
- One-on-one invitations
- Other:

PURPOSE-DRIVEN CONTENT-FOCUSED PROGRAMMING

(Be accountable to yourself—check off these guidelines as you complete each one. Attach a copy of the agenda, handouts or game instructions and props, action points assigned at the meeting, and your follow-up notes.)

- ❑ Provide the agenda in advance.
- ❑ Start on time.
- ❑ Define meeting etiquette or protocol *(example—keep an open mind, listen for understanding, honor each other's comments, have fun, etc.)*.
- ❑ Keep things moving.
- ❑ Use creativity to make meetings fun.
- ❑ Define action points.
- ❑ End on time.
- ❑ Provide follow-up notes.
- ❑ Follow through on what you decide and plan before the next meeting.

PRAYER—TRUST IN GOD

(List your prayer requests regarding the meeting, and list prayer requests generated at the meeting.)

MEETING AGENDA WORKSHEET

MEETING AGENDA

Date _____

Meeting called by: _____ Type of meeting: _____

Purpose: _____

Time: _____ Place: _____

Attendees: _____

Observers: _____

UPDATES FROM PREVIOUS MEETINGS

AGENDA ITEMS

Topic	Presenter	Time ALLOTTED

OTHER INFORMATION

Action steps:

Resources:

Special notes:

Confidential

Check desired ministry area: ❑ Middle school ❑ Senior high ❑ College-age

BASIC INFORMATION

Name _____

LAST   FIRST   MIDDLE

Address _____

CITY   STATE   ZIP

Email _____ Phone _____

Your communication preference ❑ phone call ❑ text ❑ email ❑ other:_____

Best times to reach you are _____

You are applying for an: ❑ Independent internship (not for course credit) ❑ University or seminary internship (for course credit)

If applying for university or seminary internship: School _____

Major or program _____ Anticipated graduation date _____

Program advisor and email _____

If you are currently employed: Employer _____

Employer Web site _____ Position at work _____ Years at current job _____

Church affiliation_____ ❑ Member ❑ Regular attendee

How long have you attended the church? _____

Emergency contact _____ Phone _____

NAME AND RELATIONSHIP

FAMILY INFORMATION (OPTIONAL)

Marital status (circle one): ❑ Single ❑ Married ❑ Divorced ❑ Widowed

If married, spouse's name _____

If you have children, their names and ages:

1. _____ 4. _____
2. _____ 5. _____
3. _____ 6. _____

MINISTRY EXPERIENCE OR EXPERIENCE WITH YOUTH (LIST MOST RECENT FIRST)

Church (name, city, state, and zip)	Dates	Area of service	Contact	Phone
1.				
2.				
3.				

TELL US ABOUT YOURSELF

1. Describe your faith journey.

2. What have you been doing to grow spiritually in the past year?

3. What would you do to maintain your spiritual growth as an intern?

4. What are your expectations of this youth ministry and the youth pastor?

5. Describe your background in student ministry at this church or elsewhere.

6. What are your goals as an intern? What experiences would you like to have?

7. Describe your vocational calling.

8. What education, conferences, experiences, gifts, skills, etc. have prepared you for youth ministry to this point?

REFERENCES

Please provide three character references (other than family members) who can identify your strengths and growth areas and describe your fitness for ministry. (Please mail one copy of **Letter of Reference for Applicant** and an addressed, stamped envelope to each of these references, and ask them to mail it back to the church office. If they prefer email, have them send a scanned copy, including their signature, to _____)

1. _____
     Name   Email   Home / work phone   Relationship

2. _____
     Name   Email   Home / work phone   Relationship

3. _____
     Name   Email   Home / work phone   Relationship

SELF-DESCRIPTION

Please circle the words that best describe you. Cross out words that least describe you.

trustworthy	dependable	active	compassionate	reliable	self-starter	punctual	flexible	laid-back
quick thinker	spontaneous	decisive	teachable	team player	humorous	thoughtful	solitary	leader
cautious	risk taker	patient	reflective	honest	organized	creative	disciplined	faithful

What are your spiritual gifts?

Please list any personal weaknesses, areas where you need to grow, or special concerns that could affect your ministry with students.

1. _____

2. _____

3. _____

MEDICAL INFORMATION

Have you had any prior injuries that might be aggravated by working in youth ministry?

Are you currently taking any medication prescribed by a doctor for physical or other conditions that would affect your ministry?

Do you have any medical conditions(s) that might be hazardous to others?

If you answered yes to any of the questions above, please attach another page and explain completely.

BACKGROUND INFORMATION

Have you, at any time, been involved in or accused, rightly or wrongly, of sexual abuse, maltreatment, or neglect?   ❑ Yes   ❑ No

Have you ever been accused or convicted of possession / sales of controlled substances or of driving under the influence of alcohol or drugs?   ❑ Yes   ❑ No

Are you using illegal drugs?   ❑ Yes   ❑ No

Have you been arrested or convicted for any criminal act more serious than a traffic violation?   ❑ Yes   ❑ No

Have you ever been involved romantically or sexually with any student in the youth ministry, or had sexual relations with any minor after you became an adult?   ❑ Yes   ❑ No

Have you ever been asked to step away from ministry or work with students or children in any setting, paid or volunteer? If yes, please explain.   ❑ Yes   ❑ No

Is there anything in your past or current life that might be a problem if we found out about it later? If yes, please explain.   ❑ Yes   ❑ No

I have read the _____ (church oganization) statement of faith, **Staff Expectations**, and **Reducing the Risk of Physical and Sexual Abuse** enclosures and agree to be bound by them.

❑ Yes   ❑ No   _____
                  Initial here

If the answer to any of the above questions is yes, please attach another page and write a full explanation. These will be discussed confidentially during your interview.

WAIVER / RELEASE

I, the undersigned, give my authorization to _____ representatives—hereafter

Church name

referred to as The Church—to verify the information on this form. The Church may contact my references and appropriate gov-

ernment agencies as deemed necessary in order to verify my suitability as a church youth ministry worker. I am willing to request

and submit to The Church background reports on myself from the _____ .

Background checking service

The information contained in this application is correct to the best of my knowledge. I authorize any references or churches

listed in this application to give you any information (including opinions) that they may have regarding my character and fitness for

student ministry. In consideration of the receipt and evaluation of this application by The Church, I hereby release any individual,

church, youth organization, charity, employer, reference, or any other person or organization, including record custodians, both

collectively and individually, from any and all liability for damages of whatever kind or nature that may at any time result to me,

my heirs, or family, because of compliance or any attempts to comply, with this authorization. I waive any right that I may have to

inspect any information provided about me by any person or organization identified by me in this application.

Should my application be accepted, I agree to be bound by the constitution, statement of faith and policies of The Church, and to

refrain from conduct unbecoming to Christ in the performance of my services on behalf of The Church. If I violate these guidelines,

I understand that my intern status may be terminated. By signing this application, I state that all of the information given about

myself is true.

I further state that **I HAVE CAREFULLY READ THE FOREGOING RELEASE AND KNOW THE CONTENTS THEREOF, AND

I SIGN THIS RELEASE AS MY OWN ACT.** This is a legally binding agreement that I have read and understand.

Print name _____

Signature _____ Date _____

Witness _____ Date _____

Use the following categories and questions to develop a job description for an intern.

What is the mission statement for the internship?

Is church membership an expectation?

Is church attendance an expectation?

What meetings must they attend on a regular basis?

What meetings should they attend once or twice for the experience?

When are they expected to be in the office?

What is the policy regarding days off and compensation time for events that last several days?

What is the length of the internship? Does it run concurrently with school, or does the intern commit a block of time like one year before starting seminary or a summer?

How many hours a week will the intern work? If the internship runs concurrently with school, how many hours a week is it feasible for the intern to work? Is the church willing to be flexible when finals roll around?

What is the salary or compensation package? Is insurance included? If it is an academic internship, is the church willing to help with tuition?

What age group will the intern focus on?

What programs or projects will the intern work focus on?

What *knowledge* objectives will the intern achieve by the end of the internship?

For example: By the end of this internship, the intern should be able to—

- Begin to formulate and articulate a philosophy of youth ministry.
- Identify the key characteristics of adolescence, as well as the impact on adolescents of family, society, and church.
- Explain the rationale behind the model of youth ministry the church uses.
- Articulate the demographics of the community and the services available through the local community.
- Describe the importance of the youth minister, whether professional or volunteer, in effective leadership of adolescents and their families.
- What *skills* will he achieve by the end of the internship? Include goals like these in the learning contract:

By the end of this internship, the intern should be able to—

- Write and lead a Bible study appropriate for senior high students.
- Initiate exploratory conversations with parents and with several subcultures of adolescents.
- Develop and produce a worship service.
- Put together a three-month program that includes a variety of events and topics geared toward adolescents' felt and real needs. It may include Sunday school, confirmation, and weekly activities.
- Develop and manage a youth ministry budget.
- Run an effective meeting.
- Recruit and interview potential volunteers.
- What *areas and tasks* will the intern be exposed to?

By the end of this internship, the intern will have experienced—

- Weekly church staff meetings in order to better understand how the whole church operates
- A weekly Bible study / small group as both an observer and a leader
- Participating in the organization and leadership of a weeklong missions trip

- Producing a variety of communication tools: fliers, church and youth ministry announcements, calendars, permission slips, and involvement with ministry-focused social media
- Participation in planning and strategy meetings
- What can the intern expect from you and the church?

During this internship, the intern can expect—

- Weekly or biweekly meetings with the supervisor
- Exposure to the full scope of the ministry, including administrative areas (budget development, hiring and development of volunteer staff, church staff meetings, congregational meetings, and counseling appointments when appropriate).
- Timely payment of a salary or stipend; reimbursement for approved expenses
- Medical insurance
- Conference registration for a professional seminar for youth worker
- What can the church expect from the intern?

During this internship, the church can expect that the intern will—

- Show up on time to all meetings or responsibilities
- Dress appropriately for the ministry situation
- Maintain a model lifestyle during the internship
- Immediately inform the supervisor of any areas of concern or conflict
- How will success be determined?

At the end of the internship, the intern will be evaluated—

- By means of a formal self-evaluation and a written evaluation by the supervisor.

LETTER OF REFERENCE FOR INTERN APPLICANT

Applicant's name _____

Email _____ Phone _____

The person named above is applying for a 12-month youth ministry internship with _____.

Church name

The applicant has been instructed to give you this form as part of their application process to serve as an intern. They will be working with adolescents and their families and, thus, will have contact with vulnerable populations. Please complete it to the best of your knowledge. It will become part of the application and will be used to help determine the applicant's suitability for the desired ministry. No single reference will determine acceptance or refusal, so frank appraisal will be appreciated both by the applicant and the selection committee. Your response will be kept confidential and not shared directly with the applicant. Thank you for your time on behalf of the applicant.

1. How long have you known the applicant and in what capacity?

2. What is your occupation?

3. In each category, check the characteristics that to your knowledge best describe the applicant. Add brief comments if necessary.

Achievement
- ❏ starts but often does not finish
- ❏ does only what is assigned
- ❏ meets average expectation
- ❏ resourceful and effective
- ❏ superior creative ability

Emotional stability
- ❏ somewhat over-emotional
- ❏ inclined to be apathetic
- ❏ rapidly shifting moods
- ❏ appropriate emotions for the situation
- ❏ usually well balanced
- ❏ good control in difficult situations
- ❏ learns and thinks slowly
- ❏ average mental ability
- ❏ alert, has good mind
- ❏ intelligent, makes thoughtful analysis
- ❏ brilliant, exceptional capability

Knowledge of the Bible
- ❏ sketchy, limited
- ❏ basic, but improving
- ❏ well established
- ❏ superior grasp

Leadership
- ❏ makes no attempt to lead
- ❏ tries but lacks ability
- ❏ has some leadership skills
- ❏ unusual, exceptional leadership

Personality
- ❏ avoided by others
- ❏ tolerated by others
- ❏ accepted by others
- ❏ liked by others
- ❏ sought after by others
- ❏ somewhat below par
- ❏ will face challenges in a physically rigorous setting
- ❏ fairly healthy
- ❏ good health

Responsiveness
- ❏ slow to sense how others feel
- ❏ reasonably responsive
- ❏ understanding and thoughtful
- ❏ accurately aware of others
- ❏ responds with unusual insight

Spiritual maturity
- ❏ immature faith
- ❏ has made basic commitment
- ❏ somewhat rigid beliefs
- ❏ active and growing faith
- ❏ exceptional insight and discipline

Teamwork
- ❏ frequently causes friction
- ❏ prefers to work alone
- ❏ knows how to follow
- ❏ works well with others
- ❏ most effective in teamwork

Please use the scale indicated below to further describe the applicant.
Rating scale: 1 = Outstanding, 2 = Good, 3 = Satisfactory, 4 = Fair, 5 = Poor, u/k = Unknown

1. Self-understanding

ability to identify his/her own personal strengths	1	2	3	4	5	u/k
ability to identify his/her own weaknesses	1	2	3	4	5	u/k
ability to see self as others see him/her	1	2	3	4	5	u/k
openness to growth and change	1	2	3	4	5	u/k

2. Emotional strength

ability to deal constructively with personal feelings	1	2	3	4	5	u/k
ability to receive constructive criticism	1	2	3	4	5	u/k
ability to be flexible in the face of change	1	2	3	4	5	u/k
ability to persevere through difficulties	1	2	3	4	5	u/k

3. Interpersonal relationships

shows honesty in decision-making	1	2	3	4	5	u/k
follows through on commitments	1	2	3	4	5	u/k
shows initiative and ambition	1	2	3	4	5	u/k
sets appropriate boundaries with students	1	2	3	4	5	u/k
sets appropriate boundaries with coworkers	1	2	3	4	5	u/k

4. Motivation for Ministry

ability to listen accurately to others	1	2	3	4	5	u/k
ability to respond to feelings and needs of others	1	2	3	4	5	u/k
ability to initiate friendships and care for others	1	2	3	4	5	u/k
willingness to resolve interpersonal conflicts	1	2	3	4	5	u/k

5. Ministry & Administration

desire to serve out of genuine love for Christ	1	2	3	4	5	u/k
desire to serve out of genuine love for others	1	2	3	4	5	u/k
ability to speak in front of large groups	1	2	3	4	5	u/k
willingness to do humble tasks joyfully	1	2	3	4	5	u/k
shows enthusiasm and vivacity	1	2	3	4	5	u/k
ability to take risks and respond to challenges	1	2	3	4	5	u/k
willingness to step outside personal comfort zone	1	2	3	4	5	u/k
uses diligence in studying	1	2	3	4	5	u/k
is organized and handles multiple tasks well	1	2	3	4	5	u/k
shows responsibility with finances	1	2	3	4	5	u/k
uses common sense relating to safety	1	2	3	4	5	u/k

Working in a team, working with children, youth, or people older than oneself, experiencing new ways of handling things, and getting to know new people - while all these things make being an intern exciting, they're stressful as well. Such stress may sometimes exaggerate some personality traits such as those listed below. Please check any that you feel apply to the applicant.

- ❑ Impatient
- ❑ Perfectionist
- ❑ Argumentative
- ❑ Critical of others
- ❑ Domineering
- ❑ Easily embarrassed
- ❑ Sullen

- ❑ Easily discouraged
- ❑ Cocky
- ❑ Withdrawn
- ❑ Irritable
- ❑ Anxious
- ❑ Easily offended
- ❑ Lacking a sense of humor

Additional comments:

Overall:

- ❑ I strongly recommend this applicant.
- ❑ I recommend this applicant with reservations. (Please identify your reservations.)
- ❑ I prefer to discuss this further. Please contact me at the following number:
- ❑ I cannot recommend this applicant for this internship.

Name of reference _____

Title or position _____

May we contact you? ❑ Yes ❑ No

Email _____ Phone _____ Best time to reach you _____

Signature _____ Date _____

Please send the completed form to _____
Church name   Address   City   State   Zip

Or email it with "Confidential" in the subject line, to:

Name _____ Date of evaluation _____

Internship site _____

Internship supervisor _____

Description of internship _____

_____

Please circle the number that describes you.

1 is a solid yes   **2** is a tentative yes   **3** is a tentative no   **4** is a solid no

1	2	3	4	I feel positive about my overall internship experience.
1	2	3	4	I helped set the pace in developing the ministry's identity, enthusiasm, momentum, and unity/teamwork.
1	2	3	4	My internship prepared me well for ministry.
1	2	3	4	I believe I have been able to use my gifts in my internship.
1	2	3	4	I have grown as a Christian as a result of my internship experience.
1	2	3	4	I believe that my internship experience allowed me to grow in being a leader in ministry.
1	2	3	4	I was open to evaluation and feedback from my supervisor.
1	2	3	4	I fulfilled the responsibilities of my internship in an effective manner.
1	2	3	4	I related well to other staff/coworkers.
1	2	3	4	I actively sought new experiences and challenges.
1	2	3	4	I was open to new ideas.
1	2	3	4	I believe students and parents were pleased with my work as an intern.

Please answer the following questions.

What were the highlights of your internship?

What tasks, events, and projects were you involved with in your internship? Place a star by those you led.

What skills did you acquire during your internship?

What area(s) need improvement in the youth ministry where you served?

What was the most challenging aspect of your internship for you?

How did you balance your time between your ministry and your personal time?

How has your relationship with God grown as a result of your internship?

What do you consider the most helpful aspect of the time spent as an intern?

Was there any time in which your time as an intern was a disappointment? If so, please describe.

Would you recommend other people to serve in this internship in the future? Why or why not?

As a result of your internship, rate the following—as you now see yourself—by checking the appropriate box:

POSITION DESCRIPTION CATEGORIES	Never did it	I'm hesitant	I'm strong in this area
Contacting new students			
Talking with a student about their faith journey			
Introducing a person to Christ			
Pastoral counseling			
Writing a Bible study			
Leading a Bible study			
Long-range planning: theme development, vision & mission			
Publicizing events			
Budget preparation & management			
Equipping adult leaders			
Equipping student leaders			
Working with a committee			
Working with a board			
Organizing & leading recreational activities			
Organizing & leading retreats			
Organizing & leading service projects &/or mission trips			
Teaching Sunday school &/or confirmation			
Giving a youth talk			
Leading a parents' meeting			
Leading a volunteer meeting			

What areas do you still need experience in before you graduate?

Any other comments:

Supervisor name _____ Phone _____

Supervisor's title _____ Email _____

Intern name _____ Date of evaluation _____

Description of internship _____

_____

_____

Please evaluate the following competencies of the intern as you have observed him or her in ministry. Circle the number that best describes the intern.

1 is a solid yes   **2** is a tentative yes   **3** is a tentative no   **4** is a solid no

COMPETENCIES	ADDITIONAL COMMENTS	
1 2 3 4	Appeared enthusiastic about ministry	
1 2 3 4	Was prepared to fulfill their responsibilities	
1 2 3 4	Related well to the students	
1 2 3 4	Related well to other staff and coworkers	
1 2 3 4	Took the initiative with projects and assignments	
1 2 3 4	Was open to constructive criticism from me	
1 2 3 4	Shared ideas without insisting on implementation	
1 2 3 4	Recognized when they needed help and sought it	
1 2 3 4	Demonstrated a loving, patient spirit	
1 2 3 4	Reached out to persons on the fringe	
1 2 3 4	Arrived on time	
1 2 3 4	Organized effectively	
1 2 3 4	Was resourceful	
1 2 3 4	Demonstrated gifts for ministry	

What areas of strength did you observe in this intern? (list and be specific)

What areas for further growth did you observe in this intern?

How often did you meet with the intern? What did you discuss or do in those meetings? Did the intern meet with any other staff members?

Describe the interaction between the other staff members and/or the congregation:

Did the intern display the maturity level needed for ministry?

Would you recommend this intern for ministry?

❑ Yes, enthusiastically

❑ Yes, but with the following recommendations:

❑ No, for the following reasons:

I have discussed the results of this evaluation with the intern. ❑ Yes ❑ No

Additional comments:

Supervisor's Signature: _____

Work through these questions before you take the step of proposing a youth ministry internship to your church or organization:

Do I have a clear job description with measurable goals? What exactly would an intern accomplish in the youth ministry?

Am I clear on what I expect from an intern?

Do I have time and capacity to supervise an intern? Do I have enough experience to develop another youth worker? Does anyone else on staff? What will an aspiring youth worker learn from spending time with me and this ministry?

Is church membership an expectation?

Is church attendance an expectation?

What meetings must they attend on a regular basis?

What meetings should they attend once or twice for the experience?

When do I expect them to be in the office?

What is our policy regarding days off and compensation time for events that last several days?

What is acceptable dress in the church? At ministry events? With students?

How does the intern access resources—administrative help, church vehicles, etc.?

How will the intern pay for meetings with leaders or students?

What is the length of the internship? Does it run concurrently with school, or does the intern commit a block of time like one year before starting seminary or a summer?

How many hours a week will the intern work? If the internship runs concurrently with school, how many hours a week is it feasible for the intern to work? Is the church willing to be flexible when finals roll around?

Does the internship pay enough to live on, or will the intern need a part-time job to supplement their income?

What age group will the intern work with: Middle school? High school? College-age?

What programs or projects will the intern work focus on: Vacation Bible School, day camp, small groups, worship ministry?

Who will be the intern's direct supervisor? Who else will have authority over them?

How will having an intern affect my ability to do my job?

Is my church or organization supportive of bringing on an intern? Have they hired an intern before? Has any of the leadership done an internship as part of their professional development?

Who would I need to clear the idea with before proceeding?

Does the church staff understand the job description of a youth ministry intern? Or will the church administrator expect an intern to stuff envelopes? Will the custodian expect to delegate the setup of Sunday school rooms to the intern?

Is the church willing to provide compensation to the intern? If the compensation is room and board, with whom will they live? If it's a church family, will boundaries be an issue?

If it's a small stipend, tuition credit, or cash, out of which budget will it come?

What will they use for transportation? Will the ministry loan them a car or reimburse them for travel and job expenses?

Does the church's insurance cover an intern? How about Workers' Compensation?

Does the church believe in developing future leaders for ministry, and are they willing to take on the accompanying risks? The internship is a step in the intern's discernment process. It may be that during the internship, it becomes clear that ministry is not the right direction for this person. Is the church willing to take that risk?

How can the internship be terminated if things don't work out as planned?

Is there a written description of the process involved in terminating an internship?

Is the church willing to let this person fail as well as succeed? Interns are rookies. As they try out their ministry legs, there are bound to be messes as well as successes. In what areas is the church willing to extend grace? In what areas can there be no mess-ups?

Am I ready to take appropriate and decisive action if conflict arises with an intern or about the intern? How can I be proactive in conflicts involving the intern? Can I confront based on early recognition of potential problems, or am I inclined to let things slide until I'm forced to react?

Do our students and their families understand the short-term commitment of an internship?

If this is an academic internship, what are the expectations of the sponsoring institution in regard to the intern? In regard to my supervision? In regard to my communication with the institution?

ABUSE AND HARASSMENT POLICIES AND GUIDELINES

TYPES OF ABUSE

Physical: Bruises, welts, burns, scratches, or bite marks, which are often explained away as accidental. Marks will appear in peculiar clusters, such as patterns consistent with teeth or fingernails. Wounds may appear in various stages of healing. There may be reluctance on the part of the child to discuss the "suspected" abuse and tendency will be to hide the marks that are a result of the abuse.

Emotional and Psychological: Symptoms are less obvious than those of physical abuse. Symptoms are usually observed in the behavior of the child. The child may seem unusually adult or juvenile, hard to get along with in general, or even unusually submissive. (It is important to note that these behaviors either separately or simultaneously do not always indicate abuse. Some signs may occur as part of the maturation process of the child or the result of a different problem.)

Neglect: Child may be emotionally, psychologically, physically, or developmentally impaired. Medical and dental needs may be unmet. Child may be inappropriately dressed for the weather or activities. The child may have the ongoing condition of being unclean, tired, or in trouble at school. Often times the student may be a "loner" and may steal or beg.

Sexual: Sexual abuse consists of any sexual exploitation of children under the age of 18 by an adult or a person 4 years older than the victim even if the child seems to be consenting. This form of abuse includes fondling, incest, rape, murder, assault, oral stimulation, genital or anal stimulation, or nonviolent sexual stimulation. Child sexual abuse can be inflicted in ways other than the physical assaults listed above. It can take such forms as witnessing adult sexual relations, indecent exposure, verbal sexual stimulation, peeping toms, exhibitionism, or obscene phone calls. Involving children in pornography or prostitution are also forms of child sexual abuse.

GUIDELINES

Any verbal or nonverbal sexual interaction with a child is inappropriate. Appropriate expressions of love and support include touching; however, children must be physically respected.

As much as possible, use the buddy system when working with individual youth. Let another adult know where you are.

One-on-one interaction should be male-male and female-female only.

Never take a member of the opposite sex home by yourself.

Special note: Keep a log of any unusual events or incidents involving a child that might indicate abuse.

REPORTING

Reporting child abuse or even suspected child abuse is the law. You can be held responsible in the future if a victim informs anyone of authority that you were aware of the abuse and did not report it. If you need to report proven or suspected abuse, notify the Pastor of Student Ministries immediately. The report must be made within 24 hours after you receive knowledge of the abuse.

Special note: Never promise a student you will keep a secret if they confide in you.

HARASSMENT POLICY

We are committed to providing a work environment free of unlawful harassment. Church policy prohibits sexual harassment because of race, religious creed, color, national origin or ancestry, physical or mental disability, medical condition, marital status, age, sexual orientation, or any other protected basis, including but not limited to the following behavior:

Verbal conduct such as derogatory jokes or comments, slurs or unwanted sexual advances, invitations, or gestures;

Visual conduct such as derogatory or sexually oriented posters, photography, cartoons, drawings, or gestures;

Physical conduct such as assault, unwanted touching, blocking normal movement or interfering with work because of sex, race, or any other protected basis;

Threats and demands to submit to sexual requests as a condition of continued employment, or to avoid some other loss, and offers of employment benefits in return for sexual favors;

Retaliation for having reported or threatened to report harassment.

If you believe you have been unlawfully harassed, we urge you to report the incident immediately. Follow the procedure so that your complaint can be resolved quickly and fairly:

When possible, confront the harasser and persuade him/her to stop.

Provide a written complaint to the Pastor of Student Ministries, or another pastor on staff as soon as possible after the incident. Include details of the incident(s), names of individuals involved, and the names of any witnesses.

The Pastor of Student Ministries will refer all harassment complaints to the Senior Pastor (if not the accused). The church will immediately undertake an effective, thorough, and objective investigation of the harassment allegations.

If the ministry determines that unlawful harassment has occurred, it will take effective remedial action in accordance with the circumstances. Any individual the ministry determines to be responsible for unlawful harassment will be subject to appropriate disciplinary action.

Whatever action the ministry takes against the harasser will be made known to the individual lodging the complaint. The ministry will take appropriate action to remedy any loss to you resulting from harassment.

The ministry will not retaliate against you for filing a complaint and will not tolerate or permit retaliation by volunteers or employees.

STEPS TOWARD PREVENTING SEXUAL ABUSE

1. Selection and screening
- Church membership requirement
- Clearing the applicant's name with the pastoral staff
- Requiring thorough staff application, including references that you must contact
- Conducting an application interview with two staff
- Enforcing a probationary period
- Accepting only those applicants willing to let the ministry do a thorough background check

2. Supervision
- New volunteers are paired with veterans for a time and are not alone with students.
- New volunteers are specifically evaluated at 30, 60, and 90 days.
- All volunteers receive at least yearly evaluations based on supervisory observation.
- Require two ministry-approved adults be present with a student or group of students at all times.
- Any one-on-one meeting is conducted in a visible setting such as a public coffee shop and can be accessed at any time by staff, parents, and/or caregivers.

3. Specific reporting process
Basic steps to be followed in possible abuse cases:
- All efforts to handle an incident will be well documented immediately.
- The incident will immediately be reported to ministry supervisors and, very likely, the ministry attorney.
- Contact the proper civil authorities immediately. Most states have a reporting deadline of serious allegations of 24 hours or less. These authorities, and not our ministry, will handle the investigation. Child Welfare Information Gateway has helpful resources when it comes to mandated reporting and state guidelines: https://www.childwelfare.gov.
- Notify the parents. (If notifying the parents appears to place the child at further risk, work with a licensed therapist, medical professional, or other appropriate authority.)
- Take allegations seriously; reach out to the victim and his or her family; and treat the accused with dignity and support.
- If the accused is a church worker, that person will be relieved temporarily of his or her duties until the investigation is completed.
- Use the text of a prepared public statement to answer the press and convey news to the congregation. Appoint a press liaison for your church. Typically, this is the senior pastor, executive pastor, or the chair of the board. Safeguarding the privacy and confidentiality of all involved must be a priority.

4. The following are reporting procedures for volunteer staff
- If a child or student is observed to have signs of physical abuse (bruises caused by hitting, unexplainable injuries, etc.), volunteer staff should call these things to the attention of a pastoral staff member immediately and document the report.
- If a child or student verbally accuses a family member or other person of abusing them in some way, the volunteer staff member should ask appropriate questions in an attempt to determine the veracity of the claims and the imminence of danger. If the truth of the claims seems clear, the matter should be immediately brought to the attention of a pastoral staff member. If the truth of the claims seems questionable, the claims should still be brought to the attention of a pastoral staff member on the same day that the claims are expressed.
- Whether clearly true or questionable in the estimation of the volunteer staff member, the allegations or observations should be put in writing on the day of the incident, including a verbatim/exact account

449

of the observation and/or accusation. Every detail of the event/s—including date, time of day, names of persons involved, etc.—should be included in this report. The person making the report should keep one copy, and one copy should be given to the pastoral staff member who oversees that area of ministry. These reports must be kept safe and confidential. The pastoral staff member will be responsible for making a determination as to the appropriate actions to be taken as follow-up to these observations/ accusations.

5. Defining Sexual Abuse
A. Touching
1. Fondling—touching the body on private parts
2. Inappropriate kissing
3. Intercourse (consensual or non-consensual)
4. Oral or anal intercourse

B. Non-touching
1. Sexual remarks
2. Showing pornography
3. Watching any sexual activity
4. Exhibitionism

6. Detecting sexual abuse
- Most cases of sexual abuse go undetected. There may be no apparent physical signs, or there may be physical signs detected only through medical examination.
- The cases that *are* reported are generally reported by abused children to their parents, siblings, or other caretakers—often in the form of casual remarks that lead the listener to query further.
- Most children say nothing. They may not realize that what was done to them was wrong. Or they may be too embarrassed or frightened to speak up. They may not want to get the offender in trouble—especially if a friendship has developed between offender and victim.
- In some cases, telltale physical or emotional signs may arouse your suspicion. In its publication *The Educator's Role in the Prevention and Treatment of Child Abuse and Neglect*, the National Center on Child Abuse and Neglect outlines certain indicators of sexual abuse.

Physical indicators
Difficulty in walking or sitting
Torn, stained, or bloody underclothing
Pain or itching in the genital area
Bruises or bleeding in external genitalia, vaginal or anal area
Venereal disease, especially in preteens
Pregnancy

Behavioral indicators
Unwilling to change for gym or participate in physical education class
Withdrawal, fantasy, or infantile behavior
Bizarre, sophisticated, or unusual sexual behavior or knowledge
Poor peer relationships
Delinquency or running away
Reports sexual assault by caretaker

These signs can be indicative of other problems and are not exclusively tied to sexual abuse. But the repeated occurrence of an indicator, or the presence of several indicators warrants further investigation.

STAFF GUIDELINES—SAMPLE

Because of who we are in Christ, the organization we represent, and the vulnerable age group we work with, each of us must be willing to pay the price of leadership in every area of our lives.

The following areas are very important if you are to maintain a good reputation. We need your compliance in each of these areas for you to be a staff member.

- You must not have a lifestyle that is contrary to clear Bible principles.
- Do not plan activities with students or communicate with students without formal parental approval. Activities should also be approved by the youth pastor.
- Attend church on a regular basis. Pursue spiritual growth.
- Do not form exclusive relationships, e.g., date, with junior high/middle school or senior high youth or any person under your supervision or care.
- Do not voice critical opinions about any Christian church, staff, parents, or students in front of students.
- Do not use illegal drugs.
- Do not get drunk.
- When driving students you must obey all laws and use safe driving habits.
- Never drive a student home alone.
- Male staff are expected to spend time primarily with male students, female staff with female students.
- Maintain appropriate physical and emotional boundaries at all times.

Touch

- Do not initiate or demand touch with any student. Do not force touch upon a student or leader.
- Use only appropriate touch. Appropriate touch honors physical and emotional boundaries and communicates encouragement or comfort.
- Appropriate touch should take place only when in the presence of two or more leaders.

Counseling and mentoring appointments are confidential so you should not share conversations with any person other than a pastor or supervising staff.

In our setting, we prefer that men build mentoring relationships with young men, women build mentoring relationships with young women.

Always seek to conduct meetings in a visible setting which can be accessed at any time by staff, parents, and/or caregivers.

- You **must** report to your supervisor any of the following situations **immediately. Call 911 when appropriate.**
- Physical abuse reported to you.
- Sexual abuse of any minor reported to you.
- When a student tells you he/she is suicidal (take them seriously and report **immediately**).
- When a student is in a life-threatening situation.
- When the student is threatening someone else.
- When a student discloses a pregnancy.
- When a student is involved in a runaway situation.
- When a student confesses a felony to you.
- When you have reason to believe a student is going to commit a crime.

I have read the above and accept the STAFF CONDUCT AND GUIDELINES.

Staff Signature _____

Staff Contact List Monthly

P - Personal appointment   **T** - Telephone   **L** - Letter   **C** - Card   **E** - Email

Name	Phone number	1	2	3	4	5	6	7	8	9	10	11	12	Important dates
1.														
2.														
3.														
4.														
5.														
6.														
7.														
8.														
9.														
10.														
11.														
12.														
13.														
14.														
15.														
16.														
17.														
18.														
19.														
20.														

VOLUNTEER APPLICANT CHECKLIST

Once potential youth ministry volunteers receive application packets, you should start files on them. Use this form to track their progress.

- **Date that the application packet is sent or given out** _____

- **Date when each item is returned:**

  Application _____

  Reference 1 _____

  Reference 2 _____

  Reference 3 _____

  Background check permission _____

  Reading assignment statement
  (completion of statement of faith, child abuse policy, etc.) _____

- **Fingerprinting completed** _____

  Results _____

- **Child registry/background check completed** _____

  Results _____

- **Interview date** _____

  Interviewer _____

  Notes placed in folder _____

- **Observation period started** _____

- **Observation period completed** _____

- **Observation partner** _____

- **Talked to observation partner** _____

  Notes placed in folder _____

- **Final conversation** _____

  Decision _____

- **Welcome and introduction to students and leadership team** _____

Effective year _____

Driver's name _____

Driver's license number _____

State of Issue _____ Expiration date _____

Current address _____

City _____ State _____ Zip _____

Home phone _____ Cell phone_____

Email _____

Birth date _____ Social Security no. _____

Type of license
- ❑ Operators
- ❑ Commercial (CDL)
- ❑ Chauffer
- ❑ Other (please specify)

Describe any medical conditions that could affect your ability to safely transport students or adults.

Date of your last physical:

List any medications you currently take that could potentially impair driving ability.

If you hold a CDL, please attach a copy of your current health form.

Please describe driver training that you have received:

Have you been convicted of any moving violations in the last five years?
❑ Yes ❑ No   If yes, please describe each conviction.

Do you have any restrictions or endorsements on your driver's license?
❑ Yes ❑ No   If yes, please list those restrictions or endorsements.

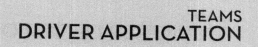

Have you been involved in any motor vehicle accidents in the last seven years?
❑ Yes ❑ No   If yes, please give the date and briefly describe each accident.

Have you been convicted of a DUI, or had your license revoked or suspended in the past 10 years?
❑ Yes ❑ No   If yes, please provide complete details.

Do you carry personal auto insurance?
❑ Yes ❑ No   If yes, please identify the insurance company and policy #.

Does our church or ministry have any reason to be concerned about your ability to be a responsible and careful driver?
❑ Yes ❑ No   If yes, please briefly describe.

I certify that all the information on this application is truthful and completely accurate. I agree to notify the church within 14 days of any changes in any of the above information. I authorize the church to verify this information with the Department of Motor Vehicles and to check references on my driving. I understand that false statements on this application will constitute grounds for immediate dismissal.

By signing, I agree to abide by safety procedures established by the church and abide by all laws.

Signature _____ Date _____

Print name clearly _____

Please attach a full color photocopy of both sides of your current driver's license to this form.

_____

Office Use Only

DMV check ❑ Yes ❑ No   Date _____

Contact name _____

Cleared with insurance company ❑ Yes ❑ No   Date _____

Contact name _____

Approved to drive _____

Date _____

TEAMS
VOLUNTEER LETTER OF REFERENCE

Confidential

_____ is applying to become a volunteer youth
worker with the student ministry at _____ Church
and has given your name as a personal reference.

The person in this staff position will be in close contact with students, and we want to ensure that these relationships will be healthy ones. Please complete the form below and use the enclosed envelope to send us your evaluation of this person's character and integrity. Your response will remain confidential.

1. Describe your relationship with this person.

2. How long have you known this person and in what context?

Please use the following scale to respond to the following questions:

1 low   **2** below average   **3** average   **4** very good   **5** excellent

How would you rate his/her ability in the following:

1. Involvement in peer relationships?   1   2   3   4   5
2. Emotional maturity?   1   2   3   4   5
3. Resolving conflict?   1   2   3   4   5
4. Following through with commitments?   1   2   3   4   5
5. Ability to relate to students?   1   2   3   4   5
6. Spiritual maturity?   1   2   3   4   5
7. What are this applicant's greatest strengths?

8. Do you have any concerns with this person working with students? If so, please explain.

❏ Please check this box if you have concerns that you would prefer discussing in person.

Thank you for taking the time to fill this out. If you have any questions regarding this reference, please contact

_____ at _____ or _____
     Name of youth pastor   phone   email

Signature _____ date _____

Please forward this document to _____
                                    Name and address of church   City   State   Zip

456

PROSPECTIVE STAFF INTERVIEW WORKSHEET

1. CHURCH BACKGROUND

How did you hear about our ministry?

Why are you interested in working with us?

How long have you been going to our church?

What brought you here?

Are you a member of the church?

2. SPIRITUAL BACKGROUND

Describe your faith journey.

How long have you been a Christian? Talk about your journey to become a Christian.

How would you describe your relationship with Christ now?

What do you do to keep your spiritual life fresh?

Who else knows you deeply? How would they describe you?

3. MINISTRY EXPERIENCE

Are you serving with any other ministries currently?

Have you served in another ministry in the past? If so, when and why did you stop serving?

What do you believe your spiritual gifts are? What do you love doing? What have other people told you you're good at?

Have you ever worked with our ministry before?

4. PERSONAL INFORMATION

What is your home situation? Are you married? Are there children? Do you have a roommate(s)?

If married, are your spouse and/or kids supportive of your commitments?

Where do you work?

Describe your job and your work environment.

Tell me about your relationship with your family growing up.

Students with whom you are in relationship pick up not only what you teach, but also what you model. What one thing in your life would you like them to learn from you? On the flip side, what one thing would you rather they didn't learn from you?

Each of us struggles with a character weakness or a stubborn bad habit. What would you say yours is?

Is there anything in your life currently, or in your past, that we should know about in your ministry to students (alcoholism, drug use, family concerns, child abuse, depression, etc.)?

Is there anything else we should discuss?

If you're new to a youth ministry position, practice interviewing by asking some of the following questions of those who have been holding down the fort till you got there. You could ask them in the past tense—"Why were you interested in working with the youth ministry?" Or you could phrase them with the future in mind—"Are you interested in continuing to work in your current role?" Comments about the purpose or value of the question is in parentheses at the end of each question.

(The **Prospective Staff Interview Worksheet** includes these same questions and space for taking notes during an interview.)

1. CHURCH BACKGROUND

How did you hear about our ministry? (This gives you insight into which forms of recruiting are giving good results.)

Why are you interested in working with us? (People's motives for joining a ministry vary. They may want to spend more time with their own kids who are in the ministry. They may want to stop teenagers from repeating the same mistakes they did. They may be bored and really like the music that the high school band plays.)

How long have you been going to our church? (Someone who's just started coming may be a church hopper, or even have a history of stirring up dissension wherever they go.)

What brought you here? (It's helpful to know if they've grown up in your denomination or if they were intrigued by the sermon topics advertised in the paper.)

Are you a member of the church? (What's your church's policy on membership and volunteering? More and more churches are leaning toward requiring volunteers to be church members, for more accountability.)

2. SPIRITUAL BACKGROUND

Tell me about your faith journey. (The reason for asking the question this way is that it invites a more comprehensive story than if you ask, "Tell me about when you became a Christian." Instead of hearing "I was saved in July 1985 at Bible camp," you'll learn details that may trigger other questions or give you a feel for experiences that equip them for particular kinds of ministry.)

How long have you been a Christian? or **Talk to me about how you became a Christian.** (If you feel the answer to any question is incomplete, reframe the question until you're satisfied with the answer.)

On a scale from one to ten, what's your relationship with Christ like now and why? (Sometimes you'll get people who have recently renewed their faith and are eager to get active in the church. You may want to give them some time to get grounded by attending a small group of their own rather than placing them in leadership. Question any extreme on the scale. If they're a one or two, find out if they expect the youth ministry to bolster their faith. If they're a nine or ten, how do they deal with the dry times in their walk?)

What do you do to keep your spiritual life sharp? (Are they active in a Bible study or small group? Do they practice spiritual disciplines like devotions and prayer? You're trying to get a sense of how they nurture their own faith. If they aren't maturing themselves, they can't lead someone else.)

Are you or have you ever been discipled or been in a small group? (This is especially appropriate if the person is applying to be a small group leader. If they've never experienced a successful small group, they'll have difficulty leading a group. You may want to suggest that, before they volunteer in the youth ministry, they take some time to ground themselves. A tough call? Yes, but it communicates that you're more interested in their spiritual growth than in their being a body serving in the youth ministry. Don't worry—they'll come back.)

3. MINISTRY EXPERIENCE

Are you serving with any other ministries? (Typically, youth ministry is one of the most time-intensive ministries of the church. Unless they're helping out in a non-relational capacity—e.g., putting together newsletters for you or entering data in the database—they won't have time or energy to serve in other ministries at the same time.)

Have you served in another ministry in the past? If so, why did you stop serving? (You're listening for patterns here. Does the person have a track record of leaving when things get tough? Do they cause conflict and leave? Do they leave if they don't get their own way? If you have a corresponding section in your application, you can do some comparing. Word of experience: if someone left their last ministry because of unresolved conflict, you can bet that conflict will follow them into this ministry.)

What do you believe your spiritual gifts are? Or what do you love doing? What have other people told you you're good at? (Do their gifts fit the needs of the job for which they're applying? They may have been "guilted" into volunteering with the youth ministry, when their talents really lie with the senior citizens or the justice and mercy committee. You're also looking to see if other people have affirmed their gifts. Often we'll hear the phrase, "God's leading me to work with the students." Don't be satisfied merely with their assertion. Ask, "Who else has seen you in action and affirmed this leading?" Probe for details.)

Have you ever worked with our ministry before? (If you're relatively new to the church—and especially if you know there was divisiveness in the ministry before you came—you'll protect the ministry by asking the question. If this person left because of your predecessor and now wants to come back, is that a good thing or a bad thing? Investigate this one.)

4. PERSONAL INFORMATION

Introduce this section by saying something like this: "It's important that we have a handle on the personal lives of our leadership team because seasons of life and relational dynamics can greatly impact our ministry. This information is strictly confidential, unless we get your permission to talk about it with a third party. Please tell what you feel we should know and what you are comfortable with sharing, with the understanding that we need to know anything that would influence or impact your ministry with students and the ministry as a whole."

(Optional) What is your home situation? Are you married? Are there children? Do you have a roommate(s)? (You're listening for issues dealing with their personal relationships. Are they divorced, separated, living with some-one where there's a romantic relationship? What is your ministry's and your church's stance on these issues? If they are divorced or widowed, how long has it been, and have they worked through the grieving and other issues affiliated with those kinds of losses?)

(Optional) If married, are your spouse and/or kids supportive of your commitments? (You're trying to avoid putting this person in conflict. If they're not being supported, their ministry can be hindered.)

Where do you work? (Be listening for jobs that may affect the applicant's fit with the ministry. For example, if she's a CPA, she may be out of commission from January until April. If she teaches high school or middle school, will she burn out if she serves students "after hours" as well?)

Are you reasonably content with your job? (Discontent is a yellow flag only; job satisfaction may or may not impact their effective ministry.)

Tell me about your relationship with your family growing up. (You're listening for unresolved issues here. Although you're not a therapist, you may learn you need to recommend one. Again, people get into ministry with mixed motives. How they dealt with (and continue to relate to) their family of origin affects how they do ministry.)

Students with whom you are in relationship pick up not only what you teach, but also what you model. What one thing in your life would you like them to learn from you? On the flip side, what one thing would you rather they didn't learn from you?

Each of us struggles with a character weakness or a stubborn bad habit. What would you say yours is? (Compare this response to the previous one. Are they similar? If not, why not?)

Is there anything in your life currently, or in your past, that we should know about in your ministry to young students? (Alcoholism, drug use, family concerns, child abuse, depression, etc.)

What are your views on the legal use of alcohol/smoking, etc.? (This question may be related to certain views they expressed on their application or that the church holds.)

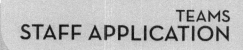

Check desired ministry area: ❑ Middle school ❑ Senior high ❑ College-age

BASIC INFORMATION

Name _____
                          LAST   FIRST   MIDDLE

Address _____
                                              CITY   STATE   ZIP

Email _____ Phone _____

Your communication preference: ❑ phone call ❑ text ❑ email ❑ other:_____

Best times to reach you are _____ May we call you at work ❑ Yes ❑ No

Employer _____ Employer address _____

Position at work _____ Years at current job _____

Email _____ Social Security # _____

Driver's License _____

Church membership: ❑ Member ❑ Regular attendee

How long have you attended our church? _____

Emergency contact_____Phone_____
                          NAME AND RELATIONSHIP

FAMILY INFORMATION

Marital status (check one): ❑ Single ❑ Married (anniversary date _____) ❑ Divorced ❑ Separated ❑ Widowed ❑ Other:

If married, spouse's name _____

If you have children, their names and ages:

1. _____   4. _____

2. _____   5. _____

3. _____   6. _____

EDUCATION

High School _____ City _____ State _____ Grad Year _____

College / tech school _____ City _____ State _____ Grad Year _____

Degree and major _____ Minor _____

Other education, training, and licenses _____

MINISTRY EXPERIENCE OR EXPERIENCE WITH YOUTH (LIST MOST RECENT FIRST)

Church (name, city, state, and zip)	Dates	Area of service	Contact	Phone
1.				
2.				
3.				

TELL US ABOUT YOURSELF

1. Describe your faith journey.

2. What have you been doing to grow spiritually in the past year?

3. What would you do to maintain your spiritual growth as a volunteer?

4. What are your expectations of the youth ministry team?

5. Explain your background in student ministry at this church or elsewhere.

6. What special qualities or qualifications would you contribute as a volunteer staff member?

7. Do your beliefs contradict the teachings of our church? If so, in which areas?

REFERENCES

Please provide three character references (other than family members) who can identify your strengths and growth areas and describe your fitness for ministry. (Please mail one copy of **Volunteer Letter of Reference** and an addressed, stamped envelope to each of these references, and ask them to mail it back to the church office. If they prefer email, have them send a scanned copy, including their signature, to _____)

1. _____
    Name   Address or Email   Home / work phone   Relationship

2. _____
    Name   Address or Email   Home / work phone   Relationship

3. _____
    Name   Address or Email   Home / work phone   Relationship

SELF-DESCRIPTION

Please circle the words that best describe you. Cross out words that least describe you.

trustworthy	dependable	active	compassionate	reliable	self-starter	punctual	flexible	laid-back
quick thinker	spontaneous	decisive	teachable	team player	humorous	thoughtful	solitary	leader
cautious	risk taker	patient	reflective	honest	organized	creative	disciplined	faithful

What are your spiritual gifts?

Please list any personal weaknesses, areas where you need to grow, or special concerns that could affect your ministry with students.

1. _____

2. _____

3. _____

MEDICAL INFORMATION

Have you had any prior injuries that might be aggravated by working in youth ministry?

Are you currently taking any medication prescribed by a doctor for physical or other conditions that would affect your ministry?

Do you have any medical conditions(s) that might be hazardous to others?

If you answered yes to any of the questions above, please attach another page and explain completely.

BACKGROUND INFORMATION

Have you, at any time, been involved in or accused, rightly or wrongly, of sexual abuse, maltreatment, or neglect?   ❏ Yes   ❏ No

Have you ever been accused or convicted of possession / sales of controlled substances or of driving under the influence of alcohol or drugs?   ❏ Yes   ❏ No

Are you using illegal drugs?   ❏ Yes   ❏ No

Have you been arrested or convicted for any criminal act more serious than a traffic violation?   ❏ Yes   ❏ No

Have you ever been involved romantically or sexually with any student in the youth ministry, or had sexual relations with any minor after you became an adult?   ❏ Yes   ❏ No

Have you ever gone through treatment for alcohol or drug abuse?   ❏ Yes   ❏ No

Have you ever been asked to step away from ministry or work with students or children in any setting, paid or volunteer? If yes, please explain.   ❏ Yes   ❏ No

Is there anything in your past or current life that might be a problem if we found out about it later? If yes, please explain.   ❏ Yes   ❏ No

I have read the _____ (church oganization) statement of faith, **Volunteer Staff Expectations**, and **Reducing the Risk of Physical and Sexual Abuse** enclosures and agree to be bound by them.

❏ Yes ❏ No   _____
Initial here

If the answer to any of the above questions is yes, please attach another page and write a full explanation. These will be discussed confidentially during your interview.

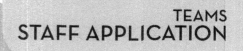
WAIVER / RELEASE

I, the undersigned, give my authorization to _____ representatives—hereafter
Church name
referred to as The Church—to verify the information on this form. The Church may contact my references and appropriate gov-

ernment agencies as deemed necessary in order to verify my suitability as a church youth ministry worker. I am willing to request

and submit to The Church background reports on myself from the _____ .
Background checking service

The information contained in this application is correct to the best of my knowledge. I authorize any references or churches

listed in this application to give you any information (including opinions) that they may have regarding my character and fitness for

student ministry. In consideration of the receipt and evaluation of this application by The Church, I hereby release any individual,

church, youth organization, charity, employer, reference, or any other person or organization, including record custodians, both

collectively and individually, from any and all liability for damages of whatever kind or nature that may at any time result to me,

my heirs, or family, because of compliance or any attempts to comply, with this authorization. I waive any right that I may have to

inspect any information provided about me by any person or organization identified by me in this application.

Should my application be accepted, I agree to be bound by the constitution, statement of faith and policies of The Church, and

to refrain from conduct unbecoming to Christ in the performance of my services on behalf of The Church. If I violate these guide-

lines, I understand that my volunteer status may be terminated. By signing this application, I state that all of the information given

about myself is true.

I further state that **I HAVE CAREFULLY READ THE FOREGOING RELEASE AND KNOW THE CONTENTS THEREOF, AND

I SIGN THIS RELEASE AS MY OWN ACT.** This is a legally binding agreement that I have read and understand.

Print name _____

Signature _____ Date _____

Witness _____ Date _____

ITEMS TO INCLUDE IN AN APPLICATION PACKET

- ❑ **Staff Application Process Letter** explaining the process

- ❑ **Staff Application**

- ❑ **Volunteer Staff Expectations**

- ❑ Church's statement of faith

- ❑ Church's constitution

- ❑ **Reducing the Risk of Physical & Sexual Abuse**

- ❑ **Volunteer Letter of Reference** form (3 copies)

- ❑ Health (medical) form

- ❑ Handouts on—

  - ❑ Child registry/background screening

  - ❑ Fingerprinting

- ❑ Optional items (depending on your church policy and state law)

❑ APPEARANCE
"People look on the outward appearance but God looks on the heart."
The first phrase is not the heart of the verse, but it's the truth. Students and adults will base their impression of our ministry on their impression of us. For this reason we wear appropriate clothing (1 Corinthians 9:19-23).
- The activity should dictate the type of clothing worn.
- All of our clothing should be clean, communicating personal discipline and recognition of self-worth, be modest, protecting the reputation and image of the Holy Spirit (1 Timothy 2:9, 1 Corinthians 8:27, 1 Thessalonians 4:6a), and avoid masking our inner qualities (1 Peter 3:1-8).

❑ STUDENT RELATIONSHIPS
Discretion in staff members' personal lives is fundamental to both spiritual integrity and to continuing to do spiritual ministry among students and their families (Ephesians 5:1-12, 15-16). To live wisely and without any hint of sexual misconduct we keep the following standards:
- Any verbal or nonverbal or technology-based sexual interaction with any student is inappropriate and will be immediately disciplined and reported to the appropriate authorities.
- Dating or any type of exclusive relationship with any junior high/middle school or senior high student is forbidden.
- Discretion must be used in physical contact with any students. Innocent behavior can be misinterpreted or misunderstood. Full body-to-body hugs, piggyback rides, sitting on laps, stroking, massaging shoulders or any other part of the body, backrubs, or affectionate kissing raises serious concerns and must be avoided. Any overt display of affection, appropriate hugging for example, should be made in a public setting in front of other group members and should not be demanded from the other party.
- Sexual gestures or overtures to a staff member by a student should be reported to one of the ministry directors or the student ministries pastor so that discussion can be held with the student.
- Staff should form male/female ministry teams whenever possible.
- One-on-one counseling with a student should always occur in a visible public place, never alone in a car or a private place. As a general rule when counseling a member of the other gender, invite a member of the same gender as the counselee to be the observing staff.
- When a situation arises where you are alone with a student of the other gender, quickly move that situation to a visible public setting.
- Driving alone with students should be avoided at all times.
- Romantic or sexual attraction for a student by an adult leader should be brought up and discussed with the ministry director for prayer and guidance.
- All suspicions of child or sexual abuse must be reported to the ministry director who will report it to the mandated reporter in the organization. That person will notify the appropriate agency.
- Any knowledge or suspicion of any youth ministry staff having an inappropriate relationship with a student must be reported promptly to the youth ministry leader. If the person in question is the leader, the report should be made to the supervisor of that person.
- No wrestling or physical horseplay should ever occur between staff and students.
- Church staff or volunteers should obtain the consent of the student's parent or guardian before going out with that student, or spending time with the student in an unsupervised situation.
- Use caution in connecting with students via social media or through other technology. Follow the church's policy on social media.

❑ DATING AND EXCLUSIVE RELATIONSHIPS
We recognize one of the greatest visible destroyers of ministries is moral impurity. The following policies should be understood in that light.

- No staff member will form any type of exclusive relationship with a student in middle school, junior high, or high school. This is ground for immediate discipline.
- Staff members involved in a dating relationship should model appropriate behavior. Particularly during church functions, our focus is to be on the Lord as well as students.
- In the case of premarital sex or extramarital sex, an immediate discipline process will be put into place.
- Model the highest standards in your relationships, whether in front of students or not.
- Be aware of what you are communicating about your relationship(s) on social media.

❏ **CHARACTER EXPECTATIONS**
- **To keep our integrity:** the motives, attitude, and actions of staff should be completely transparent to any observer. Our honesty should be testable by Luke 16:10-12.
  1. *Faithfulness in little things*—being on time, keeping our word, filling requests on time, following through with students, and other responsibilities.
  2. *Faithfulness in money*—turning in receipts, being very cautious with event cash and petty cash, remembering people have sacrificially given that dollar.
  3. *Faithfulness in that which belongs to another*—treating all the church equipment and property with utmost respect.
- **To be teachable:** None of us must claim to have arrived at infallibility. We must continually attend sessions, conferences, worship services, read, and observe with a teachable spirit, continually seeking to grow.
- **To be an appropriate role model:** Staff responsibilities naturally require frequent interaction with students and their families, as well as the community. Youth staff members come into Christian ministry from a variety of backgrounds and beliefs—especially in the gray areas of Christianity. Because staff are leaders and role models, they must use *careful discretion* when choosing movies, music, etc., for ministry activities. The use of R-rated movies is prohibited with middle school/ junior high students and parental permission is required with senior highers. Use PG-13 movies with extreme caution. *In all cases, preview a movie that you're considering showing at a youth activity.* When in doubt, check with parents or a ministry director.

  Along with entertainment choice, substances used by staff model behavior to students. Since the number one substance abused by teenagers is alcohol, staff will abstain from the use of alcoholic beverages in the presence of students.
- **To develop a servant's heart:** "Let nothing be done through strife or vain glory; but in lowliness of mind let each esteem others better than themselves. Look not every man on his own things, but every man also on the things of others. Let this mind be in you, which was also in Christ Jesus ... who made Himself of no reputation and took upon Him the form of a servant ... He humbled Himself, and became obedient ... even the death of the cross." (Phil. 2:3-8).

We aren't concerned about rank or position; the one in the pulpit is of no greater importance in God's eyes than the one leading a small group or driving the buses. As we faithfully serve one another within the ministry, the Lord expands our outreach and provides opportunities to serve those outside of the ministry. In homes, at church, and in the community, others should remember us by our willingness to serve them. "Humble yourselves in the sight of the Lord, and He will lift you up" (James 4:10 and Luke 17:10).

VOLUNTEER STAFF ORIENTATION PROCESS

Name _____ Phone _____

Address _____ Work phone _____

City _____ State _____ Zip _____ Email _____

PROCESS STEPS	DATE	COMMENTS
Initial contact	_____	_____
Run name by pastoral staff	_____	_____
Interest letter sent	_____	_____
First meeting w/_____ STAFF NAME	_____	_____
Application sent	_____	_____
Application returned	_____	_____
Background check filed	_____	_____
Background check completed	_____	_____
References checked		
1._____	_____	_____
2._____	_____	_____
3._____	_____	_____
Church membership	_____	_____
Membership seminar	_____	_____
Membership interview	_____	_____
Membership reception	_____	_____
Welcome card sent	_____	_____
Youth ministry interview _____ STAFF NAME	_____	_____
Assigned role	_____	_____
Assigned mentor	_____	_____
Training plan	_____	_____
Follow up		
30 day _____ STAFF NAME	_____	_____
60 day _____ STAFF NAME	_____	_____
90 day _____ STAFF NAME	_____	_____

Dear future youth worker,

Thanks for your interest in working with our students. We're excited that you want to make a difference in the lives of our students.

We work hard to provide an environment for spiritual growth in a context of healthy, positive relationships with adults. We take seriously our responsibility to shield our students from sexual abuse, to protect our adult leaders from accusations of sexual abuse, and to limit the exposure of the church to legal risk and liability. To accomplish this, we ask that all paid staff, as well as those volunteers who'll be working with anyone under the age of 18, complete our application process. Since you're looking into working with students under the age of 18, we need you to carefully and thoughtfully fill out the attached application and return it as quickly as possible.
So, you might be asking . . .

What's involved in the volunteer application process?
When you fill out the application, you authorize us to check personal references and to request a background check. Please thoroughly and honestly complete all forms. Send out your reference forms, including return envelopes addressed to the church, and complete the background check authorization form.

On what basis does the church approve someone to work with students?
We invite into ministry only those applicants a) who have no previous conviction for sexual or physical abuse of children; b) for whom we receive positive responses from their personal and professional references; and c) who meet the qualifications of the position for which they are applying.

If background checks raise any questions, the individual will be asked to meet with the appropriate pastor to clarify the questionable issues prior to being placed in a position relating to students.

Who will see this application?
The completed application and any subsequent information on you will be available only to the pastoral staff and church board. Once the approval process has been completed, your application and references will be maintained in a secure file.

Thanks for understanding that this paperwork is about protecting you and our students. We appreciate your willingness to help us achieve our mission to students!

Many tools for discerning spiritual gifts are currently in use in churches. Find out right away if your church offers workshops or adult classes on spiritual gifts. Prospective volunteers who have taken the classes may already know that youth ministry suits their interests and abilities. You can use the following questions to help volunteers identify their areas of interest and discern the most appropriate arena in which they might serve.

AREA OF SERVICE

Find out what triggers a person to dream and plan and take action. That arena is where they'll find most satisfaction and where you'll get their best work.

- What keeps you awake at night (besides too much coffee)?
- What do you find yourself feeling passionate about?
- What would your friends say is a recurring theme in your conversations?
- What topics do you find yourself drawn to read about?
- What themes do you find yourself following—music, movies, youth culture, counseling?

SPIRITUAL GIFTS

Sometimes these overlap; sometimes not.

- When you look back on your life, what activities brought you joy, energy, and/or success in early childhood? In grade school? Middle school? High school? College? As a young adult?
- What are the recurring themes of your memories?
- What verbs do you find yourself using—organizing, creating, discussing, building, performing, writing?
- What patterns do you discern?
- What insight have you gained in any spiritual gifts workshops or from sermons or Christian teaching?
- From the following list, choose those spiritual gifts you feel you already use. (Some of these gifts are alluded to rather than named in the Bible.)

❑ Administration	❑ Hospitality
❑ Creative communication	❑ Leadership
❑ Counseling	❑ Listening
❑ Discernment	❑ Meditation
❑ Encouragement	❑ Mercy
❑ Evangelism	❑ Shepherding
❑ Helping	❑ Teaching

- In what ways have those close to you (who are honest with you) affirmed those gifts?

ACKNOWLEDGMENTS

We (Mike and Ginny) are deeply indebted to Tim McLaughlin for helping us make our vision a reality. Thank you for your coaching and your encouragement all those many years ago. Thanks to our friend Jay Howver who has steadily encouraged us to get version 2.0 completed for some time. Thanks also to Diane Elliott who was so seminal to the first version.

Many thanks to the teams at Zondervan and Youth Specialties. Their commitment to developing great resources for youth pastors has helped many of us thrive in youth ministry. We also appreciate all the people who've helped us throughout our ministry careers with management ideas and tools.

FROM GINNY

I'm grateful for the people who coached me, networked for me, and passed on resources about management, ministry, and leadership. Many of their ideas are sprinkled in one form or another throughout these pages: Randy Black, Alison Burkhardt, Pam Magnuson Hudson, Alan Forsman, and Evelyn Johnson, just to name a few, plus a slew of youth ministry educators. I owe a debt of gratitude to Mike Work who has been a friend since we cut our teeth in junior high ministry together in Edina, Minnesota and a partner in this quest of helping youth pastors be better organized.

"Thanks" seems inadequate when I think of the youth ministry students in the Leadership and Management courses at North Park University and North Park Seminary. They have been a ministry laboratory over the years—helping me to refine, change, wrestle with, and create many of the concepts that are present in this project. They've kept in contact with me after graduation, telling me from the trenches what works and doesn't, what to add, and what to tweak. Their honesty, encouragement, and raw passion for both God and ministry often reminds me of why I keep doing what I do—and why I still love it after all these years.

Finally, I'd like to dedicate my efforts toward the creation of this project to the memory of my sister and my dad. Both of them were great business people, but their love for others is the legacy that's lasted. Their lives still continue to teach me.

FROM MIKE

I have many to thank for their significant investments in me, as well as their counsel and friendship that have shaped my ministry path.

I begin first with my mentors – Banks Corl, Dave Busby, Mark Gold, Warren Schuh, Rich Van Pelt, and Dr. Leith Anderson. Each of these leaders was a key part of my life during foundational times and represents significant periods of growth and learning in my life as a youth worker.

From the beginning of my career as a youth worker, my lifelong friend and coauthor Ginny Olson has been there as well. She was there when I learned to drive a bus, led my first junior high all-nighter, planned my first camp, gave my first talk, and lived through many of the real-life examples in this book with me. She's as significant a mentor and guide as the rest. She pushed, challenged, laughed, and did life with me (and my wife Patti) for a significant portion of my early years. And it's because of her that this book even exists. I am deeply thankful that God keeps allowing our paths to cross throughout both of our personal lives and ministry careers.

Much of what developed these pages and helped shape the creative thought and organizational strategies behind this book is attributed to my ministry partners and friends with whom I have spent hours investing in youth work – Mark Matlock, Tony Kroening, Dr. Kara Powell, Lisa Poellot, Greg Weismann, Todd Temple, Jay and Jen Howver, Heather Flies, Tic Long, Paul Alexander, Steve Logan, Mark Hallock, and Jim Hancock.

I would like to dedicate *Youth Ministry Management Tools 2.0* to my wonderful family: my wife Patti, who is my ministry partner, confidant, advisor, and professional hospitality coordinator, and our kids, Jason, Brandon, and Amy, who grew up in and around student ministry. Thank you for your amazing sacrifice, the expectations you lived with, the behind-the-scenes help you provided, and the laughter you helped create. We have so many memories to cherish. Keep investing in others with your lives.